P9-DMG-222

Culture, society and the media

Culture, society and the media

EDITED BY
MICHAEL GUREVITCH, TONY BENNETT,
JAMES CURRAN AND JANET WOOLLACOTT

Methuen

LONDON AND NEW YORK

First published in 1982 by
Methuen & Co. Ltd
11 New Fetter Lane, London EC4P 4EE

Published in the USA by
Methuen & Co.
in association with Methuen, Inc.
733 Third Avenue, New York, NY 10017

Printed in Great Britain by
Richard Clay (The Chaucer Press) Ltd
Bungay, Suffolk

British Library Cataloguing in Publication Data
Culture, society and the media.
  1. Mass media — Social aspects
  I. Gurevitch, Michael
  302.2'3   HM258

  ISBN 0-416-73500-2
  ISBN 0-416-73510-X Pbk

Library of Congress Cataloging in Publication Data
Main entry under title:
Culture, society and the media.
  Includes index.
  1. Mass media — Social aspects.   I. Gurevitch, Michael.
  HM258.C844   302.2'3   81-16986
  ISBN 0-416-73500-2   AACR2
  ISBN 0-416-73510-X

Contents

Acknowledgements	vii
Preface	1

I CLASS, IDEOLOGY AND THE MEDIA   5

Introduction   7

1 The study of the media: theoretical approaches
James Curran, Michael Gurevitch and Janet Woollacott   11

2 Theories of the media, theories of society
Tony Bennett   30

3 The rediscovery of 'ideology': return of the repressed in media studies
Stuart Hall   56

4 Messages and meanings
Janet Woollacott   91

II MEDIA ORGANIZATIONS   113

Introduction   115

5 Large corporations and the control of the communications industries
Graham Murdock   118

6 Negotiation of control in media organizations and occupations
Margaret Gallagher   151

7 Cultural dependency and the mass media
J.O. Boyd-Barrett   174

III THE POWER OF THE MEDIA   197

   Introduction   199

  8 Communications, power and social order
    James Curran   202

  9 The political effects of mass communication
    Jay G. Blumler and Michael Gurevitch   236

 10 How the media report race
    Peter Braham   268

 11 Media, 'reality', signification
    Tony Bennett   287

   Index   309

Tony Bennett is Lecturer in the Faculties of Arts and Social Sciences at the Open University; Jay G. Blumler is Director of the Centre for Television Research at the University of Leeds; J.O. Boyd-Barrett and Peter Braham are Lecturers in the Faculty of Educational Studies at the Open University; James Curran is Senior Lecturer in the School of Communication at the Polytechnic of Central London; Margaret Gallagher, formerly of the Open University, is a freelance research consultant; Michael Gurevitch is Senior Lecturer in the Faculty of Social Sciences at the Open University; Stuart Hall is in the Centre for Contemporary Cultural Studies at the University of Birmingham; Graham Murdock is in the Centre for Mass Communication Research at the University of Leicester; Janet Woollacott is Lecturer in the Faculty of Social Sciences at the Open University.

Acknowledgements

The tables appearing on pp. 248 and 251 are reprinted from Blumler, J.G. and McQuail, D. (1968) *Television and Politics: Its Uses and Influence* by permission of Faber & Faber Ltd and The University of Chicago Press. The table on p. 253 is reprinted from Robinson, J. (1974) 'The press as King-maker' by permission of *Journalism Quarterly*, and that on p. 255 from Robinson, M.J. (1976) 'American political legitimacy in an era of electronic journalism', in Cater, D. and Adler, R. (eds) *Television as a Social Force: New Approaches to TV Criticism* by permission of Praeger Publishers.

Preface

The writers of the Open University course on 'Mass Communication and Society', from which this book is substantially derived, saw the understanding of various differences and conflicts between theoretical perspectives on the mass media as an important and desirable object of study for students taking the course. Rather than aiming to show 'how the media work', the course attempted to indicate that there were a number of alternative and sometimes competing theoretical accounts of how the media work. In particular, the course focused on the division and opposition between liberal-pluralist and Marxist views of the media. As part of the pedagogic strategy of the course, students were actively encouraged to follow the history of debates between Marxists and liberal pluralists over the media and to question the assumptions of both sides. This opposition was set up and, to a certain extent, simplified for students as in the following comparison of pluralist and Marxist views.

The pluralists see society as a complex of competing groups and interests, none of them predominant all of the time. Media organisations are seen as bounded organisational systems, enjoying an important degree of autonomy from the state, political parties and institutionalised pressure groups. Control of the media is said to be in the hands of an autonomous managerial elite who allow a considerable degree of flexibility to media professionals. A basic symmetry is seen to exist between media institutions and their audiences, since in McQuail's words the 'relationship is generally entered into voluntarily and on apparently equal terms' (McQuail, 1977, p. 91): and audiences are seen as capable of manipulating the media in an infinite variety of ways according to their prior needs and dispositions, and as having access to what Halloran calls 'the plural values of society' enabling them to 'conform, accommodate, challenge or reject'. Marxists view capitalist society as being one of class domination; the media are seen as part of an ideological arena in which various class views are fought out, although within the context of the dominance of certain classes; ultimate control is increasingly concentrated in monopoly capital; media professionals, while enjoying the illusion of autonomy, are socialised into and internalise the norms of the dominant culture; the media taken as a whole, relay interpretive frameworks consonant with the interests of the dominant classes, and media audiences, while sometimes negotiating and contesting these frameworks, lack ready access to alternative meaning systems that would enable them to reject the definitions offered by the media in favour of consistently oppositional definitions. (*Mass Communication and Society*, Block 3, Introduction, p. 5)

The articulation of this kind of meta-theoretical conflict had the positive advantage of allowing students to construct and order quite disparate contributions to the field of mass communications.

However, it was not the intention of the course team to produce a course formed by the credo of news broadcasting of 'balance, neutrality and objectivity'. As reviews of the course have pointed out, the liberal pluralist/Marxist divisions make their present felt in an unequal manner.

The course is throughout an exercise in radical analysis with the liberal pluralist view serving largely as a counter-point. It counterpoints by toning the more extreme claims of the opposition and by allowing the introduction of aspects of the subject that fit awkwardly if at all into a marxist framework. By my estimate, the division of labour is about 80-20 between these orientations but drinking the course as a whole is to imbibe pretty strictly of certain versions of modern Marxism. (Carey, 1979, p. 314)

The 'unequal' weighting of Marxist and liberal pluralist views within the course stemmed largely from the task undertaken. On the one hand, we attempted a critical assessment of past developments in the field of mass communications research. On the other hand, we also sought to indicate central and pertinent contemporary theoretical developments. Increasingly, important issues and conflicts in the analysis of the mass media have been generated within and in relation to a Marxist framework.

In revising and changing the contents of the course for this reader, we have attempted to maintain the contrast between pluralist and Marxist views of the media because this contrast has been important to the history and development of mass media studies and because it remains a source of distinctive differences in the conceptualization of the media and of society generally. At the same time, the reader also makes clear significant differences within the Marxist tradition of media analysis, between, for example, those approaches which take as a starting point the base/superstructure metaphor and emphasize, as a result, the economic infra-structure of the media industries, and those approaches which are concerned to re-think a Marxist theory of ideology outside the parameters of a hierarchy of determinations, dependent always in the last analysis upon the economic. The presence of structuralism, of a linguistic paradigm, in contemporary mass communications research, with its consequent focus on the specificity and autonomy of media systems of signification and representation and the impact it has had on both Marxist and pluralist perspectives is also registered.

The reader is organized in three sections. The first, 'Class, ideology and the media, presents a series of accounts of the major theoretical traditions which have influenced the development of media theory in the past and in the present, and indicates the different foci of interest and the crucial issues around which disagreements and debates about the media could be said to be organized. The second section examines the role of media institutions: their ownership and control; the internal organization of media industries and media professionals; and the role of media institutions in the Third

World. The final section of the reader focuses on the power of the media in different areas: in terms of control of communications systems within society; in the political effects of mass communications; in the signification and reporting of race. It also reviews the theoretical issues raised by the media's apparent representation — rather than signification — of reality.

Although we have attempted to identify different theoretical perspectives on the media and the key areas in which they clash or mark strategic absences, we would not wish to suggest that the articles here provide an 'objective' map of recent mass communications research, but rather that they seek to select 'shared' theoretical problems within the field of media research and to suggest ways, albeit different ones, of thinking through those problems.

We would like to express our gratitude to all members of the 'Mass Communication and Society' course team, whose work in creating the course, and then adapting and updating it, made this book possible. We would also like to acknowledge the sterling efforts of Valerie Byrne and Deirdre Smith in helping prepare the typescript. Finally, we would like to thank the Open University for allowing us to adapt and re-use Open University course material.

REFERENCES

Carey, J. (1979) 'Mass communication and society', book review, *Media, Culture and Society*, 1 (3).
McQuail, D. (1977) 'The influence and effects of the mass media', in Curran, J., Gurevitch, M. and Woollacott, J. (eds) *Mass Communication and Society*, London, Edward Arnold.
Mass Communication and Society (1977) Milton Keynes, The Open University Press.

I

CLASS, IDEOLOGY AND
THE MEDIA

Introduction

Few areas of inquiry have expanded as rapidly as the study of the media over the last twenty years. Dominated in the late 1950s by the positivist canons of American social science, the settled view of the media which then obtained has since been profoundly challenged by a series of successive theoretical influences derived, in the main, from deviance theory, linguistics, structuralism and semiology, discourse theory (especially of late) and, perhaps most critically, from the debates in and around the area of ideology that have taken place within Marxism over the same period. Not all of these influences, however, have pulled in the same direction so that, whilst many of the orthodoxies of earlier stages in the history of mass communications research have been well and truly buried (well, nearly), no clearly articulated new orthodoxy has taken their place. Whilst some options may have been closed by means of both theoretical and empirical critique, there none the less remains a sufficient diversity of contending perspectives to guarantee a lively and productive climate of debate for some time to come.

The readings collected in this section offer a series of different but related overviews of these developments and are intended to give both students and teachers a comprehensive grasp of the key controversies which currently characterize media studies.

In 'Theories of the media: an introduction', James Curran, Michael Gurevitch and Janet Woollacott review the relationships between liberal-pluralist and Marxist approaches to the study of the media. In doing so, they dispute the conventionally held view that the liberal-pluralist approach can be characterized as theoretically cautious and empirically hard-nosed, in contrast to the supposedly more speculative, 'grand theoretical' and assertive character of Marxist approaches. Both approaches, they contend, are informed by theoretical conceptions of society and of the role of the media within it, even if these conceptions are more explicitly and self-consciously theorized in the Marxist tradition. Moreover, they argue, the empirical findings of the two traditions are not so far opposed as is usually supposed; both agree about the nature and degree of power that can be attributed to the media, albeit that they express this in different terms.

Having cleared the air in relation to what has been an important source of misunderstanding in the history of media debate, Curran, Gurevitch and Woollacott go on to argue that, in recent years, the most productive controversies have been located *within* Marxism rather than *between* the Marxist and liberal-pluralist approaches, and survey the contending paradigms — the 'structuralist', 'political economy' and 'culturalist' approaches — which currently define the main theoretical orientations within Marxist media research.

In 'Theories of the media, theories of society', Tony Bennett outlines the relationships between the more important schools of media theory and the broader concerns of the traditions of social theory on which they depend in a way that makes clear the connections between particular empirical concerns and their supporting theoretical foundations. Focusing on mass society theories, liberal-pluralism, the critical theory of the Frankfurt School and on more recent developments within the Marxist theory of ideology, Bennett places each of these in their political context and traces the historical connections between them. Entirely dominated, in its early phases, by mass society theory — a pessimistic philosophy which led to the development of the media being viewed apprehensively — opposing theoretical approaches have been developed, at least in part, by means of an engagement with and critique of the mass society position. Bennett thus shows how, from the 1930s through to the 1950s, the liberal-pluralist perspective was developed, in America, by means of a detailed empirical refutation of the mass society supposition that media audiences could be regarded as largely undifferentiated, passive and inert masses. Similarly, in the case of the Frankfurt School — the first Marxist attempt to engage theoretically with the media — he shows how the critique of the 'culture industry' contained in the writings of Theodor Adorno and Herbert Marcuse consisted of an uneasy alliance of Marxist and mass society elements. His essay concludes with a consideration of more recent developments in the Marxist theory of ideology, particularly as represented by Louis Althusser, and outlines the way in which contemporary Marxist debates about the social role and power of the media connect with the broader problems involved in the analysis of the reproduction processes of advanced capitalism.

In 'The rediscovery of "ideology": return of the repressed in media studies', Stuart Hall's central concern is with the diverse theoretical sources that have contributed to the formation of the 'critical paradigm' in media studies since the early 1960s. He prefaces this, however, with a synoptic survey of the development of media theory prior to the 1960s and, in a swingeing critique of the liberal-pluralist perspective, traces the connection between American positivist and behaviourist social science and the ideology of American pluralism in the late 1950s. To the extent that the media were viewed as reflecting an achieved consensus and, thereby, as strengthening the core value system which was alleged to hold American society together in spite of the diverse and plural groups of which it was composed, American media sociology, Hall argues, 'underwrote "pluralism"'. By contrast, during the last ten years or so, the media have been viewed 'no longer as the institutions which merely reflected and sustained the consensus, but as the institutions which *produced* consensus, "manufactured consent"'. In the main body of his essay, Hall considers those theoretical developments which ruptured the liberal-pluralist paradigm from within together with those 'outside' influences which, in founding the critical paradigm, have contributed to this change — indeed, reversal — of perspectives. In an impressive survey which takes in the contributions of deviance theory, the general perspectives of structuralism as instanced by Claude Lévi-Strauss and Roland Barthes, the psychoanalytic theories of Jacques Lacan, the work of Louis Althusser, Gramsci's concept of hegemony and its subsequent elaboration in the work of Ernesto Laclau, Hall outlines the major theoretical developments which have successively undercut and displaced the earlier analogical thinking whereby the media were said to mirror or reflect reality.

Throughout his analysis, Hall is careful to relate theoretical developments to political ones. If, as he contends, the 'critical paradigm' has been characterized by its 'rediscovery' of ideology, exiled from the heartland of American sociology, this has been closely related to the fact that ideological struggle, once optimistically thought to be over, has become more pronounced and visible. If the media are no longer viewed as reflecting an achieved consensus but as being engaged in the business of producing consent, this is due, in no small part, to the fact that there is no longer a consensus to be reflected with the result that, as the economy has plunged deeper and deeper into crisis, the need to produce consent has become more imperative yet, at the same time, increasingly difficult.

In his critique of the American social science of the 1950s, Stuart Hall argues that '*conceptually*, the media-message, as a symbolic sign-vehicle or a structured discourse, with its own internal structuration and complexity, remained theoretically wholly undeveloped' within the liberal-pluralist tradition. There can be little doubt that the centrality currently accorded such questions consitutes the most visibly distinctive feature of contemporary media theory. In the intervening period, the aggregate techniques of content analysis have been forced into the background by a veritable explosion of new methods — chiefly derived from linguistics, semiology and psychoanalysis — aimed at unlocking the structure of media messages and analysing their effects. In 'Messages and meanings', Janet Woollacott outlines some of the more important of these methods, illustrates the uses to which they have been put and considers some of the difficulties associated with them. In a discussion which ranges across the work of Lévi-Strauss, Barthes and Umberto Eco, the critical project of the film journal *Screen*, Colin MacCabe's work on the 'classic realist text' and the use of the Gramscian concept of hegemony in *Policing the Crisis*, she draws out the implications which such developments have had for traditional Marxist formulations of the concept of ideology. The general difficulty she points to has been that of reconciling semiological perspectives, with their stress on signification as an active process of the production of meaning, with 'any theory of ideology which conceives of the media as essentially reflecting the "real"'.

Viewed collectively, the readings comprising this section offer a commanding insight into the historical development of media studies together with an informed appraisal of the connections between the new developments, debates and controversies which typify recent work in this area. Albeit necessarily more cautiously and conjecturally, they also identify the directions in which future research might be expected to develop. The overall result is a useful synoptic perspective on where media studies has been, where it is now and where it is likely to be going.

1

The study of the media: theoretical approaches

JAMES CURRAN, MICHAEL GUREVITCH AND
JANET WOOLLACOTT

In this chapter we do not attempt to chart systematically all the different
approaches to the study of the mass media, each set in their different
intellectual, social and historical contexts. Instead we have chosen to
examine selectively the way in which different researchers have perceived
the *power* of the mass media and to point to the different theoretical
conceptions and empirical enquiries that have informed some of those
perceptions. In particular, we have focused on the clashes and common
ground between different accounts of the power of the media in three areas;
in the distinctions between liberal-pluralist and Marxist approaches, often
conceived of in terms of a distinction between empiricism and theory; in
different approaches to the analysis of media institutions and finally in the
different accounts of media power located in contemporary Marxist studies
of the media.

THE POWER OF THE MEDIA: THEORY AND EMPIRICISM

To a remarkable extent, there was a broad consensus during the inter-war
period — to which many researchers, writing from a 'right' as well as a 'left'
perspective subscribed — that the mass media exercised a powerful and
persuasive influence. Underlying this consensus was (1) the creation of mass
audiences on a scale that was unprecedented through the application of new
technology — the rotary press, film and radio — to the mass production of
communications; (2) a fashionable though not unchallenged view, that
urbanization and industrialization had created a society that was volatile,
unstable, rootless, alienated and inherently susceptible to manipulation; (3)
linked to a view of urbanized man as being relatively defenceless, an easy
prey to mass communication since he was no longer anchored in the
network of social relations and stable, inherited values that characterized
settled, rural communities; (4) anecdotal but seemingly persuasive evidence
that the mass media had brainwashed people during World War 1, and
engineered the rise of fascism in Europe between the wars.

This encouraged a relatively uncomplicated view of the media as all-powerful propaganda agencies brainwashing a susceptible and defenceless public. The media propelled 'word bullets' that penetrated deep into its inert and passive victims. All that needed to be done was to measure the depth and size of penetration through modern scientific techniques.

A reassessment of the impact of the mass media during the late 1940s, 1950s and 1960s gave rise to a new academic orthodoxy — that the mass media have only a very limited influence. This view was succinctly stated by Klapper (1960) in a classic summary of more than a decade's empirical research. 'Mass communications', he concludes, 'ordinarily do not serve as a necessary and sufficient cause of audience effects' (p. 8). Underlying this new orthodoxy, was a reassessment of man's susceptibility to influence. A succession of empirical enquiries, using experimental laboratory and social survey techniques, demonstrated that people tended to expose themselves to, understand and remember communications selectively, according to prior dispositions. People, it was argued, manipulated — rather than were manipulated by — the mass media. The empirical demonstration of selective audience behaviour was further reinforced by a number of uses and gratifications studies which argued that audience members are active rather than passive and bring to the media a variety of different needs and uses that influence their response to the media.

Underpinning this reassuring conclusion about the lack of media influence was a repudiation of the mass society thesis on which the presumption of media power had been based. The view of society as being composed of isolated and anomic individuals gave way to a view of society as a honeycomb of small groups bound by a rich web of personal ties and dependences. Stable group pressures, it was concluded, helped to shield the individual from media influence. This stress on the salience of small groups as a buffer against media influence was often linked to a diffusionist model of power. In particular it was stressed by a number of leading empirical researchers that the social mediation of media messages was not a hierarchical process. 'Some individuals of high social status apparently wield little independent influence', wrote Katz and Lazarsfeld (1955), 'and some of low status have considerable personal influence'. Wealth and power, it seemed, did not shape public opinion in the leading Western democracy.

Even the image of man as a natural prey to suggestion and influence was challenged by a number of persuasive theories of personality formation that apparently explained selective audience behaviour. In particular cognitive dissonance theory, which postulated that people seek to minimize the psychological discomfort of having incompatible values and beliefs, seemed to explain people's deliberate avoidance and unconscious decoding of uncongenial media messages.

In short, the conventional belief in the power of the media seemed to be demolished. A popular view based on flimsy anecdotal evidence had been confounded by systematic empirical enquiry. Even the assumptions about the nature of man and the structure of society on which the belief in media power had rested, had been 'revealed' as bankrupt and misguided.

During the late 1960s and the 1970s, the new orthodoxy was challenged from two quite different, indeed opposed, directions. Those working within the empirical effects tradition initiated what Jay Blumler has called the 'new look' in mass communications research. This has consisted partly of looking again at the small print of the pioneering studies into media effects obscured by the often polemically worded dismissals of media influence that are regularly cited in summary overviews of the literature. For although leading researchers like Katz, Lazarsfeld and Klapper reacted strongly against the conventional view of the omnipotent media in sometimes extravagantly worded generalizations, they were careful to qualify what they said by allowing a number of cases when the media may be or has been persuasive: when audience attention is casual, when information rather than attitude or opinion is involved, when the media source is prestigious, trusted or liked, when monopoly conditions are more complete, when the issue at stake is remote from the receiver's experience or concern, when personal contacts are not opposed to the direction of the message or when the recipient of the message is cross-pressured. More recently a number of scholars have also re-examined the empirical data presented in the early classic 'effects' studies and argued that they do not fully support the negative conclusions about media influence that were derived from them (Becker, McCombs and McLeod, 1975; Gitlin, 1978). Furthermore, it has been argued, social changes such as the decline of stable political allegiances and the development of a new mass medium in television require the conclusions derived from older empirical studies to be reassessed. A succinct statement of this 'new look' is presented by Michael Gurevitch and Jay Blumler later in this book.

The limited model of media influence was also attacked by scholars in the Marxist and neo-Marxist critical tradition that became a growing influence on mass communication research during the 1970s. The initial response of many Marxist and critical writers was to dismiss out of hand empirical communications research as being uniformly uninteresting. The media, they argued, were ideological agencies that played a central role in maintaining class domination: research studies that denied media influence were so disabled in their theoretical approach as to be scarcely worth confronting (or indeed, even reading).

Some empirical researchers responded with evident exasperation to this sweeping dismissal by arguing that disciplined, rigorous empirical research had revealed the inadequacy of unsubstantiated theorizing about the mass media (e.g. Blumler, 1977). Indeed, a casual reader of exchanges between these two traditions might be forgiven for thinking that a new engagement had developed in which a view of the mass media as having only limited influence, grounded in empirical research within a liberal tradition, was pitted against an alternative conception of the mass media as powerful agencies, informed by an exclusively theoretical Marxist/critical perspective.

But while the two research traditions are, in some ways, fundamentally and irreconcilably opposed, they are not divided primarily by the differences highlighted in this debate. In fact, the classical empirical studies did not demonstrate that the mass media had very little influence: on the contrary, they revealed the central role of the media in consolidating and fortifying the values and attitudes of audience members. This tended to be presented in a negative way only because the preceding orthodoxy they were attacking had defined the influence of omnipotent media in terms of changing attitudes and beliefs. The absence of media *conversion* consequently tended to be equated with the absence of influence.

Ironically, Marxist and critical commentators have also argued that the mass media play a strategic role in reinforcing dominant social norms and values that legitimize the social system. There is thus no inconsistency, at an empirical level, in the two approaches. Indeed, as Marcuse has suggested, 'the objection that we overrate greatly the indoctrinating power of the "media" . . . misses the point. The preconditioning does not start with the mass production of radio and television and the centralization of their control. The people entered this stage as preconditioned receptacles of long standing . . .' (Marcuse, 1972). He could have added with justification, that a generation of empirical research from a different tradition had provided corroboration of the reinforcement 'effect' he was attributing to the media.

Differences between the pluralist and critical schools about the power of the mass media, at the level of effectiveness, are to a certain extent based on mutual misunderstanding (notably, an over-literal acceptance by some Marxist commentators of polemical generalizations about the lack of media influence advanced by some empirical researchers). This misunderstanding has been perpetuated by the tendency for researchers in the two different traditions to examine the impact of the mass media in different contexts as a consequence of their divergent ideological and theoretical preoccupations.

Consider, for instance, the vexed issue of media portrayals of violence. Most researchers in the Marxist tradition in Britain have approached this question in terms of whether media portrayals of violence have served to legitimize the forces of law and order, build consent for the extension of coercive state regulation and de-legitimize outsiders and dissidents (Hall, 1974; Cohen, 1973; Murdock, 1973; Chibnall, 1977; Whannel, 1979). They have thus examined the impact of the mass media in situations where mediated communications are powerfully supported by other institutions such as the police, judiciary and schools, and sustained by already widely diffused attitudes favourable towards law enforcement agencies and generally unfavourable towards groups like youth gangs, student radicals, trade union militants and football hooligans. The power of the media is thus portrayed as that of renewing, amplifying and extending the existing predispositions that constitute the dominant culture, not in creating them. In contrast, empirical researchers in the liberal tradition have tended to examine media portrayals of violence in terms of whether they promote and encourage violence in everyday life. They have consequently defined the potential influence of these portrayals of violence in a form that is opposed to deeply engrained moral norms supported and maintained by a network of social relationships and powerful institutions actively opposed to 'anti-social behaviour'. That a 'limited effects' model of media influence emerged from such studies should come as no surprise: it was inherent in the way in which media influence was defined in the first place.

The same pattern of difference can be illustrated in relation to the question of voting. Some Marxist commentators have contended that media portrayals of elections constitute dramatized rituals that legitimize the power structure in liberal democracies; voting is seen as an ideological practice that helps to sustain the myth of representative democracy, political equality and collective self-determination. The impact of election coverage is thus conceived in terms of reinforcing political values that are widely shared in Western democracies and are actively endorsed by the education system, the principal political organizations and the apparatus of the state. In contrast, pioneering studies into the effects of the media on voting behaviour by Lazarsfeld *et al.* (1948), Berelson *et al.* (1954) and Trenaman and McQuail (1961) concluded that the media had only marginal influence in changing the way in which people voted. Their negative conclusions were based on an analysis of media influence in a form that was strongly opposed by powerful group norms, at a time when partisan allegiances were stable. Significantly, their conclusions have been modified as these contingent influences have weakened.

The alleged dichotomy between the 'grand-theoretical' and 'atheoretical' approaches to media study represented by the two opposed traditions of Marxism and liberalism is also a little misleading. The liberal tradition in mass communications research has been characterized by a greater attention to empirical investigation. But it does not constitute an 'atheoretical' approach: on the contrary, empirical communications research is based upon theoretical models of society even if these are often unexamined and unstated.

Indeed, the conventional characterization of liberal and Marxist traditions in mass communications research as constituting two opposed schools tends to obscure both the internal differences within each of these traditions and the reciprocal influence which each has exerted upon the other. The shift from a perception of the media as a stupefying, totally subduing force expressed, for example, by Marcuse (1972), to a more cautious assessment in which dominant meaning systems are moulded and relayed by the media, are adapted by audiences and integrated into class-based or 'situated' meaning systems articulated by McCron (1976), is characteristic of a significant shift within Marxist research that has been influenced, in part at least, by empirical communications studies. This has been accompanied by increasing interest within the Marxist tradition in empirical survey-based research into audience adaptation of media-relayed ideologies, exemplified recently for instance by Hartman (1979) and Morley (1980). At the same time, Marxist critiques have contributed to a growing recognition within empirical communications research that more attention needs to be paid to the influence of the media on the ideological categories and frames of reference through which people understand the world. Evolving from the relatively limited conception of media 'agenda-setting' (the ranking of issues, in terms of their perceived importance) in election studies, a new interest has developed in the wider 'cognitive effects' of the media that reflects a nearly universal dissatisfaction amongst researchers with the narrow conceptualization of media influence afforded by the classic effects studies.

MEDIA INSTITUTIONS

Shifting paradigms of the power of the media have had important implications for enquiry into media organizations. Clearly, recognition of the power of the media raises questions as to how and by whom this power is wielded. Answers to these questions have been sought through the investigation and analysis of the structures and practices of media organizations.

Concern with the study of media institutions, their work practices and their relationship with their socio-political environment, emerged as a mainstream feature of mass communication research only in the last two decades. Inasmuch as the early history of this field of research has been characterized by a preoccupation with the study of the effects of the media on their audiences, this new concern constituted a major shift of interest in the field. The reasons for this shift have been varied: in part it was prompted by some disillusionment with the capacity of 'effects research' to fully explain the power of the media. At the same time it also reflected an awareness of the relative neglect of media institutions as objects of study. But the more important stimuli came from theoretical developments outside the narrow confines of media research. At least three different sources of influence should be identified here: first, developments in the sociological study of large scale, formal organizations yielded theories of organizational structure and behaviour, as well as analytic tools, which were seen to be applicable to the study of media organizations and of their work practices and production processes. Secondly, the increasing influence of Marxist theorizing, with its challenge to pluralist models of power in society, prompted a reappraisal of the role of the media in society, and focused attention on the structure and the organization of the media. The media came to be seen, in this perspective, not as an autonomous organizational system, but as a set of institutions closely linked to the dominant power structure through ownership, legal regulation, the values implicit in the professional ideologies in the media, and the structures and ideological consequences of prevailing modes of newsgathering. Thirdly, increasing attention to the study of the role of the mass media in politics indicated the importance of examining the relationship between media institutions and the political institutions of society, and the ways in which political communication emerges as a subtly composite product of the interaction between these two sets of institutions.

These different influences resulted inevitably, not in a unified set of interests, but in examinations of different aspects of the institutions of the media. Having come to the study of these institutions from different perspectives and under different influences, researchers working in this field have developed at least four different foci of study, reflecting their interests in different aspects of these institutions. The four strands of interest discernible in the literature can be grouped under the following headings:
1. Institutional structures and role relationships;
2. The political economy of media institutions;
3. Professional ideologies and work practices;
4. Interaction of media institutions with the socio-political environment.

In spite of their different foci, the basic issue which underlines all four strands of study is the process of the shaping of media messages. Researchers working in this area share the assumption that an examination of the political, organizational and professional factors which impinge on the process of message production could shed considerable light on the question of the power of the media. Because different factors are selected for examination within each strand of studies, together they complement each other. When pulled together they provide a comprehensive view of the ways in which media messages are produced and shaped, and offer insights into the ways in which different influences on this process are combined in a single composite product.

Institutional structures and role relationships

This strand of studies draws its inspiration primarily from work on formal organizations. Media organizations are seen as possessing the same attributes which characterize other large-scale industrial organizations. These include: hierarchical structures; an internal division of labour and role differentiation; clearly specified and accepted institutional goals, translated into specific policies and organizational practices; clear lines of communication and accountability which generally follow and represent the hierarchical structure; modes of peer and of superior-subordinate relationships which regulate the interaction between incumbents in different roles. Most of the emphasis of this approach is thus placed on intra-organizational structures and behaviour, although some recognition is given to extra-organizational factors which impinge on the organization, such as 'shareholders', 'clients', 'sources' etc.

The various 'gatekeeper' studies, which examined the flow of news materials through the stages of the selection and editing process, as well as studies of formal and peer control in media organizations are the clearest representatives of this approach.

These studies explained the products of the media as outcomes of the interaction amongst different members of media organizations. But the interaction is not random, nor is power equally distributed amongst the occupants of different organizational positions. Rather, power and control are structured along the lines of the organizational hierarchy. But according to these studies, control in media organizations was not exerted directly or crudely. It depended on social control via informal channels more than on direct control via formal channels. The mechanisms of social control were embedded in the provision (or withholding) of organizational and professional rewards to members of the organization. They ensured the consistency of media outputs and, more important, they produced conformity by media personnel to the overall goals, policies and 'editorial lines' of the organizations for which they worked. Control, thus, is exerted from the organizational top downwards, both through formal and informal channels. It functions, however, not in a coercive fashion, but through the acceptance by occupants of the lower echelons of the legitimacy of the authority of those occupying the top positions in the organization. The conclusion which these studies reach then, is that the power of the media is located at the top of the hierarchy of media organizations.

The political economy of media institutions

Resembling the preceding strand in its focus of interest, but diametrically opposed to it, is the perspective which searches for the answers to the question of the power of the media in the analysis of their structures of ownership and control. Adopting a fundamentalist-Marxist approach, studies conducted in this vein have been based on the assumption that the dynamics of the 'culture-producing industries' can be understood primarily in terms of their economic determination (Murdock and Golding, 1977; Curran and Seaton, 1981). Thus, the contents of the media and the meanings carried by their messages are according to this view primarily determined by the economic base of the organizations in which they are produced. Commercial media organizations must cater to the needs of advertisers and produce audience-maximizing products (hence the heavy doses of sex-and-violence content) while those media institutions whose revenues are controlled by the dominant political institutions or by the state gravitate towards a middle ground, or towards the heartland of the prevailing consensus (Elliott, 1977).

The precise mechanisms and processes whereby ownership of the media or control of their economics are translated into controls over the message are, according to the proponents of this approach, rather complex and often problematic. (See Murdock's article in this book). The workings of these controls are not easy to demonstrate — or to examine empirically. The evidence quite often is circumstantial and is derived from the 'fit' between the ideology implicit in the message and the interests of those in control. The links between the economic determinants of the media on the one hand and the contents of the media on the other must, according to this analysis, be sought in the professional ideologies and the work practices of media professionals, since these are the only channel through which organizational controls can be brought to bear on the output of the media. Studies of the political economy of media organizations must therefore be closely related to, and supplemented by, analyses of the professional ideologies and practices found in these organizations.

Professional ideologies and work practices

Studies of the beliefs, values and work procedures of media professionals have their theoretical roots in the sociology of the professions. Early studies of professionalism in the media raised the question whether those employed in the media deserved the accolade of being described as a profession. The search for an answer was based on examining whether media occupations possessed the attributes of professionalism, which have defined the classic professions, such as medicine and the law. One of the attributes of professionalism has been the development of a professional ethos or ideology which defined the beliefs and values of the profession, laid down guidelines for accepted and proper professional behaviour and served to legitimate the profession's sources of control and its insistence on the right to regulate and control itself and its members. Examinations of professionalism in media occupations, particularly in journalism, identified a strong claim for professional autonomy, derived from the democratic tenets of freedom of expression and 'the public's right to know'. In addition, media professional ideology developed a commitment to values such as objectivity, impartiality, and fairness.

Academic discussions of the ideologies of media professionals reveal the diametrically opposed conclusions which might be reached when the same body of evidence is looked at from competing theoretical perspectives. A strict pluralist interpretation would accept that media professionals' claims to autonomy and their commitment to the principles of objectivity and impartiality indeed operate as guidelines for their work practices and as regulators of their professional conduct. It would, therefore, see ultimate control of the production process in the media as resting in the hands of the professionals responsible for it, in spite of the variety of pressures and influences to which they may be subjected. Some Marxist interpretations, on the other hand, challenge the validity of the claims by media personnel and dismiss the notions of objective and impartial work practices as, at best, limited and societal, masking the professionals' subservience to the dominant ideology. Control of the production process by media professionals is confined, in this view, to the production of messages whose meanings are primarily determined elsewhere within the dominant culture.

The polarity of these interpretations allows ample space for intermediate positions. Thus some proponents of the pluralist approach acknowledge the limitations on the autonomy of media professionals, and concede that the prevailing socio-political consensus defines the boundaries and constrains the space within which media professionals can be impartial. Similarly, some Marxist interpretations stress the relative autonomy of the mass media — both in the sphere of professional organization and of signification.

Some observers of these trends have suggested that as further empirical evidence is gathered, pluralist and Marxist analyses of professionalism in the media will continue to influence each other, and to discover some areas of agreement. Thus, for example researchers from both camps now share the view that powerful institutions and groups in society do have privileged access to the media, because they are regarded by media professionals as more credible and trustworthy, and because they have the resources to process information and to offer the media their views in a usable and attractive form, tailor-made to fit the requirements of the media. They also agree that the commitment of media professionals to the canons of objectivity and impartiality, however genuinely held, also serves to protect them from criticism of their performance as professionals, by partly removing their responsibility for the output of the media and placing it on their 'sources'. And they accept the analysis that this professional ideology also provides a basis for the profession's self-respect, and lays claim for respect from the public. We may tentatively conclude from this evidence of common denominators in the thinking of both schools that this strand of studies offers possibilities of further mutual influence and agreement, without necessarily leading to a convergence of the different perspectives.

Interaction of media institutions with the socio-political environment

A fourth direction which some studies of media institutions have followed has an extra-organizational focus, and examines the relationship between the media and the institutional structures and interests in their environment. This area of interest is somewhat akin to the domain of the 'political economy' approach, inasmuch as both strands of research examine the relationship between media institutions and the political and economic institutions of society. However, the macro-level at which the 'political economy' analysis is conducted leaves some micro-aspects of this relationship unexplored. In particular, questions concerning the interaction between media professionals and their 'sources' in political and state institutions appear to be crucial for understanding the production process in the media. Media organizations exist in a symbiotic relationship with their environment, drawing on it not only for their economic sustenance but also for the 'raw materials' of which their contents are made. The generation and shaping of these materials through interaction between media professionals and their sources of information, inspiration and support outside their own institutions take place at the 'interface' between the media and these institutions (Gurevitch and Blumler, 1977). Contacts at the interface, therefore, constitute a critical part of the production process, and an important area for investigating the ways in which external inputs into the production process are managed.

Here, too, it is interesting to note the differences between the pluralist and the Marxist analysis of this relationship. Pluralist analyses tend to emphasize the *mutual dependence* between media professionals and the representatives or spokesmen for other institutions. They argue that while the media are dependent on the central institutions of society for their raw material, these institutions are at the same time dependent on the media to communicate their viewpoints to the public. The capacity of the media to 'deliver' large audiences provides them, according to this analysis, with at least a semi-independent power base *vis-à-vis* other power centres in society. The implication is not that an *equality* of power obtains between the media and other powerful institutions, but rather that some measure of independent power enters into the dealings of the media with these institutions. Marxist analyses, on the other hand, regard media institutions as at best 'relatively' and marginally autonomous. The media are regarded as being locked into the power structure, and consequently as acting largely in tandem with the dominant institutions in society. The media thus reproduce the viewpoints of dominant institutions not as one among a number of alternative perspectives, but as the central and 'obvious' or 'natural' perspective.

Thus, again, competing interpretations are provided by rival perspectives, although the evidence deployed by both is similar. Questions about the power of media institutions are, therefore, less likely to be resolved empirically, than to generate further theoretical and ideological argument.

CHANGING PERSPECTIVES OF SOCIAL THEORY

In the preceding discussion, we have indicated some past shifts in the focus of interest in media studies, from a primary concern with effects to a concern with consequences which the operations of the media have for the shaping of the message. In both these areas different questions have been raised and different conclusions emerge when different theoretical frameworks are deployed. Such is the case when attempts are made to describe and define, for example, the media's relationship to their contents. One of the key issues here revolves around the degree to which the media are regarded as passive transmitters or active interveners in the shaping of the message. Probably the most familiar of the 'passive transmitter' theories is the one which employs the metaphor of the mirror to describe the role of the media in society. The notion that the media are a 'mirror to reality' could be traced to different sources. On the one hand, it is a reflection of the neutral stance implied in the concepts of objectivity and impartiality embedded in the dominant professional ideology in the media. At the same time it is rooted in a pluralist view of society, in which the media are seen to provide a forum for contending social and political positions to parade their wares and vie for public support. The media are thus expected to *reflect* a multi-faceted reality, as truthfully and objectively as possible, free from any bias, especially the biases of the professionals engaged in recording and reporting events in the outside world. This view is based on the notion that facts may be separated from opinions and hence, that while comment is free, facts are sacred. Ironically, in view of this obvious source for the 'mirror of reality' image of the media, metaphors of reflection have been almost equally influential within the Marxist tradition, if in an inverted form. Here images and definitions provided by the media have been seen to be distorted or 'false' accounts of an objective reality which are biased because they are moulded by ruling political and economic groups. Media journalism is made to appear, in Connell's phrase, as a 'kind of megaphone' by which ruling-class ideas are amplified and generalized across society (Connell, 1979).

Increasingly, however, the last decade has seen some basic shifts away from this view of the media. Essentially classical Marxism conceived of the media in terms of the metaphor of base and superstructure and little attention was paid to the specific autonomy of the mass media and to the area of its effectivity. The power of the media was simply the power of contemporary ruling classes utilizing modern communications systems to pursue their interests in line with the much quoted description of ruling-class ideology, taken from *The German Ideology*:

'The ideas of the ruling class are in every epoch the ruling ideas: i.e. the class which is the ruling *material* force in society is at the same time its ruling *intellectual* force. The class which has the means of material production at its disposal has control at the same time over the means of mental production, so that thereby, generally speaking, the ideas of those who lack the means of mental production are subject to it' (Marx and Engels, 1970, p. 64).

The effects of the mass media, in early forms of Marxist analysis were not seen as discrete and measurable but were important in the dissemination of ideologies opposed to the interests of working-class groups and the production of false consciousness in such groups. Changes in this view of the media arose in part because of internal developments in Marxism but also because of the influence of other theoretical traditions.

One of the most important shifts generally in more recent mass communications research, be it Marxist or pluralist, has been the redirection of attention to the formal qualities of media discourse. The influence of semiology and linguistics on the direction of mass communications research has been important not simply as an addition to existing studies of political effects, ownership and control and the internal workings of media organizations, but also because of the re-thinking of existing and often recognizably unsatisfactory accounts of media power which it brought about. It is worth examining the impact of structuralism on Marxist accounts of the media because, in a sense, it is around this area of theoretical convergence and contradiction that it is possible to plot some of the distinctive changes which have characterized media studies in the last few years.

A comparison of the field of media research, say, in the 1940s, with that of the present day, is instructive, not only in terms of following the seesawing estimates of media power referred to earlier but also in terms of the dominance of certain theoretical views. As we have already suggested, a simple conflict of liberal-pluralist versus Marxist approaches, conceived of in terms of the empiricism of the former and the theoreticism of the latter, does not provide an entirely adequate picture of the development of mass communications research, although it may provide an illuminating route through certain moments in the history of that research. One problem here is that the Marxism and liberal-pluralism of yesterday are not the same as those of today. During the forties the mass society theories of the Frankfurt School might have been said to represent a Marxist general theory which ran counter to the empiricist studies of attitude-change prevalent in contemporary American sociology and social psychology. The clash between the critical theorists' view of mass society and a pluralist-inspired tradition focusing on the effects of the mass media involved a major theoretical confrontation. However, the case is different now and not simply because Marxists have moved beyond the monumental pessimism incorporated within the Frankfurt School's critique of mass society. To put it bluntly, the work of the Frankfurt School was relatively marginal in developing and generating research in mass communications, in providing a theoretical paradigm within which media studies could proceed.

Recent developments in Marxist theory, in Britain for example through the 'cultural' traditions of Williams and Hall and through the importations of European 'structuralisms' (the theories of Lévi-Strauss, Althusser, Lacan and Gramsci), have meant that many of the important questions about the mass media and about 'culture' more generally are now posed within Marxism rather than between Marxism and other accounts (Johnson, 1979). Within contemporary Marxist studies of the media there are a number of different inflections in the conceptualization of the power of the media. Marxist theorists vary in their accounts of the determination of the mass media and in their accounts of the nature and power of mass media ideologies. Structuralism has played an important part in producing and illuminating distinctive differences in Marxist views of the media. The theoretical differences within Marxism have been variously described as 'three problematics' (Johnson, 1979) or the 'two paradigms' (Hall, 1980). The three different approaches which we identify here not only characterize the power of the media in different and sometimes contradictory ways but also, between them, provide the type of arena for disagreement and debate, which in the past has been a consistent feature of the differences between the pluralist and the Marxist tradition.

Structuralist studies of the media

Structuralist accounts of the media have incorporated many diverse contributions, including Saussurean linguistics, the structural anthropology of Lévi-Strauss, the semiotics of Roland Barthes and Lacan's reworking of psychoanalysis. The central and substantive concern has been with the systems and processes of signification and representation, the key to which has been seen to lie in the analysis of 'texts'; films, photographs, television programmes, literary texts and so forth. Structuralist studies in this area have been closely linked with some crucial reformulations of Marxist theories of ideology which, although bitterly attacked by those who have wished to remain on more traditional Marxist terrain, have played a positive part in by-passing and moving beyond certain impasses within Marxist accounts of the media associated with the idea of ideology as a reflection of the economic basis of media industries and society.

Althusser's reformulation of a theory of ideology, for example, clearly indicated an important shift in Marxist thinking. Althusser's view of ideology as a representation of the imaginary relationship of individuals with the real conditions of their existence moved the notion of ideology away from 'ideas' which constituted a distorted reflection of reality. Althusser's work stressed that ideology expressed the themes and representations through which men relate to the real world. For Althusser ideology always had a material existence. It is inscribed within an apparatus and its practices. Ideology operates here to interpellate individuals as subjects, 'hailing' individuals through the apparently obvious and normal rituals of everyday living. Ideology, rather than being imposed from above and being, therefore, implicitly dispensable, is the medium through which all people experience the world. Although Althusser retains both the overall form of the base/superstructure metaphor and the notion of determination in the last instance by the economic he also emphasizes the irreducibility and materiality of ideology. Determination in the last instance by the economic is a necessary but not sufficient explanation of the nature and existence of the ideological superstructures. The media within an Althusserian framework operate predominantly through ideology: they are ideological state apparatuses as opposed to more classically repressive state apparatuses. Thus the effectivity of the media lies not in an imposed false consciousness, nor in changing attitudes, but in the unconscious categories through which conditions are represented and experienced.

The combination of Althusserian Marxism and semiotics provided the initial impetus for sustained work on media texts. By largely suspending the traditional Marxist concern with the external social and economic determinants of ideology, in favour of a focus on the internal relations of signifying practices, such as film or television, structuralist media research formed the theoretical space within which to carry out detailed textual analysis. The early projects of *Screen*, for example, which examined the classic narrative cinema of Hollywood, *avant-garde* films and televisual forms, were, whatever their limitations, a very positive advance over approaches to media content which stressed 'reflection' whether in Marxist or pluralist terms. At the very least, such work showed a continuing concern to establish the autonomy and effectiveness of particular film and television forms, taking as a basis the idea that the ideology embodied in film and television is an important and necessary area of ideological struggle.

Structuralist studies have, however, moved beyond an Althusserian problematic in a number of ways. First, through attempting to combine the analysis of media-signifying practices with psychoanalysis, there has been an attempt to theorize the relationship of texts to subjects. The subject, constituted in language, in Lacanian terminology, is not the unified subject of the Althusserian formulation and traditional Marxist view, but a contra-dictory, de-centred subject displaced across the range of discourses in which he or she participates. Although this is a relatively undeveloped area in Marxist studies of the media and in Marxism generally, this line of develop-ment indicates some crucial absences both in Marxism and in earlier structuralist studies. A second movement within structuralism has involved a rejection of the base/superstructure model for a focus on the articulation of autonomous discourses. Hirst, for example, suggests that the idea of the 'relative autonomy' of ideology and the linked notion of representation is inherently unstable in its juxtaposition of ideas (the relative autonomy of the ideological and the determination of ideology by the economic base) which are logically opposed to one another. In this view there can be no middle ground between the autonomy of ideological practices such as the mass media and straightforward economic determinism.

'Political economy'

If the structuralist paradigm has directed attention at and conceived the power of the media as ideological, there have been consistent attempts to reverse the structuralist view of ideology in favour of a 'political economy' of the media. This well-established tradition in media research, which we have already touched on in relation to the analysis of media organizations, has heavily criticized structuralist accounts of the media for their over-concentration on ideological elements.

Instead of starting from a concrete analysis of economic relations and the ways in which they structure both the processes and results of cultural production, they start by analysing the form and content of cultural artefacts and then working backwards to describe their economic base. The characteristic outcome is a top-heavy analysis in which an elaborate autonomy of cultural forms balances insecurely on a schematic account of economic forces shaping their production. (Murdock and Golding, 1977, p. 17)

Similarly, Garnham characterizes the post-Althusserian position 'popular within film studies' as 'an evacuation of the field of historical materialism' for determination in the last instance by the 'unconscious as theorized within an essentially idealist' problematic (Garnham, 1979, pp. 131-2)

Of course, 'idealism' and 'economism' are terms which are readily exchanged in arguments between Marxists, each protagonist invoking the name of the master and the spirit of historical materialism. The 'political economy' account of the media is well represented by Murdock's article later in the reader, which argues for the location of media power in the economic processes and structures of media production. In a return to the base/superstructure metaphor, 'political economists' conceive of ideology both as less important than, and determined by the economic base. Ideology is returned to the confines of 'false consciousness' and denied autonomous effectiveness. Also, since the fundamental nature of class struggle is grounded in economic antagonisms, the role of the media is that of concealing and misrepresenting these fundamental antagonisms. Ideology becomes the route through which struggle is obliterated rather than the site of struggle. Murdock and Golding contend that the pressure to maximize audiences and revenues produces a consistent tendency to avoid the 'unpopular and tendentious and draw instead on the values and assumptions which are most familiar and most widely legitimated' (Murdock and Golding, 1977, p. 37). The role of the media here is that of legitimation through the production of false consciousness, in the interests of a class which owns and controls the media. The main concern of this form of media research is, therefore, the increasing monopolization of the culture industry, through concentration and diversification.

Valuable though such research may be in summarizing the evidence on the ownership of the media, there are problems with this return to the classic model of base and superstructure. As Hall suggests, the advocates of 'political economy' 'conceive the economic level as not only a "necessary" but a "sufficient" explanation of cultural and ideological effects' (Hall, 1980, p. 15). Yet the focus on general economic forms of capitalism dissipates distinctions between different media practices and allows little in the way of specific historical analysis beyond the bare bones of ownership. There is obviously some justification in the arguments by political economists that ideology has been given priority at the expense of serious consideration of the economic determinants of the mass media. Yet political economy, in its present state of development, would return us to the view of the media as a distorting mirror, a window on reality, which misrepresents reality. This view of the media, combined with a predilection for empirical analysis in the area of ownership and media organizations, frequently seems to give political economy more in common with pluralist accounts of the media than with other Marxist accounts.

'Culturalist' studies of the media

Culturalist studies of the media could be said to stand in an uneasy and ambiguous position in relation to the theoretical concerns of structuralism and political economy. On the one hand the indigenous British tradition of cultural studies, initiated through the work of Williams, Thompson and Hoggart has always been opposed to economic reductionism. This position has been effectively summarized by Hall:

It (cultural studies) stands opposed to the residual and merely reflective role assigned to the 'cultural'. In its different ways it conceptualises culture as inter-woven with all social practices; and those practices, in turn, as a common form of human activity;

sensuous human praxis, the activity through which men and women make history. It is opposed to the base superstructure way of formulating the relationship between ideal and material forces, especially, where the base is defined by the determination by the 'economic' in any simple sense. It prefers the wider formulation — the dialectic between social being and social consciousness. . . . It defines 'culture' as both the means and values which arise amongst distinctive social groups and classes, on the basis of their given historical conditions and relationships, through which they 'handle' and respond to the conditions of existence: *and* as the lived traditions and practices through which those 'understandings' are expressed and in which they are embodied. (Hall, 1980, p. 63)

On the other hand, cultural studies incorporate a stress on experience as the 'authenticating' position and a humanist emphasis on the creative, which is very much at odds with the structuralist position outlined earlier. Where structuralism had focused on the autonomy and articulation of media discourses, culturalist studies seek to place the media and other practices within a society conceived of as a complex expressive totality.

This view of media power is present in recent work which attempts a combining of culturalist and structuralist views. *Policing the Crisis* (Hall *et al.*, 1978), for example, although theoretically eclectic in its bold, if not entirely successful, compound of a theory of hegemony derived from Gramsci, a sociology of 'moral panics', and an account of the social production of news, retains a view of society as an expressive totality. The crisis in hegemony which the authors identify has its basis in the decline of the British economy after the post-war boom but is resonated in the production of popular consent through the signification of a crisis in law and order in which the mass media play the key role. The media play their part in combination with other primary institutional definers (politicians, the police, the courts) in 'representing' this crisis. In the area of news, however, media definitions are 'secondary'. The media are not the primary definers of news events but their structured relationship to powerful primary definers has the effect of giving them a crucial role in reproducing the definitions of those who have privileged access to the media as 'accredited sources' (Hall *et al.*, 1978). They are partners in the signification spiral through which distinct and local problems, such as youth cultures, student protests and industrial action, are pulled together as part of a crisis in law and order. The framework again emphasizes the expressive inter-connections of the culturalist position. There are, of course, some unresolved problems in this approach, not least of which is the unevenness of the theoretical synthesis achieved. Hence, while the media are represented as a 'key terrain where consent is won or lost', they are also in other formulations conceived of as signifying a crisis which has already occurred, both in economic and political terms (Hall *et al.*, 1978).

The conceptual difficulties and problems registered in *Policing the Crisis* are, however, paradoxically part of its positive advance, in the sense that the thesis put forward, although emerging from a culturalist perspective, involves thinking through categories which cannot be neatly placed solely in the culturalist tradition. Moreover, the writers of *Policing the Crisis* make very clear their theoretical concerns. It may well be that this theoretical concern constitutes the most important shift in this and other recent research on the mass media. The most obvious heritage of structuralism, the argument that thought does not reflect reality but works upon and appropriates it, involves a commitment to theoretical reflection which marks all three of the approaches discussed here and the interchanges between them.

The theoretical perspectives on the mass media contained within Marxism share a general agreement that the power of the media is *ideological* but there are distinct differences in the conceptualization of ideology, ranging from the focus on the internal articulation of the signifying systems of the media within structuralist analysis, through to the focus on the determination of ideology in 'political economy' perspectives and to a culturalist view of the media as a powerful shaper of public consciousness and popular consent. Although disagreements about the role of the media as an ideological force within these approaches may be similar in their intensity to earlier debates on the nature of the power of the media, these are in no sense simple repetitions of earlier debates. The theoretical ground has shifted. Increasingly, work on the media has focused on a related series of issues: the establishment of the autonomy, or relative autonomy of the media and its specific effectiveness; tracing the articulation between the media and other ideological practices; and attempting to re-think the complex unity which such practices constitute together. The way in which questions in these areas have been posed does vary in relation to diferent Marxist and other perspectives, but it is in relation to these issues within Marxism that intellectual work on the nature of media power proceeds at present.

REFERENCES

Althusser, L. (1969) *For Marx*, London, Allen Lane.
Althusser, L. (1971) *Lenin and Philosophy and other essays*, London, New Left Books.
Althusser, L. (1976) *Essays in Self Criticism*, London, New Left Books.
Becker, L., McCombs, M. and McLeod, J. (1975) 'The development of political cognitions', in Chaffee, S. (ed.) *Political Communication: Issues and strategies for research*, Beverley Hills, Sage.
Berelson, B., Lazarsfeld, P. and McPhee, W. (1954) *Voting: a study of opinion formation in a presidential campaign*, Chicago, University of Chicago Press.
Blumler, J. (1977) 'The political effects of mass communication', in DE 353, *Mass Communication and Society*, Milton Keynes, Open University Press.
Centre for Contemporary Cultural Studies (1978) *On Ideology*, London, Hutchinson.
Chibnall, S. (1977) *Law-and-Order News*, London, Tavistock.
Clarke, J., Critcher, C. and Johnson, R. (1979) *Working-class culture*, London, Hutchinson.
Cohen, S. (1973) *Folk devils and moral panics*, St Albans, Paladin.

Connell, I. (1979) 'Television, news and the social contract', *Screen*, Spring 1979, 20(1).

Curran, J. and Seaton, J. (1980) *Power Without Responsibility*, London, Fontana.

Elliott, P. (1977) 'Media organisations and occupations: an overview', in Curran, J., Gurevitch, M. and Woollacott, J. *Mass Communication and Society*, London, Edward Arnold.

Garnham, N. (1979) 'Contribution to a political economy of mass communication', *Media, Culture and Society*, 1 (2).

Gitlin, T. (1978) 'Media sociology: the dominant paradigm', *Theory and Society*, 6.

Gurevitch, M. and Blumler, J. (1977) 'Linkages between the mass media and politics', in Curran, J., Gurevitch, M. and Woollacott, J. *Mass Communication and Society*, London, Edward Arnold.

Hall, S. (1974) 'Deviance, politics and the media', in McIntosh, M. and Rock, P. (eds) *Deviance and social control*, London, Tavistock.

Hall, S. Critcher, C., Jefferson T., Clarke, J. and Roberts, B. (1978) *Policing the crisis*, London, Macmillan.

Hall, S. (1980) 'Cultural studies: two paradigms', *Media, Culture and Society*, (2).

Hartman, P. (1979) 'News and public perceptions of industrial relations', *Media, Culture and Society*, 1 (3).

Hirst, P.Q. (1976) 'Althusser's theory of ideology', *Economy and Society*, 5.

Johnson, R. (1979) 'Culture and the historians'; 'Three problematics: elements of a theory of working-class culture', in Clarke *et. al. Working-class culture*, London, Hutchinson.

Katz, E. and Lazarsfeld, P. (1955) *Personal influence*, Glencoe, Free Press.

Klapper, J. (1960) *The effects of mass communication*, Glencoe, Free Press.

Lazarsfeld, P., Berelson, B. and Gaudet, H. (1948) *The people's choice*, New York, Columbia University Press.

McCron, R. (1976) 'Changing perspectives in the study of mass media and socialisation', in Halloran, J. (ed.) *Mass media and socialisation*, International Association for Mass Communication Research.

Marcuse, H. (1972) *One-Dimensional Man*, London, Abacus.

Marx, K. and Engels, F. (1970) *The German Ideology*, London, Lawrence and Wishart.

Morley, D. (1980) *The 'Nationwide' audience: structure and decoding*, London, British Film Institute.

Murdock, G. (1973) 'Political deviance: the press presentation of a militant mass demonstration', in Cohen, S. and Young, J. (eds) *The manufacture of news*, London, Constable.

Murdock, G. and Golding, P. (1977) 'Capitalism, communication and class relations', in Curran, J., Gurevitch, M. and Woollacott, J. *Mass Communication and Society*, London, Edward Arnold.

Trenaman, J. and McQuail, D. (1961) *Television and the political image*, London, Methuen.

Whannel, G. (1979) 'Football, crowd behaviour and the press', *Media, Culture and Society*, 1 (4).

Westergaard, J. and Ressler, H. (1975) *Class in a Capitalist Society: A study of contemporary Britain*, London, Heinemann.

2

Theories of the media, theories of society

TONY BENNETT

'MASS', 'MEDIA', 'COMMUNICATIONS'?

The new media distinctively associated with the nineteenth and twentieth centuries — the press, radio and television, the cinema and the record industry — have traditionally been grouped together under the heading 'mass media' and their study developed as a part of the sociology of mass communications. At one level, this inherited vocabulary fulfils a useful descriptive function; we know what is being referred to when such terms as 'the media of mass communication' are used. At another level, however, such terms may prove positively misleading. It is clear, for example, that the media which are customarily referred to in this way resemble one another only superficially. The relationships between the state and broadcasting institutions, for example, are quite different from those which obtain between the state and the press or, different yet again, between the state and the cinema. Similarly, the relationship between industry and audience is quite differently articulated in the case of the record industry as compared with the film industry.

More important, perhaps, the vocabulary of 'mass', 'media' and 'communications' frequently involves particular assumptions about the nature of such media, the processes of which they form a part and the ways in which these are connected with broader social and political processes and relationships. In its classical usage, for instance, the term 'mass' implied that the audience created by the new media was socially undifferentiated, lacking any clear divisions along class, sex or race lines. The other, the production side of the communication process, it is true, was rarely filled in, at least not in any degree of explicit detail. But the implication was clear. If the audience which constituted the receiving end of the communication process was to be regarded as a 'mass' or 'the masses', then the business of producing and transmitting messages was viewed as being vested in the hands of an élite, however it may have been defined. It was in this way that such terms as 'mass media' and 'media of mass communication' formed a part of a ready-built theory of society which answered in advance the more pertinent questions that might be put concerning the connections between the media and social processes. Between whom do the media communicate?

Between the élite and the masses, the few and many: the answer is pre-given in the concept.

It is true that, in its contemporary use, such connotations are rarely present in this inherited vocabulary. If the term 'mass media' still enjoys a widespread currency, this is more by force of habit than anything else; a convenient way of marking out an area of study rather than a means of stating how that area should be studied or of outlining the assumptions from which research should proceed. However, it is noteworthy that in recent research the media have tended to be grouped under different headings. Theodor Adorno and Max Horkheimer, for example, coined the phrase 'the culture industry' in referring to the collective operations of the media (Horkheimer and Adorno, 1972) whereas, more recently, Louis Althusser has grouped the media with the family, the church and the education system under the heading of 'ideological state apparatuses' (Althusser, 1971). Of course, there is more at stake here than the simple question of naming. Such shifts in vocabulary have involved and been a part of the development of new approaches to the study of the media within which the connection between media processes and broader social and political relationships are construed in terms which differ significantly from those embodied in the more traditional sociology of mass communications approaches.

My purpose in this essay is to tease out some of the broader issues which lie behind this apparently simple question of naming, by identifying the nature of the expectations and presuppositions which have influenced the way in which the study of the media has been approached from within different bodies of theory. More particularly, my concern is to show how the sorts of assumptions made about the broader structure of society within different bodies of theory have determined both the sorts of questions that have been posed in relation to the media and the way in which those questions have been pursued.

I will do so by commenting on four traditions of media theory. I shall deal, firstly, with the mass society tradition which, having a pedigree reaching back into the mid-nineteenth century, has viewed the development of the media pessimistically as constituting a threat to either the integrity of élite cultural values or the viability of the political institutions of democracy, or both. I shall then examine the contrary assumptions of liberal-pluralist schools of thought. According to these the media, functioning as the 'fourth estate', play an important part in the democratic process in constituting a source of information that is independent of the government. They are also viewed as adding to the series of counterveiling sources of power which, in liberal democracies, are said to prevent a disproportionate degree of power from being concentrated in any one section of the population or organ of government. Next, I shall consider the critical theory of the Frankfurt School as an instance of an attempt to incorporate the mass society critique and put it to use from within a Marxist framework. Finally, consideration will be given to more recent attempts to develop a

Marxist approach to the media as part of a more general theory of ideology concerned with the role played by ideological institutions in the process whereby existing relations of class domination are reproduced and perpetuated or, to the contrary, challenged and overthrown.

THEORIES OF MASS SOCIETY AND THE CRITIQUE OF MASS
CULTURE

The range and diversity of the theorists who are normally regarded as having contributed to the development of mass society theory is forbidding. We have thus, to name but a few, cultural theorists such as Matthew Arnold, T.S. Eliot, Friedrich Nietzsche and Ortega y Gasset; political theorists such as John Stuart Mill and Alexis de Tocqueville; the students of crowd or mass psychology from Gustave le Bon to Wilhelm Reich and Hannah Arendt; and, finally, such representatives of the Italian school of sociology as Vilfredo Pareto and Gaetano Mosca. Although conventionally grouped together as 'mass society theorists' on the somewhat loose grounds that they share the same vocabulary, the concerns articulated within these diverse traditions are, in some respects, quite different.

These difficulties are exacerbated by the fact that the mass society conception has been complemented by the parallel perceptions of social theorists working in other areas. The writings of the founding fathers of classical sociology have been particularly important in this respect. There can be little doubt that the theories of such scholars as Ferdinand Tönnies and Emile Durkheim concerning the implications of the dissolution of traditional forms of social relationships for the maintenance of social cohesion did much to lend academic weight and credence to the thesis of social atomization which underpins most variants of mass society theory (see Bramson, 1961). It is, as a result, somewhat difficult to draw a clearly defined boundary line around the mass society tradition which tends, rather, to be 'fuzzy' at the edges, merging imperceptibly with the related theoretical traditions upon which it has drawn at various moments in its history.

The mass society tradition, then, by no means constitutes a unified and tightly integrated body of theory. It should rather be viewed as a loosely defined 'outlook' consisting of a number of intersecting themes — the decline of the 'organic community', the rise of mass culture, the social atomization of 'mass man'. Taken collectively, these have articulated a polyphony of negative and pessimistic reactions to the related processes of industrialization, urbanization, the development of political democracy, the beginnings of popular education and the emergence of contemporary forms of 'mass communication'.

The themes which comprise this outlook, however, have been orchestrated in different ways within different strands of the mass society tradition. For some theorists, responsibility for the emergence of mass society is imputed to the incorporation of 'the masses' within the formal processes of government via the extension of the franchise. For others, it is imputed to the levelling and homogenizing effects of a market economy or to the preponderance which has been given to the opinion of the 'average man' by the development of the press. Similarly, whilst some fear the threat to élite values of excellence embodied in the standards of mediocrity which the 'reign of the masses' is said to have promoted, others fear that, politically, the power attained by the masses has seriously threatened the viability of democracy to the extent that it has strengthened the role which irrational forces, the so-called psychology of the crowd, play in the political process. There are also those who consider that the primary threat embodied by mass society relates to the masses themselves to the extent that their atomization has rendered them vulnerable to manipulation by the élite, the passive prey for whatever predators might be stalking the political jungle.

Whilst an adequate treatment of the variations of stress and emphasis that have characterized the mass society tradition cannot be attempted here, a brief adumbration of its more central themes should suffice for current purposes. (More extended surveys can be found in Bramson, 1961, Giner, 1976, Kornhauser, 1960 and Swingewood, 1977.) Five such themes can be distinguished:

The tensions of liberalism

Although he cannot be regarded as a mass society theorist proper, Mill's fears for the health of the body politic reflected that sense of increasing tension between the ideals of liberty, equality and democracy which has come to typify the liberal variant of the mass society critique. Mill's central concern was that democratic forms of government gave rise to the danger of a new form of despotism — the 'tyranny of the majority'. He consequently called for a series of constitutional provisions which would curb and limit the power of the majority by defining the spheres within which that power might be legitimately exercised whilst retaining due respect for the autonomy and rights of the individual. However, Mill was as much concerned by the moral authority exerted by the majority as by its exercise of power in the formal or constitutional sense:

Protection, therefore, against the tyranny of the magistrate is not enough: there needs to be protection also against the tyranny of the prevailing opinion and feeling: against the tendency of society to impose, by other means than civil penalties, its own ideas and practices as rules of conduct on those who dissent from them; to fetter the development, and, if possible, prevent the formation, of any individuality not in harmony with its ways, and compel all characters to fashion themselves upon the model of its own. (Mill, 1969, p. 9)

The concern expressed here, the fear of social homogenization, has been central to the mass society outlook. Mill goes on to develop this theme in the chapter of his essay *On Liberty* devoted to the subject of 'individuality' where he argues that the differences between classes, regions and professions have been so blurred by the development of the market, by popular education and by new means and forms of communication as to result in a tendency toward conditions of moral and intellectual uniformity. Rather than being viewed as vehicles of enlightenment, popular education and the press are regarded as reducing intelligence to the level of the lowest common denominator, the promoters of a moral and intellectual medio-crity. It is worth noting, however, that Mill viewed the threat to moral and intellectual authority as being posed less by 'the masses', in the sense of a modern variant of the mob, than by the dull complacency of the self-satisfied middle classes.

Mass/élite theories

Although apprehensive with regard to the cultural consequences of the extension of the franchise and the development of literacy, Mill did not oppose these developments so much as merely point to their consequences and to the safeguards that would need to be taken against them. In this, he was typical of the English strand of the mass society critique which, on the whole, has been somewhat qualified in its élitism, hedging it around with a good degree of obeisance to democratic and egalitarian susceptibilities. It is thus noticeable that, for the greater part, the division between élites and masses, as it has been construed by English social and cultural theorists, has been represented as a socially and culturally produced division rather than as one resting on the differential distribution of innate natural characteristics.

The main thrust of the continental tradition of mass society theory has run in the opposite direction. Among the more important figures here are José Ortega and Friedrich Nietzsche. Stridently anti-democratic, these shared the view that men were naturally divided between the weak and the strong, between those destined to be the objects of the wills of others and those who were self-willed, and construed the social division between the élite and the masses as a product of the unequal distribution of such innate characteristics.

The difficulty, as far as Nietzsche and Ortega were concerned, was that this 'natural' balance between élites and masses had been threatened by the advent of democracy, the development of the press and of popular education and, more generally, by the dissolution of those traditional forms of social relationships which allegedly had hitherto clearly defined for the masses their subordinate 'place' within a hierarchically structured social order. In short, they feared that the rule of the élite was over and the reign of the rabble about to begin unless the former could be induced to rouse itself, to turn back the tide of democracy and liberalism which threatened to engulf it.

The masses and moral disorder

An enduring theme in the work of the founding fathers of the sociological tradition was the concern with the threat of moral disorder which was said to be posed by the disintegration of the traditional social ties binding the individual to the community and defining his or her place within it. In England where, as Perry Anderson has noted (see Anderson, 1969), questions concerning the integration of the social order have more usually been the province of literary and cultural criticism than of sociology, similar concerns have been expressed in the tradition of cultural analysis running from Matthew Arnold to T.S. Eliot and F.R. Leavis. Typifying this tradition has been the perception that social anarchy, the threat of social turbulence from 'below', can be regarded as the consequence of cultural anarchy defined as a condition in which the cultures of different classes or social groups are in competition with one another rather than coexisting, as mutually complementary parts, within a cohesively integrated system of cultural relationships. Matthew Arnold communicates this apprehension very nicely in his description of the 'Hyde Park rough', his oblique way of referring to working class political protest:

He has no visionary schemes of revolution and transformation, though of course he would like his class to rule, as the aristocratic class like their class to rule, and the middle class theirs. But meanwhile our social machine is a little out of order.... The rough has not yet quite found his groove and settled down to his work, and so he is just asserting his personal liberty a little, going where he likes, assembling where he likes, bawling as he likes, hustling as he likes. Just as the rest of us, — as the country squires in the aristocratic class, as the political dissenters in the middle class, — he has no idea of a *State*, of the nation in its collective and corporate character controlling, as government, the free swing of this or that one of its members in the name of the higher reason of all of them, his own as well as that of others. (Arnold, 1971, p. 65)

Writing in the aftermath of the popular agitation that had accompanied the progress of the 1867 Reform Bill, Arnold's fear of anarchy was a real one and he was quite unequivocal in declaring that, when and where necessary, this threat should be countered by the use of directly coercive means. The need that he articulated, however, was for the formation of a 'centre of authority', embodied in the state, that would reduce such occasions to a minimum by producing, within the members of all classes, a voluntary compliance with the direction given to social and political life by the representatives of such a 'centre of authority'. In doing so, and in this he was entirely typical of the mass society tradition, Arnold responded to the *political* problem of social disorder by redifining it as a *cultural* problem. If anarchy threatens, he argued, it is because the mechanisms of 'culture' — that is, of an integrative system of values, 'the best that has been thought and known in the world' — have broken down with the result that different classes pursue their own interests rather than subordinating them to a consensually agreed upon 'centre of authority'.

The masses and totalitarianism

Perhaps the most pessimistic current of the mass society outlook is that which seeks to argue a connection between the social conditions of 'mass man' and the rise of totalitarian social and political movements. The most influential tendency within this current of thought has been that represented by Hannah Arendt and Carl Friedrich.

Regarding Nazism and Stalinism as mere variants of an essentially similar form of totalitarianism, they have sought to explain them as the result of the entry into politics of irrational forces which the age of mass democracy is said to have inaugurated by giving political weight to the opinions of the masses during a period when their social atomization rendered them pliable to élite manipulation. Arguing that the nineteenth century witnessed the almost complete fragmentation of the social structure, the creation of a society without classes or even primary social groupings, men — and women, it needs to be added — were said to enter the twentieth century in a condition of utter isolation and alienation, totally lacking the degree of psychic self-reliance which their situation required. Rootless, lonely, directionless, 'mass man' thus constituted ready-made fodder for totalitarian parties to the extent that the chiliastic ideologies these espoused offered him a means by which he might overcome his puniness and isolation, the psychic pain of responsibility, by merging his will with that of a mass movement.

Mass culture versus folk culture

Finally, it has been argued that the development of mass society has been accompanied by the formation of a new type of culture — 'mass culture' — which, in its pervasiveness, threatens to undermine, to destroy by contamination, the qualities of moral and aesthetic excellence inscribed in the 'high culture' of the educated élite and which is construed as grossly inferior to the 'organic', supposedly more robust forms of 'folk culture' which had previously comprised the cultural life of the common people. In place of a sturdy, self-reliant and self-created culture celebrating the wholesome values of an organic folk, it is contended, we now have a weak and insipid 'mass culture' which is commercially produced and offered to the masses for their passive consumption:

Folk Art grew from below. It was a spontaneous, autochthonous expression of the people, shaped by themselves, pretty much without the benefit of High Culture, to suit their own needs. Mass Culture is imposed from above. It is fabricated by technicians hired by businessmen; its audiences are passive consumers, their participation limited to the choice between buying and not buying. . . . Folk Art was the people's own institution, their private little garden walled off from the great formal park of their masters' High Culture. But Mass Culture breaks down the wall, integrating the masses into a debased form of High Culture and thus becoming an instrument of political domination. (MacDonald, 1957, p. 60)

THE MASS SOCIETY OUTLOOK AND MEDIA RESEARCH

It can be seen from the above that the theory of mass society constructs its critique of modern society by positing a linked series of historical contrasts

between past and present. Once upon a time, it is argued, social relationships were communal and organic in nature. People knew where they were.
Their place within the order of things was clearly fixed and legitimated by a
universally binding system of beliefs and values. The distinction between
élites and masses — or, in this case, the rustic folk — was clearly constructed and culture was clearly stratified, the folk growing wise in their own way
rather than cutting their cultural teeth on the inferior, handed-down
versions of the high culture of society's élites. Since then, the development
of industry, in breaking up traditional social relationships, has thrown men
and women into isolation and self-reliance, the promise of freedom having
turned into the living nightmare of *anomie* and alienation. Democracy has
turned into its opposite as new forms of tyranny, playing on the fears and
isolation of a social atomized population, have established themselves. And
culture, in being spread, has degenerated into moral and aesthetic
barbarism.

The above sketch is, of course, a caricature. And deliberately so. For it
has been largely in such highly simplified and condensed forms that the
mass society critique has enjoyed a widespread currency outside the narrow
enclaves of academia. Daniel Bell, writing in 1960, argued that, Marxism
apart, the theory of mass society was 'probably the most influential theory
in the western world today' (Bell, 1960, p. 21). Yet, assessed as a body of
theory, the mass society critique leaves much to be desired. Its key terms,
for example, have always been notoriously imprecise. The masses and the
élite have usually been simply negatively defined as the obverse of one
another instead of each being positively identified in terms of some
objective set of social characteristics. Perhaps most important, however, is
the fact that, for all that the theory depends on establishing a series of
historical distinctions and making them work, it has notably failed to do so.
The contrast between the organic community and mass society clearly
depends on a highly romanticized conception of the past, as is evidenced by
the fact that it has proved impossible to state, with any precision, when the
one ended and the other began.

However, even assuming that the concepts of the organic community and
mass society could be given the degree of historical support they require,
there would still remain the problem of actually accounting for the
transition between the two. Here, to cite Daniel Bell once more, the theory
of mass society is crucially flawed in the respect that it 'affords us no view of
the relations of the parts of the society to each other that would enable us to
locate the sources of change' (Bell, 1960, p. 38). Why is the dominance of
élites toppled? Why are the integrated social relationships which comprise
the organic community fragmented? Unable to account for these
developments as a product of the organization of the organic community
itself in the same way, for example, that Marx accounted for the downfall of
feudal society as the result of contradictions inscribed within its very
structure, mass society theorists have had no alternative but to attribute
responsibility for the demise of the organic community to such exogenous

factors as the rise of democracy, the spread of literacy, the development of the media and so on. But, of course, unless these developments are themselves accounted for in terms of their articulation with other social forces, tendencies and contradictions, any such explanation is necessarily inadequate.

It is somewhat surprising, in view of these difficulties, that the mass society outlook should have proved so influential in defining the field of vision within which so many of the initial empirical inquiries into the social role of the media were located. Yet, until recently, its influence in this respect has been absolutely preponderant. The general philosophical reflections of the more noted exponents of the mass society outlook have, of course, always been buttressed by an underlying level of social commentary which has viewed the development of the media with apprehension. However, it was not really until the 1930s, either in this country or in America, that the media were mapped out as a field of study in a formal or academic sense. Yet, initially, this had little effect on the issues addressed. Although there were some who took exception to it, the 'force-field' exerted by the mass society outlook still determined the questions around which the debate was conducted.

Some indication of what this has meant for inquiry into the media in this country can be gleaned from the work of the *Scrutiny* group. F.R. Leavis's *Mass Civilization and Minority Culture* (1930) and Q.D. Leavis's *Fiction and the Reading Public* (1932) played a particularly important role in the formation of the *Scrutiny* perspective. 'In any period,' F.R. Leavis argued, 'it is upon a very small minority that the discerning appreciation of art and literature depends: it is only a few who are capable of unprompted first hand judgements.' Endorsing this view, Q.D. Leavis went on to argue that 'the individual has a better chance of obtaining access to the fullest (because finest) life in a community dominated by "society"' — by which she means 'a select, cultured element of the community that set the standards of behaviour and judgement, in direct opposition to the common people' — 'than in one protesting the superiority of the herd' (Q.D. Leavis, 1965, p. 202). Given this perspective, the history of the reading public which Q.D. Leavis offers becomes, inevitably, a history of deteriorating standards. As a consequence of the authority of the cultured minority having been attenuated by the intrusion of market forces into the sphere of culture, she argues, pulp journalism has replaced respectable journalism, the novel has become sentimentalized, diversion has replaced edification as the motive for reading and, oh horrors! the presumption of the middle-brow public encouraged it to argue for a place for Arnold Bennett or even Ernest Hemingway on the university curriculum.

The debate with the mass society outlook in America — chiefly conducted from the late 1930s through to the 1950s — took a different form. This was, in good part, because the debate was conducted by sociologists rather than, as in Britain, by literary or cultural theorists. This had two consequences. First, the debate focused more on the 'social organization' than on the 'cultural' end of the mass society critique: the question as to whether the thesis of social atomization could be substantiated, that is to say, was more to the fore than questions concerning the cultural consequences of the development of the media. Second, reflecting the markedly positivist theoretical culture of American sociology at the time, the debate was conducted in an empirical rather than a speculative mode as an attempt was made to check whether the central tenets of the mass society thesis would stand up to the test of controlled empirical examination.

In some studies, it is true, the central tenets of the mass society thesis seemed to be empirically corroborated. In their *Small Town in Mass Society*, for example, Vidich and Benseman argued that the media were ubiquitous, overwhelming local organs of opinion formation to produce a situation in which, politically, the small town had 'surrendered' to the mass society surrounding it. The preponderant tendency of the period, however, was to undercut rather than to underwrite the terms of the mass society critique. Detailed studies of audience reactions to and use of the media played a particularly important role in this respect, suggesting that the average member of the audience 'reacts not merely as an isolated personality but also as a member of the various groups to which he belongs and with which he communicates' (Lazarsfeld and Kendall, 1949, p. 399). Such primary groups as the family, the church, the local trade-union branch or business community, it was argued, were by no means moribund — as the mass society critique had implied — but constituted the filters, the points of mediation, between the individual and the media. In short, it was argued that the audience, far from being a homogeneous mass, was profoundly heterogeneous, the way in which media messages were received and interpreted — and, consequently, the effects that might be imputed to them — being conditioned by the primary group pressures to which they were subject *en route* to the individual. Equally, if the audience was not homogenized, neither were the media. Nor were they necessarily distant and remote, impersonally relaying messages to an anonymous audience. Morris Janowitz, in a study of community newspapers, thus showed that these tended to have flourished rather than to have declined under the pressure of the national media and, in view of this, was able to argue that the media, rather than destroying local communities, often played a vital role in their maintenance (Janowitz, 1952).

An attempt was made, as an extension of this argument, to transform the phrase 'mass society' from a pejorative into a positive term. Having condemned the mass society critique on the grounds of its excessive élitism, for example, Edward Shils proceeded to appropriate the term 'mass society' in support of a liberal-pluralist position (see Shils, 1957 and 1962). He did so by arguing that many of the developments outlined within the mass society position — the dissolution of non-rational forms of social attachment, the weakening of traditional ties and obligations, the attenuation of the power of established hierarchies — tended to augment the democratic process rather than to undermine it. If, by 'mass society', one meant a society in which 'the masses' had moved from the periphery to the centre of social, political and cultural life, then, Shils declared, he was all for it — provided that the mass was conceived not as a simple agglomeration but as a pluralist hotch-potch of differing regional, ethnic, religious and economic primary groupings.

We can see here how, in the work of such sociologists as Shils and Daniel Bell, the liberal-pluralist tradition of social theory emerged from within the mass society tradition by means of a criticism of it. This development was not restricted to the field of media sociology but formed part of a general revision of the heritage of European social theory undertaken by the younger generation of American sociologists in the war and immediately post-war years. This, in turn, was not unrelated to the need, given the war against Nazi Germany and, later, the tensions of the Cold-War period, to develop a theory that would distinguish the social structure of western democracies from those of totalitarian political systems rather than, as the mass society critique tended to, lumping them all together.

The contours of this argument were most formally stated by such political theorists as Joseph Schumpeter who defined the democratic method as 'that institutional arrangement for arriving at political decisions in which individuals acquire the power to decide by means of a competitive struggle for people's votes' (Schumpeter, 1976, p. 269). Basically, this amounted to saying that democracy, as its critics had contended, was indeed a system of government by élites but one in which the majority retained the right to determine, periodically, precisely which élite should govern. The contribution of American sociologists to this emergency repair job on the liberal-democratic tradition was to furnish a concept of social structure capable of breathing life into such dry constitutional bones. If the democratic process worked, they contended, it was because the wide range and variety of competing interest groups which constituted the bedrock of the social structure constantly checked and limited one another so as to prevent any one group from assuming a position of preponderance in relation to the others. Further, the incorporation of the masses into the political life of the nation, instead of being viewed negatively, was held to constitute a constraint which those élites temporarily vested with the responsibility for government could not afford to ignore.

These theoretical realignments had marked consequences for the way in which the media were viewed. Once regarded as the villains of mass society, they came to be viewed as the unsung heroes of liberalism-pluralism triumphant. The media, it was contended, were far from monolithic. The clash and diversity of the viewpoints contained within them contributed to the free and open circulation of ideas, thereby enabling them to play the role of a 'fourth estate' through which governing élites could be pressurized and reminded of their dependency on majority opinion. Further, in a decisive rejection of the mass culture critique, the media's role as the purveyors of culture was defended as it was pointed out that, in addition to an admittedly slushy pulp culture, they were also responsible for making the established classics of high culture available to a wider audience whose cultural standards had been lifted with rising educational standards.

There can be little doubt but that, at the empirical level, the audience research undertaken by American sociologists during the 1940s and 1950s forcibly challenged the founding assumptions of the mass society outlook. The system of concepts that they proposed in place of this, however, is not so convincing. The modified version of democracy proposed by Schumpeter was only too clearly an attempt to cut the concept down to size, to trim it so as to enable it to 'fit' the observed workings of the American political system. More important, perhaps, the revisions that were proposed in relation to the concept of democracy did not entirely escape the criticisms that had been levelled against parliamentary forms of democracy by both Marxist and élite theorists. Schumpeter's definition, for example, does not differ significantly from Marx's castigation of bourgeois democracy as a system in which the oppressed are allowed, every few years, to decide which particular representatives of the ruling class shall be allowed to represent and repress them in parliament.

More particular difficulties are posed by the structure of media ownership. It is true, as Ralph Miliband has put it, that there is no field in which 'the claims of democratic diversity and free political competition which are made on behalf of the "open societies" of advanced capitalism appear to be more valid than in the field of communications' (Miliband, 1969, p. 219). But, as Miliband goes on to argue, to accept such appearances at face value would be to ignore both the highly concentrated structure of media ownership and the fact that the range of variation within the political perspectives of the dominant media is, in fact, extraordinarily narrow. Such criticisms have induced a modification of the liberal-pluralist thesis in the respect that it now tends to seek confirmation by analyzing the relationships *within* rather than those *between* media organizations. To put the point crudely, ownership of the media may be oligopolized but, it is argued, the interests of democratic diversity are nevertheless secured by virtue of the clash and discordancy of interests which exist between owners, managers, editors and journalists. Having originated in the study of the complex heterogeneity of media audiences, the liberal-pluralist perspective has since complemented such audience studies by examining the complex heterogeneity of the other, the production end of the communications process. It is noticeable, however, that a concern with what happens in between — with the structure and content of media messages — is an extremely poorly developed part of this tradition which lacks anything approaching an adequate theory or method for the analysis of signifying systems.

THE FRANKFURT SCHOOL AND THE CRITIQUE OF THE 'CULTURE INDUSTRY'

Although predominantly a conservative tradition, the mass society outlook has also influenced the development of Marxist theories of the media. Nor is this surprising. Marx and Engels wrote suggestively on questions of the media and ideology, but they did not offer an elaborated body of theory with which to deal with such questions. Given this absence, early attempts to construct a Marxist critique of the media were virtually obliged to submit to the 'field of force' exerted by the mass society outlook. In doing so, however, they inflected its criticisms leftward, reworking them by putting them to use within the context of a critique of the media's impact in impeding the formation of a socialist political consciousness amongst members of the working class. The critique of the 'culture industry' constructed by the Frankfurt School was undoubtedly the most interesting of the attempts to fuse Marxist and mass society categories in this way.

The label of 'the Frankfurt School' is usually applied to the collective thought of those theorists — most notably, Theodor Adorno, Herbert Marcuse and Max Horkheimer — associated with the Institute for Social Research founded in Frankfurt in 1923. Recruiting largely from the cream of the young radical intellectuals of Weimar Germany, some of them disillusioned ex-Communist Party members, the Institute set itself the task of keeping the critical light of Marxism burning during the 'dark years' which its members saw ahead. Owing to this radical orientation, and to the predominantly Jewish background of its members, the accession of Hitler to the German chancellorship in 1933 forced the removal of the Institute to New York where, until 1942, it was affiliated to the Sociology Department of the University of Columbia. In 1949, Max Horkheimer, who had succeeded Carl Grunberg as director of the Institute in 1930, led the Institute back to Frankfurt — although Marcuse chose to remain in California. Horkheimer was succeeded as head of the Institute by Adorno who remained in that position until his death in 1968.

Applying the brush with broad strokes, the intellectual perspectives of the Frankfurt theorists were shaped by three major historical experiences. First, they shared a sense of monumental disappointment that the revolution of 1917 had not spread to western Europe. They were dismayed by the downturn in the revolutionary tide which resulted from this failure and by the fatal direction which, in their view, the dominance of Stalinism subsequently gave to working-class politics. Second, a deep and lasting impression was made on them by the experience of fascism which continued to haunt their works until well into the post-war epoch. Finally, they were deeply concerned by the apparent political stability which had been achieved in the post-war western world and attempted to describe and account for the ideological transformations by which this stability had been produced.

This, then, was the perspective which informed the Frankfurt theorists' historical vision. The dialectic of history, the mutually interactive relationship between the subject (human agents) and the object (the social conditions of their existence) appeared to have been fractured, the result being a complete social stasis in conditions which, so far as Adorno was concerned, were little short of hell. How had this come about? The

Frankfurt theorists sought the answer to this question on the subject rather than the object side of the equation. If the prospect of radical social change no longer seemed imminent, they argued, this was substantially because the consciousness of a need for such change had been eliminated, yielding an ideological climate in which the prospect of a horizon beyond the limits constituted by the present had been virtually lobotomized.

To do even rough justice to the Frankfurt analysis of the mechanisms whereby oppositional social and intellectual forces were said to have been thus contained and brought to heel would be a lengthy undertaking (Jay, 1973, and Slater, 1977, offer useful general surveys). We can only deal here with those aspects of the analysis which bear most closely on the media.

One of the more challenging thrusts of Marcuse's *One Dimensional Man* (1968) is the contention that the apparent rationality of production in advanced capitalism renders the social system as such immune to criticism. The system is 'sold' by its success, by its ability to produce the goods:

The productive apparatus and the goods and services which it produces 'sell' or impose the social system as a whole. The means of mass transportation and communication, the commodities of lodging, food, and clothing, the irresistible output of the entertainment and information industry carry with them prescribed attitudes and habits, certain intellectual and emotional reactions which bind the consumers more or less pleasantly to the producers and, through the latter, to the whole. The products indoctrinate and manipulate; they promote a false consciousness which is immune against its falsehood.... Thus emerges a pattern of *one-dimensional thought and behaviour* in which ideas, aspirations, and objectives that, by their content, transcend the established universe of discourse and action are either repelled or reduced to the terms of this universe. (Marcuse, 1968, pp. 26-7)

This tendency of the system of production to inoculate itself against subversion, Marcuse argued, has been reinforced by the tendency for the terms in which political issues are publicly discussed to be limited to the question of determining which techniques (for example, the debate between Keynesian and monetarist forms of economic policy) are best capable of managing the system as it is and of containing its contradictions. For the possibility of scheduling alternative political ends which qualitatively transcend or are at odds with existing social arrangements is automatically excluded from the terms of reference established by such debates. It was this tendency that Marcuse had in mind when he referred to the media's role in effecting a 'closing of the universe of discourse'.

In an analysis of the presentation of prominent public figures in the American popular press, for example, Marcuse argued that the language used tended toward an 'authoritarian identification of person and function' (Marcuse, 1968, p. 83) resulting in a 'functionalized, abridged and unified language' (ibid., p. 85) which militated against conceptual thought. Commenting on the use of 'hyphenized abridgement' in the following phrase: 'Georgia's high-handed, low-browed governor ... had the stage all set for one of his wild political rallies last week', he argues:

The governor, his function, his physical features, and his political practices are fused together into one indivisible and immutable structure which, in its natural innocence and immediacy, overwhelms the reader's mind. The structure leaves no space for distinction, development, differentiation of meaning: it moves and lives only as a whole. (ibid., p. 83)

Marcuse's objection is thus to the 'overwhelming concreteness' of newspaper copy: 'This language, which constantly imposes *images*, militates against the development and expression of *concepts*. In its immediacy and directness, it impedes conceptual thinking; thus, it impedes thinking' (ibid., p. 84).

The media, then, define for us the very terms in which we are to 'think' (or not 'think') the world. Their influence has to be assessed not in terms of what we think about or this or that particular issue, but in terms of the way in which they condition our entire intellectual *gestalt*. The threat they embody is that they inhibit thought itself by inducing us to live, mentally, in a world of hypnotic definitions and automatic ideological equations which rule out any effective cognitive mediation on our part. (Pateman, 1975, offers a useful and interesting extension of this argument.)

It was, however, perhaps in their assessment of the cultural consequences of the mass media that the negativity of the Frankfurt theorists' vision received its most acute expression. For they did not limit their concerns to the more obvious manifestations of pulp culture produced by the American film and music industries. True, they did devote considerable attention to these, describing their mechanisms and effects, which they regarded as being virtually wholly narcotic or, worse, lobotomic, in some detail (see especially, Horkheimer and Adorno, 1972). More distinctively, however, they also argued that the media had invaded and subverted the world of traditional high or bourgeois culture, making it more widely available only at the price of depriving it of the 'aura' of its separateness upon which its critical function had depended.

According to the Frankfurt theorists, the bourgeois culture of the nineteenth century had always been, if only equivocally, an oppositional culture. Sealed off from the everyday world of business and commerce, it had spoken for the ideals and aspirations which remained suppressed within the work-a-day world of the bourgeois order. Art, that is, belonged to the 'second dimension'. It embodied a vision of an alternative to existing social relationships and, in doing so, kept alive the concept of transcendence. It was, in short, subversive.

Within the social and cultural fabric of monopoly capitalism, however, art is said to have been deprived of its oppositional value. It has been tamed by being made a part of the established order. In part, this was viewed as a by-product of the nature of commodity exchange inasmuch as, concerned only with exchange values, a market economy is able to harness to its own purposes even those use values which are ostensibly opposed to it. Thus, just as Che Guevera is good for the poster business and Maoism generates a new fashion in headwear, so art — even the most subversive art — may be good for business, deprived of its critical value in being reduced to the level of a mere means for the self-reproduction of capital. I recall a particularly telling example of this in the form of an advertisement, inserted by Lloyds Bank in *The Times* in 1974, which consisted of a full-page colour reproduction of Matisse's *Le Pont* beneath which there appeared the legend: 'Business is our life, but life isn't all business'. Profoundly contradictory, what was ostensibly opposed to economic life was thus made to become a part of it, what was separate became assimilated, as any critical dimension which might once have pertained to Matisse's painting was eclipsed by its new and unsolicited function as an advertisement for the wares of finance capital.

More generally the Frankfurt theorists contended that, quite contrary to the optimism of such liberal-pluralists as Edward Shils, the media made the world of serious culture more widely accessible only at the price of depriving it of its critical substance. For the media, by bringing culture into everyday life, wrenched it from the tradition which had guaranteed it its separateness just as the techniques of mass reproduction deprived the work of art of the 'aura' of its uniqueness on which alone its critical function could be predicated. Marcuse argues the point with force and clarity:

The neo-conservative critics of leftist critics of mass culture ridicule the protest against Bach as background music in the kitchen, against Plato and Hegel, Shelley and Baudelaire, Marx and Freud in the drugstore. Instead, they insist on recognition of the fact that the classics have left the mausoleum and come to life again, that people are just so much more educated. True, but coming to life as classics, they come to life as other than themselves; they are deprived of their antagonistic force, of the estrangement which was the very dimension of their truth. The intent and function of these works have thus fundamentally changed. If they once stood in contradiction to the *status quo*, this contradiction is now flattened out. (Marcuse, 1970, p. 64)

It is this aspect of the Frankfurt critique which has been taken up most frequently by cultural theorists on the left. In particular, mention should be made of Walter Benjamin who argued that the development of techniques permitting the reproduction of works of art on a limitless scale, depriving them of their 'aura', the uniqueness of their singular existence, had created the technical preconditions whereby art, in being freed from the sacredness of its singular presence, was able to enter the domain of politics in a form in which it could be both produced and appropriated by the masses (Benjamin, 1970).

This was decidedly *not* the perspective of the Frankfurt theorists. Art, they argued, could fulfil its oppositional function only by refusing any compromise with reality. But, by the same token, it was thereby unable to have any impact on the consciousness of those whose minds are forged in the midst of a compromised reality. If art did compromise so that it might be made available to the masses it would, by the same token, lose its oppositional value. Adorno summarized this dilemma as follows:

The effect that they [works of art] would wish to have is at present absent, and they suffer from that absence greatly; but as soon as they attempt to attain that effect by accommodating themselves to prevailing needs, they deprive men of precisely that which they could ... give them. (Cited in Slater, 1977, p. 141)

The result was the advocacy of a policy of retreatism in relation to the media which, it was argued, were so compromised that they could not be used by oppositional social forces:

No work of art, no thought, has a chance of survival, unless it bears within it repudiation of the false riches and high-class production, of colour films and television, millionaire's magazines and Toscanini. The older media, not designed for mass production, take on a new timelessness: that of exemption and improvization. They alone could outflank the united front of trusts and technology. In a world where books have long lost all likeness to books, the real book can no longer be one. If the invention of the printing press inaugurated the bourgeois era, the time is at hand for its repeal by the mimeograph, the only fitting, the unobtrusive means of dissemination. (Adorno, 1974, pp. 20-1)

How one chooses to assess the Frankfurt School depends on the perspective from which one views it. Karl Popper once remarked in a radio programme that, so far as he could see, Adorno had nothing to say, and, what is more, said it in a Hegelian fashion. This, in an exaggerated way, typifies the response to the Frankfurt theorists on the part of the mainstream of Anglo-Saxon philosophy which, rather than criticizing their works in a sustained or rigorous fashion, has been content to claim that they are simply incomprehensible, Hegelian mumbo-jumbo at its worst.

The reaction from the left has been more equivocal. For there can be little doubt that the Frankfurt School has acted as an influential theoretical ginger group in relation to the mainstream of Marxism. The centrality it accorded to the study of ideology has played an important role in undermining the economism which has always been a strong tendency within Marxism. There is also little doubt that the perspective of containment — the analysis of the ideological means whereby the contradictions of capitalism are contained or held in check — has proved influential. Nevertheless, the philosophical premises on which the Frankfurt critique rested — particularly its philosophical negativity — have been, by and large, rejected; more so in Britain than in America, however, where the journal *Telos* has kept the Frankfurt flag flying. The reasons for this rejection have principally concerned the role the Frankfurt theorists assigned to the category of 'negation'. In opposition to the Leninist construction of the relationship between theory and practice — that theory must become practical by gripping the minds and directing the activities of the proletariat through the mediation of an organized political party — the Frankfurt theorists, particularly Adorno, argued that theory must give up the endeavour to change the world by transforming itself into practice. Theory thus became passive, negative in its function. Theory's purpose was not to change the world but to oppose to the world its powers of negation, to refuse to confer on it a Hegelian consecration of the rationality of its reality. By thus adopting a position of transcendence in relation to reality, theory was, at the same time, deprived of any means whereby it might connect with reality in order to change it.

The consequences of this were serious. 'For in negative fault finding,'

Hegel argued, 'one stands nobly and with proud mien above the matter without penetrating into it and without comprehending its positive aspects' (Hegel, 1953, p. 47). This exactly describes the position of the Frankfurt theorists. Although they condemned reality in round terms, they had no positive suggestions to make as to how it might be changed. Counterposing to 'that which is' an ideal conception of 'that which ought to be', but unable to locate any concrete social mechanisms whereby the gap between the two might be bridged, the result of their criticism was merely to leave everything as it is. Our current social reality was castigated as a 'bad reality', indeed as irremediably bad, but, by the same token, it was simultaneously philosophically immortalized. Their policy of retreatism in relation to the media aptly symbolized this for, as Brecht argues, its result could only be to perpetuate the conditions that had prompted the critique in the first place:

Anybody who advises us not to make use of such new apparatus [the media] just confirms the right of the apparatus to do bad work; he forgets himself out of sheer open-mindedness, for he is thus proclaiming his willingness to have nothing but dirt produced for him. (Brecht, 1964, p. 47)

MARXISM: CLASS, IDEOLOGY AND THE MEDIA

The Frankfurt theorists, although remaining committed to Marxism, broached the task of analysing the relationship between class, ideology and the media through the conceptual prism supplied by an amalgam of the mass society critique and the presuppositions of German philosophical idealism grafted on to the framework of Marxist theory. More recent developments in Marxist theory have opened up a different theoretical space within which questions pertaining to the ideological role of the media are subject to a different formulation.

Before surveying these developments, however, some more general comments on the concept of ideology are in order. As we have noted, Marx and Engels did not provide any systematic exposition of this crucial concept other than that outlined in the Introduction to *The German Ideology*, a work which many Marxists have argued cannot be taken to represent Marx's concerns during the years of his theoretical maturity. Given this caveat, two distinct areas of concern can be deciphered from Marx's handling and use of the concept.

First, the concept implies something about the social determination of signifying systems. In a much criticized passage, Marx referred to ideologies as 'definite forms of social consciousness' which, together with legal and political relationships, constitute a 'superstructure' built upon and 'corresponding' to the 'real foundation' constituted by the relations of production (Bottomore and Rubel, 1965, p. 67). Although the concept of 'correspondence' does not necessarily imply a relationship of determination, the theoretical space opened up by the concepts of 'real foundation' or 'base' and 'superstructure' clearly implies that the latter is in some way dependent on the former. Yet, as Marx argued elsewhere, particularly in the

Grundrisse, ideologies also have their relative autonomy, their own distinctive properties, so that their dependence on the 'base' must be viewed as a highly complex and mediated one. This aspect of the concept of ideology might thus be said to open up the problem regarding the precise way in which the dependence of ideological forms upon the 'base' is to be construed without depriving them of their autonomy. (It is pertinent to note, however, that the cogency of maintaining that ideology may be regarded as being *both* dependent upon and yet *also* autonomous in relation to the economy, has recently been compellingly challenged. See Cutler *et al.*, 1977.)

Second, the concept of ideology carries with it the implication of distortion. This meaning is present in the common-sense usage of the term which is usually applied to statements which are felt to be a motivated distortion of the truth. Whilst there are passages in which Marx uses the term in this way, he more typically invoked the concept to refer to the unexamined categories and assumptions which form the unacknowledged impediments to scientific investigation. It was in such terms that Marx sought to explain the limitations of classical political economy as the product not of a subjective will to falsification but of the limitations which inhere in any analysis which, implicitly, takes bourgeois society as its point of departure and its point of return. In this usage, distortion is viewed not as the result of mendacity but as the effect of the action of the dominant social relationships which, although acting on the consciousness of individuals, do so in a way that is profoundly unconscious so far as they are concerned. On this construction, then, ideology is a process which takes place 'behind our backs', producing and structuring our consciousness in ways that we are not immediately aware of. It defines, as Althusser has put it, the form in which men 'live' their relationship to the conditions of their existence, the form in which 'their relationship to their conditions of existence is represented to them' (Althusser, 1971, p. 154).

In this sense, ideology comprises the sphere of representations within which an 'imaginary' relationship to the conditions of existence is produced, a relationship which embodies a 'misrecognition' of the real nature of those conditions. Although susceptible to a more extended usage, Marxists have traditionally granted the concept of ideology a privileged purchase in relation to the ruling or dominant forms of mental representation:

The ideas of the ruling class are in every epoch the ruling ideas: i.e. the class which is the ruling *material* force is, at the same time, its ruling *intellectual* force. The class which has the means of material production at its disposal, has control at the same time over the means of mental production, so that thereby, generally speaking, the ideas of those who lack the means of mental production are subject to it. (Marx and Engels, 1965, p. 61)

Ideology, in this most distinctive of senses, is thus concerned with the transmission of systems of signification across class lines. This is conceived not as an abstract process but as being effected, in a concrete way, via 'the means of mental production' controlled by the economically dominant class. The consciousness of those subjected to this relay of ideologies is thus distorted not abstractly but in a way conducive to the perpetuation of existing relationships of class domination.

Viewed in this way, the concept of ideology suggests three main areas of concern in relation to the media. The first has to do with the nature of the social control exerted over the media. The central question here concerns the structure of the ownership of the media and, more generally, the ways and, of course, extent to which ruling-class control over the operations of the media is secured. Second, this time at the level of formal analysis, there is the question as to how, technically, the signifying systems relayed by the media work so as to achieve the effect of 'misrecognition' imputed to them. Finally, implicated in each of these areas of concern, the media — particularly such state-owned media as the BBC — occupy a critical position within the more general Marxist debates concerning the way in which the economic, political and ideological levels of the social formation should be construed as relating to one another. Needless to say, these problems are posed not abstractly but are related to concrete problems of political practice. Marxist inquiry into the media is motivated by the need to furnish a knowledge of their workings that can be put to use in the production of subversive signifying systems which might offset the effects of dominant ideology and contribute to the formation of a revolutionary consciousness within oppressed social groups and classes.

Unfortunately, the precise way in which such questions are addressed depends upon the way in which the concept of ideology is interpreted and handled — a matter on which Marxists have been by no means united. The importance of such general conceptual considerations for the specific way in which the media are to be interrogated can be illustrated by considering the contrasting approach to the concept of ideology embodied in the works of Georg Lukács and Louis Althusser.

Lukács's approach to the question of ideology is mediated through the framework of the so-called 'materialist inversion'. Whereas Hegel had construed being as the manifestation or product of consciousness, Marx argued that the relationship between these terms should be inverted. 'It is not the consciousness of men that determines their being', Marx wrote, 'but, on the contrary, their social being determines their consciousness' (Bottomore and Rubel, 1965, p. 67). The question this poses is: How is this determination of consciousness by social being effected? How are we to conceive and represent the logic of this determination? Lukács's contention was that the class relationships constituting the structure of social being determine the structure of ideological forms in the respect that they provide different conceptual vantage points which mould the consciousness of social agents in different ways. Ideological forms, that is to say, are regarded as the product or reflection of the 'already-structured' consciousness of different class-based subjects of cognition. The position that they occupy within the structure of class relationships determines the structure and content of men's and women's consciousness. The structure and content of such ideological forms as works of art, literature and philosophy are then explained as the manifestation or reflection of what is thus posited as the *already socially determined* consciousness of the social agents to which they are attributed. Lukács added to this the further argument that whereas the conceptual vantage point afforded by the class position of the proletariat enabled the proletariat to acquire a true knowledge of the workings of the capitalist system of production, the bourgeoisie was able to attain only a partial knowledge of these owing to the 'false-consciousness' necessarily engendered by its class position.

Paul Hirst has offered a useful summary of this argument:

'False consciousness' is explained . . . by the *relation* of the subject to the object. Reality (the object) determines the place of the subject within it and, therefore, the conditions of its experience of it. Reality determines the *content* of ideology; it generates false recognitions of itself by subjecting subjects to circumstances in which their experience is distorted. Reality is the *origin* of ideology because it creates the different 'places', class positions, from which subjects view it. (Hirst, 1976, p. 386)

Although the most obvious route into the problem of the social determination of consciousness, this argument is both economist and idealist. It is economist inasmuch as it views ideological forms as the product of a determination operating solely in the economic sphere. Ideology is construed as the effect of economic place. What the subject thinks and how she or he thinks it is construed as a result of the place he or she occupies in the process of production. This is to allow the level of ideology no specific determinancy of its own. Nor does it offer any account of the actual mechanisms by which the consciousness of social agents is produced; this simply 'happens', consciousness is somehow magically formed as an effect of economic relationships.

Further, the position is idealist in the respect that it seeks to explain things which have a concrete material and social existence — ideological forms as articulated in language, written or spoken, or as embodied in visual signs — with reference to something that is abstract and has no concrete existence: the concept of consciousness. Vološinov admirably exposed the weakness of this conception in his *Marxism and the Philosophy of Language*, arguing that any conception of ideology which grants the concept of consciousness, as an attribute of the subject, an existence prior to (either logically or temporarily) the forms in which it is organized must be regarded as metaphysical. It explains something which has a concrete and identifiably material existence (ideology) with reference to something which does not, a mere abstraction (consciousness).

A Marxist theory of ideology, Vološinov argues, must start from the other direction. It must start not with the abstract, consciousness, but with the concrete, the structure of ideological forms themselves. Ideology must be viewed not as the product of an evanescent consciousness but as an objective component of the material world. For ideology, Vološinov insists, has a determinate reality. It exists objectively as a distinctive organization of sound patterns (speech, music) or as a codified co-ordination of light rays (print, visual images). Its existence is thus wholly objective. It does not exist 'within' as an attribute of consciousness but 'without' as a part of material reality, articulated on and distributed through specifiable social relationships. Further, far from being regarded as the *product* of consciousness, such ideological forms must be regarded as the producers of consciousness inasmuch as they constitute the distinctive 'place' within which the social production of consciousness is actually organized and carried out. Ideology, Vološinov contends, is not an attribute of consciousness. Rather, both in general and in the particular forms it assumes, consciousness is a product of ideology. From the point of view of language as a fully developed system (and language is the home of all ideology), it is not the consciousness of individuals which determines the forms of language but rather the forms of language which, pre-existing the individuals who comprise the members of any speech community, produce the consciousness of individuals by defining the linguistic terms within which their thought is structured. And it does so not abstractly but concretely as a set of material signs relayed to individuals via the concrete mediations of home, school — and the media.

Clearly, this is a very different approach to the study of ideology. Rather than being regarded as the product of forms of consciousness whose contours are determined elsewhere, in the economic sphere, the signifying systems which constitute the sphere of ideology are themselves viewed as the vehicles through which the consciousness of social agents is produced. The consequence of this is to call into question the concerns of reflection theory, according to which ideological forms are interrogated to reveal how their determinations are 'reflected' or contained within their structure, and to put in its place a concern with the *activity* and *effectivity* of signification. The methodological import of this has been to suggest that the ideological forms relayed by the media should be read so as to decipher the signifying conventions by means of which they organize and structure the consciousness of social agents. Its more general theoretical and political significance, however, is that, escaping the economic reductionism of Lukács' position, it allows the signifying systems which constitute the sphere of the ideological to be granted their own specific role and effectivity within social life.

The work of Louis Althusser has been most influential in providing a framework within which this specific role and effectivity of the ideological can be theorized. To appreciate the role Althusser assigns to ideology, however, we must make a brief detour through Marx's *Grundrisse* where Marx distinguishes between the 'real history' of capitalism as a system of production which is already in existence and is thus 'moving on its own foundations', and the 'history of its formation'. Marx discusses this problem with reference to the so-called process of 'primitive accumulation' whereby the preconditions for production founded on capital, the separation of the labourer from the means of subsistence and the concentration of the ownership of the means of production, are brought into being. Marx's point is that the details of the actual historical mechanisms by which such preconditions of capitalist production are created can have no bearing on the actual functioning of capitalism as an economic system. For, once production is founded on a capitalist basis, it tends to *reproduce* the conditions of its own possibility, its historical presuppositions, as a result of its own internal action. The completion of every cycle of exchange between the worker and capital increases the worker's dependence on capital by impoverishing him or her at the same time as it enhances the domination of capital over the worker by augmenting its value. In this way, the social relationship of wage-labour which forms the basis of capitalist production is reproduced as a result of the logic of capitalist production itself irrespective of the way in which, historically, that relationship was first founded.

This perspective of reproduction is vital to recent developments in Marxist theory. In truth, it is not the only perspective to be found in the *Grundrisse*. For Marx went on to note that, at the same time as they reproduce themselves, the conditions of capitalist production are also 'engaged in *suspending themselves* and hence in positing the *historic presuppositions* for a new state of society' (Marx, 1874, p. 461). Nevertheless, it is the contention of such theorists as Louis Althusser and Nicos Poulantzas that it is with reference to the reproduction processes of capitalism that the precise social role of ideology is to be understood. Thus, Poulantzas has noted that the purely economic processes of capitalist production merely reproduce the *places* within the system of production that are to be occupied by the agents of production (workers, overseers, managers). There therefore remains, he argues, the task of 'the reproduction and distribution of the agents themselves to these places' (Poulantzas, 1975, p. 28). It is not enough, that is, that the worker should be reproduced as someone capable of work and socially dependent on capital; he or she must also be produced as the subject of an ideological consciousness which legitimates the dominance of capital and the subordinate place which he or she occupies within its processes. Put simply, if capitalism is to survive as an ongoing system, then concrete social individuals must be reconciled both to the class structure and to the class positions within it which they occupy. They must be induced to 'live' their exploitation and oppression in such a way that they do not experience or represent to themselves their position as one in which they are exploited and oppressed.

In a lengthier presentation of the same issue, Althusser contends that it is at the level of ideology that the reproduction of the entire system of the relations of production characterizing the capitalist mode of production is secured (see Althusser, 1971, and also chapter 1, pp. 23-5, of this collection). In maintaining this, ideology is understood not as an intellectual abstraction but as a concrete social process embodied in the material signifying practices of a collectivity of 'ideological apparatuses' — the family, school, churches and the media. There are many difficulties associated with this conception (see Bennett, 1979, chapter 7, for a brief résumé of these). Whilst this is not the place to consider these in detail, it is important to note that Althusser's position comes dangerously close to

functionalism in the respect that, by viewing all ideological forms as contributing to the reproduction of existing social relationships, it tends to
represent capitalism as a totally coherent social system ('one-dimensional'
even) lacking internal conflict at either the economic, political or ideological
levels. In this respect, Althusser's work joins a long list of 'Marxisms' which
have managed to banish the spectre of class conflict from their work. This
further means that the autonomy granted to ideology is purely nominal
inasmuch as its action is conceived as being entirely subservient to the needs
and requirements of the economy.

Finally, it should also be noted that Althusser's use of the term
'ideological state apparatuses' in relation to such institutions as the media,
the family and religious organizations has been severely criticized on the
grounds that it extends the concept of the state to such a degree that the
ability to distinguish between state and non-state institutions is called into
question.

It has been partly as a result of these criticisms that more recent developments in the Marxist theory of ideology have tended to look back beyond
Althusser to the work of Antonio Gramsci whose writings on such subjects
as culture and ideology, the role of intellectuals, and the crucial concept of
hegemony afford a more flexible, less economistic way of conceptualizing
the relationship between ideological, social, political and economic
processes and relationships. Be this as it may, the crucial role that Althusser
has played in facilitating the development of significantly new lines of
approach to the study of the media should not be underestimated. The
stress that he placed on the *active* role of ideology, on the part that it played
in shaping the consciousness of social agents, formed the central conduit
through which developments in structuralism and semiology have both
entered into and lastingly altered Marxist approaches to the media in
placing questions concerning the politics of signification at least on a par
with the traditional Marxist concern with the analysis of patterns of media
ownership and control. It may be, as subsequent critics have argued (see
Lovell, 1980), that Althusser — or, more accurately perhaps, those
following him — bent the stick too far, resulting in a tendency towards
purely formalist 'readings' or 'deconstructions' of the signifying mechanisms
of media forms which paid scant regard to the conditions of their production or to the real history of their reception by different sections of the
audience. A valid measure of Althusser's importance, however, is discernible in the fact that it has proved impossible for those who have wished
to raise such questions to do so without acknowledging that his contribution has decisively altered the ways in which they need to be posed.

REFERENCES

Adorno, T.W. (1974a) *Minima Moralia*, London, New Left Books.
Althusser, L. (1971) 'Ideology and ideological state apparatuses', in *Lenin and
Philosophy, and Other Essays*, London, New Left Books.

Anderson, P. (1969) 'Components of the national culture', in Cockburn, A. and Blackburn, R. (eds) *Student Power: Problems, Diagnosis, Action*, Harmondsworth, Penguin.

Arnold, M. (1971) *Culture and Anarchy*, Indianapolis, Bobbs-Merrill.

Bell, D. (1960) 'America as a mass society: a critique', in *The End of Ideology: on the Exhaustion of Political Ideas in the Fifties*, New York, Free Press.

Benjamin, W. (1970) 'The work of art in the age of mechanical reproduction', in *Illuminations: Essays and Reflections*, London, Jonathan Cape.

Bennett, T. (1979) *Formalism and Marxism*, London, Methuen.

Bottomore, T.B. and Rubel, M. (1965) *Karl Marx: Selected Writings in Sociology and Social Philosophy*, Harmondsworth, Penguin.

Bramson, L. (1961) *The Political Context of Sociology*, New Jersey, Princeton University Press.

Brecht, B. (1964) *On Theatre*, London, Methuen.

Cutler, A., Hindess, B., Hirst, P.Q. and Hussain, A. (1977/8) *Marx's Capital and Capitalism Today*, 2 vols, London, Routledge & Kegan Paul.

Giner, S. (1976) *Mass Society*, London, Martin Robertson.

Hegel, G.F.W. (1953) *Reason in History*, Indianapolis, Bobbs-Merrill.

Hirst, P.Q. (1976) 'Althusser and the theory of ideology', *Economy and Society*, 5 (4).

Horkheimer, M. and Adorno, T.W. (1972) 'The Culture industry: enlightenment as mass deception', in *The Dialectic of Enlightenment*, New York, Herder and Herder. Abridged version in Curran, J., Gurevitch, M. and Woollacott, J. (1977) *Mass Communication and Society*, London, Edward Arnold.

Janowitz, M. (1952) *The Community Press in an Urban Setting*, Glencoe, Illinois.

Jay, M. (1973) *The Dialectical Imagination: A History of the Frankfurt School and Institute of Social Research*, London, Heinemann.

Kornhauser, W. (1960) *The Politics of Mass Society*, London, Routledge & Kegan Paul.

Lazarsfeld, P.F. and Kendall, P.L. (1949) 'The communications behavior of the average American', in Schramm, W. (ed.) *Mass Communications*, Urbana, University of Illinois Press.

Leavis, F.R. (1930) *Mass Civilization and Minority Culture*, London, Minority Press.

Leavis, Q.D. (1968) *Fiction and the Reading Public*, London, Chatto & Windus.

Lovell, T. (1980) *Pictures of Reality: Aesthetics, Politics and Pleasure*, London, British Film Institute.

Lukács, G. (1971) *History and Class Consciousness*, London, Merlin Press.

MacDonald, D. (1957) 'A theory of mass culture', in Rosenberg, B. and White, D.M. (eds) *Mass Culture: The Popular Arts in America*, Glencoe, Free Press.

Marcuse, H. (1968) *One Dimensional Man*, London, Sphere.

Marcuse, H. (1970) *Five Lectures*, London, Allen Lane.

Marx, K. and Engels, F. (1965) *The German Ideology*, London, Lawrence & Wishart.

Marx, K. (1973) *Grundrisse: Foundations of the Critique of Political Economy*, Harmondsworth, Penguin.

Miliband, R. (1969) *The State in Capitalist Society*, London, Weidenfeld & Nicolson.

Mill, J.S. (1969) *On Liberty*, Oxford University Press, London.

Pateman, T. (1975) *Language, Truth and Politics*, Devon, Jean Stroud and Trevor

Pateman.

Poulantzas, N. (1975) *Classes in Contemporary Capitalism*, London, New Left Books.

Schumpeter, J. (1976) *Capitalism, Socialism and Democracy*, London, Allen & Unwin.

Shils, E. (1957) 'Daydreams and nightmares: reflections on the criticism of mass culture', *The Sewanee Review*, 65 (4).

Shils, E. (1962) 'The theory of mass society', *Diogenes*, 39.

Slater, P. (1977) *The Origin and Significance of the Frankfurt School*, London, Routledge & Kegan Paul.

Swingewood, A. (1977) *The Myth of Mass Culture*, London, Macmillan.

Vidich, A.J. and Benseman, J. (1960) *Small Town in Mass Society*, New York, Anchor Books.

Vološinov, V.N. (1973) *Marxism and the Philosophy of Language*, New York, Seminar Press.

3

The rediscovery of 'ideology': return of the repressed in media studies

STUART HALL

Mass communications research has had, to put it mildly, a somewhat chequered career. Since its inception as a specialist area of scientific inquiry and research — roughly, the early decades of the twentieth century — we can identify at least three distinct phases. The most dramatic break is that which occurred between the second and third phases. This marks off the massive period of research conducted within the sociological approaches of 'mainstream' American behavioural science, beginning in the 1940s and commanding the field through into the 1950s and 1960s, from the period of its decline and the emergence of an alternative, 'critical' paradigm. This paper attempts to chart this major paradigm-shift in broad outline and to identify some of the theoretical elements which have been assembled in the course of the formation of the 'critical' approach. Two basic points about this break should be made at this stage in the argument. First, though the differences between the 'mainstream' and the 'critical' approaches might appear, at first sight, to be principally methodological and procedural, this appearance is, in our view, a false one. Profound differences in theoretical perspective and in political calculation differentiate the one from the other. These differences first appear in relation to media analysis. But, behind this immediate object of attention, there lie broader differences in terms of how societies or social formations in general are to be analysed. Second, the simplest way to characterize the shift from 'mainstream' to 'critical' perspectives is in terms of the movement from, essentially, a behavioural to an ideological perspective.

'DREAM COME TRUE':
PLURALISM, THE MEDIA AND THE MYTH OF INTEGRATION

The 'mainstream' approach was behavioural in two senses. The central question that concerned American media sociologists during this period was the question of the media's effects. These effects — it was assumed — could best be identified and analysed in terms of the changes which the media were said to have effected in the behaviour of individuals exposed to their influence. The approach was also 'behavioural' in a more methodological sense. Speculation about media effects had to be subject to the kinds of empirical test which characterized positivistic social science. This approach was installed as the dominant one in the flowering of media research in the United States in the 1940s. Its ascendancy paralleled the institutional hegemony of American behavioural science on a world scale in the hey-day of the 1950s and early 1960s. Its decline paralleled that of the paradigms on which that intellectual hegemony had been founded. Though theoretical and methodological questions were of central importance in this change of direction, they certainly cannot be isolated from their historical and political contexts. This is one of the reasons why the shifts between the different phases of research can, without too much simplification, also be characterized as a sort of oscillation between the American and the European poles of intellectual influence.

To understand the nature of media research in the period of the behavioural mainstream hegemony, and its concern with a certain set of effects, we must understand the way it related, in turn, to the first phase of media research. For, behind this concern with behavioural effects lay a longer, less scientific and empirical tradition of thought, which offered, in a speculative mode, a set of challenging theses about the impact of the modern media on modern industrial societies. Basically European in focus, this larger debate assumed a very powerful, largely unmediated set of effects attributable to the media. The premise of this work was the assumption that, somewhere in the period of later industrial capitalist development, modern societies had become 'mass societies'. The mass media were seen both as instruments in this evolution, and as symptomatic of its most troubling tendencies. The 'mass society/mass culture' debate really goes back as far, at least, as the eighteenth century. Its terms were first defined in the period of the rise of an urban commercial culture, interpreted at the time as posing a threat, because of its direct dependence on cultural production for a market, to traditional cultural values. But the debate was revived in a peculiarly intense form at the end of the nineteenth century. It is common, nowadays — and we agree with this view — largely to discount the terms in which these cultural and social problems associated with the development of industrial capitalism were debated. Nonetheless, the mass culture debate did indeed identify a deep and qualitative shift in social relations which occurred in many advanced industrial capitalist societies in this period. Although the nature of these historical transformations could not be adequately grasped or properly theorized within the terms of the 'mass society' thesis, these were indeed the terms which prevailed when the 'debate' came to the fore again at the commencement of what, nowadays, we would want to characterize as the transition to monopoly forms of advanced capitalist development.

The effects which most concerned this more speculative approach can be grouped under three rough headings. Some were defined as cultural: the displacement, debasement and trivialization of high culture as a result of the dissemination of the mass culture associated with the new media. Some were defined as political: the vulnerability of the masses to the false appeals, propaganda and influence of the media. Some were defined as social: the break-up of community ties, of *gemeinschaft*, of intermediary face-to-face groups and the exposure of the masses to the commercialized influences of élites, via the media. A very specific historical image came to dominate this scenario: the breakdown of European societies under the double assault of economic depression and fascism: the latter seen in terms of the unleashing of irrational political forces, in which the propaganda media had played a key role.

The Frankfurt School gave this critique its most biting philosophical elaboration. (Their work and the mass culture debate is more extensively discussed in the previous essay in this volume.) When, in the wake of fascism, the Frankfurt School was dispersed, and its members took refuge in the United States, they brought their pessimistic forebodings about mass society with them. Briefly, their message was: 'it can happen here, too'. In a way, American behavioural science — which had already taken issue with the early versions of this mass society critique — continued, in the 1940s and 1950s, to develop a sort of displaced reply to this challenge. It argued that, though some of the tendencies of mass society were undoubtedly visible in the United States, there were strong countervailing tendencies. Primary groups had not disintegrated. Media effects were not direct, but mediated by other social processes. Essentially, to the charge that American society displayed symptoms of a sort of creeping totalitarianism, American social scientists made the optimistic response: 'pluralism works here'.

Perhaps more important than the distinction between 'pessimistic' and 'optimistic' social predictions about media effects, were the distinctions between the theoretical and methodological approaches of the two schools. The European approach was historically and philosophically sweeping, speculative, offering a rich but over-generalized set of hypotheses. The American approach was empirical, behavioural and scientistic. In fact, hypotheses proposed within one framework were often tested, refined and found wanting in an altogether different one. It is little wonder that hypotheses and findings were not commensurable. Only those who believe that there is a given and incontrovertible set of facts, innocent of the framework of theory in which they are identified, which can be subject to empirical verification according to a universal scientific method, would have expected that to be so. But this is exactly what American behavioural science offered itself as doing. There are some intriguing transitional moments here which are worth remarking — in lieu of a fuller account. They can be encapsulated in the history of two emigrés. Lazarsfeld, a distinguished European methodologist, linked with, though not a subscribing member of, the Frankfurt School, became in fact the doyen and leading luminary of behavioural methodology in the American context. (It has been speculated that his success at the latter task may have had something to do with his early sensitization to more speculative European questions: certainly, he was a more theoretically sophisticated methodologist than his more technical colleagues.) Adorno, on the other hand, the most formidable of the Frankfurt School theorists, attempted, without any conspicuous success, to adapt his speculative critique to empirical procedures. *The Authoritarian Personality* (1950) was a hybrid monster of just this kind — the product of a mixed but unholy parentage.

In the approach which succeeded the European critique, the main focus was on behavioural change. If the media had 'effects' these, it was argued, should show up empirically in terms of a direct influence on individuals, which would register as a switch of behavour. Switches of choice — between advertised consumer goods or between presidential candidates — were viewed as a paradigm case of measurable influence and effect. The model of power and influence being employed here was paradigmatically empiricist and pluralistic: its primary focus was the individual; it theorized power in terms of the direct influence of A on B's behaviour; it was preoccupied (as so-called 'political science' in this mould has been ever since) with the process of decision making. Its ideal experimental test was a before/after one: its ideal model of influence was that of the campaign. Political campaign studies conceived politics largely in terms of voting, and voting largely in terms of campaign influences and the resulting voter choices. The parallel with advertising campaigns was exact. Not only was a great deal of the research funded for the purpose of identifying how to deliver specific audiences to the advertisers — loftily entitled 'policy research' — but the commercial model tended to dominate the theory, even in the more rarified atmosphere of Academia. Larger historical shifts, questions of political process and formation before and beyond the ballot-box, issues of social and political power, of social structure and economic relations, were simply absent, not by chance, but because they were *theoretically outside the frame of reference*. But that was because the approach, though advanced as empirically-grounded and scientific, was predicated on a very specific set of political and ideological presuppositions. These presuppositions, however, were not put to the test, within the theory, but framed and underpinned it as a set of unexamined postulates. It should have asked, 'does pluralism work?' and 'how does pluralism work?' Instead, it asserted, 'pluralism works' — and then went on to measure, precisely and empirically, just how well it was doing. This mixture of prophecy and hope, with a brutal, hard-headed, behaviouristic positivism provided a heady theoretical concoction which, for a long time, passed itself off as 'pure science'.

In this model, power and influence were identical and interchangeable terms: both could be empirically demonstrated at the point of decision making. Occasionally, this reductionism was projected on to a larger canvas and the impact of the media was discussed in terms of 'society' as a whole. But this connection was made in a very specific way. And society was defined in a very limited manner. A largely cultural definition of society was assumed. Class formations, economic processes, sets of institutional power-relations were largely unacknowledged. What held society together it was agreed were its norms. In pluralist society, a fundamental broadly-

based consensus on norms was assumed to prevail throughout the population. The connection between the media and this normative consensus,
then, could only be established at the level of values. This was a tricky
term. In Parsons's 'social system' (Parsons, 1951) such values played an
absolutely pivotal role; for around them the integrative mechanisms which
held the social order together were organized. Yet what these values were —
their content and structure — or how they were produced, or how, in a
highly differentiated and dynamic modern industrial capitalist society, an
inclusive consensus on 'the core value system' had spontaneously arisen,
were questions that were not and could not be explained. Value consensus,
however, was assumed. Culturally, Edward Shils (a collaborator of
Parsons) argued, this broad band of values was so widely shared as to have
accreted to itself the power of the sacred (Shils, 1961a, p. 117). If some
groups were, unaccountably, not yet fully paid-up members of the
consensus club, they were well on the way to integration within it. The core
would gradually absorb the more 'brutal' cultures of the periphery (Shils,
1961b). Thus the democratic enfranchisement of all citizens within political
society, and the economic enfranchisement of all consumers within the free-
enterprise economy, would rapidly be paralleled by the cultural absorption
of all groups into the culture of the centre. Pluralism rested on these three
mutually reinforcing supports. In its purest form, pluralism assured that no
structural barriers or limits of class would obstruct this process of cultural
absorption: for, as we all 'knew', America was no longer a class society.
Nothing prevented the long day's journey of the American masses to the
centre. This must have been very good news to blacks, Hispanics,
Chicanos, American Injuns, New York Italians, Boston Irish, Mexican
wetbacks, California Japanese, blue-collar workers, hard-hats, Bowery
bums, Southern poor-whites and other recalcitrant elements still simmering
in the American melting pot. What is more (a comforting thought in the
depths of the Cold War) all other societies were well on their way along the
'modernizing' continuum. Pluralism thus became, not just a way of defining
American particularism, but *the model* of society as such, written into
social science. Despite the theoretical form in which this ramshackle
construction was advanced, and the refined methodologies by which its
progress was empirically confirmed, there is no mistaking the political and
ideological settlement which underpinned it. Daniel Bell assured us, in *The
End of Ideology* (1960), that the classical problem of 'ideology' had at last
been superseded. There would be a range of pluralistic conflicts of interest
and value. But they could all be resolved within the framework of the
pluralistic consensus and its 'rules of the game'. This was essentially
because, as another apologist, Seymour Lipset, forcefully put the matter:

the fundamental political problems of the industrial revolution have been solved:
the workers have achieved industrial and political citizenship; the conservatives
have accepted the welfare state; and the democratic left has recognized that an
increase in overall state power carried with it more dangers to freedom than solutions for economic problems. (Lipset, 1963, p. 406)

The installation of pluralism as *the* model of modern industrial social order represented a moment of profound theoretical and political closure. It was not, however, destined to survive the testing times of the ghetto rebellions, campus revolts, counter-cultural upheavals and anti-war movements of the late 1960s. But, for a time, it prevailed. It became a global ideology, backed by the credentials of social science. It was exported with a will around the globe. Some of its force arose from the fact that what, in theory, ought to be the case, could be shown so convincingly and empirically to be, in fact, the case. The American Dream had been empirically verified. A whole number of decisive interventions in developing countries were made in the name of hastening them along this modernizing pathway. It is sometimes asked what a moment of political settlement and theoretical hegemony looks like: this would certainly be one good candidate.

The media were articulated to this general social scientific model in, principally, two ways. In the campaign/decision-making framework, its influences were traced: directly, in behaviour changes amongst individuals; indirectly, in its influences on opinion which led, in a second step, to empirically-observable behavioural differences. Here, media messages were read and coded in terms of the intentions and biases of the communicators. Since the message was assumed as a sort of empty linguistic construct, it was held to mirror the intentions of its producers in a relatively simple way. It was simply the means by which the intentions of communicators effectively influenced the behaviour of individuals receivers. Occasionally, moves were announced to make the model of media influence more fully societal. But these, largely, remained at the level of unfulfilled programmatic promises. The methods of coding and processing a vast corpus of messages in an objective and empirically-verifiable way (content analysis) were vastly sophisticated and refined. But, conceptually, the media message, as a symbolic sign vehicle or a structured discourse, with its own internal structuration and complexity, remained theoretically wholly undeveloped.

At the broader level, the media were held to be largely reflective or expressive of an achieved consensus. The finding that, after all, the media were not very influential was predicated on the belief that, in its wider cultural sense, the media largely reinforced those values and norms which had already achieved a wide consensual foundation. Since the consensus was a 'good thing', those reinforcing effects of the media were given a benign and positive reading. The notion of selective perception was subsequently introduced, to take account of the fact that different individuals might bring their own structure of attention and selectivity to what the media offered. But these differential interpretations were not related back either to a theory of reading or to a complex map of ideologies. They were, instead, interpreted functionally. Different individuals could derive different satisfactions and fulfil different needs from the different parts of the programming. These needs and satisfactions were assumed to be universal and trans-historical. The positive assumption arising from all this was, in sum, that the media — though open to commercial and other influences — were, by and large, functional for society, because they functioned in line with and strengthened the core value system of society. They underwrote pluralism.

DEVIANTS AND THE CONSENSUS

We can identify two kinds of breaks within this theoretical synthesis which began to occur towards the closing years of the paradigm's dominance, but before it was more profoundly challenged from outside its confines. The first may be summed up as the problematizing of the term 'consensus' itself. As we suggested, the presumption of an integral and organic consensus did leave certain empirically identifiable groups beyond the pale. Since, at first, these groups were not conceived to be organized around conflicting structural or ideological principles, they were defined exclusively in terms of their deviation from the consensus. To be outside the consensus was to be, not in an alternative value-system, but simply outside of norms as such: normless — therefore, anomic. In mass society theory, anomic was viewed as a condition peculiarly vulnerable to over-influence by the media. But when these deviant formations began to be studied more closely, it became clear that they did often have alternative foci of integration. These enclaves were then defined as 'sub-cultural'. But the relation of sub-cultures to the dominant culture continued to be defined culturally. That is, sub-cultural deviation could be understood as learning or affiliating or subscribing to a 'definition of the situation' different or deviant from that institutionalized within the core value system. The career deviant in a sub-culture had subscribed positively to, say, a definition of drug-taking which the dominant consensus regarded as outside the rules (with the exception of alcohol and tobacco which, unaccountably, were given a high and positive premium within the American central value system). For a time, these different 'definitions of the situation' were simply left lying side by side. Sub-cultural theorists set about investigating the rich underlife of the deviant communities, without asking too many questions about how they connected with the larger social system. Robert Merton is one of the few sociologists who, from a position within the structural functionalist or 'anomie' perspective, took this question seriously (Merton, 1957).

But this theoretical pluralism could not survive for long. For it soon became clear that these differentiations between 'deviant' and 'consensus' formations were not natural but socially defined — as the contrast between the different attitudes towards alcohol and cannabis indicated. Moreover, they were historically variable: sub-cultural theorists were just old enough to recall the days of Prohibition, and could contrast them with the period when the positive definitions of American masculinity appeared to require a steady diet of hard liquor and king-sized filter-tips. What mattered was the power of the alcohol-takers to define the cannabis-smokers as deviant. In short, matters of cultural and social power — the power to define the rules of the game to which everyone was required to ascribe — were involved in the transactions between those who were consensus-subscribers and those who were labelled deviant. There was what Howard Becker, one of the early 'appreciators' of deviance, called a 'hierarchy of credibility' (Becker, 1967). Moreover, such 'definitions' were operational. Deviants were positively identified and labelled: the labelling process served to mobilize moral censure and social sanction against them. This had — as those who now recalled the forgotten parts of Durkheim's programme acknowledged — the consequence of reinforcing the internal solidarity of the moral community. As Durkheim puts it: 'Crime brings together upright con-sciences and concentrates them' (Durkheim, 1960, p. 102). But it also served to enforce greater conformity to society's 'rules' by punishing and stigmatizing those who departed from them. Beyond the limit of moral censure were, of course, all those sterner practices of legal processing and enforcement which punished, on behalf of society, deviant infractors. The question then arose: who had the power to define whom? And, more pertinently, in the interest of what was the disposition of power between definers and defined secured? In what interest did the consensus 'work'? What particular type of special order did it sustain and underpin?

In fact, what was at issue here was the problem of social control, and the role of social control in the maintenance of the social order. But this was no longer simply that form of social order expressively revealed in the spon-taneous 'agreement to agree on fundamentals' of the vast majority: it was not simply the 'social bond' which was enforced. It was consent to a particular kind of social order; a consensus around a particular form of society: integration within and conformity to the rules of a very definite set of social, economic and political structures. It was for these — in a direct or indirect sense — that the rules could be said to 'work'. Social order now looked like a rather different proposition. It entailed the enforcement of social, political and legal discipline. It was articulated to that which existed: to the given dispositions of class, power and authority: to the established institutions of society. This recognition radically problematized the whole notion of 'consensus'.

What is more, the question could now be asked whether the consensus did indeed spontaneously simply arise or whether it was the result of a complex process of social construction and legitimation. A society, democratic in its formal organization, committed at the same time by the concentration of economic capital and political power to the massively unequal distribution of wealth and authority, had much to gain from the continuous production of popular consent to its existing structure, to the values which supported and underwrote it, and to its continuity of existence. But this raised questions concerning the social role of the media. For if the media were not simply reflective or 'expressive' of an already achieved consensus, but instead tended to reproduce those very definitions of the situation which favoured and legitimated the existing structure of things, then what had seemed at first as merely a reinforcing role had now to be reconceptualized in terms of the media's role in the process of consensus formation.

A second break, then, arose around the notion of 'definitions of the situation'. What this term suggested was that a pivotal element in the production of consent was how things were defined. But this threw into doubt the reflexive role of the media — simply showing things as they were — and it put in question the transparent conception of language which underpinned their assumed naturalism. For reality could no longer be viewed as simply a given set of facts: it was the result of a particular way of constructing reality. The media defined, not merely reproduced, 'reality'. Definitions of reality were sustained and produced through all those linguistic practices (in the broad sense) by means of which selective definitions of 'the real' were represented. But representation is a very different notion from that of reflection. It implies the active work of selecting and presenting, of structuring and shaping: not merely the transmitting of an already-existing meaning, but the more active labour of *making things mean*. It was a practice, a production, of meaning: what subsequently came to be defined as a 'signifying practice'. The media were signifying agents. A whole new conception of the symbolic practices through which this process of signification was sustained intervened in the innocent garden of 'content analysis'. The message had now to be analysed, not in terms of its manifest 'message', but in terms of its ideological structuration. Several questions then followed: how was this ideological structuration accomplished? How was its relation to the other parts of the social structure to be conceptualized? In the words of Bachrach and Baratz, did it matter that the media appeared to underwrite systematically 'a set of predominant values, beliefs, rituals, and institutional procedures ("rules of the game") that operate systematically and consistently to the benefit of certain persons and groups at the expense of others?' (Bachrach and Baratz, 1970, pp. 43-4). In this move to take seriously the power of the media to signify reality and to define what passed as 'the real', the so-called 'end of ideology' thesis was also radically problematized.

In part, what was involved in these questions was a return of the problem of power to the powerless universe of mainstream pluralism, but also, a shift in the very conception of power. Pluralism, as Lukes has suggested (Lukes, 1976), did retain a model of power, based around the notion of 'influence'. A influenced B to make decision X. Certainly, this was a form of power. Pluralism qualified the persistence of this form of power by demonstrating that, because, in any decision-making situation, the As were different, and the various decisions made did not cohere within any single structure of domination, or favour exclusively any single interest, therefore power itself had been relatively 'pluralized'. The dispersal of power plus the randomness of decisions kept the pluralist society relatively free of an identifiable power-centre. (Various gaps in this random-power model were unconvincingly plugged by the discreet deployment of a theory of 'democratic élitism' to up-date the 'pure' pluralist model and make it square

more with contemporary realities). Lukes observes that this is a highly
behaviouristic and one-dimensional model of power. But the notion of
power which arose from the critique of consensus-theory, and which
Bachrach and Baratz, for example, proposed, was of a very different order:
'Power is also exercised when A devotes energies to creating or reinforcing
social and political values and institutional practices that limit the scope of
the political process to public consideration of only those issues which are
comparatively innocuous to A' (Bachrach and Baratz, 1970, p. 7), — a
modest way of putting the ideological question. Lukes puts this two-
dimensional model even more clearly when he refers to that power exercised
'by influencing, shaping and determining [an individual's] very wants'
(Lukes, 1975, p. 16). In fact, this is a very different order of question
altogether — a three-dimensional model, which has thoroughly broken
with the behaviourist and pluralist assumptions. It is the power which arises
from 'shaping perceptions, cognitions and preferences in such a way that
they [i.e. social agents] accept their role in the existing order of things,
either because they can see or imagine no alternative to it, or because they
see it as natural and unchangeable, or because they value it as divinely
ordained or beneficial' (Lukes, 1975, p. 24). This is an 'ideological' model of
power, by whatever other name it is called. The move from the pluralist to
the critical model of media research centrally involved a shift from a one- to
the two- and three-dimensional models of power in modern societies. From
the viewpoint of the media, what was at issue was no longer specific
message-injunctions, by A to B, to do this or that, but a shaping of the
whole ideological environment: a way of representing the order of things
which endowed its limiting perspectives with that natural or divine inevitability which makes them appear universal, natural and coterminous with
'reality' itself. This movement — towards the winning of a universal
validity and legitimacy for accounts of the world which are partial and
particular, and towards the grounding of these particular constructions in
the taken-for-grantedness of 'the real' — is indeed the characteristic and
defining mechanism of 'the ideological'.

THE CRITICAL PARADIGM

It is around the rediscovery of the ideological dimension that the critical
paradigm in media studies turned. Two aspects were involved: each is dealt
with separately below. How does the ideological process work and what are
its mechanisms? How is 'the ideological' to be conceived in relation to other
practices within a social formation? The debate developed on both these
fronts, simultaneously. The first, which concerned the production and
transformation of ideological discourses, was powerfully shaped by
theories concerning the symbolic and linguistic character of ideological
discourses — the notion that the elaboration of ideology found in language
(broadly conceived) its proper and privileged sphere of articulation. The
second, which concerned how to conceptualize the ideological instance

within a social formation, also became the site of an extensive theoretical and empirical development.

In our discussion of these two supporting elements of the critical paradigm, I shall not be concerned with identifying in detail the specific theoretical inputs of particular disciplines — linguistics, phenomenology, semiotics, psychoanalysis, for example — nor with the detailed internal arguments between these different approaches. Nor shall I attempt to offer a strict chronological account of how the succession of concepts and disciplines were integrated in sequences into the paradigm. I shall rather be concerned exclusively with identifying the broad lines through which the reconceptualization of 'the ideological' occurred, and the integration of certain key theoretical elements into the general framework of the paradigm as such.

Cultural inventories

I shall first examine how ideologies work. Here we can begin with the influence of the Sapir-Whorf hypothesis in linguistic anthropology: an idea which, though never picked up in detail, suggests some important continuities between the new paradigm and some previous work, especially in social anthropology. The Sapir-Whorf hypothesis suggested that each culture had a different way of classifying the world. These schemes would be reflected, it argued, in the linguistic and semantic structures of different societies. Lévi-Strauss worked on a similar idea, though he gradually became less interested in the cultural specificity of each society's classification system, and more involved with outlining the universal 'laws' of signification — a universal transformational cultural 'grammar', common to all cultural systems — associated with the cognitive function, the laws of the mind, and with thinking as such. Lévi-Strauss performed such an analysis on the cultural systems and myths of so-called 'primitive' societies — 'societies without history', as he called them. These examples were well fitted to his universalism, since their cultural systems were highly repetitive, consisting often of the weaving together of different transformations on the same, very limited classificatory 'sets'. Though the approach did not, clearly, hold so well for societies of more continuous and extensive historical transformation, the general idea proved a fruitful one: it showed how an apparently 'free' construction of particular ideological discourses could be viewed as transformations worked on the same, basic, ideological grid. In this, Lévi-Strauss was following Saussure's (1960) call for the development of a general 'science of signs' — semiology: the study of 'the life of signs at the heart of social life' (Lévi-Strauss, 1967, p. 16). Potentially, it was argued, the approach could be applied to all societies and a great variety of cultural systems. The name most prominently associated with this broadening of 'the science of signs' was that of Roland Barthes, whose work on modern myths, *Mythologies*, is a *locus classicus* for the study of the intersection of myth, language and ideology. The further extrapolation

— that whole societies and social practices apart from language could also be analysed 'on the model of a language' — was subsequently much developed, especially in Marxist structuralism: though the germ of the idea was to be found in Lévi-Strauss, who analysed kinship relations in primitive societies in just this way (i.e. on a communicative model — the exchange of goods, messages and women) (Lévi-Strauss, 1969).

The structuralist strand is, clearly, the most significant one, theoretically, in this development. But we should note that similar pointers could be found in theoretical approaches far removed from the universe of structuralism. It was also present in the 'social construction of reality' approach, developed by Berger and Luckmann (1966). Interactionist deviancy theory, which we earlier suggested first identified the question of 'the definition of the situation' and 'who defines whom?' also moved, though more tentatively, in the same direction. David Matza's book, *Becoming Deviant*, concluded with a strange and wayward section, intriguingly entitled 'Signification' (Matza, 1969). Also relevant was the work of the ethnomethodologists, with their concern for the strategies involved in the understandings of everyday situations, the form of practical accounting by means of which societal members produced the social knowledge they used to make themselves understood, and their increasing attention to conversational strategies.

In the structuralist approach, the issue turned on the question of signification. This implies, as we have already said, that things and events in the real world do not contain or propose their own, integral, single and intrinsic meaning, which is then merely transferred through language. Meaning is a social production, a practice. The world has to be *made to mean*. Language and symbolization is the means by which meaning is produced. This approach dethroned the referential notion of language, which had sustained previous content analysis, where the meaning of a particular term or sentence could be validated simply by looking at what, in the real world, it referenced. Instead, language had to be seen as the medium in which specific meanings are produced. What this insight put at issue, then, was the question of which kinds of meaning get systematically and regularly constructed around particular events. Because meaning was not given but produced, it followed that different kinds of meaning could be ascribed to the same events. Thus, in order for one meaning to be regularly produced, it had to win a kind of credibility, legitimacy or taken-for-grantedness for itself. That involved marginalizing, down-grading or de-legitimating alternative constructions. Indeed, there were certain kinds of explanation which, given the power of and credibility acquired by the preferred range of meanings were literally unthinkable or unsayable (see Hall *et al.*, 1977). Two questions followed from this. First, how did a dominant discourse warrant itself as *the* account, and sustain a limit, ban or proscription over alternative or competing definitions? Second, how did the institutions which were responsible for describing and explaining the events of the world — in modern societies, the mass media, *par excellence* — succeed in maintaining a preferred or delimited range of meanings in the dominant systems of communication? How was this active work of privileging or giving preference practically accomplished?

This directed attention to those many aspects of actual media practice which had previously been analysed in a purely technical way. Conventional approaches to media content had assumed that questions of selection and exclusion, the editing of accounts together, the building of an account into a 'story', the use of particular narrative types of exposition, the way the verbal and visual discourses of, say, television were articulated together to make a certain kind of sense, were all merely technical issues. They abutted on the question of the social effects of the media only in so far as bad editing or complex modes of narration might lead to incomprehension on the viewer's part, and thus prevent the pre-existing meaning of an event, or the intention of the broadcaster to communicate clearly, from passing in an uninterrupted or transparent way to the receiver. But, from the viewpoint of signification, these were all elements or elementary forms of a social practice. They were the means whereby particular accounts were constructed. Signification was a social practice because, within media institutions, a particular form of social organization had evolved which enabled the producers (broadcasters) to employ the means of meaning production at their disposal (the technical equipment) through a certain practical use of them (the combination of the elements of signification identified above) in order to produce a product (a specific meaning) (see Hall, 1975). The specificity of media institutions therefore lay precisely in the way a *social practice* was organized so as to produce a *symbolic product*. To construct *this* rather than *that* account required the specific choice of certain means (selection) and their articulation together through the practice of meaning production (combination). Structural linguists like Saussure and Jacobson had, earlier, identified selection and combination as two of the essential mechanisms of the general production of meaning or sense. Some critical researchers then assumed that the description offered above — producers, combining together in specific ways, using determinate means, to work up raw materials into a product — justified their describing signification as exactly similar to any other media labour process. Certain insights were indeed to be gained from that approach. However, signification differed from other modern labour processes precisely because the product which the social practice produced was a discursive object. What differentiated it, then, as a practice was precisely the articulation together of social and symbolic elements — if the distinction will be allowed here for the purposes of the argument. Motor cars, of course, have, in addition to their exchange and use values, a symbolic value in our culture. But, in the process of meaning construction, the exchange and use values depend on the symbolic value which the message contains. The symbolic character of the practice is the dominant element although not the only one. Critical theorists who argued that a message could be analysed as just another kind of commodity missed this crucial distinction (Garham, 1979; Golding and Murdock, 1979).

The politics of signification

As we have suggested, the more one accepts that how people act will depend in part on how the situations in which they act are defined, and the less one can assume either a natural meaning to everything or a universal consensus on what things mean — then, the more important, socially and politically, becomes the process by means of which certain events get recurrently signified in particular ways. This is especially the case where events in the world are problematic (that is, where they are unexpected); where they break the frame of our previous expectations about the world; where powerful social interests are involved; or where there are starkly opposing or conflicting interests at play. The power involved here is an ideological power: the power to signify events in a particular way.

To give an obvious example: suppose that every industrial dispute could be signified as a threat to the economic life of the country, and therefore against 'the national interest'. Then such significations would construct or define issues of economic and industrial conflict in terms which would consistently favour current economic strategies, supporting anything which maintains the continuity of production, whilst stigmatizing anything which breaks the continuity of production, favouring the general interests of employers and shareholders who have nothing to gain from production being interrupted, lending credence to the specific policies of governments which seek to curtail the right to strike or to weaken the bargaining position and political power of the trade unions. (For purposes of the later argument, note that such significations depend on taking-for-granted what the national interest is. They are predicated on an assumption that we all live in a society where the bonds which bind labour and capital together are stronger, and more legitimate, than the grievances which divide us into labour versus capital. That is to say, part of the function of a signification of this kind is to construct a subject to which the discourse applies: e.g. to translate a discourse whose subject is 'workers versus employers' into a discourse whose subject is the collective 'we, the people'). That, on the whole, industrial disputes are indeed so signified is a conclusion strongly supported by the detailed analyses subsequently provided by, for example, the Glasgow Media Group research published in *Bad News* (1976) and *More Bad News* (1980). Now, of course, an industrial dispute has no singular, given meaning. It could, alternatively, be signified as a necessary feature of all capitalist economies, part of the inalienable right of workers to withdraw their labour, and a necessary defence of working-class living standards — the very purpose of the trade unions, for which they have had to fight a long and bitter historic struggle. So, by what means is the first set of significations recurrently preferred in the ways industrial disputes are constructed in our society? By what means are the alternative definitions which we listed excluded? And how do the media, which are supposed to be impartial, square their production of definitions of industrial conflict which systematically favour one side in such disputes, with their claims to report events in a balanced and impartial manner? What emerges powerfully from this line of argument is that the power to signify is not a neutral force in society. Significations enter into controversial and conflicting social issues as a real and positive social force, affecting their outcomes. The signification of events is part of what has to be struggled over, for it is the means by which collective social understandings are created — and thus the means by which consent for particular outcomes can be effectively mobilized. Ideology, according to this perspective, has not only become a 'material force', to use an old expression — real because it is 'real' in its effects. It has also become a site of struggle (between competing definitions) and a stake — a prize to be won — in the conduct of particular struggles. This means that ideology can no longer be seen as a dependent variable, a mere reflection of a pre-given reality in the mind. Nor are its outcomes predictable by derivation from some simple determinist logic. They depend on the balance of forces in a particular historical conjuncture: on the 'politics of signification'.

Central to the question of how a particular range of privileged meanings was sustained was the question of classification and framing. Lévi-Strauss, drawing on models of transformational linguistics, suggested that signification depended, not on the intrinsic meaning of particular isolated terms, but on the organized set of interrelated elements within a discourse. Within the colour spectrum, for example, the range of colours would be subdivided in different ways in each culture. Eskimos have several words for the thing which we call 'snow'. Latin has one word, *mus*, for the animal which in English is distinguished by two terms, 'rat' and 'mouse'. Italian distinguishes between *legno* and *bosco* where English only speaks of a 'wood'. But where Italian has both *bosco* and *foresta*, German only has the single term, *wald*. (The examples are from Eco's essay, 'Social life as a sign system' (1973)). These are distinctions, not of Nature but of Culture. What matters, from the viewpoint of signification, is not the integral meaning of any single colour-term, — mauve, for example — but the system of differences between all the colours in a particular classificatory system; and where, in a particular language, the point of difference between one colour and another is positioned. It was through this play of difference that a language system secured an equivalence between its internal system (signifiers) and the systems of reference (signifieds) which it employed. Language constituted meaning by punctuating the continuum of Nature into a cultural system; such equivalences or correspondences would therefore be differently marked. Thus there was no natural coincidence between a word and its referent: everything depended on the conventions of linguistic use, and on the way language intervened in Nature in order to make sense of it. We should note that at least two, rather different epistemological positions can be derived from this argument. A Kantian or neo-Kantian position would say that, therefore, nothing exists except that which exists in and for language or discourse. Another reading is that, though the world does exist outside language, we can only make sense of it through its appropriation in discourse. There has been a good deal of epistemological heavy warfare around these positions in recent years.

What signified, in fact, was the positionality of particular terms within a set. Each positioning marked a pertinent difference in the classificatory scheme involved. To this Lévi-Strauss added a more structuralist point: that it is not the particular utterance of speakers which provides the object of analysis, but the classificatory system which underlies those utterances and from which they are produced, as a series of variant transformations. Thus, by moving from the surface narrative of particular myths to the generative system or structure out of which they were produced, one could show how apparently different myths (at the surface level) belonged in fact to the same family or constellation of myths (at the deep-structure level). If the under-lying set is a limited set of elements which can be variously combined, then the surface variants can, in their particular sense, be infinitely varied, and spontaneously produced. The theory closely corresponds in certain aspects to Chomsky's theory of language, which attempted to show how language could be both free and spontaneous, and yet regular and 'grammatical'. Changes in meaning, therefore, depended on the classificatory systems involved, and the ways different elements were selected and combined to make different meanings. Variations in the surface meaning of a statement, however, could not in themselves resolve the question as to whether or not it was a transformation of the same classificatory set.

This move from content to structure or from manifest meaning to the level of code is an absolutely characteristic one in the critical approach. It entailed a redefinition of what ideology was — or, at least, of how ideology worked. The point is clearly put by Veron:

If ideologies are structures . . . then they are not 'images' nor 'concepts' (we can say, they are not contents) but are sets of rules which determine an organization and the functioning of images and concepts. . . . Ideology is a system of coding reality and not a determined set of coded messages . . . in this way, ideology becomes autonomous in relation to the consciousness or intention of its agents: these may be conscious of their points of view about social forms but not of the semantic conditions (rules and categories or codification) which make possible these points of view. . . . From this point of view, then, an 'ideology' may be defined as a system of semantic rules to generate messages . . . it is one of the many levels of organization of messages, from the viewpoint of their semantic properties . . . (Veron, 1971, p. 68)

Critics have argued that this approach forsakes the content of particular messages too much for the sake of identifying their underlying structure. Also, that it omits any consideration of how speakers themselves interpret the world — even if this is always within the framework of those shared sets of meanings which mediate between individual actors/speakers and the discursive formations in which they are speaking. But, provided the thesis is not pushed too far in a structuralist direction, it provides a fruitful way of reconceptualizing ideology. Lévi-Strauss regarded the classificatory schemes of a culture as a set of 'pure', formal elements (though, in his earlier work, he was more concerned with the social contradictions which were articulated in myths, through the combined operations on their generative sets). Later theorists have proposed that the ideological discourses of a particular society function in an analogous way. The classificatory schemes of a society, according to this view, could therefore be said to consist of ideological elements or premises. Particular discursive formulations would, then, be ideological, not because of the manifest bias or distortions of their surface contents, but because they were generated out of, or were transformations based on, a limited ideological matrix or set. Just as the myth-teller may be unaware of the basic elements out of which his particular version of the myth is generated, so broadcasters may not be aware of the fact that the frameworks and classifications they were drawing on reproduced the ideological inventories of their society. Native speakers can usually produce grammatical sentences in their native language but only rarely can they describe the rules of syntax in use which make their sentences orderly, intelligible to others and grammatical in form. In the same way, statements may be unconsciously drawing on the ideological frameworks and classifying schemes of a society and reproducing them — so that they appear ideologically 'grammatical' — without those making them being aware of so doing. It was in this sense that the structuralists insisted that, though speech and individual speech-acts may be an individual matter, the language-system (elements, rules of combination, classificatory sets) was a social system: and therefore that speakers were as much 'spoken' by their language as speaking it. The rules of discourse functioned in such a way as to position the speaker as if he or she were the intentional author of what was spoken. The system on which this authorship depended remained, however, profoundly unconscious. Subsequent theorists noticed that, although this de-centered the authorial 'I', making it dependent on the language systems speaking through the subject, this left an empty space where, in the Cartesian conception of the subject, the all-encompassing 'I' had previously existed. In theories influenced by Freudian and Lacanian psychoanalysis (also drawing on Lévi-Strauss), this question of how the speaker, the subject of enunciation, was positioned in language became, not simply one of the mechanisms through which ideology was articulated, but the principal mechanism of ideology itself (Coward and Ellis, 1977). More generally, however, it is not difficult to see how Lévi-Strauss's proposition — 'speakers produce meaning, but only on the basis of conditions which are not of the speaker's making, and which pass through him/her into language, unconsciously' — could be assimilated to the more classic Marxist proposition that 'people make history, but only in determinate conditions which are not of their making, and which pass behind their backs'. In later developments, these theoretical homologies were vigorously exploited, developed — and contested.

Historicizing the structures

Of course, in addition to the homologies with Lévi-Strauss's approach, there were also significant differences. If the inventories from which particular significations were generated were conceived, not simply as a formal scheme of elements and rules, but as a set of ideological elements, then the conceptions of the ideological matrix had to be radically historicized. The 'deep structure' of a statement had to be conceived as the network of elements, premises and assumptions drawn from the long-standing and historically-elaborated discourses which had accreted over the years, into which the whole history of the social formation had sedimented, and which now constituted a reservoir of themes and premises on which, for example, broadcasters could draw for the work of signifying new and troubling events. Gramsci, who referred, in a less formal way, to the inventory of traditional ideas, the forms of episodic thinking which provide us with the taken-for-granted elements of our practical knowledge, called this inventory 'common sense'.

What must be explained is how it happens that in all periods there coexist many systems and currents of philosophical thought, how these currents are born, how they are diffused, and why in the process of diffusion they fracture along certain lines and in certain directions ... it is this history which shows how thought has been elaborated over the centuries and what a collective effort has gone into the creation of our present method of thought which has subsumed and absorbed all this past history, including all its follies and mistakes. (Gramsci, 1971, p. 327)

In another context, he argued:

Every social stratum has its own 'common sense' and its own 'good sense', which are basically the most widespread conception of life and of men. Every philosophical current leaves behind a sedimentation of 'common sense': this is the document of its historical effectiveness. Common sense is not something rigid and immobile, but is continually transforming itself, enriching itself with scientific ideas and with philosophical opinions which have entered ordinary life.... Common sense creates the folklore of the future, that is as a relatively rigid phase of popular knowledge at a given place and time. (Gramsci, 1971, p. 326)

The formalist conception of the 'cultural inventory' suggested by structuralism was not, in my view, available as a theoretical support for the elaboration of an adequate conception of ideology until it had been thoroughly historicized in this way. Only thus did the preoccupation, which Lévi-Strauss initiated, with the universal 'grammars' of culture begin to yield insights into the historical grammars which divided and classified the knowledge of particular societies into their distinctive ideological inventories.

The structural study of myth suggested that, in addition to the ways in which knowledge about the social world was classified and framed, there would be a distinctive logic about the ways in which the elements in an inventory could yield certain stories or statements about the world. It was, according to Lévi-Strauss, the 'logic of arrangement' rather than the particular contents of a myth which 'signified'. It was at this level that the pertinent regularities and recurrences could best be observed. By 'logic' he did not, certainly, mean logic in the philosophical sense adopted by western rationalism. Indeed, his purpose was to demonstrate that Western rationalism was only one of the many types of discursive arrangement possible; no different intrinsically, in terms of how it worked, from the logic of so-called pre-scientific thinking or mythic thought. Logic here simply meant an apparently necessary chain of implication between statement and premise. In western logic, propositions are said to be logical if they obey certain rules of inference and deduction. What the cultural analyst meant by logic was simply that all ideological propositions about the social world were similarly premised, predicated or inferenced. They entailed a framework of linked propositions, even if they failed the test of logical deduction. The premises had to be assumed to be true, for the propositions which depended on them to be taken as true. This notion of 'the entailment of propositions', or, as the semanticists would say, the embeddedness of statements, proved of seminal value in the development of ideological analysis. To put the point in its extreme form, a statement like 'the strike of Leyland tool-makers today further weakened Britain's economic position' was premised on a whole set of taken-for-granted propositions about how the economy worked, what the national interest was, and so on. For it to win credibility, the whole logic of capitalist production had to be assumed to be true. Much the same could be said about any item in a conventional news bulletin, that, without a whole range of unstated premises or pieces of taken-for-granted knowledge about the world, each descriptive statement would be literally unintelligible. But this 'deep structure' of pre-suppositions, which made the statement ideologically 'grammatical', were rarely made explicit and were largely unconscious, either to those who deployed them to make sense of the world or to those who were required to make sense of it. Indeed, the very declarative and descriptive form of the statement rendered invisible the implied logic in which it was embedded. This gave the statement an unchallenged obviousness, and obvious truth-value. What were in fact propositions about how things were, disappeared into and acquired the substantive affirmation of merely descriptive statements: 'facts of the case'. The logic of their entailment being occluded, the statements seemed to work, so to speak, by themselves. They appeared as proposition-free — natural and spontaneous affirmations about 'reality'.

The reality effect

In this way, the critical paradigm began to dissect the so-called 'reality' of discourse. In the referential approach, language was thought to be transparent to the truth of 'reality itself' — merely transferring this originating meaning to the receiver. The real world was both origin and warrant for the truth of any statement about it. But in the conventional or constructivist theory of language, reality came to be understood, instead, as the result or effect of how things had been signified. It was because a statement generated a sort of 'recognition effect' in the receiver that it was taken or 'read' as a simple empirical statement. The work of formulation which produced it secured this closing of the pragmatic circle of knowledge.

But this recognition effect was not a recognition of the reality behind the words, but a sort of confirmation of the obviousness, the taken-for-grantedness of the way the discourse was organized and of the underlying premises on which the statement in fact depended. If one regards the laws of a capitalist economy as fixed and immutable, then its notions acquire a natural inevitability. Any statement which is so embedded will thus appear to be merely a statement about 'how things really are'. Discourse, in short, had the effect of sustaining certain 'closures', of establishing certain systems of equivalence between what could be assumed about the world and what could be said to be true. 'True' means credible, or at least capable of winning credibility as a statement of fact. New, problematic or troubling events, which breached the taken-for-granted expectancies about how the world should be, could then be 'explained' by extending to them the forms of explanation which had served 'for all practical purposes', in other cases. In this sense, Althusser was subsequently to argue that ideology, as opposed to science, moved constantly within a closed circle, producing, not knowledge, but a recognition of the things we already knew. It did so because it took as already established fact exactly the premises which ought to have been put in question. Later still, this theory was to be complemented by psychoanalytic theories of the subject which tried to demonstrate how certain kinds of narrative exposition construct a place or position of empirical knowledge for each subject at the centre of any discourse — a position or point of view from which alone the discourse 'makes sense'. It, accordingly, defined such narrative procedures, which established an empirical-pragmatic closure in discourse, as all belonging to the discourse of 'realism'.

More generally, this approach suggested, discourses not only referenced themselves in the structure of already objectivated social knowledge (the 'already known') but established the viewer in a complicitous relationship of pragmatic knowledge to the 'reality' of the discourse itself. 'Point of view' is not, of course, limited to visual texts — written texts also have their preferred positions of knowledge. But the visual nature of the point-of-view metaphor made it particularly appropriate to those media in which the visual discourse appeared to be dominant. The theory was therefore most fully elaborated in relation to film: but it applied, *tout court*, to television as well — the dominant medium of social discourse and representation in our society. Much of television's power to signify lay in its visual and documentary character — its inscription of itself as merely a 'window on the world', showing things as they really are. Its propositions and explanations were underpinned by this grounding of its discourse in 'the real' — in the evidence of one's eyes. Its discourse therefore appeared peculiarly a naturalistic discourse of fact, statement and description. But in the light of the theoretical argument sketched above, it would be more appropriate to define the typical discourse of this medium not as naturalistic but as *naturalized*: not grounded in nature but producing nature as a sort of guarantee of its truth. Visual discourse is peculiarly vulnerable in this way because the systems of visual recognition on which they depend are so widely available in any culture that they appear to involve no intervention of coding, selection or arrangement. They appear to reproduce the actual trace of reality in the images they transmit. This, of course, is an illusion — the 'naturalistic illusion' — since the combination of verbal and visual discourse which produces this effect of 'reality' requires the most skilful and elaborate procedures of coding: mounting, linking and stitching elements together, working them into a system of narration or exposition which 'makes sense'.

This argument obviously connects with the classical materialist definition of how ideologies work. Marx, you will recall, argued that ideology works because it appears to ground itself in the mere surface appearance of things. In doing so, it represses any recognition of the contingency of the historical conditions on which all social relations depend. It represents them, instead, as outside of history: unchangeable, inevitable and natural. It also disguises its premises as already known facts. Thus, despite its scientific discoveries, Marx described even classical political economy as, ultimately, 'ideological' because it took the social relations and the capitalist form of economic organization as the only, and inevitable, kind of economic order. It therefore presented capitalist production 'as encased in eternal natural laws independent of history'. Bourgeois relations were then smuggled in 'as the inviolable laws on which society in the abstract is founded'. This eternalization or naturalization of historical conditions and historical change he called 'a forgetting'. Its effect, he argued, was to reproduce, at the heart of economic theory, the categories of vulgar, bourgeois common sense. Statements about economic relations thus lost their conditional and premised character, and appeared simply to arise from 'how things are' and, by implication, 'how they must forever be'. But this 'reality-effect' arose precisely from the circularity, the presupposition-less character, the self-generating and self-confirming nature, of the process of representation itself.

The 'class struggle in language'

Later, within the framework of a more linguistic approach, theorists like Pêcheux were to demonstrate how the logic and sense of particular discourses depended on the referencing, within the discourse, of these pre-constructed elements (Pêcheux, 1975). Also, how discourse, in its systems of narration and exposition, signalled its conclusions forward, enabling it to realize certain potential meanings within the chain or logic of its inferences, and closing off other possibilities. Any particular discursive string, they showed, was anchored within a whole discursive field or complex of existing discourses (the 'inter-discourse'); and these constituted the pre-signifieds of its statements or enunciations. Clearly, the 'pre-constituted' was a way of identifying, linguistically, what, in a more historical sense, Gramsci called the inventory of 'common sense'. Thus, once again, the link was forged, in ideological analysis, between linguistic or semiological concerns, on the one hand, and the historical analysis of the discursive formations of 'common sense' on the other. In referencing, within its system of narration, 'what was already known', ideological discourses both warranted themselves in and selectively reproduced the common stock of knowledge in society.

Because meaning no longer depended on 'how things were' but on how things were signified, it followed, as we have said, that the same event could be signified in different ways. Since signification was a practice, and 'practice' was defined as 'any process of transformation of a determinate raw material into a determinate product, a transformation effected by a determinate human labour, using determinate means (of "production")' (Althusser, 1969, p. 166), it also followed that signification involved a determinate form of labour, a specific 'work': the work of meaning-production, in this case. Meaning was, therefore, not determined, say, by the structure of reality itself, but conditional on the work of signification being successfully conducted through a social practice. It followed, also, that this work need not necessarily be successfully effected: because it was a 'determinate' form of labour it was subject to contingent conditions. The work of signification was a social accomplishment — to use ethnomethodological terminology for a moment. Its outcome did not flow in a strictly predictable or necessary manner from a given reality. In this, the emergent theory diverged significantly, both from the reflexive or referential theories of language embodied in positivist theory, and from the reflexive kind of theory also implicit in the classical Marxist theory of language and the superstructures.

Three important lines of development followed from this break with early theories of language. Firstly, one had to explain how it was possible for language to have this multiple referentiality to the real world. Here, the polysemic nature of language — the fact that the same set of signifiers could be variously accented in those meanings — proved of immense value. Vološinov put this point best when he observed:

Existence reflected in the sign is not merely reflected but refracted. How is this refraction of existence in the ideological sign determined? By an intersecting of differently oriented social interests in every ideological sign. Sign becomes an arena of class struggle. This social multi-accentuality of the ideological sign is a very crucial aspect.... A sign that has been withdrawn from the pressures of the social struggle — which, so to speak, crosses beyond the whole of the class struggle — inevitably loses force, degenerates into allegory, becoming the object not of a live social intelligibility but of a philological comprehension. (Vološinov, 1973, p. 23)

The second point is also addressed as an addendum, in Vološinov's remark. Meaning, once it is problematized, must be the result, not of a functional reproduction of the world in language, but of a social struggle — a struggle for mastery in discourse — over which kind of social accenting is to prevail and to win credibility. This reintroduced both the notion of 'differently oriented social interests' and a conception of the sign as 'an arena of struggle' into the consideration of language and of signifying 'work'.

Althusser, who transposed some of this kind of thinking into his general theory of ideology, tended to present the process as too uni-accentual, too functionally adapted to the reproduction of the dominant ideology (Althusser, 1971). Indeed, it was difficult, from the base-line of this theory, to discern how anything but the 'dominant ideology' could ever be reproduced in discourse. The work of Vološinov and Gramsci offered a significant correction to this functionalism by reintroducing into the domain of ideology and language the notion of a 'struggle over meaning' (which Vološinov substantiated theoretically with his argument about the multi-accentuality of the sign). What Vološinov argued was that the mastery of the struggle over meaning in discourse had, as its most pertinent effect or result, the imparting of a 'supraclass, eternal character to the ideological sign, to extinguish or drive inward the struggle between social value judgements which occurs in it, to make the sign uni-accentual' (1973, p. 23). To go back for a moment to the earlier argument about the reality-effect: Vološinov's point was that uni-accentuality — where things appeared to have only one, given, unalterable and 'supraclass' meaning — was the result of a practice of closure: the establishment of an *achieved system of equivalence* between language and reality, which the effective mastery of the struggle over meaning produced as its most pertinent effect. These equivalences, however, were not given in reality, since, as we have seen, the same reference can be differently signified in different semantic systems; and some systems can constitute differences which other systems have no way of recognizing or punctuating. Equivalences, then, were secured through discursive practice. But this also meant that such a practice was conditional. It depended on certain conditions being fulfilled. Meanings which had been effectively coupled could also be un-coupled. The 'struggle in discourse' therefore consisted precisely of this process of discursive articulation and disarticulation. Its outcomes, in the final result, could only depend on the relative strength of the 'forces in struggle', the balance between them at any strategic moment, and the effective conduct of the 'politics of signification'. We can think of many pertinent historical examples where the conduct of a social struggle depended, at a particular moment, precisely on the effective dis-articulation of certain key terms, e.g. 'democracy', the 'rule of law', 'civil rights', 'the nation', 'the people', 'Man'kind', from their previous couplings, and their extrapolation to new meanings, representing the emergence of new political subjects.

The third point, then, concerned the mechanisms within signs and language, which made the 'struggle' possible. Sometimes, the class struggle in language occurred between two different terms: the struggle, for example, to replace the term 'immigrant' with the term 'black'. But often, the struggle took the form of a different accenting of the *same* term: e.g. the process by means of which the derogatory colour 'black' became the enhanced value 'Black' (as in 'Black is Beautiful'). In the latter case, the struggle was not over the term itself but over its connotative meaning. Barthes, in his essay on 'Myth', argued that the associative field of meanings of a single term — its connotative field of reference — was, *par excellence*, the domain through which ideology invaded the language system. It did so by exploiting the associative, the variable, connotative, 'social value' of language. For some time, this point was misunderstood as arguing that the denotative or relatively fixed meanings of a discourse were not open to multiple accentuation, but constituted a 'natural' language system; and only the connotative levels of discourse were open to different ideological inflexion. But this was simply a misunderstanding. Denotative meanings, of course, are not uncoded; they, too, entail systems of classification and recognition in much the same way as connotative meanings do; they are not natural but 'motivated' signs. The distinction between denotation and connotation was an analytic, not a substantive one (see Camargo, 1980; Hall, 1980a). It suggested, only, that the connotative levels of language, being more open-ended and associative, were peculiarly vulnerable to contrary or contradictory ideological inflexions.

Hegemony and articulation

The real sting in the tail did not reside there, but in a largely unnoticed extension of Vološinov's argument. For if the social struggle in language could be conducted over the same sign, it followed that signs(and, by a further extension, whole chains of signifiers, whole discourses) could not be assigned, in a determinate way, permanently to any one side in the struggle. Of course, a native language is not equally distributed amongst all native speakers regardless of class, socio-economic postion, gender, education and culture: nor is competence to perform in language randomly distributed. Linguistic performance and competence is socially distributed, not only by class but also by gender. Key institutions — in this respect, the family-education couple — play a highly significant role in the social distribution of cultural 'capital', in which language played a pivotal role, as educational theorists like Bernstein and social theorists like Bourdieu have demonstrated. But, even where access for everyone to the same language system could be guaranteed, this did not suspend what Vološinov called the 'class struggle in language'. Of course, the same term, e.g. 'black', belonged in both the vocabularies of the oppressed and the oppressors. What was being struggled over was not the 'class belongingness' of the term, but the inflexion it could be given, its connotative field of reference. In the discourse of the Black movement, the denigratory connotation 'black = the despised race' could be inverted into its opposite: 'black = beautiful'. There was thus a 'class struggle in language'; but not one in which whole discourses could be unproblematically assigned to whole social classes or social groups. Thus Vološinov argued:

Class does not coincide with the sign community i.e. with the community which is the totality of users of the same set of signs for ideological communication. Thus various different classes will use one and the same language. As a result, differently oriented accents intersect in every ideological sign. Sign becomes an arena of class struggle. (Vološinov, 1973, p. 23)

This was an important step: the ramifications are briefly traced through below. But one could infer, immediately, two things from this. First, since ideology could be realized by the semantic accenting of the same linguistic sign, it followed that, though ideology and language were intimately linked, they could not be one and the same thing. An analytic distinction needed to be maintained between the two terms. This is a point which later theorists, who identified the entry of the child into his/her linguistic culture as one and the same mechanism as the entry of the child into the ideology of its society neglected to show. But the two processes, though obviously connected (one cannot learn a language without learning something of its current ideological inflexions) cannot be identified or equated in that perfectly homologous way. Ideological discourses can win to their ways of representing the world already-languaged subjects, i.e. subjects already positioned within a range of existing discourses, fully-social speakers. This underlined the necessity to consider, instead, the 'articulation' of ideology in and through language and discourse.

Second, though discourse could become an arena of social struggle, and all discourses entailed certain definite premises about the world, this was not the same thing as ascribing ideologies to classes in a fixed, necessary or determinate way. Ideological terms and elements do not necessarily 'belong' in this definite way to classes: and they do not necessarily and inevitably flow from class position. The same elementary term, 'democracy' for example, could be articulated with other elements and condensed into very different ideologies: democracy of the Free West and the German Democratic Republic, for example. The same term could be disarticulated from its place within one discourse and articulated in a different position: the Queen acknowledging the homage of 'her people', for example, as against that sense of 'the people' or 'the popular' which is oppositional in meaning to everything which connotes the élite, the powerful, the ruler, the power bloc. What mattered was the way in which different social interests or forces might conduct an ideological struggle to disarticulate a signifier from one, preferred or dominant meaning-system, and rearticulate it within another, different chain of connotations. This might be accomplished, formally, by different means. The switch from 'black = despised' to 'black = beautiful' is accomplished by inversion. The shift from 'pig = animal with dirty habits' to 'pig = brutal policeman' in the language of the radical movements of the 1960s to 'pig = male-chauvinist pig' in the language of feminism, is a metonymic mechanism — sliding the negative meaning along a chain of connotative signifiers. This theory of the 'no necessary class belongingness' of ideological elements and the possibilities of ideological struggle to articulate/disarticulate meaning, was an insight drawn mainly from Gramsci's work, but considerably developed in more recent writings by theorists like Laclau (1977).

But the 'struggle over meaning' is not exclusively played out in the discursive condensations to which different ideological elements are subject. There was also the struggle over access to the very means of signification: the difference between those accredited witnesses and spokesmen who had a privileged access, as of right, to the world of public discourse and whose statements carried the representativeness and authority which permitted them to establish the primary framework or terms of an argument; as contrasted with those who had to struggle to gain access to the world of public discourse at all; whose 'definitions' were always more partial, fragmentary and delegitimated; and who, when they did gain access, had to *perform with the established terms of the problematic in play*.

A simple but recurrent example of this point in current media discourse is the setting of the terms of the debate about black immigrants to Britain as a problem 'about numbers'. Liberal or radical spokesmen on race issues could gain all the physical access to the media which they were able to muster. But they would be powerfully constrained if they then had to argue within the terrain of a debate in which 'the numbers game' was accepted as *the privileged* definition of the problem. To enter the debate on these terms was tantamount to giving credibility to the dominant problematic: e.g. 'racial tension is the result of too many black people in the country, not a problem of white racialism'. When the 'numbers game' logic is in play, opposing arguments can be put as forcefully as anyone speaking is capable of: but the terms define the 'rationality' of the argument, and constrain how the discourse will 'freely' develop. A counter argument — that the numbers are *not* too high — makes an opposite case: but inevitably, it *also reproduces the given terms of the argument*. It accepts the premise that the argument is 'about numbers'. Opposing arguments are easy to mount. Changing the terms of an argument is exceedingly difficult, since the dominant definition of the problem acquires, by repetition, and by the weight and credibility of those who propose or subscribe it, the warrant of 'common sense'. Arguments which hold to this definition of the problem are accounted as following 'logically'. Arguments which seek to change the terms of reference are read as 'straying from the point'. So part of the struggle is over the way the problem is formulated: the terms of the debate, and the 'logic' it entails.

A similar case is the way in which the 'problem of the welfare state' has come, in the era of economic recession and extreme monetarism, to be defined as 'the problem of the scrounger', rather than the 'problem of the vast numbers who could legally claim benefits, and need them, but don't'. Each framework of course, has real social consequences. The first lays down a base-line from which public perceptions of the 'black problem' can develop — linking an old explanation to a new aspect. The next outbreak of violence between blacks and whites is therefore seen as a 'numbers problem' too — giving credence to those who advance the political platform that 'they should all be sent home', or that immigration controls should be strengthened. The definition of the welfare state as a 'problem of the illegal claimant' does considerable duty in a society which needs convincing that 'we cannot afford welfare', that it 'weakens the moral fibre of the nation', and therefore, that public welfare spending ought to be drastically reduced. Other aspects of the same process — for example, the establishment of the range of issues which demand public attention (or as it is more commonly known, the question of 'who sets the national agenda?') — were elaborated as part of the same concern with extending and filling out precisely what we could mean by saying that signification was a site of social struggle.

The fact that one could not read off the ideological position of a social group or individual from class position, but that one would have to take into account how the struggle over meaning was conducted, meant that ideology ceased to be a mere reflection of struggles taking place or determined elsewhere (for example, at the level of the economic struggle). It gave to ideology a relative independence or 'relative autonomy'. Ideologies ceased to be simply the dependent variable in social struggle: instead, ideological struggle acquired a specificity and a pertinence of its own — needing to be analysed in its own terms, and with real effects on the outcomes of particular struggles. This weakened, and finally overthrew altogether, the classic conception of ideas as wholly determined by other determining factors (e.g. class position). Ideology might provide sets of representations and discourses through which we lived out, 'in an imaginary way, our relation to our real conditions of existence' (Althusser, 1969, p. 233). But it was every bit as 'real' or 'material', as so-called non-ideological practices, because it affected their outcome. It was 'real' because it was *real in its effects*. It was determinate, because it depended on other conditions being fulfilled. 'Black' could not be converted into 'black = beautiful' simply by wishing it were so. It had to become part of an organized practice of struggles requiring the building up of collective forms of black resistance as well as the development of new forms of black consciousness. But, at the same time, ideology was also determining, because, depending on how the ideological struggle was conducted, material outcomes would be positively or negatively affected. The traditional role of the trade unions is to secure and improve the material conditions of their members. But a trade-union movement which lost the ideological struggle, and was successfully cast in the folk-devil role of the 'enemy of the national interest', would be one which could be limited, checked and curtailed by legal and political means: one, that is, in a weaker position relative to other forces on the social stage; and thus less able to conduct a successful struggle in the defence of working-class standards of living. In the very period in which the critical paradigm was being advanced, this lesson had to be learned the hard way. The limitations of a trade-union struggle which pursued economic goals exclusively at the expense of the political and ideological dimensions of the struggle were starkly revealed when obliged to come to terms with a political conjuncture where the very balance of forces and the terms of struggle had been profoundly altered by an intensive ideological campaign conducted with peculiar force, subtlety and persistence by the radical Right. The theory that the working class was permanently and inevitably attached to democratic socialism, the Labour Party and the trade-union movement, for example, could not survive a period in which the intensity of the Thatcher campaigns preceding the General Election of 1979 made strategic and decisive inroads, precisely into major sectors of the working-class vote (Hall, 1979; Hall, 1980b). And one of the key turning-points in the ideological struggle was the way the revolt of the lower-paid public-service workers against inflation, in the 'Winter of Discontent' of 1978-9, was successfully signified, not as a defence of eroded living standards and differentials, but as a callous and inhuman exercise of overweening 'trade-union power', directed against the defenceless sick, aged, dying and indeed the dead but unburied 'members of the ordinary public'.

Ideology in the social formation

This may be a convenient point in the argument to turn, briefly, to the second strand: concerning the way ideology was conceived in relation to other practices in a social formation. Many of the points in this part of the argument have already been sketched in. Complex social formations had to be analysed in terms of the economic, political and ideological institutions and practices through which they were elaborated. Each of these elements had to be accorded a specific weight in determining the outcomes of particular conjunctures. The question of ideology could not be extrapolated from some other level — the economic, for example — as some versions of classical Marxism proposed. But nor could the question of value-consensus be assumed, or treated as a dependent process merely reflecting in practice that consensus already achieved at the level of ideas, as pluralism supposed. Economic, political and ideological conditions had to be identified and analysed before any single event could be explained. Further, as we have already shown, the presupposition that the reflection of economic reality at the level of ideas could be replaced by a straightforward 'class-determination', also proved to be a false and misleading trail. It did not sufficiently recognize the relative autonomy of ideological processes, or the real effects of ideology on other practices. It treated classes as 'historical givens' — their ideological 'unity' already given by their position in the economic structure — whereas, in the new perspective, classes had to be understood only as the complex result of the successful prosecution of different forms of social struggle at all the levels of social practice, including the ideological. This gave to the struggle around and over the media — the dominant means of social signification in modern societies — a specificity and a centrality which, in previous theories, they had altogether lacked. It raised them to a central, relatively independent, position in any analysis of the question of the 'politics of signification'.

Though these arguments were cast within a materialist framework, they clearly departed radically from certain conventional ways of putting the Marxist question. In their most extended text on the question, *The German*

Ideology, Marx and Engels had written, 'The ideas of the ruling classes are in every epoch the ruling ideas i.e. the class which is the ruling material force is at the same time its ruling intellectual force' (p. 64). The passage is, in fact, more subtle and qualified than that classic and unforgettable opening suggests. But, in the simple form in which it appeared, it could no longer — for reasons partly sketched out earlier — be sustained. Some theorists took this to mean that any relationship between ruling-class and dominant ideas had therefore to be abandoned. My own view is that this threw the baby out with the bath water, in two senses. It was based on the unsupported, but apparently persuasive idea that, since 'ideas' could not be given a *necessary* 'class belongingness', therefore there could be no relation of any kind between the processes through which ideologies were generated in society and the constitution of a dominant alliance or power bloc based on a specific configuration of classes and other social forces. But clearly it was not necessary to go so far in breaking the theory of ideology free of a necessitarian logic. A more satisfactory approach was to take the point of 'no necessary class belongingness': and then to ask under what circumstances and through what mechanisms certain class articulations of ideology might be actively secured. It is clear, for example, that even though there is no necessary belongingness of the term 'freedom' to the bourgeoisie, historically, a certain class articulation of the term has indeed been effectively secured, over long historical periods: that which articulated 'freedom' with the liberty of the individual, with the 'free' market and liberal political values, but which disarticulated it from its possible condensations in a discourse predicated on the 'freedom' of the worker to withdraw his labour or the 'freedom' of the 'freedom-fighter'. These historical traces are neither necessary nor determined in a final fashion. But such articulations have been historically secured. And they do have effects. The equivalences having been sustained, they are constantly reproduced in other discourses, in social practices and institutions, in 'free societies'. These traditional couplings, or 'traces' as Gramsci called them, exert a powerful traditional force over the ways in which subsequent discourses, employing the same elements, can be developed. They give such terms, not an absolutely determined class character, but a tendential class articulation. The question as to how the articulation of ideological discourses to particular class formations can be conceptualized, without falling back into a simple class reductionism, is a matter on which important work has since been done (the work of Laclau referred to earlier here is, once again, seminal).

Second, to lose the ruling-class/ruling-ideas proposition altogether is, of course, also to run the risk of losing altogether the notion of 'dominance'. But dominance is central if the propositions of pluralism are to be put in question. And, as we have shown, the critical paradigm has done a great deal of work in showing how a non-reductionist conception of dominance can be worked out in the context of a theory of ideology. However, important modifications to our way of conceiving dominance had to be effected before the idea was rescuable. That notion of dominance which meant the direct imposition of one framework, by overt force or ideological compulsion, on a subordinate class, was not sophisticated enough to match the real complexities of the case. One had also to see that dominance was accomplished at the unconscious as well as the conscious level: to see it as a property of the system of relations involved, rather than as the overt and intentional biases of individuals; and to recognize its play in the very activity of regulation and exclusion which functioned through language and discourse before an adequate conception of dominance could be theoretically secured. Much of this debate revolved around the replacement of all the terms signifying the external imposition of ideas or total incorporation into 'ruling ideas' by the enlarged concept of 'hegemony'. Hegemony implied that the dominance of certain formations was secured, not by ideological compulsion, but by cultural leadership. It circumscribed all those processes by means of which a dominant class alliance or ruling bloc, which has effectively secured mastery over the primary economic processes in society, extends and expands its mastery over society in such a way that it can transform and re-fashion its ways of life, its *mores* and conceptualization, its very form and level of culture and civilization in a direction which, while not directly paying immediate profits to the narrow interests of any particular class, favours the development and expansion of the dominant social and productive system of life as a whole. The critical point about this conception of 'leadership' — which was Gramsci's most distinguished contribution — is that hegemony is understood as accomplished, not without the due measure of legal and legitimate compulsion, but principally by means of winning the active consent of those classes and groups who were subordinated within it.

From the 'reflection of consensus' to the 'production of consent'

This was a vital issue — and a critical revision. For the weakness of the earlier Marxist positions lay precisely in their inability to explain the role of the 'free consent' of the governed to the leadership of the governing classes under capitalism. The great value of pluralist theory was precisely that it included this element of consent — though it gave to it a highly idealist and power-free gloss or interpretation. But, especially in formally democratic class societies, of which the US and Britain are archetypal cases, what had to be explained was exactly the *combination* of the maintained rule of powerful classes *with* the active or inactive consent of the powerless majority. The ruling-class/ruling-ideas formula did not go far enough in explaining what was clearly the most stabilizing element in such societies — consent. 'Consensus theory' however, gave an unproblematic reading to this element — recognizing the aspect of consent, but having to repress the complementary notions of power and dominance. But hegemony attempted to provide the outlines, at least, of an explanation of how power functioned in such societies which held both ends of the chain at once. The question of 'leadership' then, became, not merely a minor qualification to the theory of ideology, but the principal point of difference between a more and a less adequate explanatory framework. The critical point for us is that, in any theory which seeks to explain both the monopoly of power and the diffusion of consent, the question of the place and role of ideology becomes absolutely pivotal. It turned out, then, that the consensus question, in pluralist theory, was not so much wrong as incorrectly or inadequately posed. As is often the case in theoretical matters, a whole configuration of ideas can be revealed by taking an inadequate premise and showing the unexamined conditions on which it rested. The 'break' therefore, occurred precisely at the point where theorists asked, 'but who produces the consensus?' 'In what interests does it function?' 'On what conditions does it depend?' Here, the media and other signifying institutions came back into the question — no longer as the institutions which merely reflected and sustained the consensus, but as the institutions which helped to produce consensus and which manufactured consent.

This approach could also be used to demonstrate how media institutions could be articulated to the production and reproduction of the dominant ideologies, while at the same time being 'free' of direct compulsion, and 'independent' of any direct attempt by the powerful to nobble them. Such institutions powerfully secure consent precisely because their claim to be independent of the direct play of political or economic interests, or of the state, is not wholly fictitious. The claim is ideological, not because it is false but because it does not adequately grasp all the conditions which make freedom and impartiality possible. It is ideological because it offers a partial explanation as if it were a comprehensive and adequate one — it takes the part for the whole (fetishism). Nevertheless, its legitimacy depends on that part of the truth, which it mistakes for the whole, being real in fact, and not merely a polite fiction.

This insight was the basis for all of that work which tried to demonstrate how it could be true that media institutions were both, in fact, free of direct compulsion and constraint, and yet freely articulated themselves systematically around definitions of the situation which favoured the hegemony of the powerful. The complexities of this demonstration cannot be entered into here and a single argument, relating to consensus, will have to stand. We might put it this way. Formally, the legitimacy of the continued leadership and authority of the dominant classes in capitalist society derives from their accountability to the opinions of the popular majority — the 'sovereign will of the people'. In the formal mechanisms of election and the universal franchise they are required to submit themselves at regular intervals to the will or consensus of the majority. One of the means by which the powerful can continue to rule with consent and legitimacy is, therefore, if the interests of a particular class or power bloc can be aligned with or made equivalent to the general interests of the majority. Once this system of equivalences has been achieved, the interests of the minority and the will of the majority can be 'squared' because they can both be represented as coinciding in the consensus, on which all sides agree. The consensus is the medium, the regulator, by means of which this necessary alignment (or equalization) between power and consent is accomplished. But if the consensus of the majority can be so shaped that it squares with the will of the powerful, then particular (class) interests can be represented as identical with the consensus will of the people. This, however, requires the shaping, the education and tutoring of consent: it also involves all those processes of representation which we outlined earlier.

Now consider the media — the means of representation. To be impartial and independent in their daily operations, they cannot be seen to take directives from the powerful, or consciously to be bending their accounts of the world to square with dominant definitions. But they must be sensitive to, and can only survive legitimately by operating within, the general boundaries or framework of 'what everyone agrees' to: the consensus. When the late Director General of the BBC, Sir Charles Curran remarked that 'the BBC could not exist outside the terms of parliamentary democracy', what he was pointing to was the fact that broadcasting, like every other institution of state in Britain, must subscribe to the fundamental form of political regime of the society, since it is the foundation of society itself and has been legitimated by the will of the majority. Indeed, the independence and impartiality on which broadcasters pride themselves depends on this broader coincidence between the formal protocols of broadcasting and the form of state and political system which licenses them. But, in orienting themselves in 'the consensus' and, at the same time, attempting to shape up the consensus, operating on it in a formative fashion, the media become part and parcel of that dialectical process of the 'production of consent' — shaping the consensus while reflecting it — which orientates them within the field of force of the dominant social interests represented within the state.

Notice that we have said 'the state', not particular political parties or economic interests. The media, in dealing with contentious public or political issues, would be rightly held to be partisan if they systematically adopted the point of view of a particular political party or of a particular section of capitalist interests. It is only in so far as (a) these parties or interests have acquired legitimate ascendancy in the state, and (b) that ascendancy has been legitimately secured through the formal exercise of the 'will of the majority' that their strategies can be represented as coincident with the 'national interest' — and therefore form the legitimate basis or framework which the media can assume. The 'impartiality' of the media thus requires the mediation of the state — that set of processes through which particular interests become generalized, and, having secured the consent of 'the nation', carry the stamp of legitimacy. In this way a particular interest is represented as 'the general interest' and 'the general interest as "ruling"'. This is an important point, since some critics have read the argument that the operations of the media depend on the mediation of the state in too literal a way — as if it were merely a matter of whether the institution is state-controlled or not. The argument is then said to 'work better for the BBC than for ITV'. But it should be clear that the connections which make the operations of the media in political matters legitimate and 'impartial' are not institutional matters, but a wider question of the role of the State in the mediation of social conflicts. It is at this level that the media can be said (with plausibility — though the terms continue to be confusing) to be 'ideological state apparatuses'. (Althusser, however, whose phrase this is, did not take the argument far enough, leaving himself open to the charge of illegitimately assimilating all ideological institutions into the state, and of giving this identification a functionalist gloss).

This connection is a systemic one: that is, it operates at the level where systems and structures coincide and overlap. It does not function, as we have tried to show, at the level of the conscious intentions and biases of the broadcasters. When in phrasing a question, in the era of monetarism, a broadasting interviewer simply takes it for granted that rising wage demands are the sole cause of inflation, he is both 'freely formulating a question' on behalf of the public and establishing a logic which is compatible with the dominant interests in society. And this would be the case regardless of whether or not the particular broadcaster was a lifelong supporter of some left-wing Trotskyist sect. This is a simple instance; but its point is to reinforce the argument that, in the critical paradigm, ideology is a function of the discourse and of the logic of social processes, rather than an intention of the agent. The broadcaster's consciousness of what he is doing — how he explains to himself his practice, how he accounts for the connection between his 'free' actions and the systematic inferential inclination of what he produces — is indeed, an interesting and important question. But it does not substantially affect the theoretical issue. The ideology has 'worked' in such a case because the discourse has spoken itself through him/her. Unwittingly, unconsciously, the broadcaster has served as a support for the reproduction of a dominant ideological discursive field.

The critical paradigm is by no means fully developed; nor is it in all respects theoretically secure. Extensive empirical work is required to demonstrate the adequacy of its explanatory terms, and to refine, elaborate and develop its infant insights. What cannot be doubted is the profound theoretical revolution which it has already accomplished. It has set the analysis of the media and media studies on the foundations of a quite new problematic. It has encouraged a fresh start in media studies when the traditional framework of analysis had manifestly broken down and when the hard-nosed empirical postivisim of the halcyon days of 'media research' had all but ground to a stuttering halt. This is its value and importance. And at the centre of this paradigm shift was the rediscovery of ideology and the social and political significance of language and the politics of sign and discourse: the *re*-discovery of ideology, it would be more appropriate to say — the return of the repressed.

REFERENCES

Adorno, T.W. *et al.* (1950) *The Authoritarian Personality*, New York, Harper & Bros.

Althusser, L. (1969) *For Marx*, London, Allen Lane.

Althusser, L. (1971) 'Ideology and ideological state apparatuses', in *Lenin and Philosophy and Other Essays*, London, New Left Books.

Bachrach, P. and Baratz, M. (1970) *Power and Poverty, Theory and Practice*, Oxford, Oxford University Press.

Barthes, R. (1972) *Mythologies*, London, Jonathan Cape.

Becker, H. (1967) 'Whose side are we on?', *Social Problems*, 14, Winter.

Bell, D. (1960) *The End of Ideology*, New York, Free Press.

Berger, P. and Luckmann, T. (1966) *The Social Construction of Reality*, Harmonds-worth, Penguin.

Camargo, M. (1980) 'Ideological dimension of media messages', in Hall, S. *et al.* (eds) *Culture, Media, Language*, London, Hutchinson.

Coward, R. and Ellis, J. (1977) *Language and Materialism*, London, Routledge & Kegan Paul.

Durkheim, E. (1960) *The Division of Labour in Society*, Glencoe, Free Press.

Eco, U. (1973) 'Social life as a sign system', in Robey, D. (ed.) *Structuralism: An Introduction*, Oxford, Clarendon Press.

Garnham, N. (1979) 'Contribution to a political economy of mass communication', *Media, Culture and Society*, 1 (2), April.

Glasgow University Media Group (1976) *Bad News*, London, Routledge & Kegan Paul.

Glasgow University Media Group (1980), *More Bad News*, London, Routledge & Kegan Paul.

Golding, P. and Murdock, G. (1979) 'Ideology and mass communication: the question of determination', in Barrett, M., Corrigan, P., Kuhn A. and Wolff J. (eds) *Ideology and Cultural Reproduction*, London, Croom Helm.

Gramsci, A. (1971) *Selections from the Prison Notebooks*, London, Lawrence & Wishart.

Hall, S. (1975) 'Encoding and decoding in the television discourse', *Education and Culture*, 6, Council of Europe, Strasbourg.

Hall, S. (1979) 'The great right moving show', *Marxism Today*, January.

Hall, S. (1980a) 'Encoding and decoding' (revised extract), in Hall, S. *et al.* (eds) *Culture, Media, Language*, London, Hutchinson.

Hall, S. (1980b) 'Popular democratic vs authoritarian populism', in Hunt, A. (ed.) *Marxism and Democracy*, London, Lawrence & Wishart.

Hall, S., Connell, I. and Curti, L. (1977) 'The "unity" of current affairs television', *Cultural Studies*, 9.

Laclau, E. (1977) *Politics and Ideology in Marxist Theory*, London, New Left Books.

Lévi-Strauss, C. (1969) *The Elementary Structures of Kinship*, London, Eyre & Spottiswoode.

Lévi-Strauss, C. (1967) *The Scope of Anthropology*, London, Jonathan Cape.

Lipset, S. (1963) *Political Man*, London, Heinemann.

Lukes, S. (1975) *Power: A Radical View*, London, Macmillan.

Marx, K. and Engels, F. (1970), *The German Ideology*, London, Lawrence & Wishart.

Matza, D. (1969) *Becoming Deviant*, New Jersey, Prentice Hall.

Merton, R. (1957) *Social Theory and Social Structure*, New York, Free Press.

Parsons, T. (1951) *The Social System*, New York, Free Press.

Pêcheux, P. (1975) *Les Verités de la Police*, Paris, Maspero.

Saussure, F. de (1960) *Course in General Linguistics*, London, P. Owen.

Shils, E. (1961a) 'Centre and periphery', in *The Logic of Personal Knowledge*, London, Routledge & Kegan Paul.

Shils, E. (1961b) 'Mass society and its culture', in Jacobs, N. (ed.) *Culture for the Millions*, New York, Van Nostrand.

Veron, E. (1971) 'Ideology and the social sciences', *Semiotica*, III (2), Mouton.

Vološinov, V.N. (1973) *Marxism and the Philosophy of Language*, New York, Seminar Press.

4

Messages and meanings

JANET WOOLLACOTT

Ideology is the final connotation of the totality of connotations of the sign or the context of signs. (Umberto Eco, 1971, p. 83)

Interest in and discussion of the mass media has come from a variety of theoretical and disciplinary sources. Within these wide-ranging and some-times contradictory approaches, the analysis of media messages has been seen as of varying importance. American concern with mass communications has tended to focus on a model of communication which stressed the relationships between the *individuals* involved. In this tradition the communication process was conceived of as a relationship between a sender of messages on the one hand and a receiver of messages on the other. The mass communication process merely converted the receiver from being one to being many individuals. Given this image of the workings of the mass media, the attention of researchers was directed at the psychological dispositions of the producers of mass media messages and at the effects of the message on the members of the audience. The analysis of the meaning of media messages came to be subsumed in these areas of study.

Moreover, early Marxist studies of the media, whilst based on very different theoretical premises, tended to be more concerned with the overall ideological role of the mass media in capitalist societies and less concerned with the meaning of and the production of meaning within specific media messages. When such questions were addressed they were inflected with a form of cultural pessimism. Members of the Frankfurt School, for example, attempted to show that mass culture, and particularly, American mass culture with which they had acquired a forced familiarity, was a debased culture. Adorno and Horkheimer (1977) suggested that the culture of a society under monopoly capitalism was peculiarly repressive in that while bourgeois culture offered a better and more valuable world realizable by every individual from within, mass culture produced a more totalitarian state in which even the illusory advantage of inner freedom of the individual was lost.

In the culture industry the individual is an illusion not merely because of the standardization of the means of production. He is tolerated only so long as his complete identification with the generality is unquestioned. Pseudo-individuality is rife: from the standardized jazz improvisation to the exceptional film star whose hair curls over her eye to demonstrate her originality. What is individual is no more than the generality's power to stamp the the accidental detail so firmly that it is accepted as such. (Adorno and Horkheimer, 1977, p. 374)

Adorno's contention that the mass media provided the ideological counterpart to the economic development of capitalist societies, although very different from the propositions of researchers who concentrated on the 'effects' on audiences of violent or sexual aspects of the media, led to a similar intellectual lacuna in the concrete analysis of media messages.

The distinctive feature of production in the mass media as opposed to general economic production, is that it is concerned with the production and articulation of *messages* within specific signifying systems, the rules and meanings of which we tend to take for granted. The messages in the media are both composed and interpreted in accordance with certain rules or codes. When we see a news event on television or film, we do not see that event 'raw' but we see a message about that event. We can read the message and interpret it but we take for granted the rules and codes through which we read and interpret. The analysis of mass media messages and their discourses of meaning are clearly important for an understanding of mass communications. As Hall has suggested: 'we must recognize that the symbolic form of the message has a privileged position in the communication exchange: and that moments of "encoding" and "decoding", though only "relatively autonomous" in relation to the communication process as a whole, are *determinate* moments' (Hall, 1973, p. 2).

The last ten years have seen an increasing concern with the formal semiological analysis of the mass media message, in news coverage advertising, feature films and television fiction and this has gone hand in hand with developments in theories of ideology. This article will seek to explore some of the developments and problems of this theoretical alliance.

The traditional method for the analysis of the meaning of mass communications messages was *content analysis*. Content analysts operated by establishing certain conceptual categories in relation to media content and then quantitatively assessing the presence or absence of these categories with varying degrees of sophistication. Content analysis as a method was used by researchers of quite different theoretical backgrounds and with varying degrees of success but the method inevitably stresses the manifest content of the message as the most important area for social scientific analysis. The manifest content of the message was taken to provide 'the common universe between the emission, the reception and the researcher' (Camargo, 1972, p. 124). While content analysis was much used in research operating on an individualistic model, it has also been successfully employed to support research on race and the area of news values (Glasgow University Media Group, 1976). Content analysis clearly has advantages for the systematic investigation of a wide range of material. Cantril's original study of the impact of *The Invasion from Mars*, for example, simply reproduced the script of the radio play, but if a researcher wanted to look at 200 plays this was no longer feasible (Cantril *et al.*, 1940). At the same time, however, content analysis has usually proved to be quite limited in conveying the meaning of specific media messages.

More recent research has tended to conceptualize the problems of under-standing media messages rather differently. Semiological or structuralist studies, deriving many of their theoretical premises from linguistics, re-asserted a concern with media messages as *structured wholes* rather than with the quantified explicit content of fragmented parts of messages. Semiology as Burgelin points out, is not only rarely quantitative but also contains an implicit critique of the quantitative pre-occupation of content analysis.

But above all there is no reason to assume that the item which recurs most frequently is the most important or the most significant, for a text is, clearly, a *structured* whole, and the place occupied by the different elements is more important than the number of times they recur. Let us imagine a film in which the gangster hero is seen performing a long succession of actions which show his character in an extremely vicious light, but he is also seen performing one single action which reveals to a striking degree that he has finer feelings. So the gangster's actions are to be evaluated in terms of two sets of opposites: bad/good and frequent/exceptional. The polarity frequent/exceptional is perceptible at first sight and needs no quantification. Moreover we clearly cannot draw any valid inferences from a simple enumeration of his vicious acts (it makes no difference if there are ten or twenty of them) for the crux of the matter obviously is: what meaning is conferred on the vicious acts by the fact of their juxtaposition with the single good action? Only by taking into account the structural relationship of this one good action with the totality of the gangster's vicious behaviour in the film can we make any inference concerning the film as a whole. (Burgelin, 1972, p. 319)

This fairly familiar gangster plot, Burgelin contends, cannot be understood in terms of the quantification of its manifest content but necessitates an examination of the relationship of the different parts of the plot and the way in which they are articulated to form a specific and complex message with various levels of signification.

Some of the early sound gangster films such as *Public Enemy* (1931) aroused considerable official concern because of their violence. Similarly later television programmes on crime and other genres such as Westerns or spy films have aroused the kind of concern that led researchers (who in many ways knew better) to conceptualize the mass communications process in terms of a behaviourist model in which representations of violence were seen to effect in an unmediated way the opinions and actions of individual members of the audience. Content analysis was often used as a tool in this kind of research and its focus on a simple level of manifest content allowed a straightforward transition to be made between violence on the screen and delinquency, gangfights and muggings elsewhere. Semiological studies, on the other hand, focused on film as a *discourse*, on the film as a communi-cation about violence rather than violence itself, and in that sense, re-oriented research towards the system of rules which governed that discourse generally, and the gangster film in particular, rather than specific violent episodes. Within this kind of analysis the codes governing the genre of *film noir* gave different violent episodes different meanings. Indeed, the violent act could only be understood in relation to other elements in the film and in terms of the conventions of the genre. Such acts were no longer seen to have a single fixed meaning but to be capable of signifying different values and presenting different codes of behaviour depending upon how they are articulated as signs amongst other signifying elements within a discourse.

Semiological studies present their own ambiguities and difficulties not least because semiology, unlike content analysis, is not a method but constitutes a constellation of studies in art, literature, anthropology and the mass media which in some way developed or made use of linguistic theory. As a philosophy, as a theory, as a set of concepts and as a method of analysis, semiology has had many facets and has been subject to various interpretations, debates and polemics. Semiology emerged from the study of language problems and the structure of language. Barthes once defined structuralism as a method for the study of cultural artefacts which orginated in the methods of contemporary linguistics. The early structuralist studies attempted to uncover the internal relationships which gave different languages their form and function. Later semiological work took a broader view and attempted to lay down the basis for a science of signs which would include not only languages but also any other signifying system.

The contributions that linguistic analogies made to the study of other cultural forms did not rest solely on the blind application of the methods of one discipline to another, but developed in rather different ways in relation to different theoretical contexts. For our purpose, in working out the methods through which semiologists examine the mass media, it is worth noting some distinctive features of semiological studies in which there is a certain tension. Semiology is distinguished by its insistence on the importance of the sign. This involves the initial isolation of the *signifier* as an object of study from the *signified*. This is relatively easy to understand when the object of investigation is language but is perhaps less easy to comprehend when the object of research is a non-verbal sign system. One famous structuralist anthropological study is Lévi-Strauss's analysis of kinship. Here Lévi-Strauss (1969) considers marriage rules and systems of kinship in a number of 'primitive' societies as a 'kind of language', that is to say, 'a set of operations designed to ensure a certain type of communication between individuals and groups' (Jameson, 1972, p. 111). The message is made up of the women of the group who circulate between the clans, dynasties and families, whereas in language it would be the 'word of the group' which circulated between individuals. The priority of the language model suggested here is typical of semiological treatment whether it be of kinship systems, furniture and fashion, of films and television programmes or of toys and cars. Saussure, who laid down the outlines of semiology as a 'science of signs', contended that the advantage of the linguistic model was that it cut through the apparent naturalness of actions or objects, to show that their meaning is founded on shared assumptions or conventions. In this sense, the methods of linguistics compel the researcher to study the system of rules underlying speech rather than any external influences or determinants.

As the example of gangster films referred to earlier indicates, another characteristic feature of semiological analysis is that it appears to concentrate on the internal structuring of a text or message. Barthes points to this concern of semiologists with immanent analysis:

The relevance shown by semiological research concerns by definition, the meaning of the analysed objects: we consider the objects solely in relation to their meaning without bringing in, at least not prematurely, that is, not before the system be reconstituted as far as possible, the other determinants (psychological, sociological or physical) of these objects; we must certainly not deny these other determinants, which each depend upon another relevancy; but we must treat them also in semiological terms, that situate their place and function in the system of meaning.... The principle of relevancy obviously requires of the analyst a situation of 'immanence', we observe the given system from within. (Barthes, 1967, p. 95)

The internal relationships of any structure are therefore, what gives meaning to any element in the structure. Hence if a particular action is impolite, it is not because of its intrinsic qualities but because of certain relational features which differentiate it from polite actions. Structural analysis tends to stress binary oppositions of this type as a heuristic device, 'a technique for stimulating perception, when faced with a mass of apparently homogenous data to which the mind and eye are numb: a way of forcing ourselves to perceive difference and identity in a wholly new language the sounds of which we cannot yet distinguish from each other. It is a decoding or deciphering device, or alternatively a technique of language learning' (Jameson, 1972, p. 113).

The focus on the internal relationships of a text does raise certain problems. Many of the Russian formalist studies, for example, attempt to examine literature in terms of its internal structure. Propp's *The morphology of the folk tale* (1968) attempts to identify the narrative structure of the Russian folk tale. Propp was reacting strongly against the treatment of isolated elements in folk tales whereby tales were separated and classified according to whether their principal characters are animals, ogres, magical figures, humorous figures and so forth. Propp argues that the identity of character and landscape and the nature of obstacles is less important than their *function*. 'Function is understood as an act of character defined from the point of view of its significance for the course of the action' (Propp, 1968, p. 21). Propp establishes that the narrative of the folk tale follows a certain pattern. The story begins with either an injury to a victim or the lack of some important object and ends with retribution for the injury or the acquisition of the thing lacked. The hero is sent for on the occasion of the injury or the discovery of the lack and two key events follow:

1. He meets the donor (a toad, a hag, a bearded old man, etc.) who after 'testing' him, supplies him with a magical agent which enables him to pass victoriously through his ordeal.

2. He meets the villain in decisive combat *or* he finds himself with a series of tasks or labours which, with the help of his agent, he is ultimately able to solve properly.

The latter part of the tale may constitute a series of retarding devices before the ultimate transfiguration of marriage or coronation.... Propp identifies 31 narrative functions through which it is possible to classify folk tales.

The main problem of this focus on the internal relationships of a particular group of texts is that the specificity of any one text both in the context of its production and its reading, through which meaning is established, is lost. Russian folk tales become indistinguishable from the latest episode of *The Sweeney*, from *Star Wars* or from a Raymond Chandler novel. Indeed, Eco's analysis of the narrative structure of the James Bond novels which suggests that the novels are fixed as a sequence of moves inspired by a code of binary oppositions comes remarkably close to Propp's typical narrative. Eco suggests that the invariable scheme of the Bond novels is as follows:

A. M moves and gives a task to Bond.
B. The villain moves and appears to Bond (perhaps in alternating forms).
C. Bond moves and gives a first check to the villain or the villain gives first check to Bond.
D. Woman moves and shows herself to Bond.
E. Bond consumes woman: possesses her or begins her seduction.
F. The villain captures Bond (with or without woman, or at different moments).
G. The villain tortures Bond (with or without woman).
H. Bond conquers the villain (kills him or kills his representative or helps at their killing).
I. Bond convalescing enjoys woman, whom he then loses. (Eco, 1960, p. 52)

What takes Eco's analysis of Bond beyond some universal fairy tale is that Eco shows that this coded schema, which forms the basis for all the Bond novels (with the exception of *The Spy Who Loved Me*) is closely linked to a series of oppositions. So the opposition of Bond and the villain is accompanied by an opposition between the western world and the Soviet Union, between Britain and non anglo-saxon countries, between ideals and cupidity, between chance and planning, between excess and moderation, between perversion and innocence, between loyalty and disloyalty.

The internal oppositions within the text are obviously part of wider ideological discourses, notably the ideology of the Cold War. Eco makes this clear in the character of some of the oppositions, particularly that of Bond and the villain.

The villain is born in an ethnic area that stretches from central Europe to the Slav countries and to the Mediterranean basin: as a rule he is of mixed blood and his origins are complex and obscure; he is asexual or homosexual or at any rate, is not sexually normal; he has exceptional inventive and organizational qualities which help him to acquire immense wealth and by means of which he usually works to help Russia: to this end he conceives a plan of fantastic character and dimensions, worked out to the smallest detail, intended to create serious difficulties either for England or the Free World in general. In the figure of the villain in fact, there are gathered the negative values which we have distinguished in some pairs of opposites, the Soviet Union and countries which are not Anglo-Saxon (the racial convention blames particularly the Jews, the Germans, the Slavs and the Italians, always depicted as half-breeds), Cupidity elevated to the dignity of paranoia, Planning as technological methodology, satrapic luxury, physical and psychical excess, physical and moral Perversion, radical Disloyalty. (Eco, 1960, p. 44)

Moreover, Eco takes his concern beyond the structure of the text (the Bond novels) in other ways in examining the relationship between the 'literary inheritance and the crude chronicle, between eighteenth-century tradition and science fiction, between adventurous excitement and hypnosis' (Eco, 1960, p. 74). In seeking to establish relationships both with previous literary forms and more minimally and dubiously with audience response, Eco attempts to go beyond a predominantly inductive analysis such as that of Propp to place the narrative structure of the Bond novels within literary discourse and to suggest the necessity of placing the reading and understanding of the meaning of the novels in specific social practices.

Eco's analysis also indicates the tension in semiology between formal textual analysis and the realm of the *signified* and between different texts and between different signifying systems. It is in this area that semiology becomes vitally concerned with ideology. The principal conceptual tool of Saussurean linguistics was the *sign* and the concept of the sign distinguished between various elements in the process of speech, in the now classic formulation:

Signifier — Sign — Signified

The relationships involved here are not those between the word and the real world but between the signifier (an acoustic image, for example) and the signified (the concept). In this sense, semiology excludes consideration of the 'real world' but at the same time the notion of the sign inevitably suggests a reality beyond itself. There is then a certain ambivalence in semiological studies between the analysis of signifying systems such as the mass media as internally and logically structured and the search for underlying structures. Different theorists have attempted to locate the underlying structures, in areas as different as 'literariness' or the universal qualities of the human mind. The theoretical alliance of semiology and Marxism in the study of the mass media has produced the argument that the underlying structure is that of 'myth' or 'ideology'.

Roland Barthes' *Mythologies* (1972) suggested both that semiotics could be applied to areas which had not previously been noted for their 'meaning' and that the results of such an analysis constituted an account of contemporary ideology, as in the following passage.

If we are to believe the weekly *Elle* which some time ago mustered twenty women novelists on one photograph, the woman of letters is a remarkable zoological species: she brings forth pell-mell, novels and children. We are introduced, for example, to *Jaqueline Lenoir* (*two daughters, one novel*); *Marina Grey* (*one son, one novel*); *Nicole Dutreil* (*two sons, four novels*), etc. What does this mean? This: to write is a glorious but bold activity; the writer is an 'artist', one recognizes that he is entitled to a little bohemianism. As he is in general entrusted — at least in the France of *Elle* — with giving society reasons for its clear conscience, he must, after all, be paid for his services: one tacitly grants him the right to some individuality. But make no mistake: let no women believe that they can take advantage of this pace without having first submitted to the eternal statute of womanhood. Women are on the earth to give children to men; let them write as much as they like, let them decorate their condition, but above all, let them not depart from it: let their biblical fate not be disturbed by the promotion which is conceded to them, and let them pay immediately, by the tribute of their motherhood for this bohemianism which has a natural link with a writer's life. (Barthes, 1972, p. 50)

Barthes was in no sense remarkable for his identification of ideological forms. After all Marxists had been describing paintings, novels and the mass media as ideological for many years, and rather more occasionally had analysed the meanings of specific ideological forms. What Barthes established was the use of semiology as a preamble to the study of myth or ideology and in so doing, he pointed to some of the specific problems of analysing the mass media as signifying systems.

In abstract it is not difficult to apply the central concepts of the structuralist conceptual apparatus, 'sign', 'code' (language) and 'message' (speech) to the mass media. Art historians for example, such as Panofsky, rapidly identified the fixed iconography of early movies.

There arose, identifiable by standardised appearance, behaviour and attributes, the wel-remembered types of the vamp and the straight girl (perhaps the most convincing modern equivalents of the medieval personifications of the vices and virtues), the family man and the villain, the latter marked by a black moustache and a walking-stick. Nocturnal scenes were printed on blue or green film. A checkered tablecloth meant once for all, a 'poor but honest' milieu, a happy marriage soon to be endangered by a shadow from the past was symbolised by the young wife's pouring the breakfast coffee for her husband; the first kiss was invariably announced by her kicking out with her left foot. (Panofsky, 1934, p. 25)

At the same time, however, there was a sense in which film and photography involved some crucial changes from preceding signifying systems, such as painting. Benjamin, in seeking to indicate the changes for works of art brought about by the process of mechanical reproduction, suggests that such changes can be illuminated by comparing the painter and the cameraman. 'The painter', he states, 'maintains in his work a natural distance from reality, the cameraman penetrates deeply into its web' (Benjamin, 1977). Even naturalistic painting usually makes clearer the painter's presence, his techniques and codes, than does photography or film.

There is a tremendous difference between the pictures they obtain. That of the painter is a total one, that of the cameraman consists of multiple fragments which are assembled under a new law. Thus for contemporary man the representation of reality by film is incomparably more significant than that of the painter since it offers precisely because of the thoroughgoing permeation of reality with mechanical equipment, an aspect of reality which is free of all equipment. (Benjamin, 1977, p. 400)

The problem is that photography and film, unlike many other signifying forms, appears to *record* rather than to *transform*. Barthes suggests, for example, in his initial analyses of advertisements that the photographic component constituted the paradox of being 'a message without a code' (Barthes, 1971).

Barthes then continues, however, to establish the codes through which advertisements and other mass media messages are constructed while simultaneously carrying the claim of *having-been-there*, the evidence of *'this-is-what-happened-and-how'*. In his analysis of a Panzani advertisement, he points to the signs of marketing, the string-bag, stocked with Panzani tins, spaghetti and pepper and tomato, with the connotations of freshness of product and household use; to the colour tints of the poster (yellow, green and red) which signify Italianness reinforced by the Italian assonance of the Italian name, Panzani; to the assembly of different objects which suggest the idea of a whole culinary service and in which Panzani tins are equated with the natural products surrounding them; and finally to the aesthetic signified of still life. Barthes identifies three messages in the Panzani advertisement; a linguistic message, a coded iconic message and an uncoded iconic message. He suggests that one way of approaching the apparently uncoded message, that is, the literal image of the photograph, is to start with the linguistic message, then examine the literal image and finally examine the overall symbolic meaning of the message. This method of dealing with the uncoded iconic message (the literal image, the photograph) Barthes calls denotation while the analysis of the coded iconic message (the overall symbolic meaning of the advertisement) Barthes calls connotation. Clearly these modes of analysis are only analytically distinct in that there is no way to read a 'literal image' neutrally, which is not in some way dependent on coding and cultural conventions.

The distinguishing feature of Barthes' formal readings of advertisements and other media messages is the identification of second-order meanings, meanings beyond those initially noted. In the case of the example from *Elle*, the connection between women, novels and children in the message signifies that women are only allowed to write if they have children — but it also goes beyond this in terms of the second-order meaning, whereby the complex of pictures and words and their meaning come to constitute a signifier for the idea that it is the natural place of women to produce children even if they also produce novels. Film and photography, Barthes suggests, operate upon us in a manner which suppresses and conceals their ideological function because they appear to record rather than to *transform* or *signify*. Hall uses this kind of analysis to establish the ideological character of news photographs:

New photos operate under a hidden sign marked 'this really happened, see for yourself'. Of course the choice of this moment of an event as against that, of *this* person rather than that, of *this* angle rather than any other, indeed the selection of this photographed incident to represent a whole complex chain of events and meanings is a highly ideological procedure. But by appearing literally to produce the event as it

really happened news photos repress their selective/interpretive/ideological function. They seek a warrant in that ever-pre-given neutral structure, which is beyond
question, beyond interpretation: the 'real' world. At this level, news photos not only
support the credibility of the newspaper as an accurate medium. They also guarantee
and underwrite its objectivity (that is they neutralize its ideological function). (Hall,
1972, p. 84)

The analysis of news photographs is obviously very similar to that of
Barthes but it perhaps registers more acutely because the conventions of
news-reporting rely heavily on accepted canons of impartiality. News-
reporting presents itself as a selection of and impartial comment on 'reality'
as it unfolds and uses photographs and films as evidence of reality
'unfolding'. Yet a range of research studies on the position of women, on
race, on the treatment of industrial relations and in particular on the role of
the trade unions, would show quite clearly that such subjects have rarely
been treated 'impartially' in news-reporting in the press or in broadcasting.
A BBC survey conducted in 1962 showed that 58 per cent of the population
used television as their main source of news and, even more significantly,
that 68 per cent of the group interviewed believed that television news was a
trustworthy medium. For this reason alone it could be seen to be important
to establish that the claims of the news to 'impartiality' are dubious.

Semiotics, with its focus on the internal mechanisms through which
meanings are produced in texts appeared to offer in relation to news
coverage and many other areas, a way of engaging with the meaning of
particular texts and of talking about more general ways through which
signifying systems operate. Yet at the same time, if semiology was to be
anything other than a set of formalist techniques, it had to be used and
articulated within a general theory of ideology. I would suggest that
semiology has been appropriated in a number of ways and has thereby been
elided into a series of theoretical positions with which it is not altogether at
one. I want to trace some of the problems of these theoretical elisions in
relation to three positions, three arguments which take as a point of
reference a semiological reading of a specific media message but which carry
with them more general arguments about the nature of ideology.

Fiske and Hartley's recent introduction to reading television, for example,
purports to be a first attempt to combine a theory of the cultural role of
television with a 'semiotic-based method of analysis whereby individual
broadcast items can be critically "read"' (Fiske and Hartley, 1978). Fiske
and Hartley appear at least initially to follow Barthes's ideas quite closely.
Their own text is littered with concepts taken from Barthes although their
argument about the role of television is very different, suggesting that while
television may present messages with 'preferred meanings' and those
preferred meanings 'usually coincide with the perceptions of the dominant
sections of society', the form of television, its 'constraints' and 'internal
contradictions', is one which allows 'freedom of perception to all its
viewers'. Essentially, Fiske and Hartley suggest that television functions to
'de-familiarize' the viewer precisely because the viewer is 'spontaneously

and continuously confronted' with the necessity to negotiate a stance which will allow him to decode television programmes. Despite their expressed faith in the techniques of semiotics, these are largely eschewed. Lip-service is given to the terms but the authors proceed to analyse television programmes in a rather different way. Hence, the analysis of 'News at Ten' (7 January 1976) appears at first glance to follow closely Barthes's explanation of second-order signification in relation to the now famous example of the black soldier saluting the French flag on the cover of *Paris-Match*.

Thus the image in our film of a soldier clipping a magazine on to his rifle as he peers from his sandbagged bunker fortress in Belfast can activate the myth by which we currently 'understand' the army. This myth, as we shall show, is that the army consists of ordinary men, doing a professional and highly technological job. In order to trigger this myth the sign must be robbed of its specific signified, in this case, perhaps, of 'Private J. Smith, 14.00 hours, January 4th 1976'. The sign loses this specificity and becomes now the second-order signifier; so the signified becomes one-of-our-lads-professional-well-equipped (not Private J. Smith) and the sign in this second order activates or triggers our mental 'myth chain' by which we apprehend the reality of the British soldier/army in Northern Ireland. (Fiske and Hartley, 1978, p. 42)

However, Fiske and Hartley move quickly from this to suggest both that myth meets our cultural needs and that those 'needs require the myth to relate accurately to reality out there'.

Indeed, Fiske and Hartley go on to argue that their Belfast news film is part of a general process whereby television tests myths against reality and upon apprehending inaccuracy, initiates change.

Our news film from Belfast provides us with a particularly clear example of the way television can hint at the inadequacy of our present myths and thus contribute to their development. The sequence of army shots is followed immediately by a sequence showing the funerals of some of the victims of the violence. The last shot of the army sequence is of an armoured troop carrier moving right to left across the screen. There is then a cut to a coffin of a victim being carried right to left at much the same pace and in the same position on the screen. The visual similarity of the two signifiers brings their meanings into close association. The coffin contains the death that should have been presented by the soldiers in the troop carrier. Thus the myth of the army that underlies the whole army sequence has been negated by television's characteristic of quick-cutting from one vivid scene to another. (Fiske and Hartley, 1978, p. 44.)

There are a number of problems with this reading. Although the basic claim that Fiske and Hartley make (that television news is critical of institutions) is not implausible, the reading that supports it is. Buscome calls it 'nothing more than a piece of free association', pointing out that in order for the two shots of the army and coffin to have the meaning claimed, it would be necessary to show that it is a general rule of television news-editing that two subjects moving in the same direction across the screen will be read as 'linked' by more than space and time, or alternatively that the interpretation offered of the inter-cutting is in some way marked in the text, if for example, the second track said something like 'Where the army goes, death is not far behind' (Buscombe, 1979, p. 88). Basically Buscombe argues that the readings given by Fiske and Hartley are not 'semiotic' because they are not dependent on the idea of a set of structured relationships but are dependent on notions of similarity of content.

Moreover, Fiske and Hartley frequently seem to treat ideology as a functional, if mediated, reflection of reality.

The myths ... cannot themselves be discrete and unorganized, for that would negate their prime function (which is to organize meaning): they are themselves organized into a coherence that we might call a *mythology* or an ideology. This, the third order of signification reflects the broad principles by which a culture organizes and interprets the reality with which it has to cope. (Fiske and Hartley, 1978, p. 46)

Television overall, they argue, is better than the literary traditions of the past both at using this area of mythology or ideology and disrupting it. Television, they suggest, performs a 'bardic function' operating as a mediator of language, producing messages not 'according to the internal demands of the text', 'nor of the individual communicator' but 'according to the *needs* of the culture'. Similarly they explain the centralized institutionalization of television as a response to the culture's 'need for a common centre' and the 'oral' quality of television as a compensatory discourse for cementing the 'non-literate' working class into a culture which places 'an enormous investment in the abstract elaborated codes of literacy' (Fiske and Hartley, 1978, p. 86). Semiology is taken over and into this set of arguments with rather curious consequences. The systems of signification embodied in television are handed over to a formulation quite alien to what one would have thought were the first principles in a semiological ABC. The meanings of television programmes are seen to be structured not in accordance with any internal logic but in response to reality 'out there'. Television as an historically specific social institution which constitutes the material base for specific discourses is reduced to the 'needs of the culture'; and finally and most strangely for the work of two such enthusiastic espousers of the semiotic cause, the authors suggest that the overall form of television, with its contradictory and 'de-familiarizing' effects, operates to give the audience the 'freedom to decode as they collectively choose' (Fiske and Hartley, 1978, p. 193). Although, of course, it is perfectly possible to decode oppositionally in the sense of reading a television text while disagreeing with and reversing its ideological message, it is certainly not the case that the audience is free to decode as it wishes. Oppositional readings are dependent upon an accurate decoding in the first place. (Buscombe, 1979)

Fiske and Hartley clearly set out to avoid a crude and reductionist analysis of the ideology of television forms, but their own position involves certain ambiguities. The confusion between freedom to decode and freedom to read oppositionally is echoed throughout their work. Hence while accepting that television performs an ideological function at a general level, they are anxious to avoid either a conspiracy theory on the part of media professionals, on the one hand, or a view of media audiences which sees them as mindless dupes. They are compelled therefore to assume that the ideological function is a *general* one in which the material practices of the television industry have no part and that the ideology of television is also avoidable by collective aberrant decoding on the part of the audience. Their own readings, if somewhat erratically, stress the ideological meanings of television programmes but they attempt to use these readings in a pluralist theoretical framework which stresses the universal character of the ideologies involved (ideology answers 'cultural needs') and glosses over specific ideological forms. This sometimes seems to lead them into the worst forms of the reductionism they sought to avoid. Their reading of 'The Sweeney', for example, focuses on the relationship between Carter and Regan, comparing them with their West Coast counterparts, 'Starsky and Hutch'. At the same time, their view of cultural needs is drawn in, and on the basis of the way in which Regan and Carter work together with Regan dramatically privileged and in a higher position in the police hierarchy, they suggest that 'The Sweeney' tells us that 'in a period when real life offers us wage restraint, inflation and a fall in living standards, there is no need for class hostility' (Fiske and Hartley, 1978, p. 188). Although Regan and Carter are in different positions in the police hierarchy, it seems curious to assume that the Regan and Carter relationship represents class relationships when both men share within the series the same class position and both articulate populist resentments against a system which inextricably entangles class and crime, against them. It is one thing to suggest that 'The Sweeney', like 'Starsky and Hutch' and 'Ironside' operates to personalize status relationships: quite another, to suggest that 'The Sweeney' 'presents a society where class divisions are overcome because both "classes" — Regan and Carter — share the same outlook on life, methods and language'. This kind of dubious leap tells us little about the specific ideological message of 'The Sweeney' and assumes a relationship of *reflection* between television and society. The Sweeney's mythology of defensive determination, we are told, is peculiarly appropriate for a society in a period of recession.

Since ideologies operate in a manner generally concomitant with the needs of the culture and since audiences are free to decode as they will in the Fiske and Hartley formulation, there is little need to examine specific developments and changes within ideological and televisual discourses or the relationship between mass media texts and systems of production or the inter-connections between the media, the state and the class system. The production of 'readings' becomes an end in itself, an exercise in establishing different interpretations in a manner not dissimilar to certain traditional forms of literary criticism, although without the search for excellence which normally preoccupies those forms.

Marxist negotiations with and appropriations of semiology as a linguistic paradigm have taken different directions in the sense that semiology has been articulated with an existing and a developing theory of ideology. For Marx, ideology constituted a specific part of his theory about the nature and internal dynamics of capitalist society. Marx never wrote systematically about ideology and culture but nevertheless a theory of ideology is contained within his work and scattered throughout his work are a series of programmatic outlines. Marx's concept of ideology rested on a substructure/superstructure model which is clearly set out in the much quoted passage from the Preface to a *Contribution to the critique of political economy:*

In the social production of their life, men enter into definite relations which are indispensible and independent of their will, relations of production which correspond to a definite stage of development of their material productive forces. The sum total of these relations of production constitutes the economic structure of society, the real foundation on which rises a legal and political superstructure and to which correspond definite forms of social consciousness. The mode of production of material life conditions the social, political and intellectual life process in general. It is not the consciousness of men that determines their being but, on the contrary, their social being that determines their consciousness. At a certain stage of their development, the material productive forces of society come in conflict with the existing relations of production, or — what is but a legal expression for the same thing, with the property relations within which they have been at work hitherto. From forms of development of the productive forces these relations turn into their fetters. Then begins an epoch of social revolution. With the change of the economic foundation the entire immense superstructure is more or less rapidly transformed. In considering such transformations a distinction should always be made between the material transformation of the economic conditions of production, which can be determined with the precision of natural science, and the legal, political, religious, aesthetic or philosophic — in short ideological forms in which men become conscious of this conflict and fight it out. Just as our opinion of an individual is not based on what he thinks of himself, so can we not judge of such a period of transformation by its own consciousness; on the contrary, this consciousness must be explained rather from the contradictions of material life, from the existing conflict between the social productive forces and the relations of production. (Marx and Engels, 1962, pp. 262-3)

This passage has often been read as an economically determinist view of ideology in which both the 'ideological forms' and the 'consciousness of men' are moulded by the economic substructure. This has been the justification for the focus in Marxism on the problem of transforming the capitalist infrastructure. Yet, Marx was well aware that the superstructural forms — the organization of the state, religion, etc. — could exert considerable influence on the course of events and his empirical work often points to the relative autonomy of these areas of society in specific historical circumstances. A great deal would seem to hinge on the use of the word 'determines'. The term 'determination' can be used to suggest rather different forms of relationship. Williams has argued that it is possible for the term to indicate either a process 'of setting limits and exerting pressures' or a quite different process in which 'subsequent content is essentially prefigured, predicted and controlled by a pre-existing external force', and that Marx uses the term in the former sense (Williams, 1973, p. 4). Marx certainly uses the language of determinism but it is worth noting that he was writing in opposition to idealist and theological accounts of the world, in which the language of determinism was the expected form. It is noticeable that it is in statements that reverse received propositions that Marx uses the word 'determines' most forcibly as in: 'It is not the consciousness of men that determines their being but rather their social being which determines their consciousness' (Marx and Engels, 1962, p. 363).

Debates within Marxism have consistently revolved around the problems associated with economic determinism, although Williams accurately identifies and develops the elements within Marxism which militate against a crude determinism. Marx certainly emphasizes the necessity both for specific historical analysis and for viewing capitalist society as a totality in which the tendencies of the determining base are mediated at other levels. Some formulations, however, have, in stressing the class basis of ideology, lent themselves to various forms of reductionism:

The ideas of the ruling class are in every epoch the ruling ideas: i.e. the class which is the ruling *material* force in society is at the same time its ruling *intellectual* force. The class which has the means of material production at its disposal has control at the same time over the means of mental production so that thereby, generally speaking, the ideas of those who lack the means of mental production are subject to it. The ruling ideas are nothing more than the ideal expression of the dominant material relationships grasped as ideas: hence of the relationships which make the one class the ruling one, therefore, the ideas of its dominance. (Marx and Engels, 1970, p. 64.)

The idea of ruling-class ideology is a well-known one and has coloured a great deal of thinking about the mass media. Traditional Marxist accounts of the media reveal two important characteristics in the conceptualization of the media. Firstly, ideology is conceived as 'false consciousness'. The work of members of the Frankfurt School, for example, gives to the mass media and the culture industry a role of ideological dominance which destroys both bourgeois individualism and the revolutionary potential of the working class. Secondly, the base/superstructure model applied to the mass media generated a continuing concern with the ownership and control of the mass media which gives the signifying capacity of the media a second place, an essentially reflective place, within its theorizing.

Structuralist or semiological investigations of the media allowed a temporary, or in some cases permanent, suspension of involvement in these problems of determination associated with the base/superstructure metaphor. The representation of the media within Marxism as, on the one hand, a purveyor of ruling-class ideology and on the other hand, the inculcator of false consciousness was, in any case, threatened by the Althusserian reformulations of a theory of ideology. Although the Althusserian view retained the notion of determination in the last instance by the economic, it also stressed the autonomy and materiality of the ideological and effected a decisive break with ideological reductionism of an economist and reflective nature. The Althusserian conceptualization of ideology as the themes, concepts and representations through which men and women 'live' in an imaginary relation, their relation to their real conditions of existence also involved a shift away from problems of determination in favour of articulation between the parts in a structure in the focus on the terrains, apparatuses and practices of ideology. In this theoretical context, there have been a number of efforts to combine and synthesize Marxist studies with a semiological paradigm.

The project of the periodical *Screen*, in attempting to generate the theoretical basis for film and television studies in the education system, has involved just such efforts. In particular there has been continuous attention within *Screen* to the dominant codes of narrative cinema, one focus of which has been the contention that such codes are 'realist' and that this form of realism has to be critically engaged with in order to understand the ideological character of the cinema and in order to effect changes within it. Of course, the 'window on reality' effect of photography, film and television has become almost a commonplace of media research. By the early 1970s, there was a general recognition of the inadequacies of a conceptualization of the media which stressed its neutral and reflective role. The arguments in *Screen* surrounding MacCabe's identification of a 'classic realist text' had a rather different focus. MacCabe argued that the 'realism' of the cinema is tied to the characteristics of a particular type of literary production — that of the nineteenth-century realist novel. MacCabe defined the 'classic realist text' as one in which there is 'a hierarchy among the discourses which compose the text and this hierarchy is defined in terms of an empirical notion of truth' (MacCabe, 1974, p. 10). The essential features of the 'classic realist text' MacCabe proposed, were, firstly, its inability to deal with the real as contradictory and secondly its positioning of the subject in a relationship of 'dominant specularity'. The dominant discourse in a classic realist text effects a closure of the subordinated discourses and the reader is placed in a position 'from which everything becomes obvious'. This is achieved through the effacement of the text's signifying practice, through the concealment of its construction. MacCabe used the notion of the 'classic realist text' in an illustrative example of the analysis of Pakula's film, *Klute*. The dominant discourse in *Klute*, according to MacCabe, is the unfolding of the narrative as reality revealing itself. Against this can be measured other subordinate discourses, notably the subjective account provided by the heroine, Bree, talking to her psychiatrist, in a series of fragmentary scenes throughout the film. This subjective discourse in which Bree talks about her desire for independence is seen to be illusionary in relation to the dominant discourse.

The final scene [it is suggested] is particularly telling in this respect. While Klute and Bree pack their bags to leave, the soundtrack records Bree at her last meeting with her psychiatrist. Her own estimation of the situation is that it most probably won't work but the reality of the image ensures us that this is the way it will really be. (MacCabe, 1974, p. 10)

This analysis allowed MacCabe to dispute contemporary critical accounts of the film which stressed the realistic and liberated character of the heroine, played by Jane Fonda. Rather MacCabe contended that the hero, Klute, the detective, played by Donald Sutherland, is privileged within the narrative as a character whose discourse is also a discourse of knowledge. As a man and a detective, he both solves the problems of his friend's disappearance and comes to know the truth about Bree, thereby guaranteeing that the essential woman can only be defined and known by a man. Moreover, this possession of knowledge is also shared by the reader of the film as the narrative unfolds: 'if a progression towards knowledge is what marks Bree, it is possession of knowledge which marks the narrative, the reader of the film and John Klute himself' (MacCabe, 1974, p. 11).

The linguistic paradigm, the form of 'immanent' analysis familiar to us from earlier examples, is clearly present in this type of reading. What distinguishes MacCabe's argument, however, is the setting up of the category of 'classic realism' as the dominant mode of film and television production and endowing that category with certain *essential* ideological characteristics. MacCabe does not suggest that classic realist texts cannot be progressive but he does argue that such texts can only be progressive in so far as they espouse an ideological or political position which is at odds with the *status quo*. Realist texts remain unprogressive in their *form* in the sense that realist texts always interpellate or pull in spectators as unified non-contradictory subjects in a position of dominant specularity. In *Klute*, for example, there is a process of identification involved in the progression of the narrative and the sequence and form of shots which positions the viewer in relation to the narrative in a position of knowledge, which makes it appear as if he or she knows reality. But this position of knowledge is created by the film rather than produced by the viewer. The classic realist text is, in MacCabe's formulation highly 'closed'. It is for this reason that MacCabe favours, as progressive texts, certain *avant garde* films in which there is no dominant discourse but on which the reader has to work and produce a meaning for the film.

There are a number of problems with the notion of the 'classic realist text' not least of which is the extent to which films and television programmes conform to and effectively realize a classic realist project. The rather general nature of the category also raises difficulties. The idea of the classic realist text has a tendency to conceal as much as it illuminates inasmuch as it becomes difficult to distinguish between a nineteenth-century novel and a Hollywood movie or between different groups of Hollywood films. At the same time, the thesis of the 'classic realist text' and the subsequent debate around the term, did have the considerable merit of bringing to the forefront of discussion the formal and ideological characteristics of film and television. It is worth remembering that the implicit modes of pluralist mass communications research against which *Screen* and MacCabe wrote conceived of the media as transparent and neutral communicators and that early semiological inquiries focused on individual texts and general categories of ideology. MacCabe's argument in its suggestion that texts embodied even in terms of their formal characteristics a political signification moved beyond a view of the media as passive transmitters and beyond the reading of single texts. It also undoubtedly led to an élitist concern with *avant garde* texts and with texts which reflected upon themselves.

The *Screen* arguments around realism also involved an explicit rejection of traditional Marxist views of the media as reflective. MacCabe makes it clear that his own work 'does not understand cinema to have an ideological function determined by its representational relationship to other ideological, political and economic struggles' (MacCabe, 1978, p. 32). The theory of ideology which lies behind this takes as its central conceptions the notions of *discourse* and the *subject*. The idea of discourse focuses attention on the internal characteristics and processes of signifying systems. Relationships between discourses are conceived of in terms of articulation rather than determination. This use of the linguistic paradigm would replace the operations of the base/superstructure metaphor and in an extreme form suggest that there is a necessary non-correspondence of all practices. A central concern of this theory of ideology has been the development of theorizing the neglected area of the subject and subjectivity, using Lacanian psychoanalytic concepts to indicate how subjects are constituted in language and other discourses as a non-unified and contradictory set of positions.

The debate around realism and the analysis of realist texts moved the conceptualization of ideology closer to a linguistic or structuralist model of society. There are advantages here in terms of the internal coherence of the conceptual apparatus employed and in the space provided for the concrete analysis of particular ideological and discursive formations. However, there have also been attempts to register the autonomy of discursive practices and signifying systems within a Marxist framework. *Policing the crisis*, for example, represents a formidably ambitious attempt to reconcile a re-working of Gramsci's theory of hegemony with an analysis of the signifying practices of the media in an account of 'a crisis in hegemony' in post-war Britain (Hall *et al.*, 1978). The authors attempt to map out the shifting ideological configurations of the period, characterizing them as culminating in a crisis in hegemony. The study is not confined to an analysis of the ideological superstructures but involves tracing 'the "passage" of a crisis from its material base in productive life through to the complex spheres of the superstructures' (Gramsci, quoted in Hall, 1978). Beginning from the orchestration by the media of mugging as a 'moral panic', the writers attempt to establish that the mugging panic represents a movement from a 'consensual' to a more 'coercive' management of the class struggle which in itself stems from the declining international competitiveness of the British economy following the post-war boom. The analysis suggests that there was a form of hegemonic equilibrium in the immediate post-war period, the erosion of which led to attempts to secure 'consent' by more coercive although 'legitimate' means. The immediate post-war period saw the construction of a consensus as the condition for the stabilization of capitalism in the circumstances of the Cold War and this provided a period of extensive hegemony in the 1950s. Economic decline triggered the disintegration of this 'miracle of spontaneous consent' and there was an attempt to put forward a 'Labourist' variant of consent to replace it. The exhaustion of this form of consent, however, combined with the rise of social and political conflict, the deepening of the economic crisis and the resumption of a more explicit class struggle culminated in the 'exceptional' form of class domination in the 1970s through the state (Hall *et al.*, 1978, p. 218). (There is a further discussion of *Policing the Crisis* in chapter II, pp. 30-55.)

The media appear to play a particularly important part in this analysis. They are described as 'a key terrain where "consent" is won or lost', 'a field of ideological struggle' (Hall *et al.*, 1978, p. 220). The media are also the focal point for the authors' conception of the autonomy of the superstructure for, while rejecting the idea of a 'set of monolithic interpretations systematically generated by the ruling class for the explicit purpose of fooling the public', *Policing the Crisis* does contend that the media serve to reproduce — although through their own 'constructions and inflections' — 'the interpretations of the crisis subscribed to by the ruling-class alliance' (Hall *et al.*, 1978, p. 220). The crisis has its basis in changes in the economy. Although avoiding a heavily determinist stance and relying more on a culturalist view of determination, *Policing the Crisis* retains a hierarchy of determinations, while at the same time seeking to establish the specificity and relative autonomy of the media signification system.

The key to the media's involvement in the construction of consent lies in the authors' analysis of news as performing a crucial transformative but *secondary* role in defining social events. The primary definers are those to whom the media turn, their accredited sources in government and other institutions. Although *Policing the Crisis* emphasizes the transformative nature of media news-reporting in the selection and inflection of items and topics, the conception of the media role is one of 'structured subordination' to the primary definers. Further the 'creative' media role serves to reinforce a consensual viewpoint by using public idioms and by claiming to voice public opinion. Thus in the crisis described the media have endorsed and enforced primary definitions of industrial militancy, troublesome youth cultures, mugging, student protest movements as part of a 'law and order' problem pulling discrete and local events into an amplification spiral and registering them all within a discourse of 'law and order'.

The thesis put forward in *Policing the Crisis* raises certain problems in relation to the siting of signifying systems within a Marxist theory of ideology. It is clear that the autonomy of media significations within the argument is very limited. Basically, the media serve, in the specific historical conditions analysed, to reproduce and reinforce 'primary definitions'. They are assumed thereby to signify a crisis which already exists for the primary definers, a crisis already in operation in the realm of politics and economics. Moreover, given this view of the operations of the media, it is difficult to see how the media operate as 'a field of ideological struggle'. Since the news is read as 'the media' and the news is characterized by its reproduction of primary, 'dominant' definitions in a consensual form, struggle, along with those primary definitions, would seem to lie outside this area of media signification. The area of 'struggle' or opposition would seem to lie in *Policing the Crisis*, insofar as it lies anywhere, in the areas of class experience and the cultural forms through which men and women live that experience; but those cultural forms are largely neglected in favour of the focus on 'news'. Some of the difficulties present in *Policing the Crisis* undoubtedly stem from the attempted synthesis of this form of Marxist culturalist theory, inflected through Gramsci, with an Althusserian conception of the media as an ideological state apparatus largely concerned with the reproduction of dominant ideologies and with an attempt to recognize the autonomy and specificity of the media. With this kind of multiple 'grafting' going on, it is not entirely surprising that some shoots do not flourish. In this case, attention to the internally ordered characteristics of the media suffers, since the media is conceived of as representing 'reality' in a manner inflected in the interests of dominant groups. In effect a sophisticated version of the notion of 'false consciousness' is proposed; 'by consenting to the view of the crisis which has won credibility in the echelons of power, popular consciousness is also won to support too the measures of control and containment which this version of social reality entails' (Hall *et al.*, 1978, p. 221).

Semiology or structuralism and in particular the semiological analysis of media texts have been woven into various formulations of a theory of ideology with a range of subsequent problems in the internal coherence of such theories. It is through the endless thinking through of this kind of incoherence, that intellectual work proceeds. The problems raised in the texts discussed here indicate the general difficulty of reconciling semiotics with any theory of ideology which conceives of the media as essentially reflecting the 'real'. Yet the treatment of systems of signification as autonomous, not bound in a relationship of reflection or representation to an external reality, does not exclude relationships of articulation between different forms of signification nor does it necessarily exclude the analysis of the determinations of signifying systems. Indeed, an effective theory of signification would necessarily involve examining the overall pattern of signifying systems and the configuration of ideological practices. In this sense, *Policing the Crisis*, with all its problems, suggests the theoretical ambitions which a materialist theory of signification and ideology should have.

REFERENCES

Adorno, T.W. and Horkheimer, M. (1977) 'The culture industry: enlightenment as mass deception', in Curran, J. *et al. Mass Communication and Society*, London, Edward Arnold.
Barthes, R. (1967) *Elements of semiology*, London, Jonathan Cape.
Barthes, R. (1971) 'The rhetoric of the image', *Working Papers in Cultural Studies*, Spring.
Barthes, R. (1972) *Mythologies*, London, Jonathan Cape.

Benjamin, W. (1977) 'The work of art in an age of mechanical reproduction', in Curran, J. *et al. Mass Communication and Society*, London, Edward Arnold.

Buono, E. del and Eco, U. (eds) (1966) *The Bond Affair*, London, Macdonald.

Burgelin, O. (1972) 'Structuralist analysis and mass communication', in McQuail, D. (ed) (1972) *The Sociology of mass communications*, Harmondsworth, Penguin.

Buscombe, E. (1978/9) 'Unscrambling semiotics', *Screen Education*, (29).

Camargo, M. de (1972) 'Ideological analysis of the message: a bibliography', *Working Papers in Cultural Studies*, 3, Autumn.

Cantril, H. (1966) *The Invasion from Mars*, New York, Harper Torchbooks.

Curran, J., Gurevitch, M. and Woollacott, J. (eds) (1977) *Mass Communication and Society*, London, Edward Arnold.

Eco, U. (1966) 'Narrative structure in Fleming', in Buono, E. del and Eco U. (eds) *The Bond Affair*, London, Macdonald.

Eco, U. (1971) *A Estrutura Ausente*, S. Paolo, Perspectiva.

Fiske, J. and Hartley, J. (1978) *Reading Television*, London, Methuen.

Hall, S. (1972) 'The determination of news photographs', *Working Papers in Cultural Studies*, 3.

Hall, S. (1973) 'Encoding and decoding in the television discourse', *CCS occasional paper*.

Hall, S., Critcher, C., Jefferson, T., Clarke, J. and Roberts, B. (1978) *Policing the crisis: Mugging, the State and Law and Order*, London, Macmillan.

Jameson, F. (1972) *The Prison-House of Language*, New Jersey, Princeton University Press.

Lévi-Strauss, C. (1970) *The Elementary Structures of Kinship*, London, Social Science Paperbacks in association with Eyre & Spottiswoode.

MacCabe, C. (1974) 'Realism and the cinema', *Screen*, 15 (2).

MacCabe, C. (1978) 'Discourse, cinema and politics', *Screen*, 19 (4).

McQuail, D. (1972) *The Sociology of Mass Communications*, Harmondsworth, Penguin.

Marx, K. and Engels, F. (1962) *Selected Works*, London, Lawrence & Wishart.

Marx, K. and Engels, F. (1970) *The German Ideology*, London, Lawrence and Wishart.

Panofsky, E. (1934) 'Style and medium in the moving pictures', reproduced in Talbot, D. (1967) *Film, An Anthology*, Berkeley, Cal., University of California Press.

Propp, V. (1968) *The Morphology of the Folktale*, Austin, Texas, and London, University of Texas Press.

Saussure, F. de (1966) *Course in General Linguistics*, New York, McGraw-Hill.

Williams, R. (1973) 'Base and superstructure', *New Left Review*, 82.

II

MEDIA ORGANIZATIONS

Introduction

Discussions of the power of the media commonly focus on two different sets of questions. The first is concerned with the *nature* of the power of the media. Do they change people's views and opinions? Do they influence people to believe in certain ways, e.g. buy Brand X of soap-powder or vote for Party Y in an election? Do they 'shape the climate of opinion' in society (and what specifically is implied by that statement)? Do they 'set the agenda' for society? Do they contribute to the 'shaping and reproduction of the hegemony of the dominant values' in society? These, and similar questions, focus on the impact of the media on society, both at the micro- and at the macro-levels, and result in a variety of explanations and analyses of that impact. Some of these are discussed both in the first and in the last sections of this book.

The second set of questions are concerned with locating the centres of power in the media. Clearly, whatever the answers to the first set of questions, the wielding of power in the media must be in the hands of those who have control over the content and shape of the messages disseminated by the media. But where or with whom does that power reside? Indeed is it possible to pinpoint precisely the location of power and control in the media? Should the search focus on any specific individuals, such as the proprietors of newspapers, or the managing directors or editors-in-chief of press and broadcasting organizations? Or alternatively should the examination focus on the *relationships* between them and those professionals who are responsible for, or involved in, the production process in the media? Can the power of the media be explained by examining the norms and rules which govern the behaviour of media professionals? To what extent is the socio-political environment within which the media operate crucial for determining and explaining the performance of the media and in prescribing their impact? These questions, like those concerned with explaining the *nature* of media power, also represent a variety of theoretical approaches to the study of the media, and suggest different foci of examination and different kinds of inquiry. But irrespective of these differences, their starting point is similar. They all regard media organizations as the 'correct' setting within which the search for locating the power in the media ought to be conducted.

Having power in, or control over, the media must imply the capacity to determine or significantly to influence the contents of media products and the meanings carried by them. Any other form of control is secondary, because ultimately whatever power the media may be said to have, either over their mass audiences, or over the performance of various élites or over the 'climate of opinions', this power resides in what they say and the way in which they say it. This *potential* distinction between direct control over the contents of the messages and all other forms of institutional control (e.g. financial, bureaucratic, technological) lies at the root of the debate over the issue of 'ownership and control' in the media. An exposition of the different positions and schools of thought which take part in this debate opens the second section of the book, in the chapter by Graham Murdock. The Marxist position, which takes as its text Marx's argument that 'the class which has the means of material production at its disposal has control at the same time over the means of mental production' and hence regards ownership in the media (and more generally, *economic control*) as the critical factor in determining control over media messages, is juxtaposed with the 'managerialist' thesis, which argues that in analysing the structure of control in media organizations a distinction should be made between control over long-term policies and the allocation of resources (labelled 'allocative control') and control over the day-to-day operation of the production of media products. Murdock presents a four-fold classification of approaches to corporate control, and illustrates his analysis with examples from contemporary work in Britain, although the general arguments, he claims, are applicable to all advanced capitalist economies.

The following chapter by Margaret Gallagher focuses on problems and issues of control *within* media organizations. Different sources of *external* constraints on the media (e.g. political, commercial and technical) are examined, and the discussion illustrates how these constraints helped to shape the structure of control in British broadcasting. The second half of the paper examines the ways in which organizational pressures toward structuring and regulating the work of media professionals are negotiated through the invocation of the notion of professionalism, and the attendant claims for professional autonomy. The implicit conclusion is that the very capacity of media organizations to perform in a creative and innovative manner is dependent on the way in which, in the author's phrase, the 'politics of accommodation' in the mass media is played out. Media audiences — the consumers of media products — must judge for themselves the extent to which creativity, and indeed courage, are reflected in the products disseminated by the media.

Finally, Oliver Boyd-Barrett widens the scope of the discussion and raises some of the issues in the 'media imperialism' debate, i.e. 'the role of the mass media in relations of cultural dependency between nations'. This debate still provides the site for one of the more lively controversies in discussions of communication policies. On the one hand are arraigned the proponents of a *laissez-faire* approach to the flow of communication between nations, and on the other those who argue for the need to restrict and regulate this flow, in order to counter situations of cultural dependency and to preserve the sovereignty of weaker nations. Like most other debates among media scholars, the origins of this debate are easily traceable to a neo-Weberian position on the one hand, and a neo-Marxist position on the other. The author, however, is not content to adopt one position or the other but examines both of them critically since, in his view, many attempts at evaluating the role of the mass media in the process of cultural dependency 'tend to select or give undue weight to evidence which will support a condemnatory attitude. A more fruitful line of investigation', he argues, 'may be to review and evaluate the kinds of claims which some western consultants originally made in support of harnessing the mass media to developmental objectives.' In other words, issues of policy should be judged by the discrepancies, if any, between the promises and the consequences of such policies, rather than on purely ideological grounds.

5

Large corporations and the control of the communications industries

GRAHAM MURDOCK

INTRODUCTION

The communications industries produce peculiar commodities. At one level they are goods and services like any others: cans of fruit, automobiles or insurance. But they are also something more. By providing accounts of the contemporary world and images of the 'good life', they play a pivotal role in shaping social consciousness, and it is this 'special relationship' between economic and cultural power that has made the issue of their control a continuing focus of academic and political concern. Ever since the joint-stock company or corporation emerged as the dominant form of mass media enterprise in the latter part of the last century, questions about the nature of and limits to corporate power have occupied a key place in debates about the control of modern communications. This paper sets out to review the major strands in this debate and to evaluate the contending positions in the light of recent research. Although most of my examples and illustrations will be drawn from contemporary work on Britain, the general arguments are applicable to all advanced capitalist economies.

CORPORATE CONTROL IN THE CONGLOMERATE ERA

The potential reach and power of the leading media corporations is greater now than at any time in the past, due to two interlinked movements in the structure of the communications industries — concentration and conglomeration.

As I have shown elsewhere (Murdock and Golding, 1977) production in the major British mass media markets is increasingly concentrated in the hands of a few large companies. In central sectors such as daily and Sunday newspapers, paperback books, records, and commercial television programming, two-thirds or more of the total audience are reading, hearing or looking at material produced by the top five firms in that sector. Other markets, notably cinema exhibition and women's and children's magazines are even more concentrated, with the lion's share of sales going to the top two companies in each. Even areas such as local weekly newspapers where production has traditionally been highly dispersed are now showing a significant increase in concentration. In 1947 for example, the leading five publishers of national newspapers accounted for only 8 per cent of the weekly market. By 1976, their share had risen to 25 per cent (Curran, 1979, p. 64). As well as illustrating the growth of concentration within particular media sectors, this example also points to the other major source of the large corporations' increasing control over the communications industries — conglomeration.

Conglomeration is a product of the merger movement which has been accelerating since the mid 1950s. In the ten years between 1957 and 1968 for example, over a third (38 per cent) of all the companies quoted on the London Stock Exchange disappeared through mergers and acquisitions (Hannah, 1974). Since then the pace has quickened still further. In 1967-8 for example, there were 1709 mergers among manufacturing and commercial companies. By 1972-3 the figure had risen to 2415 (Ministry of Prices, 1978, p. 16). As well as reinforcing the dominance of the leading firms in most major sectors, this 'take-over boom' (as it is popularly known) has produced a distinctly new kind of corporation — the conglomerate — with significant stakes in a range of different markets, which may or may not be related to one another.

S. Pearson and Son provides a good example of one of the two main types of conglomerates. Although the firm was already highly diversified by the end of the Second World War with sizeable interests in ceramics, oil, banking and local newspapers, in common with most conglomerates it has acquired its major stakes in communications since the mid 1950s. In 1957, the Group bought *The Financial Times* from the Eyre family and took a substantial minority holding in Lord Illiffe's press company (*BPM Holdings*) which is currently the country's fifth largest publishers of provincial evening papers. Throughout the 1950s and 1960s they also made a series of smaller acquisitions to strengthen their stake in the weekly and bi-weekly market, and by 1974 they had a total of 96 titles (treble the number they had in 1941) making them far and away the most important force in the sector. In the late 1960s the company branched out into book publishing with the acquisition of Longman in 1968 and the merger with the country's leading paperback house, Penguin Books, in 1970. More recently, they have diversified into the general area of leisure provision with the purchase of Madame Tussauds, and the London Planetarium in 1977 and Warwick Castle the following year. Pearson is an example of a *general conglomerate* whose interests in communications (although significant for the relevant media sectors) are secondary to its interests in other areas of industry and commerce. General conglomerates have recently been most active in Britain in the field of newspaper publishing with Trafalgar House's acquisition of the Beaverbrook Group, and Lonrho's purchase of *The Observer* and take-over of Scottish and Universal Investments with its important Scottish press interests.

Communications conglomerates on the other hand, operate mainly or solely within the media and leisure industries, using the profits from their original operating base to buy into other sectors. In Britain the profits from commercial television have provided a particularly important source of finance for this kind of diversification. In addition to operating one of Britain's five network television companies for example, the Granada Group Ltd own the country's second largest television rental chain and the fourth largest paperback publishing group, and have interests in cinema, bingo clubs, motorway service areas, and music publishing. Similarly, the Midlands contractor ATV has branched out into the music business, film production and cinema exhibition, while London Weekend Television has recently bought the major publishing house of Hutchinson with its successful Arrow paperbacks division. Other leading communications conglomerates like EMI, were built on the profits from other bases in the post-war boom in leisure and entertainment spending.

Although EMI was the dominant force in the British record industry throughout the 1950s, its activities remained concentrated in the music business and certain sectors of electronics. Then in the early 1960s the company signed The Beatles and a clutch of other beat groups, and reaped enormous profits from the subsequent pop explosion. This sudden inflow of cash provided the base for a massive programme of diversification, notably into the film and television industries. In 1966 EMI bought the Shipman and King cinema chain, and two years later they launched their bid for Associated British Pictures. Their success brought them another 270 cinemas, the Elstree Studios, a major film distribution company, and a quarter share in Thames Television, the company that had secured the lucrative London weekday franchise in 1967. By 1970, EMI had bought up sufficient extra shares to give them a controlling edge over their other main partner in Thames, Rediffusion(a subsidiary of a major industrial conglomerate, British Electric Traction). EMI continued to diversify throughout the 1970s, buying bingo halls, hotels, sports clubs, and a range of other leisure facilities. In December 1979 however, the company was itself taken over by another leading conglomerate, Thorn Electrical Industries, and a new corporation Thorn-EMI formed.

At the present time, then, the communications industries are increasing dominated by conglomerates with significant stakes in a range of major media markets giving them an unprecedented degree of potential control over the range and direction of cultural production. Moreover, the effective reach of these corporations is likely to extend still further during the 1980s, due to their strategic command over the new information and video technologies (see, for example, Robins and Webster, 1979). Nor does their influence end there. As the recent history of the BBC illustrates, in addition to the market power they wield directly, the major media corporations increasingly structure the business environment within which public communications organizations operate.

The BBC is one of the largest culture-producing institutions in Britain, and through its national television and radio networks and its regional and local studios, its products reach most members of the population on most

days of the year. However, it is misleading to see the BBC as an equal or
countervailing force to the leading communications conglomerates. On the
contrary, their activities and goals are determinant and exercise a significant
influence on the Corporation's general allocative policies. In surveying the
BBC's relationship to its operating environment, however, recent
commentators have tended to gloss this over and to concentrate instead on
the 'special relationship' between the corporation and the government of the
day, although, here again, some aspects have received more attention than
others. Recent work has focused particularly on instances of political interference in programme making (see Tracey, chaps. 8-10, and Briggs chap. 4)
and on the growth of internal controls on production as a mechanism for
forestalling further intervention. Rather less attention has been given to the
government's potential influence over policy through its control of the
compulsory licence fee which finances the corporation's activities.

However, the level of the licence fee only sets the limit points to allocative
decision making. Within these parameters the options for resource
allocation and overall programme policy are crucially influenced by the
BBC's involvement in markets where the terms of the competition are set by
the large corporations. They determine the general level of production
costs, both directly through their role as suppliers of equipment, raw
materials and programmes, and indirectly by fixing the market price for
creative labour and technical expertise. Hence the BBC is locked in a
constant competition for talent in which the dynamics of inflation put it at a
permanent disadvantage since unlike the commercial companies it cannot
pass on increases in costs by raising the price of its services. On the other
hand, it cannot cut production costs significantly since it is competing for
audiences.

In order to sustain its claim to the compulsory licence fee and justify
requests for increases, the BBC cannot let its total share of the audience slip
below 50 per cent for any length of time, and so it is drawn into a battle
with the commercial companies in which it has to offer comparable
products. Consequently, the heartland of its popular programming (BBC 1
and Radio 1) is increasingly commandeered by the same sorts of formats
and content as dominate the commercial sector, while the public-service
function is increasingly concentrated in the minority sectors such as adult
education and Radio 3. Nor is the BBC an isolated example. Public
broadcasting in France and Italy is already under similar pressures from the
newly introduced commercial sector, and West Germany seems set to
follow suit in the near future.

The increasing reach and power of the large communications
corporations gives a new urgency to the long-standing arguments about
who controls them and whose interests they serve. As we shall see, a good
deal of this debate has centred around the changing relationship between
share ownership and control of corporate activity, and it is this central issue
that I want to concentrate on here. Unfortunately however, discussions in
this area have been dogged by loose definition so, before we examine the

main strands in the debate, we need to clarify the two main terms: 'control' and 'ownership'.

DEFINING CONTROL AND OWNERSHIP

Following Pahl and Winkler (1974, p. 114-15), we can distinguish two basic levels of control — the *allocative* and the *operational*. Allocative control consists of the power to define the overall goals and scope of the corporation and determine the general way it deploys its productive resources (see Kotz, 1978, p. 14-18). It therefore covers four main areas of corporate activity:

1. The formulation of overall policy and strategy.
2. Decisions on whether and where to expand (through mergers and acquisitions or the development of new markets) and when and how to cut back by selling off parts of the enterprise or laying off labour.
3. The development of basic financial policy, such as when to launch a new share issue and whether to seek a major loan, from whom and on what terms.
4. Control over the distribution of profits, including the size of the dividends paid out to shareholders and the level of remuneration paid to directors and key executives.

Operational control on the other hand, works at a lower level and is confined to decisions about the effective use of resources already allocated and the implementation of policies already decided upon at the allocative level. This does not mean that operational controllers have no creative elbow-room or effective choices to make. On the contrary, at the level of control over immediate production they are likely to have a good deal of autonomy. Nevertheless, their range of options is still limited by the goals of the organizations they work for and by the level of resources they have been allocated.

This distinction between operational and allocative control allows us to replace the ambiguous question of 'who controls the media corporations?' which is often asked, with three rather more precise questions: 'where is allocative control over large communications corporations concentrated?', 'whose interests does it serve?' and 'how does it shape the range and content of day-to-day production?'.

The answer most often given to the first of these questions is that allocative control is concentrated in the hands of the corporation's legal owners — the shareholders — and it is their interests (notably their desire to get a good return on their investment by maximizing profits) that determine the overall goals and direction of corporate activity. However, as with 'control', we need to distinguish between two levels of 'ownership': *legal ownership* and *economic ownership* (see Poulantzas, 1975, p. 18-19). This distinction draws attention to the fact that not all shareholders are equal and that owning shares in a company does not necessarily confer any influence or control over its activities and policies. For legal ownership to become economic ownership, two conditions have to be met. First, the shares held need to be 'voting' shares entitling the holder to vote in the elections to the board of directors — the company's central decision-making forum. Second, holders must be able to translate their voting power into effective representation on the board or that sub-section of it responsible for key allocative decisions (since each share usually carries one vote, the largest holders are normally in the strongest position to enforce their wishes). As a result, economic ownership in large corporations is typically structured like a pyramid with the largest and best organized voting shareholders determining the composition of the executive board who formulate policy on behalf of the mass of small investors who make up the company's capital base. Associated Communications Corporation (the parent company of ATV Network) provides a particularly clear example of this structure. According to the last published accounts the legal ownership of the company is highly diversified with some 54.2 million 'A' ordinary shares in circulation, divided up among over thirteen thousand separate investors, mostly in small parcels of between a hundred and a thousand units. Economic ownership on the other hand is highly concentrated with the company's three key executives holding a majority of the voting shares. The founder and current chairman, Sir Lew Grade, has a total of 27 per cent while the two managing directors hold a further 25 per cent between them, giving the three men a numerical majority over the other voting shareholders. However, it is not necessary to hold over 50 per cent of the voting shares in order to exercise effective allocative control. Where the other main blocs of voting shares are small and fragmented, a well-organized individual or group can assert control with less than 5 per cent.

When we are talking about the relationship between control and ownership then, we are talking first and foremost about the connections between allocative control and economic ownership. Unfortunately, as we shall see presently, a number of commentators have failed to make these crucial distinctions with the result that there has been a good deal of arguing at cross purposes. Nevertheless, when the confusions of terminology have been cleared away there remains a fundamental division of opinion over the relative importance of share-ownership as a source of command over the activities of the modern corporation and the general direction of the corporate economy.

FOUR APPROACHES TO CORPORATE CONTROL

Approaches to the control of large corporations can be usefully divided up according to the general conception of the socio-economic order that underpins them (capitalism v. industrial society) and the primary focus of their analysis (whether it emphasizes action and agency or structural context and constraint). This produces the basic classification of approaches summarized in Table 1.

Table 1: *Varieties of approach to corporate control*

Focus of analysis	Conception of the socio-economic order	
	Capitalism	Industrial society
ACTION/POWER Asks the question: 'Who controls the corporations?'	*Instrumental Approaches* stress the continuing centrality of ownership as a source of control over the policies and activities of large communications corporations. They operate at two levels: (a) At the *specific level* they focus on the control exercised by individual capitalists to advance their own particular interests. (b) At the *general level* they examine the ways in which the communications industries as a whole operate to bolster the general interests of the capitalist class, or of dominant factions within it.	*Pluralist approaches* start from the position that ownership is a relatively unimportant and declining source of effective control over the activities of large modern corporations. They also operate at two levels: (a) *Specific* approaches emphasize the use and power of the managerial strata and the relative autonomy of creative personnel within communications corporations. (b) More general analyses stress the autonomy of media élites and their competitive relation to other institutional élites.
STRUCTURE/ DETERMINATION Asks the question: 'What factors constrain corporate controllers?'	*Neo-Marxist political economies* focus on the ways in which the policies and operations of corporations are limited and circumscribed by the general dynamics of media industries and capitalist economies.	*Commercial* laissez-faire *models* stress the centrality of 'consumer sovereignty' and focus on the ways in which the range and nature of the goods supplied is shaped by the demands of consumers expressed through their choice between competing products in the 'free' market.

Action approaches to corporate activity revolve around the concept of power. They focus on the way in which people, acting either individually or collectively, persuade or coerce others into complying with their demands and wishes. They concentrate on identifying the key allocative controllers and examining how they promote their own interests, ideas and policies. Structural analysis, on the other hand, is concerned with the ways the options open to allocative controllers are constrained and limited by the general economic and political environment in which the corporation operates. The pivotal concept here is not power but determination. Structural analysis looks beyond intentional action to examine the limits to choice and the pressures on decision making.

There has been a tendency for these two approaches to develop separately and even antagonistically. As I have argued elsewhere (Murdock, 1980) this is a false dichotomy. An adequate analysis needs to incorporate both. A structural analysis is necessary to map the range of options open to allocative controllers and the pressures operating on them. It specifies the limit points to feasible action. But within these limits there is always a range of possibilities and the choice between them is important and does have significant effects on what gets produced and how it is presented. To explain the direction and impact of these choices however, we need an action approach which looks in detail at the biographies and interests of key allocative personnel and traces the consequences of their decisions for the organization and output of production. As Steven Lukes has pointed out, the concept of power is a necessary complement to structural analysis.

To use the vocabulary of power in the context of social relationships is to speak of human agents, separately or together, in groups or organisations, significantly affecting the thoughts and actions of others. In speaking thus, one assumes that, although the agents operate within structurally determined limits, they nonetheless have a certain relative autonomy and could have acted differently. The future, though it is not entirely open, is not entirely closed either. (Lukes, 1974, p. 54)

A full analysis of control then, needs to look at the complex interplay *between* intentional action and structural constraint at every level of the production process.

As well as this division between action and structural approaches, the analysis of corporate control has been caught up in the basic opposition betwen what Giddens has called *'theories of industrial society'* and *'theories of capitalism'* (see Giddens, 1979, p. 100-1). These theories offer fundamentally opposed models of the socio-economic order produced by industrial capitalism. The basic positions began to polarize in the mid-nineteenth century with Marx on the one side, and Saint Simon and his personal secretary Auguste Comte (one of the founding fathers of modern sociology) on the other (see Stanworth, 1974).

Although both 'theories' start from an analysis of the economic system, they approach it in very different ways. Marx begins with the unequal distribution of wealth and property and its convertibility into productive industrial capital through the purchase of raw materials, machinery and labour power. For Marx, the defining feature of the emerging industrial order was that effective possession of the means of production was concentrated in the hands of the capitalist class, enabling them to direct production (including cultural production) in line with their interests, and to appropriate the lion's share of the resulting surplus in the form of profit. However, Marx argued, capitalists are not free to do exactly as they like. On the contrary, he suggests that they were in much the same position as 'the sorcerer who is no longer able to control the powers of the nether world whom he has called up by his spells' (Marx and Engels, 1968, p. 40). The economic system created by the pursuit of profit has, he argued, a momentum of its own which produces periodic commercial crises and social conflicts which threaten profitability. Consequently, many of the actions of capitalists are in fact reactions — attempts to maintain profits in the face of the pressures exerted by shifts in the general economic and political system. Marx's general model, therefore, contains both an action and a structural approach to control over the cultural industries and both these strands have been pursued by later writers.

The action strand in Marxism focuses on the way in which capitalists use communications corporations as instruments to further their interests and consolidate their power and privilege. In its simplest version, this kind of *instrumental* analysis concentrates on how individual capitalists pursue their specific interests within particular communications companies. The second main variant, however, works at a more general level and looks at the way the cultural industries as a whole operate to advance the collective interests of the capitalist class, or at least of dominant factions within it. Marx's best-known statement of this position occurs in one of his earliest works, *The German Ideology*, where he argues that:

The class which has the means of material production at its disposal, has control at the same time over the means of mental production.... Insofar as they rule as a class and determine the extent and compass of an epoch, they do this in its whole range, hence among other things (they) also regulate the production and distribution of the ideas of their age: thus their ideas are the ruling ideas of the epoch. (Marx and Engels, 1974a, p. 64-5)

As Marx saw it, then, the owners of the new communications companies were members of the general capitalist class and they used their control over cultural production to ensure that the dominant images and representations supported the existing social arrangements. Subsequent work has attempted to develop this general argument by looking in more detail at the ideological and material links between the communications industries and the capitalist class. At the ideological level commentators have tried to specify the ways in which the dominant media images bolster the central tenets of capitalism, while at the material level studies have focused on the economic and social links binding the key controllers of communications facilities with other core sectors of the capitalist class. Marx himself provided a model for these kinds of analyses in his article, 'The Opinion of the Press and the Opinion of the People', which he wrote for the Viennese newspaper *Die Presse*, on Christmas Day 1861.

The American Civil War was at its height at the time and Marx was trying to explain why the leading London newspapers were calling for intervention on the side of the South when popular opinion seemed to support the North. His answer was that intervention was in the interests of a significant sector of the English ruling class headed by the Prime Minister, Lord Palmerston, and that this group was able to influence the press coverage through their ownership of leading newspapers and their social and political connections with key editors.

Consider the London press. At its head stands *The Times*, whose chief editor, Bob Lowe, is a subordinate member of the cabinet and a mere creature of Palmerston. The Principal Editor of *Punch* was accommodated by Palmerston with a seat on the Board of Health and an annual salary of a thousand pounds sterling. *The Morning Post* is in part Palmerston's private property.... *The Morning Advertiser* is the joint property of the licenced victuallers.... The editor, Mr Grant, has had the honour to get invited to Palmerston's private soirées.... It must be added that the pious patrons of this liquor-journal stand under the ruling rod of the Earl of Shaftesbury and that Shaftesbury is Palmerston's son-in-law. (Marx and Engels, 1974b, p. 124-5)

By pointing to the various links between newspaper editors and proprietors and the Palmerston circle, Marx usefully underscores the need to see the ownership and control of communications as part of the overall structure of property and power relations. (As we shall see, this is an important point of difference between Marxists and the proponents of 'the managerial revolution thesis', who tend to focus on the balance of power *within* media corporations.) At the same time, however, Marx's argument illustrates the fundamental problems with this kind of instrumentalist approach.

He begins the article by asserting that the fact that the London newspapers had faithfully followed every twist and turn in Palmerston's policy provides clear evidence of his control over the press. But this argument mistakes correlation for causality. By showing that there is a close correspondence between Palmerston's views and press presentations, Marx simply poses the question of control; he does not offer an answer. Nor is one provided by his description of the economic and social ties linking press personnel to the Palmerston clique. While this exercise points to *potential* sources of control and influence and identifies *possible* sources along which it might flow, it does not show whether this control was actually exercised or how it impinged on production. This problem of inference, from patterns of ownership and interconnection to processes of control, has dogged every subsequent analysis of this type. For as Connell has rightly pointed out:

Studies of networks of directors and family ownership provide evidence not of organisation itself, but of the potential for organisation. From inferring that they could function as systems of power within business, it is a long step to showing that they do. This requires a case-by-case study. (Connell, 1977, p. 46)

Marx himself, however, never relied solely or even mainly on this type of analysis, and alongside the action-oriented strands in his work he developed a powerful structural approach.

Analysis at this level is focused not on the interests and activities of capitalists, but on the structure of the capitalist economy and its underlying dynamics. For the purposes of structural analysis, it does not particularly matter who the key owners and controllers are. What is important is their location in the general economic system and the constraints and limits that it imposes on their range of feasible options. As Marx put it in a well-known passage:

The will of the capitalist is certainly to take as much as possible. What we have to do is not to talk about his will, but to inquire into his power, *the limits of that power*, and *the character of those limits*. (Marx and Engels, 1968, p. 188)

It is this structural strand in Marx's thought that has provided the main impetus behind the various neo-Marxist political economies of communication.

This same division between structural approaches on the one hand and action-oriented approaches on the other, is also evident in the 'theories of industrial society' which have provided the main counter to Marxist models of modern capitalism.

In contrast to Marxist accounts, 'theories of industrial society' start with the organization of industrial production rather than the distribution of property and the fact of private ownership. The central argument was already evident in the writings of Marx's contemporary Saint Simon, who saw property as a steadily declining source of power. As the new industrial order developed, he argued, ownership would become less and less significant, and effective control over production would pass to the groups who commanded the necessary industrial technologies and organizations: the scientists, engineers and administrators. This theme of the declining importance of ownership and the rise of property-less professionals as a key power group, was pursued by a number of later writers. But it found its most powerful and influential expression in Adolf Berle and Gardiner Mean's book, *The Modern Corporation and Private Property*, published in 1932. According to their analysis, the modern corporation had witnessed a bloodless revolution in which the professional managers had seized control. They had quietly deposed the old captains of industry and become the new rulers of the economic order — 'the new princes'. For Berle and Means:

The concentration of economic power separate from ownership [had] created new economic empires, and delivered these empires into the hands of a new form of absolutism, relegating 'owners' to the position of those who supply the means whereby the new princes may exercise their power. (Berle and Means, 1968, p. 116)

This argument made an immediate impact and was widely taken up in books like James Burnham's *The Managerial Revolution*, whose title provided the popular tag by which this thesis came to be known. This idea of a 'managerial revolution' in industry is still very much with us and commands support from a number of eminent political and economic commentators, including John Galbraith, who made it one of the major themes in his best-selling book, *The New Industrial State*.

Seventy years ago the corporation was the instrument of its owners and a projection of their personalities. The names of these principals — Rockefeller, Mellon, Ford — were known across the land. . . . The men who now head the great corporations are unknown . . . (they) own no appreciable share of the enterprise. (Galbraith, 1969, p. 22)

As we shall see later, the 'managerial revolution thesis' is open to a number of empirical and conceptual criticisms. Not least, it tends to blur the crucial distinctions between the levels of ownership and control we distinguished earlier.

Despite these problems, however, it has had an enormous influence on current thinking and has supported two important currents of analysis which correspond to the two levels of instrumentalism in the Marxist approach. The first of these concentrates on the balance of power and influence within individual corporations. Where Marxists emphasize the continuing power of effective possession operating directly through specific interventions in the production process or indirectly through the limits set by allocative decisions, managerialists stress the relative impotence of owners and the autonomy of administrative and professional personnel. At the second, more general level managerialism feeds into pluralist accounts of power. Where Marxists insist that the capitalist class is still the most significant power bloc within advanced capitalism, pluralists regard it as one élite among a number of others composed of the leading personnel from the key institutional spheres — parliament, the military, the civil service, and so on. These élites are seen as engaged in a constant competition to extend their influence and advance their interests, and although some may have an edge at particular times or in particular situations, none has a permanent advantage. Hence, instead of seeing the effective owners of the communications corporations as pursuing the interests of a dominant capitalist class (as in the Marxist version of general instrumentalism), pluralists see the controllers of the various cultural industries as relatively autonomous power blocs competing with the other significant blocs in society, including industrial and financial élites.

This pluralist conception of the power structure is linked in turn to the *laissez-faire* model of the economy which provides the basis for the structural level of analysis within the theory of industrial society. Both conceptions are dominated by the image of the market. Just as there is a competition for power and influence between institutional élites, so media corporations are seen as having to compete for the attention and loyalty of consumers in the market. And, in the final analysis, so the argument goes, it is the demands and wants of consumers that determine the range and nature of the goods that corporations will supply. Like the capitalists in Marxist accounts, the 'new princes' of managerialism are not free to pursue their interests just as they like; their actions and options are limited by the power and veto of consumers. This notion of 'consumer sovereignty' is central not only to many academic analyses but also to the rationalizations that the communications industries give of their own operations. Here are two recent examples, the first from the eminent British journalist John Whale, and the second from the American marketing analyst, Martin Seiden:

The central truth about newspapers (is) that they cannot go beyond the range of their readers. It is therefore the readers, in the end, who are the figures of power.... That is the answer to the riddle of proprietorial influence. Where it survives at all, it must still defer to the influence of readers.... The broad shape and nature of the press is ultimately determined by no one but its readers. (Whale, 1977, p. 82-5)

It is with the audience and not with the media that the power resides.... By being constantly polled, the audience determines the type of programming that is offered by television. Because the audience's attention is so essential to the success of the system, its influence over the media is exercised in its day-to-day operation rather than as some vague, intangible desire on the part of those who own the media. (Seiden, 1974, p. 5)

Having outlined the main approaches to the question of corporate control we can now begin to examine them in more detail and see how adequate they are conceptually and how well they fit the available empirical evidence.

BEYOND CAPITALISM?
THE IDEA OF 'THE MANAGERIAL REVOLUTION'

The second half of the nineteenth century saw an important shift in the nature of industrial enterprise. Whereas in the earlier part of the century most firms were owned by individuals or families, the Victorian era saw the rapid development of the joint-stock company or corporation in which entrepreneurs expanded their capital-base by selling shares in their enterprises to outsiders with money to invest. These shareholders became the legal owners of the company. As the century progressed, this new system rapidly gained ground in all sectors of industry including the major mass medium of the time — the press. With the repeal of the newspaper taxes and the changes in company law in the mid 1850s, investing in newspapers became both easier and more attractive. The next thirty years saw the launching of well over four hundred press companies and by the end of the century most publishers had adopted some form of joint-stock organization (Lee, 1976, p. 79-80). By then, a number had also begun to offer shares not only to small groups of select investors but to the general public. The first significant media company to 'go public' in Britain was Northcliffe's *Daily Mail* in 1897.

As well as dispersing the legal ownership of companies among a steadily widening group of shareholders, the rise of the modern corporation significantly altered the relationship between ownership and control. Unlike the old style owner-entrepreneurs who had actively intervened in the routine running of their enterprises, the new shareholder-proprietors tended to be 'absentee owners', who left the business of supervising production to paid professional managers. Marx was one of the first commentators to highlight this development, noting that:

Stock companies in general have an increasing tendency to separate this work of management from the ownership of capital ... the mere manager who has no title whatever to the capital performs all the functions pertaining to the functioning capitalist ... and the capitalist disappears as superfluous from the production process. (Marx, 1974, p. 387-88)

Along with other types of enterprise the press of Marx's day was also caught up in this general shift in industrial organization. Whereas in the earlier part of the century it had been common for newspaper proprietors to double as editors, as the scale of newspaper organizations increased, so more owners relinquished their control over day-to-day operations and left the routine management of their papers to full-time editors.

Marx saw the rise of professional managers simply as a further elaboration in the division of industrial labour. He did not see it as the basis for a shift in the locus of control within corporations. Although they had delegated operational control, he argued, the leading owners still retained their effective control over overall policy and resource allocation through the board of directors which they elected and on which some of them sat. Consequently, the managers' operational autonomy (and their continued employment with the company) ultimately depended on their willingness to comply with the interests of the owners.

Marx's own awareness of the limits to managerial autonomy was underscored by his experience of working as one of the *New York Daily Tribune's* European correspondents. To begin with his articles were very highly regarded and when money troubles forced the paper to lay off its foreign staff, he was one of the two people retained. However, the proprietor, Horace Greely, was becoming increasingly alarmed by Marx's views and he asked the editor, Charles Dana, to sack him. Dana refused, but publication of Marx's articles was suspended for several months and soon afterwards the paper dispensed with his services on the grounds that the space was needed for their coverage of the Civil War. The owners' interests had finally outweighed respect for Marx's undoubted journalistic skills (see McLellan, 1973, p. 284-89).

This basic imbalance of power between owners and managers has recently been re-emphasized in an interview with Sir James Goldsmith, the flamboyant proprietor of Britain's short-lived weekly news magazine, *Now*.

Interviewer: If the editor and you disagree, what do you do?
Goldsmith: It's the same as in any other business. If you disagree with the editor, it's give and take — and sometimes you give in, sometimes he gives in. If a disagreement becomes such that you can't live together, then the editor goes, just like a managing director would. (Dimbleby, 1979, p. 230)

Opponents of the Marxist argument might well object to this example on the grounds that Goldsmith's interventionist stance is untypical of owner-manager relations in modern corporations. However, it is by no means an isolated instance. Take for example the case of London Weekend Television. When the British commercial television franchises came up for re-allocation in 1967, the company successfully bid for the contract to serve the London area at weekends. Their submission promised innovations in all major areas of programming and pledged that the company would 'respect the creative talents of those who, within the sound and decent commercial disciplines, will conceive and make the programmes'. On this basis they attracted an experienced and highly-regarded management team headed by Michael Peacock, a former Controller of BBC 1. As economic conditions in the television industry worsened, however, the 'commercial disciplines' increasingly prevailed over 'respect for creative talents'. Programme innovations were shelved and relatively unprofitable drama and arts programmes had their budgets cut and were broadcast at non-peak times. By the spring of 1969, peak-time viewing was almost completely dominated by American material, cinema films, comedy shows and successful series from other companies. Despite this concentration on relatively low-cost, high-audience programmes, however, LWT made a loss of 1.1 million pounds in its first year of operation. Then, in September 1969, under pressure from the leading interests on the board, Michael Peacock's contract was terminated. This action precipitated a crisis among the creative management and six of those in senior positions resigned. As one of them, Frank Muir (the head of Entertainment) explained to the press afterwards:

We thought we had the programme creative element built into their business board with Michael Peacock on it. But, it wasn't enough. What it boils down to is the divine right of boards to have the final say in TV-programme companies.

Theorists of capitalism see this and similar instances as confirming Marx's general argument that the interests of owners operating through key members of the board, continue to determine the basic allocative policies of modern corporations. Supporters of the 'managerial revolution thesis' on the other hand, strongly oppose this conclusion and insist that the dispersal of shareholding and separation of ownership from management have brought about a fundamental shift in the locus of corporate control. As modern corporations expand and become more complex, they argue, only the full-time executives are in a position to keep track of developments and since they control the flow of information to the board, they can present the available options in ways that favour the policies they would like to see implemented. Moreover, with the progressive expansion of legal ownership through new share issues, the larger holders command a steadily diminishing proportion of the total and are less and less able to enforce their interests. Consequently, although the directors still formally control the corporation on behalf of the shareholders, in reality they are reduced to rubber-stamping the strategies and policies devised by the managers. They have replaced owners as the primary allocative controllers.

Managerialists see this shift in the locus of corporate control as laying the basis for a new kind of advanced industrial order which Berle dubbed 'People's Capitalism' (Berle, 1960). According to this argument the fact that most managers own few, if any, shares in the enterprises they run separates them not only from the capitalist class but from the underlying aims and interests of that class. Berle and Means, for example, were adamant that the 'managerial revolution' raised 'for re-examintion the whole question of the motive force back [*sic*] of industry, and the ends to which the modern corporation can or will be run' (Berle and Means, 1968, p. 9). They were convinced that as managers were progressively released from the demands of shareholders they would develop new aims and motivations. In particular, they suggested that profit maximization would cease to be the major driving force behind industrial enterprise and that as a result corporations would become less exploitative and more socially responsible, more 'soulful' to use a contemporary term.

Berle and Means's general thesis gained enormously in credibility from being backed by detailed empirical evidence derived from their research into patterns of ownership and control in all 200 of the top American corporations. The results of this study are still frequently quoted today, and their approach has been widely adopted by subsequent commentators. However, a closer look at their work reveals several major problems.

Critics have attacked the managerialist argument for underestimating the continuing power of capital ownership and for failing to take adequate account of the structural constraints on corporate behaviour. Berle and Means regarded 20 per cent as the minimum holding that an owner needed to enforce his control. Consequently, if the largest identifiable holding of voting shares fell short of this, they defined the corporation as management controlled. Using this criterion, they were able to classify two-thirds of their total sample as under management control. However, there are problems with this impressive-looking finding. Firstly, the fact that they were unable to obtain reliable information on a number of companies means, as they point out, that their 'classification is attended by a large measure of error' (Berle and Means, 1968, p. 84). In fact, as Zeitlin has shown (1974, p. 1081-2) their data only allowed them to classify 22 per cent of their total sample and 3.8 per cent of the leading industrial corporations as definitely under management control. In the absence of reliable data either way, they simply 'presumed' that the rest were also manager-controlled. However, this is a dubious assumption for several reasons. In the first place, the true extent of proprietal holdings is often disguised through the use of 'nominees' (usually banks) who hold shares on behalf of owners whose identity they are not required to declare. Prior to the take-over by Thorn of EMI, for example, both of EMI's two largest shareholders were controlled by nominees; Guaranty Nominees with 6 per cent and Bank of England Nominees with 4.6 per cent. But even where the identity of all the major shareholders is known, Berle and Means's method still leads them to underestimate the degree of potential owner control. According to the last shareholders' list, for example, the largest holding in Thames Valley Broadcasting (the commercial radio station) was Thames Television's 19.88 per cent, which falls just short of Berle and Means's 20 per cent cut-off point for owner control. What was not apparent from the list, however, was that one of the other leading holders, EMI (with 4.52 per cent) also held the controlling interest in Thames TV which gave the company command over 24.4 per cent of the station's total shares, enough for owner control in Berle and Means's terms. This failure to take account of the interconnections between shareholders is symptomatic of a more general limitation in the managerialist approach.

As I indicated earlier, effective economic ownership depends not only on the *absolute* size of the largest shareholding bloc, but also on the *relative* dispersal of the other voting shares and on their holders' capacity for common action and collective mobilization. Hence control is not a quantity but a social relation. Consequently, its analysis requires a dynamic perspective which takes account of the shifting balance of power between shareholders, rather than the static enumerative approach of Berle and Means.

As well as neglecting the interrelations between shareholders, Berle and Means also ignore the potential influence of other forms of capital relations on corporate behaviour. In particular, critics have drawn attention to the power of banks and other suppliers of loan capital. As Kotz has argued:

A corporation that requires a large supply of external funds, even if it is financially sound, may have to yield a certain amount of informal influence to a big lender or investment bank.... The ultimate source of power obtained by financial institutions in such situations is the threat of denying further funds, which could prevent the corporation from carrying out its plans. (Kotz, 1978, p. 21)

A good example is provided by the American Telephone and Telegraph Company (ATTC), the giant communications corporation which Berle and Means singled out to illustrate the principle of management control. At first sight, it looked like a text-book example. The voting shares were very widely dispersed with the top twenty shareholders accounting for less than 5 per cent (4.6 per cent) of the total between them. Consequently, Berle and Means concluded that the corporation was under complete management control and operated independently of any significant property-owning group. However, a closer look revealed that ATTC was tied in with two of the largest owner groups in the US economy — the Morgans and the Rockefellers. At the time (1932), the Morgans' influence extended across a quarter of America's corporate wealth, with the Rockefellers running a close second.

Both had significant banking relations with ATTC and both were well represented on the board. No less than fourteen of the nineteen members had links with other Morgan interests, with fifteen representing the Rockefeller interest (see Klingender and Legg, 1937, p. 71). How exactly the two groups influenced ATTC policy is open to dispute, but clearly the social and economic ties between them and the corporation's senior management provided convenient channels along which influence and control might *potentially* flow. By sticking so closely to what we might call the 'capitalism in one company' approach, however, Berle and Means gloss over the existence and extent of these indirect sources of influence, and present a truncated account of the relations between property ownership and allocative control.

This failure to examine the contextural constraints on corporate behaviour provides the starting point for the critiques of managerialism mounted by neo-Marxist political economists. As De Vroey has emphasized:

While Managerialists just ask the question 'who rules the corporations?', Marxists' main question is: 'For which class interests are the corporations ruled?' Here, one questions the logic of the actions, and this logic goes beyond motivations, being inherent to the mode of production and the place of the individuals within it. (De Vroey, 1975, p. 6-7)

As we saw earlier, supporters of the 'managerial revolution' thesis stress the fact that managers do not share the traditional capitalists' concern with profit maximization. Since most of them have few shares in the companies they run, the argument goes, their motivations tend to revolve around career and promotion rather than profit. Their main concerns are with building up the autonomy and influence of their departments, gaining prestige and status, and advancing the ideas they favour. However, by emphasizing personal motivations this analysis conveniently neglects the ways in which managers' actions are constrained by the economic context in which they are obliged to operate. No matter who controls the corporations, opponents argue, profit maximization remains the basic *structural* imperative around which the capitalist economy revolves; hence,

Professional managers have to worry about profits, just as much as the traditional tycoon.... Even if they are subjectively interested not in profits but in the growth of the firm and the power and prestige which this brings them, profits are still essential to secure this growth. Profits provide directly much of the finance for growth; they are also necessary for raising extra funds from outside. (Glyn and Sutcliffe, 1972, p. 52)

This structuralist argument also casts doubt on the idea of the 'soulful' corporation. This is not to say that corporations are only interested in making profits or that their support for cultural and community activities is not informed by a genuine philanthropy. However, these activities also bolster the effective pursuit of profit by enhancing the corporation's general image and deflecting criticism of its operations. Atlantic Richfield, the American oil company that owned *The Observer*, provides a good illustration of this mixture of motives. The company's involvements in arts patronage and social-welfare programmes have been hailed as a prime example of the 'soulful' corporation in action, and there is no doubt that these moves are partly motivated by a genuine concern for the quality of communal life. However, as the chairman pointed out to shareholders in 1978, they also help considerably with the main business of profit maximization.

Atlantic Richfield is aggressively seeking out the economic opportunities afforded by our free enterprise system and taking full advantage of them. Despite the social upheaval of the last few years (including increasingly critical appraisals of business), *Atlantic Richfield's primary task remains what it has always been — to conduct its business within accepted rules to generate profits, thereby protecting and enhancing the investments of its owners.* But ... senior management recognize that the Company cannot expect to operate freely or advantageously without public approval. And today the public expects a corporation to contribute to the quality, as well as the quantity, of life — or go out of business altogether. (Atlantic Richfield, 1978, p. 27) [my italics]

Far from replacing the pursuit of profit as Berle and Means had hoped, then, corporate excursions into social responsibility have become a way of pursuing this goal more effectively in an unstable social and political climate.

Analysing the nature of these constraints on profitability and their implications for corporate behaviour provides the basis for the structuralist strand in Marxist approaches to corporate control. In contrast, the instrumentalist's current stresses the continuing centrality and power of individual owners and of the capitalist class.

PATTERNS OF OWNERSHIP: RECENT EVIDENCE

According to the most recent detailed study of the largest 250 firms in the UK economy, well over a half (56.25 per cent) have 'an effective locus of control connected with an identifiable group of proprietary interests' and can be classified as owner controlled (Nyman and Silbertson, 1978, p. 80). However, the composition of these proprietary interests has changed considerably over the last two decades. In 1957, almost two thirds (65.8 per cent) of the shares quoted on the London Stock Exchange were held by individuals. By 1975, this proportion had shrunk to just over a third (37.5 per cent). Over the same period, the proportion held by major insurance companies, investment trusts and pension funds, increased from 19 per cent to 42.7 per cent. There was also a small rise in the proportion held by other industrial and commercial companies and by overseas interests (Royal Commission on the Distribution of Income and Wealth, 1979, p. 141). Not surprisingly, communications corporations show the impact of these shifts somewhat unevenly.

As I have shown elsewhere (Murdock, 1980), the national press, as one of the oldest media sectors, is still largely dominated by companies controlled by the descendants of the original founding families and their associates. In fact, five out of the top seven concerns are of this type (they are: Associated Newspapers, The Daily Telegraph Limited, The Thomson Organisation, News International and S. Pearson and Son). However, the resilience of individual ownership is by no means confined to the press or to the British media. The American entertainment industries also boast a number of well-known instances of proprietal power. They include: Mr Kirk Kerkorian, who has a 25.5 per cent stake in Columbia Pictures and a sizeable stake in another Hollywood major, MGM; and Mr William Paley, chairman and key stockholder in CBS Inc., the major music publishing and commercial broadcasting company (see Halberstam, 1976).

Proprietorial interests are also well to the fore in Britain's commercial television industry. This is a particularly relevant case given the managerialist argument that the withering-away of owner power is a developing trend which is likely to be furthest advanced in the most recently established branches of economic activity.

As Table 2 shows, almost all the leading corporations involved in commercial television display a highly-concentrated pattern of ownership centred on identifiable groups of proprietary interests. Indeed, five out of the eight qualify as 'owner controlled', even on Berle and Means's restrictive definition. In fact, the only major holding company that approximates to the managerialist model is EMI, although the presence of substantial nominee holdings make it impossible to assess the real extent of owner interests. However, the table also shows that the pattern of ownership is rather more variable than in the press. This reflects both the general shifts in share ownership since the mid-1950s when commercial television was first launched, and the specific characteristics of investment in the industry (notably the heavy involvement of newspaper companies and corporations engaged in set rental and entertainment). In three out of the eight leading concerns (Granada, Associated Communications and Scottish Television) the locus of proprietorial control lies with the leading members of the boards. In all but one of the remainder, control is held by the major institutional investors, operating through their representatives on the relevant boards. The current board of Southern Television, for example, includes the chairmen of two of the major investors — The Rank Organisation and D.C. Thomson (the Scottish press company) — and the managing director of the third, Associated Newspapers. Similarly, Lord Hartwell, the deputy chairman of LWT (Holdings), is also the chairman of one of the company's major shareholders, The Daily Telegraph Ltd, while the Anglia Group is headed by the Marquis Townsend of Raynham, vice-chairman of one of the leading investors, Norwich Union Life Insurance. As I have shown elsewhere (Murdock, 1979), these shareholding and directorial links between media companies and other leading corporations are by no means unique to television. On the contrary, they are part of an expanding network of connections binding the major communications corporations to other core sectors of British capital.

These patterns of media ownership appear to breathe new life into the instrumentalist argument in both its versions. The resilience of individual ownership fits easily into the long-standing debate about the nature and scope of proprietorial intervention in media production, while the inter-meshing of communications companies and general capital re-emphasizes the question of how far media corporations operate in the interests of the capitalist class as a whole.

DYNAMICS OF CONTROL

Specific interventions and particular interests

All owners of media corporations have a basic interest in increasing the profitability of their enterprises. They may or may not also be interested in influencing the output in line with their views and values. When commentators talk about proprietorial intervention, however, they mostly have in mind this second, ideological, dimension. Concern about this reached its height in Britain between the two world wars, when the activities of press barons provided almost daily examples of owners using their papers to promote the social and political views they favoured. As Lord Beaverbrook, the celebrated proprietor of the *Daily Express*, told the 1948 Royal Commission on the Press, he ran the paper 'purely for propaganda and with no other object', although he quickly added that a paper is no good 'for propaganda unless it has a thoroughly good financial position', and admitted that he had 'worked very hard to build up a commercial position' (Royal Commission on the Press 1948, para. 8656 et seq.). For him, high circulations were a means to a mainly ideological end. For the present owners, Trafalgar House Ltd, profitability has become the

Table 2: *Britain's leading commercial television companies: major voting shareholders in the relevant holding companies 1979 (1)*

Operating company	Holding company	Major holdings (given in percentage) by:			
		Individuals (per cent)	Financial Institutions	Corporations with communications interests	Industrial Corporations, Nominees, and overseas interests
Thames Television Ltd	EMI Ltd (2)		Prudential Assurance 3.5 Pearl Assurance 1.1 M & G (Unit Trust) 3.4 National Coal Board Pensions 2.2 Midland Bank Trust 2.0		Guarantee Nominees 6.0 Bank of England Nominees 4.6 West Unit Nominees 2.6
London Weekend Television Ltd	LWT (Holdings) Ltd	Robert Clark (director) 12.0	Pearl Assurance 12.0 Imperial Tobacco Pension Fund 12.0	New International Ltd 12.0 The Daily Telegraph Ltd 11.0 *The Observer* (Atlantic Richfield) 11.0	Samuel Montagu (Nominees) 6.0
ATV Network Ltd	Associated Communications Corporation	Lord Grade (chmn) 27.5 Jack Gill (co. managing director) 15.0 Louis Benjamin (co. managing director) 15.0 Norman Collins (director) 6.5		Trafalgar House Ltd 8.0 BPM Holdings 5.0	
Granada Television	Granada Group Ltd (3)	Bernstein family trusts 40.0			

Company	Holding company / Director	%
Yorkshire Television Tyne Tees Television	Trident Television Ltd	
	Lord Bernstein (President)	11.0
	Alex Bernstein (chairman)	6.0
	Cecil Bernstein (director)	5.0
	Sir James Hanson (director)	7.0
	Telefusion Ltd (includes 7% held personally by the chairman, John Wilkinson)	20.23
	United Newspapers	8.2
	May Gurney Holdings (contractors)	7.0
Anglia Television	Anglia Television Group Ltd	
	Marquis Townsend of Raynham (chmn)	7.0
	Norwich Union Life Insurance	6.0
	The *Guardian* and *Manchester Evening News*	22.0
	Romulus Films	22.0
	Eastern Counties Newspapers	10.0
Southern Television Ltd	Associated Newspapers	37.5
	Rank Organisation	37.5
	D C Thomson	25.0
Scottish Television Ltd	William Brown (managing director)	12.0
	Gavin Boyd (dir.)	14.0
	Earl of Wemyss (director)	8.0
	Sir Ian Stewart (dir.)	7.0

NOTES: (1) Information taken from the last available company depositions at the time of writing. All figures refer to the situation before the reallocation of the franchises in 1980.

(2) Date for EMI Ltd relates to the period prior to the recent take-over by Thorn Electrical Industries.

(3) These holdings may overlap to a certain extent since from the share register it is impossible to separate fully the personal holdings of the various members of the Bernstein family from their holdings through the various family trusts.

primary goal, although ideological intervention is not entirely unknown. According to one inside account, *Daily Express* editors were still subject to pressure from the board, in the person of Victor Matthews, the Chief Executive who

would delight in pouring out home-spun wisdom at considerable length often at the busiest time of the day. This would sometimes have to be recreated by a journalist in the form of an editorial. He would hold hour-long post-mortems, and would discuss at length the main headline on the front page. (Jenkins, 1979, p. 101)

Over and above these sorts of individual interests, recent changes in patterns of ownership have added a new corporate impetus to ideological intervention.

Because of the trend towards conglomeration and the growth of institutional investment, media enterprises are increasingly linked to companies operating in socially and politically contentious areas such as oil and military technology. This, as Neal Ascherson has argued, leads to 'the increase of potential "no go" areas for critical reporting' and presentation, as corporations seek to use their media enterprises to promote a favourable image of their other activities (Ascherson, 1978, p. 131). According to Richard Bunce, for example, American communications conglomerates systematically use their television production wings to defend and advance their other interests. By way of illustration he cites a WBC documentary on urban mass transportation-systems which he claims stemmed directly from the fact that the company's parent corporation, Westinghouse Electric, is the country's main supplier of such systems. Similarly, he maintains that the major reason that the three main television networks turned down the first option on the 'Pentagon Papers' (exposing American military strategies in Vietnam) was that their parent companies were all heavily involved in servicing the war effort (see Bunce, 1976, chap. 6).

Although such interventions cannot be entirely discounted in a complete account of corporate power, critics have pointed out that very few instances have been convincingly documented and that those that have been are generally atypical. However, the fact that allocative controllers may not intervene in routine operations on a regular basis does not mean that there is no relationship between the owners' ideological interests and what gets produced. For as Westergaard and Resler have pointed out, the exclusive concentration on the active exercise of control

neglects the point that individuals or groups may have the effective benefits of 'power' without needing to exercise it in positive action.... They do not need to do so — for much of the time at least — simply because things work their way in any case. (Westergaard and Resler, 1975, p. 142-3)

According to this view, proprietors do not normally have to intervene directly since their ideological interests are guaranteed by the implicit understandings governing production.

As I pointed out earlier, even where they have absolute operational autonomy, newspaper editors are still bound by the overall policies set by the board. As The Mirror Group told the last Royal Commission on the Press, although

the heavy hand of the proprietor has been generally removed from editors ... their freedom is and must always be limited by the traditional policy of their papers. ... The editor of *The Times* is not free for example to convert his paper into a left-wing tabloid. (Royal Commission on the Press, 1975a, p. 21)

Other commentators have pointed to the way that reporters exercise self-censorship by holding back from investigating areas that might prove problematic for their employing organizations. Here again, the intermeshing of media and general corporate ownership has significantly increased the range of potentially sensitive areas. As one recent American analysis of interlocks concluded:

Because of the tremendous shared interests at the top coverage is limited and certain questions never get asked. Reporters who think about delving into institutional behaviour may think twice. They worry about the editing. They worry about being removed from choice beats, or being fired. (Dreier and Weinberg, 1979, p. 68)

Against this however, there are numerous instances of creative personnel asserting their autonomy and producing material that criticizes or challenges the interests of their parent conglomerates. Penguin Books provide a good example. As we noted earlier, this is a subsidiary of S. Pearson and S. Pearson and Son, a general conglomerate which owns Lazards, the prominent merchant bank, and significant stakes in a range of important British and American industrial corporations. Yet Penguin have regularly published books attacking the activities and interests of large corporations, including those to which Pearson is connected.

In an attempt to get around the contradictory evidence from particular cases the other major variant of instrumentalism has raised the level of analysis from the specific to the general, and focused on the coincidence between the values and views promoted by the general run of media output and the overall interests of the capitalist class.

Capital sociometrics: the contours of class cohesion

The general version of instrumentalism starts from the celebrated passage in Marx's *German Ideology* quoted earlier, and follows Ralph Miliband in arguing that although the original formulation now needs

to be amended in certain respects ... there is one respect in which the text [still] points to one of the dominant features of life in advanced capitalist societies, namely the fact that the largest part of what is produced in the cultural domain is produced by capitalism; and is therefore *quite naturally intended* to help in the defence of capitalism [by preventing] the development of class-consciousness in the working class. (Miliband, 1977, p. 50) [my italics]

Supporters of this view have tried to bolster this somewhat bald assertion with two main sorts of evidence. Firstly, they have drawn on the results of content studies to try to show how the routine media fare produced for mass audiences legitimates the central values and interests of capitalism. At its simplest, this argument points to the ways in which media material celebrates the openness and fairness of the present system and denigrates oppositional ideas and movements. More sophisticated versions focus on the less direct inhibitions to the development of critical consciousness. They stress the way the popular media misrepresent structural inequalities and evoke the communalities of consumerism, community and nationality; the way they fragment and disconnect the major areas of social experience by counterposing production against consumption, work against leisure; the way they displace power from the economic to the political sphere, from property ownership to administration; and the way that structural inequalities are transformed into personal differences. And a certain amount of supporting evidence for these arguments can be found in a number of recent content studies, including those conducted by researchers who reject Marxist models of the media.

Having outlined these general trends in popular media output however, instrumentalists are faced with the problem of explaining them and it is at this point that they turn to the evidence on interlocks between media corporations and other key sectors of capital. The aim here is to produce a sociometric map of capitalism on the assumption that shared patterns of economic and social life produce a coincidence of basic interests and result in 'a cluster of common ideological positions and perspectives' (Miliband, 1977, p. 69).

Once again, recent research lends considerable support to this general argument. As I have shown elsewhere (Murdock, 1979 and 1980), the ownership pattern noted earlier for commercial television — of conglomeration coupled with growing shareholding links with other leading corporations — is increasingly characteristic of the press and the other major media sectors. Moreover, these direct ownership connections with leading capitalist interests are considerably extended by interlocking directorships. In 1978, for example, nine out of the top ten British communications concerns had directorial links with at least one of Britain's top 250 industrial corporations, and six had links with a company in the top twenty. In addition, seven out of the ten had boardroom connections with leading insurance companies, five had links with major merchant banks, and six shared directors with other significant banks and discount houses. These business links are further consolidated by communalities in social life. In 1978, for example, all fifteen of the top media corporations had board members who belonged to one or more of the élite London clubs. Moreover, the clubs most frequently favoured by directors of media corporations — Whites, Pratts, the Beefsteak, the Garrick, Carlton and Brooks's — were also among the most popular with the directors of leading financial institutions, and to a lesser extent, business corporations (see Whitley, 1973 and Wakeford *et al.*, 1974). As well as offering further points of contact between the major media concerns and other leading corporations, club memberships provide channels for informal exchange between the leading media enterprises themselves. The older-established firms are particularly well connected through the club network. In 1978, for example, S. Pearson and Son was linked by club membership to twelve of the other top fifteen communications companies; and EMI and Associated Newspapers were each linked to ten.

At one level then, the available evidence gives reasonable support to the instrumentalist position. Media corporations are increasingly integrated into the core of British capitalism and the material they produce for mass consumption does tend to support, or at least not to undermine, capitalism's central values of private property, 'free' enterprise, and profit. However, this evidence *only describes* the general coincidence between patterns of ownership and patterns of output. *It does not explain it*, although instrumentalists often present it as though it did, as in the *Morning Star's* evidence to the last Royal Commission on the Press.

All the national newspapers have property holdings and substantial links with a wide range of financial and industrial undertakings. They are thus closely integrated with Monopoly Capital as a whole. [Hence] it is not surprising that the national capitalist newspapers strongly defend private enterprise. (Royal Commission on the Press, 1975b, p. 2)

This argument moves from correlation to causality by assuming that the capitalist class act more or less coherently to defend their shared interests. At its crudest, this produces a version of conspiracy theory. At the very least, it has to assume that the owning class intentionally pursue their collective ideological interests through their control over cultural production. There are fundamental problems with this position.

Although it ultimately depends upon an empirical account of influence and control it cannot supply the necessary evidence due to the difficulties of investigating corporate decision making at the higher levels. So in the absence of direct evidence instrumentalists are obliged to fall back on the second-hand sources provided by inside accounts together with what can be gleaned from the publicity surrounding take-overs and board struggles and scandals of various kinds. Apart from their obvious partiality, these accounts necessarily deal with atypical situations and so they cannot offer an adequate base for analysing the routine exercise of power and control. It is very easy to become fascinated by what goes on in the corridors of corporate power, by the personality clashes, the clandestine deals, the back-stabbings and so on. But even if a reliable range of relevant information were available, this version of instrumentalism would still be open to the theoretical objections that it concentrates solely on the level of action and agency and that it identifies the core interests of capitalists with the active defence of key ideological tenets.

This second assumption is not absolutely necessary, however. Other variants of instrumentalism stress the centrality of economic interests and see the production of legitimating ideology as the logical outcome of the search for profits. In Ralph Miliband's words:

Making money is not at all incompatible with indoctrination ... the purpose of the 'entertainment' industry, in its various forms, may be profit; but the content of its output is not by any means free from ideological connotations of a more or less definite kind. (Miliband, 1973, p. 202)

This version avoids slipping into a conspiratorial view of the capitalist class as a tightly-knit group of ideologically motivated men. 'No evil-minded capitalistic plotters need be assumed, because the production of ideology is seen as the more or less automatic outcome of the normal, regular processes by which commercial mass communications work in a capitalist system' (Connell, 1977, p. 195). Nevertheless, it remains tied to an action approach, which as Nicos Poulantzas has forcefully pointed out, ultimately identifies the origins of social action with the interests and motivations of the actors involved, operating either individually or collectively (Poulantzas, 1969).

In contrast, structuralist approaches shift the emphasis from action to context, from power to determination. Although recent neo-Marxist political economies of communications have also focused on the pursuit of profit they have concentrated on the ways that this is shaped and directed by the underlying logic of the capitalist system rather than on the identity, motivations and activities of the actors involved.

Demands and determinations

As we noted earlier, commentators differ fundamentally in the way they characterize the external constraints on corporate activity. Opponents of Marxism maintain that the range and content of cultural productions is ultimately determined by the wants and wishes of audiences. If certain values or views of the world are missing or poorly represented in the popular media, they argue, it is primarily because there is no effective demand for them. Hence, this notion of 'consumer sovereignty' focuses on the spheres of exchange and consumption and the operations of the market. In contrast 'theorists of capitalism' start with the organization of production and the way it is shaped by the prior distribution of property and wealth. They see the structure of capital as determining production in a variety of ways and at a variety of levels.

First of all, they point out that the escalating costs of entering the major mass media markets means that they are only effectively open to those with substantial capital. As a result, the enterprises that survive and prosper will 'largely belong to those least likely to criticize the prevailing distribution of wealth and power' while 'those most likely to challenge these arrangements' will be 'unable to command the resources needed for effective communication to a broad audience' (Murdock and Golding, 1977, p. 37). This argument has also found supporters outside the ranks of 'theorists of capitalism'. After reviewing the evidence on newspaper costs, for example, the last Royal Commission on the Press concluded that although 'anyone is free to start a national daily newspaper, few can afford even to contemplate the prospect' (Royal Commission on the Press, 1977, p. 9). Moreover, after launching, a new paper faces the problem of building up a readership while paying the market price for raw materials, labour and publicity. Increasingly these costs require capital backing of the kind that is only available to the conglomerates, who can subsidize the initial loss-making period out of the profits from their other enterprises. It is no accident that Britain's latest national daily, the *Star*, is backed by the Trafalgar House shipping and property consortium, or that the (short-lived) weekly news magazine *Now* was able to draw on the resources of Sir James Goldsmith's Cavenham food group. Without this kind of support a successful launch is more or less impossible as the collapse of the *Scottish Daily News* clearly illustrated (see McKay and Barr, 1976). Other sectors, such as record and film making, where production costs are relatively low, are rather more open at the level of initial market entry. But independent producers still face the problem of securing adequate national and international distribution for their products, and here again the power of the large corporations is crucial since they increasingly command the major channels of dissemination. For supporters of the 'consumer sovereignty' position, however, arguments about the barriers to effective competition are ultimately irrelevant since they see all cultural producers, large or small, as equally subject to the final veto of consumer demand. At this point in the Marxist argument capital makes an appearance in another form — advertising.

'Theorists of capitalism' start from the undisputed fact that the core commercial media of television, radio and the press get most of their income and profits from their advertisers and not from their audiences. This they argue turns the ideal of 'consumer sovereignty' on its head and makes the advertisers the real figures of power and their demands for predictable audiences the major determinant of supply (see Smythe, 1977). However, the advertisers' dominant role in financing the core commercial media need not necessarily mean that audience wants are secondary or insignificant. On the contrary, opponents argue, since advertisers are interested in reaching as many of their target audience as possible, consumer preferences are still the most important factor in the situation. This counter argument is persuasive, but oversimple. For, as James Curran has pointed out: 'advertisers are not equally interested in reaching all people. Some people have more disposable income or greater power over corporate spending than others, and consequently are more sought after by advertisers' (Curran, 1978, p. 246). As a result, the distribution of advertising (and therefore commercial viability) follows the general distribution of social wealth with media producers trying to attract either mass audience or affluent minorities while paying relatively little attention to the poor and disadvantaged. The effects of this imbalance are particularly evident in the national press where even Marxism's sternest critics admit that the fact that an editor 'must either produce a newspaper which will be read by the millions or one which will attract the big spenders' means that 'the rich and the business executives are the only minority groups fully catered for' (Beloff, 1976, p. 14). As well as affecting the number and range of available titles, this economic logic has had important effects on press coverage and style at both the 'quality' and 'popular' ends of the market.

James Curran's research, for example, has highlighted the impact of advertising on the coverage of the 'quality' papers as they compete to offer advertisers a conducive 'editorial environment' for their products. By way of example he cites the case of financial advertising, arguing that the concentration on advertisements for personal investment schemes is matched by an editorial focus on share advice and Stock Exchange dealings which unintentionally produce a misleading picture of modern capital and the corporate economy (Curran, 1978, p. 239-45). Among the 'popular' papers, the effects of advertising dependence are even more pervasive. Here, the accelerating search for the largest possible audience has produced a marked decline in overt partisanship (and particularly in support for left of centre positions within the Labour movement) and a concentration on the non-contentious and consumer-oriented areas of leisure and personal life (see Murdock, 1980). Another interesting example of advertising-induced withdrawal from class and controversy is provided by the history of American television drama. In the years immediately after the war, drama slots were dominated by anthologies of single plays, many of which dealt with working-class life. While these were popular with audiences and regularly attracted high ratings, they increasingly worried advertisers who saw plays with lower-class settings as damaging to the images of mobility and affluence they wanted to build up around their products. Accordingly, in 1955 they begin to switch their sponsorship to the action-adventure series that were beginning to emerge from the old Hollywood studios. The business advantages were obvious. 'Drama moved outdoors into active, glamorous settings. Handsome heroes and heroines set the tone — and some proved willing to do commercials, and even appear at sales meetings and become company spokesmen' (Barnouw, 1978, p. 107). The series also had distinct advantages for the production companies. The fact that they contained the minimum of dialogue and the maximum of action made them ideal export material. They were intelligible anywhere that audiences were familiar with Hollywood westerns and thrillers. Where the American studios lead, everyone else has followed in varying degrees, and the international market is now central to the economics of commercial television. It enables companies to cut costs (through co-production agreements) while massively increasing their potential sales to other broad-coasting organizations. At the same time it imposes certain constraints on the themes that can be profitably dealt with. In addition to action-adventure series on the American model (such as 'The Persuaders' and 'The Avengers'), British television's most successful drama exports have been historical series that capitalize on the dominant overseas images of England such as the interest in the Victorian and Edwardian eras, and the fascination with the English Royal Family and upper class. The economic imperatives of the international market therefore create a further interruption to the perfect relationship between domestic demand and domestic production assumed by the idea of 'consumer sovereignty'.

SELECTIVE INCORPORATIONS

Nevertheless, historical and action-adventure series do command large domestic audiences and regularly feature in the ten most popular programmes. Similarly, the formula of crime, sex, sport and scandal employed by the *Sun* does attract a mass readership. Does this mean then that these products are an accurate reflection of popular consciousness and popular culture? The answer is 'no', not entirely. As Raymond Williams (1979) has pointed out, the popular media work by incorporation rather than imposition. They pick up particular elements within working-class culture, transform them into pleasurable products and offer them back to working-class audiences. This process of selection works unevenly, however. Recent studies have convincingly shown that popular consciousness is both complex and contradictory (see, for example, Nichols and Armstrong, 1976 and Davis, 1979). There is ample evidence that British working-class culture is saturated with sexism, fatalism, admiration and affection for royalty and the aristocracy, and a deep-seated distrust of politicians, intellectuals and foreigners. At the same time it also contains a powerful critique of capitalism organized around a grass-roots socialist tradition. However, the need to attract and keep large, politically heterogeneous audiences means that the popular media tend to play safe and pick up the conservative rather than the radical strands in popular culture. Hence the structural opposition between Capital and Labour is regularly transformed into a series of political opposition between 'them' and 'us'; citizens versus bureaucrats; the moderate majority versus the militant minority; the law abiding versus the deviant; Britain versus its enemies. As a result, critique is incorporated into a diffuse kind of populism that can be easily mobilized in defence of the *status quo*. The relationship between popular ideologies and popular media output is therefore more usefully viewed as partial and incomplete rather than distorted.

CONCLUSION

This chapter has set out to review the major approaches to the location of control over the mass communications systems of the advanced western societies and to highlight some of the problems with their organizing concepts and supporting evidence. In particular, I have tried to show how the central divisions in the literature are rooted in broader and more fundamental divisions between 'theories of capitalism' and 'theories of industrial society' and between models of action and power and models of structure and determination. I have also tried to suggest that the central issues raised by these conflicts remain open both theoretically and empirically. Consequently, I have been more concerned to indicate the extent of the questions we now need to ask than to offer pre-emptive answers.

148   *Culture, society and the media*

REFERENCES

Atlantic Richfield Company (1978) *Annual Report*, Los Angeles.

Ascherson, N. (1978) 'Newspapers and internal democracy', in Curran, J. (ed.) *The British Press, A Manifesto*, London, Macmillan.

Barnouw, E. (1978) *The Sponsor: Notes on a Modern Potentate*, New York, Oxford University Press.

Beloff, N. (1976) *Freedom Under Foot: The Battle over the Closed Shop in British Journalism*, London, Temple Smith.

Berle, A. (1960) *Power without Property*, New York, Harcourt Brace.

Berle, A. and Means, G. (1968) *The Modern Corporation and Private Property*, New York, Harcourt Brace.

Briggs, A. (1979) *Governing The BBC*, London, British Broadcasting Corporation.

Bunce, R. (1976) *Television in the Corporate Interest*, New York, Praeger Publishers.

Burnham, J. (1960) *The Managerial Revolution*, Bloomington, Indiana, Indiana University Press.

Connell, B. (1977) *Ruling Class, Ruling Culture*, London, Cambridge University Press.

Curran, J. (1978) 'Advertising and the press', in Curran, J. (ed.) *The British Press: A Manifesto*, London, Macmillan.

Curran, J. (1979), 'Press freedom as a property right: the crisis of press legitimacy', *Media, Culture and Society*, 1 (1).

Davis, H. H. (1979) *Beyond Class Images: Explorations in the Structure of Social Consciousness*, London, Croom Helm.

DeVroey, M. (1975), 'The separation of ownership and control in large corporations', *The Review of Radical Political Economics*, 7 (2).

Dimbleby, D. (1979) Interview with Sir James Goldsmith, *The Listener*, 102 (2625).

Dreier, P. and Weinberg, S. (1979) 'The ties that bind: interlocking directorships', *Columbia Journalism Review*, November/December.

Galbraith, J. K. (1969) *The New Industrial State*, Harmondsworth, Penguin.

Giddens, A. (1979) *Central Problems in Social Theory: Action, Structure and Contradiction in Social Analysis*, London, Macmillan.

Glyn, A. and Sutcliffe, B. (1972) *British Capitalism, Workers and the Profits Squeeze*, Harmondsworth, Penguin.

Halberstam, D. (1976) 'CBS: The power and the profits', *The Atlantic*, 237 (1).

Hannah, L. (1974) 'Takeover bids in Britain before 1950: an exercise in business pre-history, *Business History*, XVI (1).

Jenkins, S. (1979) *Newspapers: The Power and the Money*, London, Faber & Faber.

Klingender, F. and Legg, S. (1937) *Money Behind the Screen*, London, Lawrence & Wishart.

Kotz, D. M. (1978) *Bank Control of Large Corporations in the United States*, Los Angeles, University of California Press.

Lee, A. (1976) *The Origins of the Popular Press in England 1855-1914*, London, Croom Helm.

Lukes, S. (1974) *Power: A Radical View*, London, Macmillan.

McKay, R. and Barr, B. (1976) *The Story of the Scottish Daily News*, Edinburgh, Canongate.

McLellan, D. (1973) *Karl Marx: His Life and Thought*, London, Macmillan.

Marx, K. (1974) *Capital, Volume three: the Process of Capitalist Production as a whole*, London, Lawrence & Wishart.

Marx, K. and Engels, F. (1968) *Selected Works*, one volume, London, Lawrence & Wishart.

Marx, K. and Engels, F. (1974a) *The German Ideology*, London, Lawrence & Wishart.

Marx, K. and Engels, F. (1974b) *The Civil War in the United States*, New York, International Publishers.

Miliband, R. (1973) *The State in Capitalist Society*, London, Quartet Books.

Miliband, R. (1977) *Marxism and Politics*, London, Oxford University Press.

Ministry of Prices and Consumer Protection (1978) *A Review of Monopolies and Mergers Policy: A Consultative Document*, HMSO, Cmnd. 7198.

Murdock, G. (1979) *Mass Media and The Class Structure: An Exploratory Study in Britain*, Final Report to the Social Science Research Council.

Murdock, G. (1980) 'Class, power, and the press: problems of conceptualization and evidence', in Christian, H. (ed.) *The Sociology of Journalism and the Press*, University of Keele, Sociological Review Monographs, no. 29.

Murdock, G. and Golding, P. (1974) 'For a political economy of mass communications', in Miliband, R. and Saville, J. (eds) *The Socialist Register 1973*, London, Merlin Press.

Murdock, G. and Golding, P. (1977) 'Capitalism, communication and class relations', in Curran, J. *et al.* (eds) *Mass Communication and Society*, London, Edward Arnold.

Nichols, T. and Armstrong, P. (1976) *Workers Divided*, London, Fontana.

Nyman, S. and Silbertson, A. (1978) 'The ownership and control of industry', *Oxford Economic Papers*, 30 (1).

Pahl, R. and Winkler, J. (1974) 'The economic élite: theory and practice', in Stanworth, P. and Giddens, A. (eds) *Elites and Power in British Society*, London, Cambridge University Press.

Poulantzas, N. (1969) 'The problem of the capitalist state', *New Left Review*, (58).

Poulantzas, N. (1975) *Classes in Contemporary Capitalism*, London, New Left Books.

Robins, K. and Webster, F. (1979) 'Mass communications and information technology', in Miliband, R. and Saville, J. (eds) *The Socialist Register 1979*, London, Merlin Press.

Royal Commission on the Distribution of Income and Wealth (1979) *Report No. 7: Fourth Report on the Standing Reference*, London, HMSO, Cmnd. 7595.

Royal Commission on the Press (1948) *Minutes of Evidence: Twenty Sixth Day*, London, HMSO, Cmnd. 7416.

Royal Commission on the Press (1975a) *Minutes of Evidence: Docket 9E1 — Mirror Group Newspapers*.

Royal Commission on the Press (1975b) *Minutes of Evidence: Docket 10E1 — Morning Star Co-Operative Society Ltd.*

Royal Commission on the Press (1977) *Final Report*, London, HMSO, Cmnd. 6810.

Seiden, M. (1974) *Who Controls the Mass Media? Popular Myths and Economic Realities*, New York, Basic Books.

Smythe, D. (1977) 'Communications: blindspot of western Marxism', *Canadian Journal of Social and Political Theory*, 1 (3).

Stanworth, P. (1974) 'Property, class and the corporate élite', in Crewe, I. (ed.) *British Political Sociology Yearbook*, vol. 1, London, Croom Helm.

Tracey, M. (1978) *The Production of Political Television*, London, Routledge & Kegan Paul.

Wakeford, J. *et al.* (1974) 'Some social and educational characteristics of selected élite groups in contemporary Britain', in Crewe, I. (ed.) *British Political Sociology Yearbook*, vol. 1, London, Croom Helm.

Westergaard, J. and Resler, H. (1975) *Class in a Capitalist Society: A Study of Contemporary Britain*, London, Heinemann.

Whale, J. (1977) *The Politics of the Media*, London, Fontana.

Whitley, R. (1973) 'Communalities and connections among directors of large financial institutions', *Sociological Review*, 21 (4).

Williams, R. (1979) 'The growth and role of the mass media', in Gardner, C. (ed.) *Media, Politics and Culture*, London, Macmillan.

Zeitlin, M. (1974) 'Corporate ownership and control: the large corporation and the capitalist class', *The American Journal of Sociology*, 79 (5).

6

Negotiation of control in media organizations and occupations

MARGARET GALLAGHER

THE MEANING OF CONTROL IN THE MEDIA

Media organizations and occupations lie right at the heart of any study of mass communication, for they embody the processes through which the *output* of the media comes into being. The assumption that media messages and images constitute a powerful social, cultural and political force dominates both public debate and perspectives of research in the field of mass communication. Whether expressed in terms of a search for 'measurable effects' or formulated as a more macro-analysis of the 'agenda-setting' or 'reality-defining' function of the media, this assumption underlies practically all questions concerned with the link between media output and social consciousness.

In the decade since Jeremy Tunstall suggested that:

a more organization-oriented view of the media in general seems essential if we are not to perpetuate the predominant view in which the media messages sometimes appear to be reaching the audience members' eyes and ears as if from heaven above or (in some perspectives) hell below (Tunstall, 1970, p. 15)

an increasing number of British and American studies have begun to redress a longstanding imbalance in media research, which has historically tended to be preoccupied with mass media 'effects', rather than with how and why media output comes to be as it is. More recent research, however (for example, Halloran *et al.*, 1970; Cantor, 1971; Elliott, 1972; Epstein, 1973; Tuchman, 1974; Burns, 1977; Tracey, 1978; Steen, 1979), examining the interaction of organizational, production, professional and personal factors and their influence on the output of the media, has broken new ground in opening up the previously obscure contexts within which mass communicators operate.

Reasons for the concentration of media research on the end, rather than on the beginning, of the mass communication process are not hard to find (see Blumler and Gurevitch). Quite apart from the particular origins and development of research into the media — its sources of question and problem formulation, of institutional support, of funding, not to mention the theoretical and methodological influences of its contributory disciplines

— it is clear that from the outset the audience has been a much more *accessible* focus of enquiry than the communicators themselves.

Paul Lazarsfeld was one of the first to note the problems for research in this area:

If there is any one institutional disease to which the media of mass communications seem particularly subject, it is a nervous reaction to criticism. As a student of mass media I have been continually struck and occasionally puzzled by this reaction, for it is the media themselves which so vigorously defend principles guaranteeing the right to criticize. (Lazarsfeld, 1972, p. 123)

In Britain, Tom Burns has documented the BBC's refusal to permit publication of his 1963 study of the organization (Burns, 1977). Burns is at pains to point out the Corporation's complete reversal, in 1972, of its initial decision — and indeed its invitation to update the original study; and the very accumulation of a body of serious work on the media has contributed to a climate of greater acceptance of the role of research in this field. Nevertheless, access to media organizations remains difficult — in some cases impossible — to negotiate in terms acceptable to both researchers and communicators. Different levels of problems and different attempts at their solution are evident in, for example, Elliott, 1972; Glasgow University Media Group, 1976; Tracey, 1978.

If the relative inaccessibility of media organizations is in one sense a testament to their power in controlling the communication channels of society, the very fact of media sensitivity to external criticism, and the mechanisms developed to deal with it, are also an acknowledgement that this power is by no means absolute, and that the means and limits of control must be negotiated. Study of these processes of negotiation — with agencies both external and internal to the organizations themselves — is essential to an understanding of the *nature* of control in the media. For while the question of *who* controls (see Murdock, 1977) is fundamental, the *significance* of that control rests in the way in which it is, or can be, exercised. In other words, 'control' in the media has meaning primarily in terms of the extent to which communicators are able to shape output. What is the interplay of factors which determines this ability? What is the relative importance, for example, of external political, economic and social factors against internal factors such as professional ideologies, ownership and management structures, editorial polices, and technical and financial constraints? How does the communicator preserve creative autonomy within the organizational setting? How and why, finally, does media output come to be as it is?

Research has so far provided only very partial answers to these questions. A number of early American studies of the communicator (White, 1950; Breed, 1955; Gieber, 1956) did attempt to highlight some of the organizational constraints on media production, within a framework which could broadly be described as that of functional or systems analysis, although this framework was more frequently implicit in the research design than expressed as an explicit theoretical formulation. From this early work emerged the concept of the 'gatekeeper' — the powerful and often overtly prejudiced 'Mr Gates' who selects, processes and organizes the information to be made available to an audience which is — by implication at least — passive and unsuspecting. Subjected to numerous refinements since its first appearance in the work of David White in 1950, the gatekeeper concept is still prominent. It remains, however, essentially narrow in its treatment of communicators whom it casts as agents for system maintenance and control:

Processes of 'gatekeeping' in mass communication may be viewed within a framework of a total social system, made up of a series of subsystems whose primary concerns include the control of information in the interest of gaining other social ends. (Donahue *et al.*, 1972, p. 42)

The problems of functional or social systems analysis need not be detailed here. It is perhaps sufficient to note that its limited ability, in theoretical terms, to account for conflict and its causes, change, individual purpose, the relationship between organizations and social structure has, when applied to the study of mass communicators, resulted in very restricted conceptualizations of the context in which media output is produced.

Other theoretical perspectives can be seen to underly some of the more recent studies of media organizations and occupations, though again these theories more often exist at an implicit than at an explicit level. There is the liberal-pluralist view, which sees media and media practitioners as autonomous, responsible institutions and individuals (for example, Seymour-Ure, 1968; Blumler, 1969). This contrasts with class-based or Marxist analyses which view the media as inextricable from society's dominant institutions and ideologies, and see media output as an articulation and legitimation of the controlling interests in those institutions and ideologies (for example, Hall, 1977; Murdock and Golding, 1977; elements of this approach can also be traced in less explicitly political contexts in, for example, Elliott, 1972; Glasgow University Media Group, 1976). Yet it seems that neither the liberal-pluralist nor the Marxist perspective has so far been really successful in moving from theoretical formulation to empirical validation (q.v. Bennett for an analysis of some of the problems involved in 'operationalizing' theory). Moreover, both Richard Hoggart — in Glasgow University Media Group (1976) — and Michael Tracey (1978) have argued that each of these perspectives obscures the complexities of the internal and external relations of media production.

A further approach, in fact that adopted by Tracey (1978) in his study of the production of political television in Britain, derives from a paradigm for the social action analysis of organizations proposed by Silverman (1968). This calls for a more actor-based perspective, an analysis of the process relating an organization to the wider environment, the development of hypotheses based on internal and external factors and the interrelationship of these factors. Such an approach, which informs the direction of the arguments which follow here, would see media output as the 'present outcome of the ends sought by different groups and the actions which they have chosen to pursue in the light of the means available to them' (Silverman, 1968).

This perspective views organizations and occupations as dynamic, as part of a social process, as change-oriented. It demands an examination of the relationships of the wider environments of media organizations to routines and practices in their operations; an analysis of this relationship as part of a socio-historical development, within which mass communication organizations can be placed in particular social contexts; and a consideration of the relative importance of organizational and occupational factors in shaping media output.

MEDIA ORGANIZATIONS: SOURCES OF EXTERNAL CONSTRAINT

A central feature of mass communication organizations is their ambivalent relationship to other sources of power in society. Mass communicators are typically characterized as a potentially powerful social group with access to scarce societal resources — the channels of communication. This power, however, is exercised in the context of a network of public controls and constraints external to the organization. Such controls are used to counterbalance the potentially disruptive power of the mass communicators: access to large diffuse audiences, for instance, could be used to threaten accepted social distributions of knowledge and ideas which, in stable societies, tend to be integrated with established hierarchies of power and social control.

However, it cannot be assumed that mass communication organizations are *directly* or even particularly *effectively* controlled by other powerful social institutions. External constraints, for example, are paralleled by equally influential demands internal to the organizations themselves. In part, these relate to the claims of individual communicators to a sense of professional autonomy and are manifested primarily in terms of intra-organizational conflict or tension. At the same time, this drive towards autonomy or independence is expressed collectively in organizational terms in the delicate set of balances which maintain the separation of media institutions from the apparatus of the state. Overriding all these individual and organizational demands, however, is the problem of survival: communication organizations are concerned to stay in business. Consequently, they are involved in a continual and evolving process of negotiation or bargaining with other sources of civil and social power. This means that the operation of a mass media organization will be bounded by rules and conventions which may not be explicit, but which fit the prevailing notions about more general social organization, and which are mediated by such factors as media ownership, finance, organizational conceptions of the audience, and the development of professional or occupational ideologies.

Limits of organizational autonomy: the case of monopoly control in British broadcasting

One of the most important features of media history has been the location of broadcasting within centrally controlled systems. There have been countries — for example, Holland — which developed systems partly analogous to publishing, where control of the wavelength and editorial control were separated, but these were very few indeed. Even in America, with its powerful doctrine of personal cultural freedom and its lack of prescription on cultural choice, a central licensing authority, the Federal Communications Commission, was set up to regulate the allocation of wavelengths. Moreover, the rapid development of three great networks with their own codes and editorial and commercial demands helped to create a central ethos in American broadcasting.

The United States presents a different picture from much of the rest of the world, especially from Europe where the central national authority (modelled in many cases on the BBC) was accepted with seeming inevitability. Commentators have ascribed this tendency to various factors. In Britain, for example, the BBC's first Chief Engineer Peter Eckersley has described the origins of centralization in broadcasting organization solely in terms of a technical problem — the wavelength shortage: 'The BBC was formed as the expedient solution of a technical problem; it owes its existence solely to the scarcity of wavelengths' (Eckersley, 1942, p. 48).

But although the wavelength problem was clearly of importance in influencing the decision to confine broadcasting within a single *national* institution — the chaos of early radio broadcasting in America, where thousands of stations sprang up in the early 1920s before the establishment of the FCC, had an important effect in pushing Britain towards a highly disciplined system — there was no *technical* need to concentrate wavelength and editorial control in the same hands. The decision to create a broadcasting monopoly in Britain can be traced, rather, to an historical period when developments in wireless telephone and telegraphy had already been brought firmly under a form of government control, via the Post Office; and when World War I had underlined the major importance of the new medium of wireless. Moreover, centralization was in part a response to the demands of the growing public of radio hams who pushed for the setting up of some central broadcasting of programmes for general entertainment (Smith, 1974).

Although a *variety* of technical, historical and social pressures pushed towards centralization, the particular *form* of centralized control eventually adopted in Britain — the public service monopoly — has in large part been attributed to the lobbying of one particular man, John Reith, the General Manager of the British Broadcasting Company, and later the first Director-General of the British Broadcasting Corporation. Reith saw the 'brute force of monopoly' as one of four fundamentals necessary to the development of a particular type of broadcasting — the other three being the motive of public service, a sense of moral obligation, and assured finance. Reith's version of the public role of broadcasting was, in Raymond Williams' definition, an 'authoritarian system with a conscience' (Williams, 1962):

There was to hand a mighty instrument to instruct and fashion public opinion; to banish ignorance and misery; to contribute richly and in many ways to the sum total of human well-being. The present concern of those to whom the stewardship had, by accident, been committed was that those basic ideals should be sealed and safeguarded, so that broadcasting might play its destined part.... (Reith, 1949, p. 103)

So the responsibility at the outset conceived, and despite all discouragements pursued, was to carry into the greatest number of homes everything that was best in every department of human knowledge, endeavour and achievement; and to avoid whatever was or might be hurtful. In the earliest years accused of setting out to give the public not what it wanted but what it needed, the answer was that few knew what they wanted, fewer what they needed. (Ibid., 101)

Since its inception, then, the type of *programming* broadcast by the BBC was inextricably bound up with, indeed consciously dictated by, the nature of the organization itself, its system of internal control and its relationship to external controls. Anthony Smith has described the Reithian 'idea of serving a public by forcing it to confront the frontiers of its own taste' as a powerful, *political* measure, which ensured the success of Reith's enterprise, and was to have a lasting influence on the ways in which the BBC would address its audience (Smith, 1974).

The 'public service monopoly' in Britain lasted for almost thirty years until the advent of commercial television in the 1950s. During that time the BBC had expanded from a service which barely filled a single radio channel to one which had three national radio programmes, extensive regional and overseas services and a television channel. To what extent can the persistence of monopolistic paternalism in British broadcasting be ascribed to the prevailing dynamic influence of Reith alone? To what extent was it the result of the convergence of interests of certain dominant institutional forces in society? Peter Eckersley, the BBC's Chief Engineer, adhered strongly to the importance of Reith's personal influence, seeing it as 'one man's conception of the role of broadcasting in a modern democracy' (Eckersley, 1942, p. 55). R.L. Coase, in his study of monopoly in British broadcasting, also subscribed to the power of the Reithian influence but saw it — along with that of the political parties, the Press and the Post Office — as just one *combination* of forces which led to widespread support for monopoly:

Had the Labour Party been in power at the time of the formation of the BBC; had independent broadcasting systems not been associated in the minds of the Press with commercial broadcasting and finance by means of advertisements; had another department, say the Board of Trade, been responsible for broadcasting policy; had the views of the first chief executive of the BBC been like those of the second; with this combination of circumstances, there would be no reason to suppose that such a formidable body of support for a monopoly of broadcasting would ever have arisen. (Coase, 1950, p. 195)

Given the context in which it emerged, it is difficult to accept the Reithian concept of monopolistic control as a 'brute force' either in preserving organizational autonomy or in fostering a particular approach to programming. Rather, supported by the governing party, the bureaucracy and the other media, the form and output of the organization reflected the social forces which had brought it into being. Subsequent changes in the arrangement of those forces (beginning after World War II) were fed into parallel changes in the structure of British broadcasting and its programming.

The diffuse nature of the social controls within which the media are rooted make those controls no less influential, however. From this perspective, the limits to organizational and individual communicator autonomy are well-defined. For example, the development of distinguishing organizational codes, practices and rituals within media institutions may well be professional responses to the tensions involved in finding the boundaries of institutional autonomy. But in the sense that they arise within organizational contexts pre-defined by the wider socio-political environment, such responses remain fundamentally limited and even ambiguous as a means of tension resolution. Two of the most important sources of external constraint on media organizations derive from the commercial and political environments in which they operate.

The commercial context of control

The early development of broadcasting in Britain illustrates the complexity of the external forces which shape and constrain mass media organizations, and the dynamic nature of the relationship in which the organization draws on, incorporates and transforms prevailing social attitudes before transmitting them again according to its own formula. In this light definitions of the media as either 'the tools of government' or 'the fourth estate' become untenable. What can be said is that the mass media arise from, reflect, may reinforce or even change prevalent social hierarchies, but that the strength and direction of this relationship will vary greatly according to specific historical and social contexts.

Perhaps the biggest single change in direction and emphasis in British broadcasting, for example, occurred with the breaking of the BBC's monopoly in the 1950s and the advent of commercial television. This arrived as the result of pressure for an expansion in advertising — an expansion which coincided with the career and financial interests of those who lobbied for the introduction of a commercial system. Wilson argues that the change of direction was made politically possible by changes within the governing Conservative party, changes which in turn reflected and expressed forces which were shaping British society: 'Throughout the controversy it was apparent that the commercial advocates were contemptuous of efforts to uphold either cultural or intellectual standards; the decisive consideration was that television was a great marketing device' (Wilson, 1961, pp. 214-15).

What was involved here was a change in the *purpose* of communication. The implications should have been far-reaching. In the event, for a variety of reasons some of which will be dealt with later, the fundamental difference between the 'public service' commitment of the BBC and the 'independence' of the commercial system did not become a reality. Nevertheless, the competitive relationship which of necessity developed between the two systems had important consequences for programming in both the BBC and the independent companies. Tracey (1978) in his case study of one of these (ATV), concluded that the output of its programme departments was as much a 'product for consumption' as were the products advertised in the commercial breaks. But, he argues, the 'logic' of commercialism is not escaped by the BBC because it too must compete for a share of the audience. In the mid-1950s, for example, the full impact of ITV's competition was apparent to the BBC through the 30:70 ratio of audience ratings. If the Corporation was to be able to rely on its revenue from the public licence fee, it had to demonstrate its *public* appeal by attracting a larger share of the audience: the pursuit of the ratings was conducted with a vigour which resulted in the achievement of a roughly 50:50 ratio during the 1960s.

Two devices were crucially important in the ratings battle. First, there was the emergence of the programme 'series' built around a production team, rather than resting with an individual producer. These series, such as 'Tonight', 'Panorama', 'Sportsview', 'Maigret', and 'This is Your Life', were immensely popular — 'the shock troops of the BBC's effective counter-attack on the commercial opposition' (Jay, 1972, p. 23) — guaranteed the viewers a predictable programme and guaranteed the BBC an audience. These were devised as much from a need to impose an 'administrative logic' on a rapidly expanding and increasingly cost-conscious organization as in the interests of audience maximization:

Production teams responsible for output right through the year meant that . . . orders and contracts could be placed for 12 months, with the consequent advantages of price to the BBC and security to suppliers, writers and performers. And the relationship between the production team's budget and the audience research figures gave a quick and easy measure of cost-effectiveness. (Jay, 1972, p. 23)

The other strategy developed to cope with competition was the 'art of scheduling'. Huw Wheldon, former Managing Director of BBC Television, has commented that 'It is always difficult for people to accept the brutal proposition that competition means putting Like against Like but the fact remains that it is so' (quoted in Smith, 1974, p. 136). The knowledge that certain sorts of programme attracted a much larger audience than others and the discovery in the 1960s of the 'inheritance factor' — the factor which tended to cause the viewer, once 'caught', to stay with whatever channel had originally grabbed him — has led to a drive not only to fight like with like, but to begin the fight earlier and earlier. This drive is evidenced not simply in a standardization in the substance or content of programmes but also in their form and style.

In Britain, certain potential excesses of commercial competition are to an extent limited by the relationship of both the BBC and ITV to government: in fact Burns (1977), who describes the programe scheduling activities of both organizations as a mutually convenient 'pacing' rather than competition in any real sense, finds the competitive relationships ambivalent and in some respects fictional. In the United States, on the other hand, the spirit of the First Amendment and the tradition of complete personal economic freedom militate against any governmental control of the editorial process and result in an immensely powerful competitive ethic. At the same time, the dominant social ethos of private enterprise creates its own constraints: if the British media are rooted in a broadly-based *social* control, American media organizations are bounded by powerful *economic* control mechanisms which are extremely influential on both the organizational context of media production and the nature of media output.

In the early days of network broadcasting the production of programmes was the almost exclusive province of advertising agencies. During this period the networks — NBC, CBS and later ABC — contented themselves with profits made from the purchase and resale (to advertisers) of transmission time on groups of stations. But in the 1940s each network began to develop programme packages for commercial sale. This meant increased revenue, which now came from the sale of programmes as well as of time. This development has, of course, led to further concentration of network control: since the network holds an option on the most desirable transmission times on stations coast to coast it will inevitably fill those times with programmes in which it has a financial stake. Indeed the three networks now originate 95 per cent of all programmes transmitted throughout the USA.

Supported by revenues from advertisers, the network is primarily interested in reaching the largest possible number of 'buyers' for the products advertised. The function of the local station is to deliver this audience to the network, which in turn sells it to the advertiser. Various systems — for example, the Nielsen Marketing Research Territory groupings, or Arbitron's Area of Dominant Influence markets — provide potential advertisers with minutely detailed information needed to determine the most efficient way of achieving the desired coverage in specific market areas. In the 'TV marketplace' the advertiser 'buys' his viewers at anything between $2¼ per thousand 'unassorted' to $10½ a thousand if they can be refined down to particular categories like young women, teenagers and so on, who can be more valuable in that form to sellers of specific products. The sums involved are vast: the average 30-second prime-time network television announcement costs about $60,000 (the highest cost to date, for commercials during the first television broadcast of the film *Gone With the Wind*, was $130,000); even low-rated spots average about $45,000. In 1977, commercial television had total revenues of $5.9 billion and profits of $1.4 billion (Broadcast Yearbook, 1979).

The collective financial and social pressures under which American broadcasting operates affect programme policy and production in profound ways. Epstein (1975) has documented in considerable detail how, in the struggle to attain a competitive rating for its failing news programme, ABC completely changed not just the format, style and pace of the broadcast but the political perspective which it encapsulated, in order to meet the 'Middle America' predilections of its affiliated station managers. While the price of advertising time during the news broadcast did rise dramatically (by more than 100 per cent) this, concludes Epstein, was achieved only at the cost of a fundamental change in the journalistic product.

The political dimension of constraint

Probably the most crucial of all the relationships which bind any media organization to its society is that between the organization and the government. In essence this relationship is characterized by the links of both media and government to the electorate, whose support is necessary to both sets of institution. In Britain, it is particularly important in mediating the commercial imperative which dominates the US media system. Thus, whether one chooses to describe the British broadcast media as 'industrial and commercial organizations' (Golding, 1974) — stressing the predominantly market situation in which they compete — or as 'two state-owned networks' (Beadle, 1963) — emphasizing the failure of the pressure for decentralization of control — the broadcasting system remains essentially unitary in character.

From time to time all broadcasting organizations undergo review by the state in order to obtain re-licensing or re-chartering. These periods of scrutiny have profound effects on all internal decision making over programmes, since the organizations tend to construct their programme schedules in ways designed to gain the political support of various sections of the community. Since the BBC was established fifty years ago, it has been subjected to at least twelve major reviews which have affected its internal interests. Smith (1973) describes the history of broadcasting as 'a history of crises, each causing a wave of special caution, sometimes lasting for years, inside the organization.' Sykes, Crawford, Beveridge, Pilkington, and Annan — names of the men who headed the influential Committees which have investigated broadcasting's structure and practices in Britain — are names which loom large in the mythology of the broadcasting organizations. 'The story of broadcasting is in many ways a history of how broadcasting organizations set about the task of staying in business. The actual programmes reveal the institution's needs as much as the interests of the audience' (Smith, 1973, p. 59).

The relationship with government means that the broadcasting organization is constantly under review, at times under direct scrutiny, and occasionally — at least in the perception of the broadcasters — under threat. For instance, Sir Hugh Greene, former Director General of the BBC,

has tellingly described the Corporation's response to the Pilkington Committee as a 'battle campaign' to be won by ensuring that no public row
broke out over any programme during the period of investigation (Greene,
1969). The 'battle' analogy, suggesting that positions can be fought for,
boundaries defined and redefined, hostages exchanged, and so on,
illustrates well the complexity of the positions involved, and the limits of
control exercised by either 'side' in what could be described as a 'war game'
(rather than a war) where the unwritten rules are as important as the
written.

Because of the close and complex relationship between media organizations and other dominant social and political institutions, it is arguable that
the mass media will essentially tend to reinforce — even though they may
ostensibly, or in passing, challenge or question — prevailing social and
political hierarchies. Examples of such reinforcement can be found in
Britain, for instance, as far back as the General Strike in 1926 and in current
coverage, or lack of coverage, of events in Northern Ireland.

We discussed the problem of reporting Northern Ireland affairs on many occasions
with people at all levels, and on our visit to the Province. The BBC told us that they
could not be impartial about people dedicated to using violent methods to break up
the unity of the state. The views of illegal organizations like the IRA should be
broadcast only 'when it is of value to the people that they should be heard and not
when it is in the IRA's interest to be heard'. The BBC said that before 1965 they had
tried in their reports on Northern Ireland to maintain a consensus and build up the
middle ground, but when that policy failed they abandoned it. In their programme
in 1972, 'The Question of Ulster', they had examined the range of views in Northern
Ireland, in order 'to bring the information to the attention of the British public
because in the end it was their opinions which were going to decide'. In considering
what should be broadcast the BBC had intensified the 'reference-up' system; and
they told us that they gave particular consideration to the effect of BBC broadcasts
on the army in Northern Ireland. The IBA told us that they had to consider under the
IBA Act whether a programme was likely to encourage or incite to crime or to lead
to disorder, and they also took into account what the public believed might be the
effect of such a programme. They did not consider the right course was to hive
Northern Ireland off from the rest of the network while programmes on Northern
Ireland affairs were being shown to the rest of the UK. The IBA's policy has been
criticized as unduly restrictive. Journalists at Thames Television and London
Weekend Television have both protested to us about IBA decisions to stop the
transmission of material. (Annan, 1977, p. 269-70)

It must also be clear, however, that the degree of reinforcement and the
nature of the controls within which it operates will vary enormously with
differing historical and social circumstances. Tracey (1978) illustrates this
through a chronological series of case studies of political broadcasting. The
complexity of the relationship between the media and dominant social
institutions, he contends, is highlighted by 'alternate moments of apparent
autonomy and real subjection'. Tracey argues convincingly that external
controls or constraints on the mass media have functioned indirectly
through 'the defining of impartiality, the underpinning of conventional
forms and a commitment to the productive and consumptive practices of a

commercial process', rather than through the exercise of any direct authority. Instead there operates, according to Burns (1977) a 'politics of accommodation', in which the relationship between communication organizations and the central social authority is mediated by, for example, organizational conceptions of audience interests and the professional or occupational ideologies of the communicators themselves.

THE COMMUNICATOR IN THE ORGANIZATION: SOURCES OF INTERNAL TENSION

The fact that the structure and organization of mass media institutions can be shown — at least in a partial sense — to arise from and be shaped by extrinsic factors has implications for the individuals who work within the media organizations. Mass communicators must operate within the context of institutionalized values and criteria of success, which are not simply the particular values of their peers or reference groups but are to some extent the central values of normative order in society. Moreover, it can be argued that structural constraints are implicit in the social organization of mass communicators and the ways the organization helps or precludes the achievement of occupational goals. The structural organization of production is important primarily because of the way in which individual roles are defined: for example, television organizations have found it useful to leave the position of creative roles, such as the producer, structurally imprecise. At the same time, the existence of creative, ambiguous roles within organizations of bureaucratic centralization is a potential source of conflict or tension. Indeed, the very terms 'structure' and 'organization' imply a pressure towards bureaucratic methods of problem solution, methods which may take various forms — from the use of standardized decision-making processes to the development of institutionalized expectations — but whose overall aim is to deal with potentially conflict-ridden situations or relationships.

Professionalism as a response to conflict

The term 'professional' is commonly used in at least three different ways. First, there is the use of the term to denote the 'expert', in contrast to the 'amateur'. This is a usage which Burns (1969) found widespread in the BBC. Second, there is the Weberian view of the professional as the rational, bureaucratic, efficient role embodying an ethic of 'service' to the client or public. The third, Durkheimian use describes the way in which professionals invest their work and organizations with moral values and norms.

It is often argued that a central dilemma for mass communicators concerns the extent to which the large-scale media organization tends to 'bureaucratize' the creative role of its members. Demands for stability, regularity and continuity may be said to drive media institutions towards the rationalization of staff roles — to create professionals in the sense described by Weber. However, it can also be argued that the negative effects of bureaucratization on individual roles can be countered by the development of professional pride and values — in the sense used by Durkheim — which may at times even run counter to the interests of the organization. It follows, therefore, that media 'professionalism', while perhaps arising from one basic source of conflict — that between organizational goal and creative occupational role — can actually be used to respond to that conflict in two quite different ways, which may in themselves promote conflict.

Elliott (1977) suggests that claims to professionalism in the mass media represent, on the one hand, an *occupational adaptation* or response to the dilemmas of role conflict and, on the other, an *organizational strategy* to meet the demands of significant constituents in the environment of media institutions. Examining the contradictory demands of 'art' and 'commerce' in media organizations, Elliott points out that this simple dichotomy actually fuses a number of interrelated dilemmas for the communicator, notably the pursuit of ideas such as 'creativity' and 'autonomy' within organizational milieus which may tend to foster more pragmatic responses to day-to-day events. The basic dilemmas are complex and may encompass such contradictory demands as those between high and low culture, professional standards and commercial judgement, self-regulation and bureaucratic control, self-motivation and financial inducement, self-monitoring and serving an audience, using one's talents to some artistic, social or political purpose and having them used solely for the commercial ends of the organization. Given this complexity, the responses or adaptations made by communicators are equally complex. However, Elliott argues, the end result — the media output — will only vary if the response of the individual communicator is supported by the organizational system in which the communicator is working.

A focus on the twin dilemmas posed by the professional pursuit of 'creativity' and 'autonomy' within an organizational context raises a further dimension or set of tensions in relation to media production. This concerns the relative importance of structural and of operational factors in the development of media output. In a general sense, it should become clear that although structural considerations partly, at least, determine both the nature of mass media operations and the approaches adopted in their execution, in the main they impinge more on the general organization of communicators' activities than on the day-to-day implementation of individuals' roles. These are affected at least as much by immediate, operational considerations as by their structural location within the organization.

Creativity in an organizational context

The 'mass' character of mass communication presents the media organization with its first all-pervasive dilemma: how can 'mass media industries' reconcile the dictates of organizational efficiency — for example, towards regularity, routine, control — with the commitment of individual 'creators' to their skills or craft?

The real trouble is that the 'industrial revolution' in entertainment inevitably revolutionizes the production as well as the distribution of art. It must, for the output required is too great for individual craft creation; and even plagiarism, in which the industry indulges on a scale undreamed of in the previous history of mankind, implies some industrial processing. (Newton, 1961)

This analogy with industrial organization is a prevalent one in the analysis of mass media roles and production processes. Newton goes on to argue that the impossibility of individual craft is paralleled by the organization of production for quantity, speed and marketability, rather than for quality. Because of the industrialized distribution system in the field of popular music, for example, and its reliance on large audiences, the mass media can afford neither the unreliability of the individual music creator nor the tastes of sophisticated minorities. This, the argument goes, produces an inevitable drive towards standardized, commercial, musical pap, which leads to a further worsening in audience taste and the alienation of the professional musician. Other studies (for example, Coser, 1965) have described alienation as a typical communicator response, and pointed to the development of occupational ideologies and values which dismiss general audiences as unappreciative 'outsiders'.

It is not difficult to identify a number of inadequacies in arguments of this kind. In the first place, by baldly confronting the needs of the artist or producer with the demands of the audience, the argument fails to take account of the role of the intermediary organization, which can provide a sort of refuge or shield for its employees: the distance between producer and audience can allow the former to avoid any precise definition of relationship and attitude towards the latter. Seen in this light, the bureaucracy of the organization may have a dual function for the producer: while regulating his integration into the organizational system, it may also allow him considerable autonomy. Second, it can be argued that specialization and professionalization within media organizations have led to the growth of powerful professional reference groups — either formal or informal in organization — which both protect individual producers and provide alternative definitions of success. Third, the argument ignores economic variations between different media which allow those sectors with low unit costs (and the music or record industry is one of these) to overproduce, balancing failures against successes, in an attempt to ensure that no potential 'hit' is missed. This allows for provision for minorities, which may indeed evolve into mass markets — as, for instance, in the development of reggae music — and provides scope for innovation and idiosyncracy on the part of producers. Finally, there is a distinction to be made between standardization of product style and standardization of productive role.

There is a tendency, in arguments which create a dichotomy between creativity and industrial process, to blur the line between production and dissemination activities in mass media organizations. The fact that mass production techniques and the bureaucratic formal organizaton that goes with them play a vital role in the circulation of mass media artefacts does not necessarily mean that industrial techniques are applied to their production. Yet when Lewis Coser describes the formal organization as an 'emasculator' of the individual's creativity, resulting in alienation, he ascribes this to the 'industrial mode of production' within media organizations:

The industries engaged in the production of mass culture share basic characteristics with other mass-production industries. In both, the process of production involves a highly developed division of labour and the hierarchical co-ordination of many specialised activities. In these industries, no worker, no matter how highly placed in the organisational structure, has individual control over a particular product. The product emerges from the co-ordinated efforts of the whole production team, and it is therefore difficult for an individual producer to specify clearly his particular contribution. (Coser, 1965, p. 325)

Coser's conclusion is that the individual creative producer, in alienation, holding his work in contempt, is robbed by the production team of his need to make a unique contribution. However, such an interpretation begs a number of important questions concerning, for example, the nature of 'creativity', perceived needs and goals of individual producers, distinctions between 'art' and 'craft', and so on. The views of a producer from the original production team responsible for 'Tonight', one of the most successful of Britain's early 'formula' shows, indicate a different set of priorities from that imagined by Coser:

It was on 'Tonight' that I learned the creative logic of a production team.... Although an idea can only originate in one person's mind, it often emerges in a half-formed state: it can be greatly improved if six or seven people question it and add to it and elaborate it and refine it. In the same way, after the programme was over, six or seven people were much better than one at evaluating it, drawing conclusions, seeing new possibilities to exploit or errors to be corrected.... It makes a production team the best place for any novice to learn the craft.... It also offers him a variety of different roles — writer, film director, researcher, studio director, interviewer, producer — with a correspondingly better chance of finding a suitable niche than he would have if apprenticed to a single producer. (Jay, 1972, pp. 24-5)

'Formula' styles do not necessarily mean standardized trivia, any more than they apparently mean standardized roles: while the range of styles may be dictated by the organization and technology of the medium, the quality of the finished product may have more to do with the ability of those performing the major creative functions and with the general socio-economic and socio-cultural milieus.

Nevertheless, the power of general economic and commercial factors in determining the creative freedom of individuals in the production process should not be underestimated. In times of financial stringency, particularly, experimentation and originality tend to be subordinated to predominantly market considerations.

Whereas, in the early sixties, a schedule of ten to twelve weeks was considered acceptable for a half-hour documentary, nowadays a standard series (such as 'Horizon') will think itself lucky to get more than five weeks for an hour. But, as a fellow-editor remarked to me recently: 'In those days we were developing the conventions. Now we merely apply them'. It is the technician's pride in his work-manship which leads him to tolerate and hence to perpetuate, this condition.... He will show that he can do a good job regardless of the difficulties (for if he does not, someone else will).... Haste necessitates the adoption of rules-of-thumb for calculating the viewer's response, and this in turn requires the adoption of methods to which such calculation is appropriate.... It is really not good enough for me to say that we employ the commercial and authoritarian models of communication only as a shorthand, since shorthand is all we have time for. What has happened is that we have adopted towards our own work a mode of sensitivity born of the need of others to pass snap judgement upon it. Professionalism is the technician's bad faith. (Vaughan, 1976, p. 19)

The question of control of media operations and output is thus very much broader and more complex than the attempt at a simple polarization of creativity and industrial process. This can be pursued further by examining the extent and nature of the autonomy enjoyed by the individual communicator within the media organization, and by looking at the effect of this on the products which ensue. The fundamental question here is: to what extent and in what ways can media personnel exercise operational control over their institutionally transmitted messages?

Communicator autonomy and organizational control

It has already been argued that organizational structure and policy both arise from and confront the social and political contexts within which they are located. In looking at the communicator within the organization, a similar iteration can be found: the individual is drawn to, and recruited by, an organization with whose operation and practices he generally feels some sympathy; at the same time, he has some scope for making a personal impact and for shaping the product in a particular way. Again, the extent of his potential impact will vary depending on the type of organization and on the nature of his individual role within it.

Roles and goals Media organizations and the communicators who work within them may have different goals. Three dominant sets of goals confront most media organizations, all determining the shape of the media output. Audience maximization, for instance, is a major *economic goal* whose attainment pushes for the application of certain criteria (broadly associated with 'entertainment' values) to output. *Organizational goals* can derive from the relationship to the controlling authority or the external legal, cultural, political and economic demands: the organization co-ordinates its output within an overall policy or strategy. *Professional goals* relate both to output — the use of inexplicit and diffuse criteria to charac-terize 'good television' or 'good journalism' — and to personnel, in terms of career patterns and criteria of success and appraisal.

In his study of news-gathering journalists, Tunstall (1972) provides an alternative categorization of the goals of news organizations: an audience goal, an advertising goal, and a non-revenue goal, which refers to any other objective — the pursuit of policy, political influence, prestige and so on. Through an examination of the relationship of these goals to the prevailing work roles, Tunstall explores the issue of autonomy and control in news journalism. His study indicates that role/goal conflict is generally controlled by a somewhat subtle process of negotiation, and rarely becomes overt: specialist journalists tend to have the same views as their major sources — those who cover trade unions vote Labour, those who cover the police vote Conservative, and so on. Any specialist has a variety of defences he or she can use against the organization, and both journalists and news organizations are able largely to have their way with what most concerns them.

Tactical autonomy and strategic control Despite some real auto-nomy in *tactical* detail (at the operational level), however, communicators can be *strategically* controlled (at the level of policy implementation) by notions accepted within their own occupation and more broadly within the media organization. For example, accepted 'professional truths' about how an interview should be conducted, what kinds of people are 'names', the appropriate budget for a particular 'time-slot' and so on are all important; above all, communicators can be constrained by the past performance of their organization in terms of learning what is 'acceptable'. This comes through clearly in Tom Burns's study of BBC professionals: 'What is drummed into producers is that if there is any doubt in their minds about a topic, or viewpoint, or film sequence, or contributor they must refer up to their chief editor, or head of department' (Burns, 1977, p. 195). At the same time, of course, it is open to the individual to push forward the boundaries of acceptability, but this is more likely to be allowed to happen at times of economic buoyancy or, in the case of the BBC, when the spectre of the Royal Commission is less visible. Thus, in the middle 1960s, the BBC could pioneer new forms of political satire in 'That Was the Week That Was', of drama in the Wednesday Play slot, of comedy in 'Monty Python'. These forms provoked an enormous amount of public comment and protest which the BBC firmly withstood.

By the beginning of the 1970s, with Annan appearing in the middle distance, the mood had changed. A programme entitled 'Yesterday's Men', concerned with the Labour opposition leaders one year after their ousting in the General Election of 1970, produced a violent political storm to which the BBC was forced to react publicly — by setting up the Complaints Com-mission. Tracey (1978) in his case study of the episode highlights the dual role of the BBC in both controlling and protecting its employees. Despite sanctions and changes imposed after the event, the programme-makers had, in fact, a great deal of freedom to develop and implement their conception of what the programme should be like. Little overt censorship was apparent at any stage. The policy of 'referral upwards' appeared to work in favour of the communicators through the invocation of 'professionalism' as a joint response — of both executives and producer — to outside attack. However, there is little doubt that the 'Yesterday's Men' episode has entered into the organizational lore as an example of what is, or is not, 'acceptable'. As the programme's producer said: 'Nobody must do "Yesterday's Men" again. You mustn't. Better be safe than imaginative' (Tracey, 1978, p. 201). The Annan Committee itself subsequently related these events to changes in the social and political climate:

Hitherto it had been assumed — apart from the occasional flurry over a programme — that Britain had 'solved' the problem of the political relations of broadcasting to Government, Parliament and the public. Now people of all political persuasions began to object that many programmes were biased or obnoxious.... The appointment of Lord Hill as Chairman of the BBC, and the subsequent appointment in his place at the ITA of Lord Aylestone, was widely interpreted as a sign that Government was firing a shot across the bows of the broadcasters to warn them that many members of the viewing public thought they were off course.... When Lord Hill and the Governors decided ... to assert the editorial independence of broadcasters by refusing to ban 'Yesterday's Men' ... politicians may have wondered whether they had appointed an admiral who habitually turned a blind eye when the Admiralty made a signal. The broadcasters realized they were heading for trouble, so they battened down the hatches. (Annan, 1977, p. 15)

The economic control mechanism The possibilities for, and limitations of, the autonomy of individual communicators within any media organization cannot be considered without reference to the economic base of the organization. The effects of the introduction of a competitive commercial element to British broadcasting have already been related to the programme policy orientations of the organizations. In another sense, and although it has been argued that British media professionals — particularly in the BBC — are primarily limited by a form of social control (by rather vague reference to standards, taste, acceptability), communicators in Britain are also subject to controls rooted in straightforward notions of business efficiency. For example, the emergence of a strong new stratum of middle management in the BBC in the late 1960s is conventionally attributed to the impact of the McKinsey Report. An unofficial submission to the Annan Commission pointed to the repercussions of this for programme-makers:

The BBC initiated the McKinsey Report which recommended a stricter internal system of control over financial expenditure. The BBC understandably complied. We do not dispute the necessity for rigorous financial stringency but we submit that we have now not only unrealistically elaborate financial procedures but that these have led to an even more Byzantine system of planning and control over programmes themselves....

Programme-makers feel strongly that real control, artistic as well as financial, has moved further and further away from themselves. We submit that this has had a correspondingly ill effect on programmes for which producers often feel accountable rather than responsible. (Quoted in Vaughan, 1976, p. 12)

It is in the United States, however, that the strictest limitations are imposed by a decidedly economic mechanism of control — by direct and measurable reference to what will sell. This stringent economic imperative leaves American communicators in an extremely weak position *vis-à-vis* the powerful networks.

The people at the networks say they want something fresh, they want something new, they want something different. You come in with something new, fresh and different. You work on it a little more and they say, wait a minute — that's a little too different. They pay lip-service to the idea of originality but in actuality the activity takes place along areas that are somewhat familiar to them. They will buy anything they can relate to success. They don't want it exactly like it was before. If you wanted to do a western that was similar to 'Gunsmoke' but not 'Gunsmoke', you are in pretty good shape. But if you do something that is totally different or something that is exactly 'Gunsmoke' chances are you are dead. (Cantor, 1971, pp. 128-9)

Paralysed by the ferocious competition in which they engage, the networks respond by minimizing all possible risks, hedging all bets. Every year they commission about 100 pilot shows for projected new series. These shows are then rigorously pre-tested according to the most sophisticated marketing techniques available, vetted in special annual screening sessions by the biggest advertisers, and finally weeded down to the twenty or twenty-five which are most likely to deliver the goods. The networks commission work to detailed and rigid specifications in terms of established formulae, and particularly of those which succeeded best in the previous season.

The image of the audience The economic mechanism is closely linked to organizational perceptions of audience requirements and behaviour. However, the relationship of media organizations and communicators to their audience is essentially ambiguous: Tracey (1978) defined it as an 'absent framework' in his study of the production of political television in Britain. Indeed, there is a sense in which the organization can be said to develop a model of the audience to suit its own needs:

It can be shown that the role of the audience extends beyond the creation and the contents of the mass media product, but affects the structure and the culture of the mass media industries themselves. . . . Every mass media creator, whatever his skill, is to some degree dependent on the validity of his audience image for his status and standing in the industry. (Gans, 1957, p. 322)

This struggle — between the communicator's image of the audience, and the organizational or institutional image of an audience or society in whose name the organization has been constructed — is illustrated by a particular form of transaction which emerged in the late 1970s.

A disastrous 1975-6 American television season, in which ratings indicated average viewing down by nine to fifteen minutes a day, and in which sixteen of the twenty-seven new shows launched at the beginning of the season were cancelled and replaced, led to speculation about the possibility of a change in American tastes and leisure patterns. Paralleled by a boom in the export of British television programmes to the United States, the move was interpreted as a triumph for 'quality programming': 'What has happened is that U.S. TV audiences have grown up. They will not take a steady diet of junk, and Britain produces quality material' (Mason, 1976, p. 40). The British imports receiving most acclaim in the United States were the big, long-running glossies: 'The Forsyte Saga', 'The Six Wives of Henry VIII', 'America', 'Elizabeth R'. Some British imports inspired American imitations, such as 'All in the Family' (from 'Till Death Us Do Part' and also shown in Britain), 'Sanford and Son' ('Steptoe and Son'), and a costly failure 'Beacon Hill' ('Upstairs, Downstairs').

To what extent might this actually reflect the emergence of a deep-seated audience need for a certain type of programming? (This would imply a personalized, communicator image of the audience.) Or how much could it be due to the expansion of big-business interests with capital to invest in long-term promotion (implying an institutionalized, organizational need)? For one thing, the selling of British programming was not an easy matter. Richard Price Associates, a company formed to market abroad the programmes of several commercial companies, took eighteen months and twelve major sales presentations to sell 'Upstairs, Downstairs' to the United States. For another, the foreign film arm of Sir Lew Grade's ATV, Independent Television Corporation (ITC), was at that time developing one of the largest production schedules in Europe, being involved not only in co-productions with Radiotelevision Italiana (RAI), but also in a major export drive to the United States. ITC-RAI co-productions of the late 1970s, such as 'The Life and Times of William Shakespeare', and 'The Life of Jesus' starred some of Hollywood's and Britain's biggest names.

In this context, it is difficult to see the purely 'quality' explanation as holding water (moreover, the falling pound in the late 1970s meant that British programmes were a cheap buy). An alternative explanation is that this is an example of the external 'survival' needs of the organization being fed into the communicators as intellectual attitudes, ideals and values which, although organizational in origin, may be expressed, interpreted, or even experienced as occupational or professional tenets.

THE LIMITS OF CONTROL

Consideration of the external and internal contexts of media organizations and occupations, it has been argued, is fundamental to an understanding of the sources, nature and directions of control in the media, particularly in relation to the shaping of output. The complex of constraints which has been outlined, and within which communication organizations and professionals operate, makes it difficult to sustain a view of the media and media practitioners as autonomous 'watch-dogs'. On the other hand, to the extent that the media can be observed to negotiate the parameters of constraint — exercising, at least at times, a policy of 'brinkmanship' — they cannot be dismissed as subservient 'tools of government'. Rather, the general conclusion must be that mass communication is indeed bound with, and bounded by, the interests of the dominant institutions in society, but that these interests are continually redefined through a process to which the media themselves contribute.

Tracey (1978, p. 242) concludes that 'the external political and commercial context locks the programme-making process into a cycle of dependency'. The external context of programme making, he argues, functions as a latent 'presence'. Thus, 'broadcasting is always conducted with a certain degree of fear; an error or misjudgement by a producer can by damaging the public image . . . severely endanger its essential economic or political interests' (Smith, 1972, p. 4). Consequently, the capacity to influence, if not control, rests on an understanding of the powers and consequences which may for the most part remain latent.

Yet the process is not wholly contained. For example, the 'Yesterday's Men' episode, as both Burns (1977) and Tracey (1978) suggest, indicates the limits within which both influence is possible and criticism tolerable. Burns contends that the limits of criticism have, since the mid-1950s, actually been proven extensible. His thesis that the broadcasters' historical acceptance that the 'national interest' must be served is a price which they pay for their dedication to professionalism is intriguing. Put the other way round, certain professional stances — such as those of the investigative or adversary journalist, or the anti-establishment tone of certain items of output — are a reaction against the restraints imposed by the accommodation reached between professionalism and the national interest: they gained acceptance as the 'price' which it has been found possible to exact for that accommodation.

The politics of accommodation in the mass media is played out at different levels — between the professionals and the management, between the organization and the establishment. Within this accommodation, the limits of control are in constant negotiation: from the trivial 'You put in a "crap" to get two "hells" and a "damn"' (US programme producer, in Levine, 1975, p. 22) to the politically resonant 'At the time of the General Strike . . . the compromises [Reith] accepted made it possible for his successors to be much more firm and uncompromising when they faced the anger of governments about the BBC's treatment of such crises as Suez' (Greene, 1972, p. 549). Through these negotiations and accommodations different interests are served. The precise nature and the implications of the controls expressed through those interests have, as yet, been only very loosely defined and interpreted by media research. However, the questions which such definitions and interpretations raise are as much political as sociological.

REFERENCES

Annan (1977) *Report of the Committee on the Future of Broadcasting*, London, HMSO.

Beadle, G. (1963) *Television: a critical view*, London, Allen & Unwin.

Blumler, J.G. (1969) 'Producers' attitudes towards television coverage of an election campaign: a case study', *Sociological Review Monograph*, 13.

Breed, W. (1955) 'Social control in the newsroom: a functional analysis', *Social Forces*, 33.

Broadcasting Yearbook (1979), Washington DC, Broadcasting Publications.

Brown, L. (1971) *Television: the business behind the box*, New York, Harcourt-Brace Jovanovich.

Burns, T. (1969) 'Public service and private world', *Sociological Review Monograph*, 13.

Burns, T. (1977) *The BBC: Public Institution and Private World*, London, Macmillan.

Cantor, M. (1971) *The Hollywood TV Producer*, New York, Basic Books.

Coase, R.L. (1950) *British Broadcasting: a study in monopoly*, London, Longman.

Coser, L. (1965) *Men of Ideas*, Glencoe, Free Press.

Donohue, G., Tichenor, P. and Olien, C. (1972) 'Gatekeeping: mass media systems and information control', in Kline, G. and Tichenor, P. (eds) *Current Perspectives in Mass Communication Research*, Beverley Hills, Cal., Sage.

Eckersley, P. (1942) *The Power behind the Microphone*, London, Scientific Book Club.

Elliott, P. (1972) *The Making of a Television Series: a case study in the sociology of culture*, London, Constable.

Elliott, P. (1977) 'Media organisations and occupations: an overview', in Curran, J., Gurevitch, M. and Woollacott, J. (eds) *Mass communication and Society*, London, Edward Arnold.

Epstein, E. (1973) *News from Nowhere: television and the news*, New York, Random House.

Epstein, E. (1975) 'Broadcast journalism: the rating game', in *Between Fact and Fiction: the problem of journalism*, New York, Vintage Books.

Gans, H.J. (1963) 'The creator-audience relationship in the mass media: an analysis of movie making', in Rosenberg, B. and White, D.M. (eds) *Mass Culture: the popular arts in America*, Glencoe, Free Press.

Gieber, W. (1956) 'Across the desk: a study of 16 telegraph editors', *Journalism Quarterly*, 34.

Glasgow University Media Group (1976) *Bad News*, London, Routledge & Kegan Paul.

Golding, P. (1974) *The Mass Media*, London, Longman.

Greene, H. (1969) '*The Third Floor Front*', London, Bodley Head.

Greene, H. (1972) 'The future of broadcasting in Britain', *New Statesman*, 20 October.

Hall, S. (1977) 'Culture, the media and the "ideological effect"', in Curran, J. *et al.* (eds) *Mass Communication and Society*, London, Edward Arnold.

Halloran, J.D. *et al.* (1970) *Demonstration and Communications: a case study*, Harmondsworth, Penguin.

Jay, A. (1972) *Corporation Man*, London, Jonathan Cape.

Lazarsfeld, P. (1972) *Qualitative Analysis: Historical and Critical Essays*, Boston, Allyn and Bacon.

Levine, R. (1975) 'As the TV world turns', *New York Times Magazine*, 14 December.

Mason, M. (1976) 'The great British video invasion', *Signature*, February.

Murdock, G. and Golding, P. (1977) 'Capitalism, Communication and Class Relations', in Curran, J. *et al.* (eds) *Mass Communication and Society*, London, Edward Arnold.

Newton, F. (1961) *The Jazz Scene*, Harmondsworth, Penguin.

Reith, J. (1949) *Into the Wind*, London, Hodder & Stoughton.

Seymour-Ure, C. (1968) *The Press, Politics and the Public*, London, Methuen.

Silverman, D. (1968) 'Formal organisation or industrial sociology: towards a social action analysis of organisation', *Sociology*, 2 (2).

Smith, A. (1972) 'Internal pressures in broadcasting', *New Outlook*, 4.

Smith, A. (1973) *The Shadow in the Cave*, London, Allen & Unwin.

Smith, A. (1974) *British Broadcasting*, Newton Abbot, David & Charles.

Steen, B. (1979) *The view from Sunset Boulevard*, New York, Basic Books.

Tracey, M. (1978) *The Production of Political Television*, London, Routledge & Kegan Paul.

Tuchman, G. (1978) *Making News: a Study in the Construction of Reality*, New York, Free Press.

Tunstall, J. (1970) *Media sociology: a reader*, London, Constable.

Tunstall, J. (1972) 'News organisation goals and specialist newsgathering journalists', in McQuail, D. (ed.) *Sociology of Mass Communications*, Harmondsworth, Penguin.

Vaughan, D. (1976) *Television documentary usage*, British Film Institute Television Monograph, 6.

White, D.M. (1950) 'The gatekeeper: a case study in the selection of news', *Journalism Quarterly*, 27.

Williams, R. (1962) *Communications*, Harmondsworth, Penguin.

Wilson, H.H. (1961) *Pressure group*, London, Secker & Warburg.

7

Cultural dependency and the mass media

J.O. BOYD-BARRETT

The focus of this chapter is on the role of the mass media in the poorer countries of the world, how the functions of the media relate to one or more definitions of 'national development', and especially on whether and how the media serve as channels for inter-cultural 'invasion' of the poorer countries by the more affluent and powerful nations. In other words, the central theme is the role of the mass media in relations of cultural dependency between nations. The title might suggest to some that this theme belongs in the study of 'inter-cultural communication'. But others might argue that the heart of the problem lies in the imbalance of power between nations. Either way, this chapter can do little more than signpost some issues that are central to the question of the contribution of the media to dependency. At the same time it should be kept in mind that cultural dependency can also reflect, and may reinforce, imbalances of socio-economic power among the affluent nations, or among cultures within nations. Nor must it be assumed that the mass media are necessarily the most significant contributors to cultural dependency, let alone to other forms of dependency.

FROM IMPERIALISM TO DEPENDENCY

Space is insufficient here to examine the concept of 'dependency' in any detail. To some readers the term 'imperialism' may be more familiar. But 'imperialism' is strongly associated with the act of territorial annexation for the purpose of formal political control. 'Dependency' theory asserts that national sovereignty is not a sufficient safeguard against the possibility of *de facto* control of a nation's economy by alien interests. In most Marxist theory, imperialism is regarded as an inevitable outcome of capitalism. There is no essential reason in dependency theory why the economic and political interests of the communist superpowers should not sometimes also distort or stunt the autonomous development of poorer nations. Imperialism, in Marxist theory, can be superseded only by international socialism. In contemporary dependency theory there is a greater element of doubt as to whether the circle of dependency processes, whereby the structural imperatives of developed economies enslave the weaker, is or is not absolutely vicious, and as to whether significant change is possible within the existing international order. In this paper it will be taken 'as read' that there is substantial evidence to show that many weaknesses in the economies of poorer nations are partly caused by and sometimes reinforced by the political and commercial interests of the stronger economies. But no position will be taken *a priori* as to the long-term inevitability of dependency, or as to the significance of media communication in relation to dependency.

Outline of the argument

The purpose of this paper is first to look at the major different approaches to the role of mass media in what, for the sake of convenience, will loosely be termed 'Third-World development'. It will be suggested that these approaches reflect different underlying ideologies. It will be seen that for both ideological and technological reasons there is considerable debate as to what constitutes the appropriate range of phenomena to which the study of the media and dependency should confine itself. A brief account will then be given of the different ways in which inter-cultural penetration is found to occur. Certain shortcomings in the evidence will be discussed. It will be suggested that a key factor in any evaluation of the role of the mass media in the process of 'cultural dependency' is the significance to be attributed to the power of any state or government apparatus to combat this process. Many attempts at such evaluation tend, as a result of the kind of questions they ask, to select or give undue weight to evidence which will support a condemnatory attitude. A more fruitful line of investigation may be to review and evaluate the kinds of claim which some western consultants originally made in support of the harnessing of the mass media to developmental objectives.

THE POLITICS OF A CHANGING PARADIGM

Nordenstreng and Schiller (1979) identified three successive paradigms in the study of the relationship between communication and development. In the first of these the emphasis was on the contribution of the mass media to the promotion of western-style (capitalist) development. I will term this the 'missionary' approach. A second paradigm sought to expose the more evident elements of ethnocentricity of the first, and to relate the mass media to different models of development. This may be labelled the 'pluralist' approach. But a third and more recent school of thought took the view that there could be no real understanding of the media unless priority was given to an understanding of the fundamental relationship between 'developed' and 'developing' economies, 'the international socio-politico-economic system that *decisively determines* the course of development within the sphere of each nation' (my emphasis). This paradigm I will tag 'totalistic'.

Corresponding sociological models

Each approach or paradigm corresponds with one of three major sociological models of society. The 'missionary' approach develops from *structural functionalism*. Functionalism tended to reify certain postulated features of complex industrial societies as essential for their reproduction and survival. This in turn encouraged the assumption that industrialization would be facilitated in other societies if these essential features were in some way engendered. The media 'missionaries' sought to transplant western media technologies to the poorer economies so that one day these economies would be facsimiles of the western economies. In sociological theory, functionalism was superseded by *Neo-Weberianism* which reacted against the functionalist reification of society and against the inability of functionalism to explain social change. Neo-Weberianism gave primacy to conflict as a driving force of change, and in particular, the conflict between groups for income, power and status. In doing so, it 'rediscovered' motive, interest, and perception, and 'redelivered' society to human beings. But it could also be seen to legitimate a pluralistic view of society as made up of equally competing and bargaining groups, a society in which belief-systems could operate independently as sources of change. There are similarities here, therefore, with what I have called the 'pluralist' approach to the study of the relationship between communication and development. While it pays equal regard to different modes of development, this approach may underestimate the extent to which the pattern of development in any given economy may be determined by a stronger economy. Thus it precludes the kind of analysis advocated by the media 'totalists' whose view of society derives from *neo-Marxism*, in which all social relations are seen in terms of their derivation from the mode of production.

'TOTALIZATION' AND THEORY DEVELOPMENT

The major strategic consequence of the 'totalistic' approach in the study of the mass media and 'development' is that it greatly widens the range of phenomena that must be considered essentially relevant. The theoretical core of analysis is located at ever higher levels of global social structure. In Schiller's work, as represented in Chapter 2 of the 1979 volume, the theoretical core is located in the relationship between the multi-national corporations and the global market economy. (The relationship between multi-nationals and nation states, on the other hand, is seen as relatively unproblematic: governments of parent nations and élites of host nations simply work in support of these giant enterprises.) In this scenario, transnational media are seen as constituting the 'ideologically supportive informational infrastructure for the MNC's' (Schiller, 1979, p. 21). Thus in addition to the generalized informational activities in which all such enterprises engage (e.g. generation and transmission of business data, export of management techniques), there are various categories of transmedia support activities, most important of which are advertising agencies, market survey and opinion polling services, public relations firms, government information and propaganda services and traditional media.

It is perhaps significant that traditional mass media are relegated to such a low position in this hierarchy (with the implication that they are mere creatures of advertising agencies) and that some other forms of socio-cultural imperalism are barely considered. This is partly explicable in terms of the rhetorical usefulness of highlighting the less familiar features of cultural dependency, but Schiller's agenda may also, in its ordering of issues, serve to underemphasize the role of state regulation.

A second major expansionary pressure upon the framework of analysis is represented by the pace of technological change, which may in turn be related to the development and commercialization of innovations in the defence and aerospace industries of the major economies (Mattalart, 1979). Satellite communication, for instance, introduces the growing potential for direct broadcast television and greatly complicates the task of global allocation of communication space. The rapid but uneven pace of satellite development intensifies the conflict between those countries that lag in technology but wish to preserve access for future use, and those which believe that existing capacity should be fully exploited by those with the means to do so. Developments of computer technology and digital communication greatly intensify the capacity for 'transborder data flows' at a pace possibly beyond the ability of international bodies to regulate. The 'electronic' revolution in the dissemination of information, whereby the same digital signal can be transformed into a number of different final formats requires that equivalent attention be given to both 'traditional' media (for example, newspapers, television) and more recent dissemination technologies (for example, home terminal publishing, videotext) (Hamelink, 1979; Marvin, 1980). The task presented by the need for international regulation of these developments itself represents a further pressure on the framework of analysis, one that requires consideration not simply of the socio-economic structures of dependency, but also of the highly legalistic contexts in which much international bargaining on such matters tends to occur (cf. the proceedings of the World Administrative Radio Conference, 1979, or the UNESCO debate on the final report of the International Commission for the Study of Communication Problems, 1980).

The benefits and costs of 'totalization'

There can be little question as to the generally beneficial impact that these trends towards 'totalization' have had on the quality of media-related theory and insight. For instance, they brilliantly de-neutralize the concepts of 'development', 'media', 'technology', etc., so that the signification of each of these is shown to be profoundly political. Among other things, they alert researchers to the danger of uncritical adoption of western assumptions about which particular vehicles of cultural or media influence are the most 'significant': media technology, comics, and advertising, for example, may be just as significant as, respectively, media content, 'élite' news, and drama. 'Totalization' also alerts researchers to the assumptions about the channels of control which actually carry most influence: in the assessment of communication impact, for instance, an owner cannot be assumed to have more overall influence than an advertiser or supplier.

But 'totalization' also brings certain dangers. It not only de-neutralizes the phenomena under investigation, but effectively de-neutralizes itself at the same time. Its emergent priorities are curiously in line with the political strategies and bargaining poses of the nationalist-Marxist alliance of southern nations in their international negotiations with nations of the north. In certain formulations it is ahistorically and naively determinist: thus Nordenstreng and Schiller speak of the 'decisive determination' of national development by the global economy. This formulation is as rigid as the structural functionalism which neo-Marxism helped to surmount, indeed more so, in its incapacity to account for change. The totalistic approach adopts too uncritically a relatively simplistic version of dependency theory, in a manner which appears unduly concerned to eliminate as insignificant the machinery of the national state. For example, it is by no means generally accepted that capitalist expansion everywhere or even typically destroyed viable patterns of desirable or indigenous forms of development; nor is it beyond dispute that dominant nations 'de-capitalize' peripheral nations or 'de-nationalize' their successful local business in the manner in which dependency theory asserts (Smith, 1979). ('Decapitalize' is to direct or deflect indigenous capital or sources of capital away from locally-controlled enterprise and investment. 'Denationalize' is to remove the locus of real control of indigenous enterprise from local to non-local interests.) It is still too early to determine what significance should be attributed to the fact that India, for example, has doubled its food production in twenty years; is, in 1980, the eighth largest industrial country in the world, with the third largest pool of technically trained manpower; and has exerted considerable government control over industrial development. Simplistic referencing to dependency theory is not enough. What is required is a two-way process in which grounded theoretical research informs and modifies dependency theory as much as it draws sustenance from it.

FORMS OF INTER-CULTURAL MEDIA PENETRATION

The remainder of this paper is concerned primarily with the inter-cultural dimensions of traditional mass media processes and with particular reference to the poorer economies of the world. The discussion will be contextualized, where appropriate, in relation to the range of factors discussed in preceding paragraphs. Perhaps the most overt form of inter-cultural media penetration is the ownership of national media by multinational interests. Linked to, but by no means coincidental with this, is the question of the locus of formal managerial control. But regardless of ownership or formal control, inter-cultural penetration may also be exercised by external customers for media services — in particular, the multi-national companies which buy advertising space, or any advertisers who channel their custom through multi-national advertising agencies, or both. Both media and advertising organizations may have resort to multi-national public relations, market survey, and opinion-poll organizations in order to appraise the size and social composition of media audiences and the potential audience demand for various commodities. Advertising itself ranks as part of programme content and as such exerts influence, but it also exerts influence on the content of other programming. The extent of such influence depends, first, on how far media executives consider it necessary to maximize audiences or to attract certain kinds of audience for the benefit of advertisers; second, on the extent of competition for advertisers' custom; and third, on the extent of government or professional regulation of the volume and range of advertising. Next there is the question of programme contents that are imported or simply received from extra-national sources. The role of imports should also be seen in the light of the objectives and economics of the exporting organizations. This introduces, for example, questions concerning the conditions of sale: are the sales package-deals or is there collusion between the major exporters to maintain given price levels? The notion of 'exporter' should be defined broadly enough to encompass both those organizations whose primary concern is organizational profit, and those whose primary concern is to promote general or specific attitude change in relation to given political, religious or other objectives.

It is not only specific programme contents that are exported. Directly or indirectly there is also the 'export' from the stronger economies of particular conceptual models that affect, for instance, prevailing views as to how programme contents should be arranged or presented, or the components which are deemed to constitute an appropriate 'schedule' or 'format'. These models incorporate certain profound assumptions: for example, that certain complexes of media technology should be applied in particular ways. The news-entertainment-advertising mix of the daily newspaper is an instance; likewise, the association of media technologies with certain periodicities of use as in the daily or weekly newspaper, the weekly or monthly magazine, or evening television. But the technology itself, not just its application, is cultural, and occurs in the form that it does for complex social and economic reasons which have to do with the histories of social relations in the metropolitan centres and which embody certain consequences of class relations (as in élite-mass one-way communication). The adaptation of particular kinds of media receiver to given international communication facilities (radio, cable, satellite) raises issues to do with the ownership and control of such facilities, differential rates of access to them, and procedures for international allocation. These considerations overlap with the process of the transmission of situationally-specific professional ideologies from metropolitan to peripheral centres of the world economy, through such means as formal education and training schemes, or simply through constant exposure to imported media products.

Theory or propaganda?

There is almost certainly a good case to be made for the hypothesis that the mass media have, to an as yet unspecified extent, contributed to the complex of processes referred to as dependency. Yet much of the evidence and argumentation is presented as though it were in illustration of an established and incontrovertible fact. There is a rough division, in the catalogue of forms of media-related cultural penetration already outlined, between those which are susceptible to precise measurement (e.g. the number of newspapers owned by multi-nationals; the number of hours of imported television programming in peak viewing times) and those which are not nearly as amenable to positivistic methodologies (e.g. cultural changes attributable to mass media). Yet the weight of evidence for theses of media imperialism often relies heavily on the latter. Caution with respect to available evidence is frequently absent. Instances may be noted where there is no simple acknowledgement of the non-availability of certain kinds of relevant data. Too much weight may sometimes be given to western influences on one particular medium without reference to the general character of all media output or to evidence concerning respective media impacts. The totality of relevant exogenous media influences may sometimes be evaluated in isolation from an evaluation of countervailing indigenous influences. It tends to be assumed that the adoption of any given western media practice represents a stage in the process of social change that would not have occurred solely in response to indigenous pressures. The role of the demand for cultural imports is underemphasized or glibly explained away as 'created'. Analysis of actual effects or consequences is especially rudimentary. The contours of the debate have perhaps been too much influenced by the Latin American experience, where specifically North American penetration of technology, advertising, low-brow canned US media fodder, has been especially acute in conditions of relatively low national government regulation. There is a general tendency towards exaggerated claims for media impact. When the particular dangers predicted in relation to one innovation fail to materialize, or do not materialize as unambiguously as expected, attention moves on to the next incipient weapon of imperialism. In the case of direct broadcast satellites, for example, insufficient attention was given by the pessimists to the wide variety of means available to governments for controlling or preventing the reception of such transmissions (for example, by prohibiting the sale of particular kinds of receiver). It is very curious that a phenomenon as pervasive and as elusive as that of inter-cultural media influence should so rarely be seen to contribute at least some positive factors to the process of social change in poorer economies. Finally, in consideration of the macro-political implications of cultural imperialism, there is often a strange reluctance to speculate on the global consequences of a unilateral decision of one power-block not to thus pursue its interests.

State regulation and resistance

An historical trend which suggests the necessity for a less deterministic model than that suggested by Nordenstreng and Schiller is the marked decline in direct foreign ownership and control of national media systems in many parts of the so-called developing world. This in itself suggests one reason why research interest has shifted to less obvious transcultural media influences. The shift in ownership and control highlights two factors: the importance of state regulation of media control and the declining diversity of media outlets in many ex-colonial territories. Very many of the colonial countries actually enjoyed a wider spread of media diversity than was later allowed by post-colonial regimes. In many British, French and Dutch territories, for instance, there had developed strong anti-colonial or at least indigenous press media pursuing religious, racial, nationalist or more diffuse political and cultural objectives. Many leaders of the first wave of independent states came to power on the back of political news-sheets that they themselves had founded and/or edited. Once in power, many regimes experimented with a measure of press diversity and decontrol, but such experiments hardly anywhere survived for long without severe modification and restriction. Even where foreign interests did retain an ownership presence, their freedom with regard to political and social comment was greatly constrained by a gamut of devices, examples of most of which are to be found in Lent's (1978) description of Asia's 'completed revolution', namely, the achievement of state control over the mass media.

Even with respect to many of the less direct forms of trans-cultural media influence, the possibility of state regulation is clearly available. Katz and Wedell (1978) provide instances of countries actively and successfully engaged in reducing the proportions of imported television-fare or foreign radio music on local media networks. Even some of the most subtle of cultural imports (for example, the 'import' of the standard western television schedule) are not self-evidently beyond the reforming capacity of any determined government convinced of the desirability of change. Nor is state regulation of media self-evidently inhibited by fear of the loss of advertising revenue, especially where there are few competing outlets for advertising.

But some influences are especially difficult to eradicate. For instance it is argued that television technology inevitably distorts local culture in non-western societies. Television cannot easily accommodate the cultural diversity common to many such societies. 'Authentic' local cultural expression requires the full social membership and engagement of those who participate in it, while television permits only a passive viewing of selected elements. Governments of new nation states are often more concerned with the construction and diffusion of a nationally-integrative culture which may borrow familiar elements of traditional cultures but which is designed to transcend their boundaries. Such governments may actively resist attempts to preserve what they may see as the politically destabilizing vitality of diverse cultures. There is, in any case, a tendency on the part of some critics of cultural imperialism to employ the terms 'authentic' or 'traditional' in respect to local culture in a manner similar to the frequent use of the term 'community' in some western countries, that is, with mythological, '*gemein-schaft*' connotations of cosy togetherness.

It is also true that resistance to inter-cultural media penetration can at times be expensive. For a nation that is committed to television, a decision to reduce dependence on cheap programme imports may well require a much heavier outlay on expensive home productions which, because of poor facilities or inexperience, may seem to lack some of the polished gloss of western soap opera. But the decision to restrict television time, or even do without television, is still available, even if politically difficult. Resources for indigenous media development may be affected by the availability of international advertising. Even where there is no direct restriction on such advertising, however, its availability can be reduced indirectly by policies such as import restriction or nationalization. In Guyana, for instance, where such policies were adopted in the 1970s, the proportion of total media advertising accounted for by non-local adverti-sers declined from 70 per cent to 10 per cent in the period 1964-76, and this was responsible in part for a deterioration of programme standards, a reduction in newspaper titles and cancellation of plans for expansion of regional broadcast stations (Sanders, 1978).

There can be no adequate evaluation of inter-cultural media penetration which does not take into full account the variability of mass media policies adopted by individual governments. The infrastructure of global communi-cation may be very much the development of, and in the control of, the super-powers. But it does not necessarily determine what happens within particular nations. Nor is it free of internal strains: many western multi-national corporations are in competition with one another; there are political and economic conflicts between the more affluent nations; and smaller nations have found ways and means of bringing collective pressure to bear on the more powerful nations.

The danger of assuming a simple one-way responsibility for the short-comings of the international communication system is illustrated by the case of the major western news agencies, which are frequently accused of ethnocentricity in their handling of news coverage on which most Third-World nations rely. Such criticism tends to underestimate the extent to which the agencies have regionalized their services, the increase over time in the overall volume of news which they provide, and the problems inherent in defining what in fact constitutes adequate regionalization. The major agencies are heavily dependent on the output of national news agencies and the national media, partly because their resources are in many areas thinly spread, and partly because more and more restrictions are imposed upon the news-gathering activities of foreign newsmen. Of equal importance is the willingness of many non-western media to depend on western agency coverage even where alternative courses of action are available. Matta (1979) has demonstrated the reluctance of élite Latin American media to provide independent coverage not only of world news but of continent-wide affairs. If there were more independent coverage, the major agencies might better be able to gauge the real nature of Third-World news requirements. A substantial proportion of all world agency news distributed in Latin America is, in any case, gathered in Latin America by Latin American nationals working for the western agencies, transmitting mainly in Spanish. While the agencies are often accused of ignoring authentic 'Third-World' angles in news coverage, Matta also gives examples of important development-related stories carried by the world agencies but not used by the Latin American media.

COMMUNICATION AND DEVELOPMENT

It has been suggested that the 'totalistic' approach has resolutely concentrated on negative evaluations of western media influence. It is useful, therefore, to review some of the more optimistic claims originally entertained by some western researchers, among others, not because such claims can easily be upheld — far from it — but because the evidence suggests a greater element of ambiguity and diversity than 'totalistic' theorists would allow.

Media availability

Any general discussion of media impact should include an assessment of the extent to which populations are actually exposed to the media. The most important factor helping to account for exposure is physical availability of the media. This is still something that cannot be taken for granted in very many of the poorer countries. The major obstacles to media development pertain to market conditions, political insecurity, linguistic diversity, illiteracy, and technology. In the west, the press developed as a form of 'mass' communication because it could 'sell' large audiences to advertisers, and advertising revenue made it possible to sell newspapers at below-cost levels. In many poorer countries there are relatively small markets for the commodities that major advertisers want to sell. Even the purchasing ability for mass media products themselves is still extremely low in many countries. The conditions of production, and particularly of distribution, are often very much more difficult than in most industrialized economies, for reasons of distance, terrain, shortages of equipment and skills, shortages of foreign exchange. Advertising is directed disproportionately towards the small circulation élite media. This contributes to the information gap between rich and poor, since the greater revenue enjoyed by the 'élite' media improves their coverage and presentation. Media diversity is constrained by the nationalization of media systems by governments, which tend to feel threatened by privately-owned media, and which are often the only sources of substantial media investment available. Political insecurity often dissuades governments from attempting to decentralize media systems or from encouraging cultural pluralism through the media. Government control does not of itself help to overcome print illiteracy. If priority has been given to the need to establish centralized systems of communication for the benefit of 'social order', the development of broadcasting may be seen to by-pass the need for literacy. The existence of linguistic diversity has in many countries actually helped to sustain the life of the language of the ex-imperial power, given the need for a lingua franca, a language of convenience. The élite media are more likely to adopt the old imperial language, while poorly resourced vernacular papers may have to undertake their own translations of news agency and similar copy. Broadcast media, especially radio, can cater more adequately for linguistic diversity, but the resources for multi-linguistic programming and dissemination may not be forthcoming, especially where linguistic divisions correspond with imbalances of social and political power. Radio is by far the most influential and important mass medium in most poorer economies, but its impact is still restricted by technological constraints — atmospheric sources of reception interference, inadequacy of technical data, inadequate numbers and strength of transmitting stations, etc. The availability of radio receivers did greatly increase with the introduction of transistors, but repair facilities may be non-existent and quality of reception very bad. In most non-industrialized economies, television is primarily an urban phenomenon, sometimes confined to élite audiences. The total degree of exposure to media for any single individual in most parts of the so-called Third World is far less than the average for citizens of the industrialized economies and this is likely to remain so for some considerable time.

Positive claims for a media contribution to development

The belief that the media would play an important role in relation to national development, in terms both of information dissemination and of attitude change, was promoted by some western researchers in interesting contrast to an established view that in the already 'developed' world the media performed a mainly reinforcing role with respect to attitude change. While state regulation of media control in the Soviet Union and Eastern Europe, for example, was still widely regarded as totalitarian and reprehensible in the west, state control in the 'developing' countries won the sympathy of some western apologists who considered it to be the necessary, if sad, price to be paid for political integration and national prosperity, given the conditions of tribalism that were said to threaten the security of new nations. Some research studies had suggested a causal link between media growth and industrialization. It seemed more important to establish the basic media infrastructure, first, than to worry unduly about content.

At least four benefits could be claimed on behalf of the role of the mass media in relation to development. These were that the mass media could, first, break down traditional values thought to be inimical to the process of industrialization and modernization; second, help promote the attainment of an autonomous and integrated national identity; third, assist in the dissemination of specific technical skills; fourth, they could be harnessed to the task of rapid expansion of formal education and improvement of educational attainment in schools.

In the early promotion of these benefits, at least two important general obstacles to success were frequently overlooked. The first of these was the culturally-bound model of development which characterized much of the thinking about the role of the media. Rogers (1976) argued that economic growth did not necessarily have to come about through industrialization. Development was not adequately measured by such questionable devices as GNP, nor was it to be equated with such features as capital-intensive technology or international loans. The western model had failed to bring about the anticipated levels of development in many countries, and even in the west the process of industrialization had brought about grave problems (for example, environmental pollution) as well as benefits. A second obstacle that was overlooked was the wide range of factors that limited actual levels of government or private commitment to development-related objectives. It was assumed either that the mass media, of themselves, would bring about attitude changes conducive to the requirements of a developing society, or that the formal objectives of development were so obvious and so compelling that any right-minded media organization or its government would not hesitate to harness the media to these objectives. But left to themselves, established privately-owned media systems had no motive to engage in development-type programming if profit was to be made in other ways, and if production costs could be cut by reliance on cheap imports of popular programming from western countries. Exposure to such material might conceivably enhance individual empathy, which for Lerner (1958) was a major prerequisite for the acceptance of other aspects of what, in his view, constituted the modern society. But it could just as well breed a consumer-oriented attitude inimical to the requirements of a developing society (Wells, 1972). As for the role of governments, many studies suggested that these were far more likely to intervene in media programming on matters that concerned their own political security than on development-related issues, and that rhetoric was rarely matched by the reality (for example, Barghouti, 1974 and Hachten, 1975). Other relevant factors that were often overlooked included the low pay and status of journalists in many countries, the vulnerability of media systems to the bribery and corruption of political machines, the widespread intolerance of media independence and initiative, and even the corrupt journalism practices which in some countries took the form of black-mailing vulnerable news 'sources' (see, for example, Cole, 1975; Jones, 1979; Lent, 1978).

Breakdown of traditional values

In addition to these general obstacles to successful exploitation of the media for developmental purposes, there were many further considerations specific to particular claims. Take, first, the claim that the media could play an important role in breaking down traditional values considered inimical to development. This claim implicitly justified cultural penetration by more 'developed' societies, and had a substantial intellectual heritage. Several studies had found a relationship between mass media availability or exposure and other indices of industrialization or 'modernity' (see Schramm, 1964). It was hypothesized (Lerner, 1958) that the link was causal, that the mass media contributed to the process of becoming 'modern'. One possible link in the causal chain lay in the area of attitude change and conceptual skill. This in turn could be related to some studies of western industrialization which had attached considerable importance to social-psychological variables such as in Weber's (1965) description of the 'protestant ethic' and its associated syndrome of deferred gratification. (Weber's thesis was discredited by Trevor-Roper (1977), who argued, amongst other things, that many Calvinist entrepreneurs lived far from frugal lives, and that rational capitalism existed in southern Catholic Europe before the growth of Calvinism.) A related application was McClelland's (1961) concept of 'achievement motivation', propensity for which was associated with, among many other factors, the content characteristics of traditional children's stories. Lerner (1958) in his study of development in the Middle East identified 'empathy' as the crucial modernizing component of the human psyche and defined the concept in terms of a high capacity for rearranging the self-system at short notice. The mass media were important facilitators of this process of interior manipulation.

Elaboration of theory along lines such these was problematic. The model of development, as we have seen, was ethnocentric. Not only did it obscure the reality about some of the conditions of developing countries, but it even obscured the reality of the nature of the so-called developed countries. For instance, certain features that had been considered typical of 'traditional' societies and inimical to 'development' were to be later identified in 'developed' societies. It was not obvious that all or even most 'traditional' values were inimical to development: in Japan they were very likely positive facilitators. Nor was it obvious that supposedly 'modern' features necessarily facilitated development. Lerner's 'empathy' concept might, for example, appear to be a facilitating quality, especially in relation to entrepreneurship and other innovative processes. But it could also be seen as an obstacle in the way of cementing the kind of work discipline 'appropriate' for the masses in developed industrial countries. High 'empathy' might have a destructive impact on industrial society by generating a critical approach to authority and by kindling an impatience with the constraints imposed by industrialism on certain possibilities for individual development.

One important way the media were seen as being able to promote economic growth through attitude change was in their role as vehicles for the advertising and the display of consumer goods. This, it was believed, would promote consumption, which in turn would promote local industrialization, higher incomes and yet further consumption. But this view was attacked by critics of 'cultural imperialism' on the grounds that it greatly underestimated the extent to which, first, production of consumer goods continued to be controlled by or in the interests of the major western-based corporations; and second, the consumer goods in question continued to be largely irrelevant to basic housing, clothing and food requirements of the masses of the people, only serving to draw away existing funds from socially productive investment. Wells (1972) claimed to find empirical evidence to demonstrate the view that the impact of North American television programming in South America was 'consumerist': the rewards for sectoral inequality were displayed but the means to attain a more widespread material culture were not. However, an attitude study of adult residents of Barquisimeto, Venezuela (Martin *et al.*, 1979) was unable to find any significant evidence of a high correlation between exposure to mass media entertainment and a consumerist attitude orientation, except possibly among the already well off.

The view that mass media could help to break down traditional values thought to be inimical to development has therefore been found unhelpful in a number of ways. The concept of 'development' is itself an especially value-laden term; the relationship between given social values and a western model of development is peculiarly complex, and possibly requires a better understanding of both 'developing' and 'developed' societies than at present exists, if indeed it is still meaningful to refer to either independently of the other. The evidence in favour of the 'consumerist' thesis is inconclusive. It is too broad an issue to be determined simply by reference to attitudes. Evaluation of whether a consumerist impact, if such there is, is negative or positive in relation to development, is an especially complex task. Not enough is known of media systems which have been systematically exploited for 'producerist' ends to be able to evaluate whether these may be said to have an independent impact in relation to their respective developmental contexts.

Consolidating national identity

The second major claim for a positive media role in relation to development concerns its potential for the establishment of a popular sense of national identity. This potential perhaps has been more widely recognized by new Third-World élites than the media's potential for more specific economic or educational objectives. It would be difficult to argue that nationalized media systems, disseminating news and information of government activities, very often in the absence of any competition, have not achieved some degree of national consolidation. But the simple claim that mass media contribute to national integration and hence to development requires considerable modification.

Even where the mass media have been nationalized, there remains an important conflict, identified by Katz and Wedell (1978) between the exploitation of mass media in order to achieve national integration and the exploitation of mass media in order to bring about changes in attitudes that would hasten the process of modernization. The importance of the mass media in relation to national unity is evident at each of three stages in the development process: the stage of political integration in the early phase of independence, the onset of 'modernization', and then the reaction against it. The initial concern for political integration is seen to require a stress on common traditional symbols, or the creation of symbols that are then made to seem commonly traditional. But this use of media proves insufficiently competitive with western-style programming, which is seen either as economically inevitable or as positively related to modernization, or both. Attempts to preserve the 'traditional' may not survive the transfer of traditional arts to the new technology of mass media for mass audiences, while resources for local production may be too tight to allow real competition with dubbed imports. The use of media for modernization, unlike its use for national integration, is fundamentally divisive and may cancel out any impact attributable to integrative goals. Modernization sets generation against generation, old élites (for example, tribal elders) against new (for example, urban professionals); it may itself be associated with the newly achieved dominance of a particular tribe or social grouping and in this way can become an anti-integrative symbol against which the disadvantaged, the minority tribes and the dispossessed may be mobilized. There then re-emerges a concern for national integration to overcome such conflicts, and this may involve a deliberate identification of the agents of 'neo-imperialism' as the common enemy. This in itself may expose the illusory character of the original claim for a positive relationship between mass media and national integration, inasmuch as the mass media may have been sponsored by western corporations, based on western technology, carried western programming and in other ways illustrated the general socio-economic process of dependency. If integration has been achieved, it may now seem that it has been achieved at least as much in respect to a particular world order as to a particular national system of government.

The claim of many early researchers that the media had an important role to play in the establishment of a national consciousness directly or indirectly endorsed a model of development in which an urban political élite, often advised by international agencies or western governments, determined the goals of society and set about manipulating the masses towards these goals. The very models of broadcasting imported from the west confirmed the notion of heavily concentrated media systems, physically and structurally located close to the centres of political and military power, employing technologies equipped only for one-way communication as in the west. In this sense the claim entailed a basically conservative view of the role of the media. This was then enhanced by the particular contents that governments often used to promote national integration, often involving a focus on inherently conservative national symbols: the presidency, the state religion, an urban and élitist version of 'national news', a particular language or group of favoured languages, etc.

Dissemination of skills

The claim that the media could assist in the dissemination of specific technical skills was a considerably more limited and verifiable claim. While it is probable that over time the growing sophistication of dissemination strategies is likely to have greater pay-offs, the specific role of the mass media has been rather more limited than many first anticipated. Early strategies were often based on studies of the diffusion of innovations, which showed that adopters of innovations could be classified according to their receptivity to innovation, and that early adopters could play an important role as opinion-leaders or trend-setters. It was of great importance to identify the characteristics of early adopters, so that these could be sought out as targets for communication about innovations, and so that interpersonal processes could take over in the percolation of the new ideas throughout the community.

This approach was both convenient and simplistic. It was convenient because it meant that field-service agents for agricultural innovation programmes had to concentrate on only a small proportion of the total community. Because early adopters tended to be wealthier and to have larger farms, the impact was greater. The early adopters were also easiest to talk to and persuade. The model was simplistic because it assumed a more homogeneous community than was usually the case: instead of a single set of opinion-leaders, there was usually a stratified community, with opinion-leaders in each strata. By concentrating only on the wealthier farmers, therefore, the diffusion approach may have accentuated the gap between rich and poor, because there was no continuous line of influence and because the poor were not sufficiently motivated or were unable to innovate. The poor needed more attention, possibly of a different kind (see Roling *et al.*, 1976). These considerations had important implications for the role of the mass media in diffusion programmes, and raised difficult questions concerning the resources available for highly differentiated approaches.

The idea that a major innovation programme could depend entirely on the mass media alone came to be discredited, certainly. It could not be assumed that governments or private media systems would necessarily make the resources available for media dissemination. More important, effective communication and diffusion was seen to extend well beyond the explicit content of the message and beyond the confines of media organizations. Two important additional considerations involved, first, the situational characteristics of the explicit message, and second, the situational characteristics at point of reception.

Simple provision of the message was insufficient. It had to be provided at a time, in a language or in a style acceptable to the listener, which would make effective comprehension possible and likely. But broadcasting in many 'developing' nations had to cater for many linguistic groups, requiring the apportionment of staffing resources and air-space to different groups, with possibly a great reduction in effective listening-time for any one group and considerable content duplication. This meant there was less overall time available for a station to pick up the 'casual' listener, and less opportunity for listeners to estabish regular listening habits. Motivation to listen could quickly be dissipated if presentation and reception were poor or inappropriate. In Rao's (1966) study of two Indian villages the number of villagers who mentioned unintelligibility as the reason for not listening to the radio was so high that the author advocated a major change of announcers' vocabulary. It could be the right language, but the level of abstraction or formality could be too great. Presentation could influence the chances of effective implementation. Kearl (1977) warned against the tendency for 'scientific' knowledge to be converted into an unsuitable authoritarian mode of traditional knowledge in the process of dissemination, and argued that more stress should be placed on trial and error procedures.

By the late 1970s, therefore, it was widely considered that the conditions for effective mass communication, in relation to the dissemination of specific technical skills, extended well beyond the communication message itself and involved an important measure of interpersonal communication, at least in those societies where interpersonal communication was still the primary source of non-local information and values. But where there was less dependence on interpersonal communication, the mass media may have become more self-sufficient as effective disseminators (see Schneider and Fett, 1978). The necessary scale of investment for dissemination was considerably greater than allowed for in original models of the media's role in development, and often required greater dependence on the aid programmes of international organizations and western governments.

Media for formal education

Whereas diffusion programmes have generally been concerned with particular kinds of skill or information for adults, it was also claimed that the mass media, especially broadcasting, could achieve rapid improvements in a country's formal educational system and in the numbers it could educate. Schramm (1964) claimed that the mass media could overcome problems of teacher shortage, and could provide a means of education even in areas where there were not yet any schools. Just as in the case of diffusion research, so in respect of educational broadcasting, most of the literature appears to originate from sources committed to these kinds of objective. But there was considerably more caution by the late 1970s than in the early 1960s. This reflected greater experience of the problems of organizational logistics, technology and programme quality. First, the need to deliver specific programme material at a specific time on a stated day to classes of pupils in a particular grade in all schools of a given educational system could cause immense logistic difficulties (Katz and Wedell, 1975), which in the developed countries were only overcome with considerable co-ordination of services and resources. Nationwide coverage, second, was difficult for transmission reasons, especially in the case of television, which was mostly confined to affluent urban sectors. But even with radio there were many problems related to quality of reception, supply of receivers and maintenance. Many broadcast organizations, finally, found it difficult to infuse the high levels of talent and resources required to sustain quality of programming over time, in order to sustain, in turn, listeners' motivation and the pedagogic impact of the material transmitted.

Re-interpreting the evidence from a number of early experiments in educational television, Carnoy (1975) argued that educational television (ETV) did not provide instruction that was cheaper than alternative methods of improving education, methods that involved the addition of more trained teachers to the school system; and that the introduction of ETV did not obviate the need to retrain teachers. There was a tendency for the educational benefits to be concentrated in the first year of pupils' exposure to such programming, and it was uncertain whether these improvements would extend throughout school life. Carnoy was doubtful if such improvements would seem significant if compared, not with tradi-tional educational systems, but with non-ETV innovations in teaching methods. There was also some doubt, he claimed, whether there was a high pecuniary rate of return on investment in educational expansion *per se*: evidence of the rate of return on increased student attainment indicated that it was greater at the lower levels of schooling than at higher levels, but there was no conclusive evidence that this pay-off compared favourably with other public investments. Nor could it be said that ETV contributed significantly to equalization of opportunity and income in society: in none of the projects he examined did he find any features of design or execution that would have redistributed education itself or the income associated with more schooling.

But the future of broadcasting for education in the 'developing' countries is more likely to rest with radio than with television. Jamison and McAnany (1978) identified three objectives for radio in relation to formal education: improving educational quality and relevance; lowering educational costs; and improving access to education. Examining the strategies available for the achievement of these objectives, they concluded that only distance learning (replacing teacher and school) definitely seemed to improve access and reduce cost, but that improvements in the quality of education were not generally associated with this strategy. Their findings also suggested that radio was much less likely to be effective in teaching cognitive skills, work skills and in changing behaviour than it was likely to be effective in motivating and informing. But unless resources were made available to enable motivation to be translated into action, the effective benefit could be negligible.

Katz and Wedell (1975) have argued that 'extensive' use of broadcasting is more likely to be successful than 'intensive' use. By 'extensive' they refer to programming that is not associated with formal education, that is received in private homes in the normal course of broadcast transmissions, and which may take the form either of informational or entertainment matter, but which is designed with certain developmental goals in mind. Intensive use of broadcasting, on the other hand, of the kind reviewed by Carnoy (1975) or Jamison and McAnany (1978), was already on the way to being outdated by the trend towards greater individualization of the learning process, and with advances in educational technology which were adapting to the demand for individualization and flexibility, such as audio and visual cassettes, teaching machines, programmed learning texts, overhead projectors and film loops, portable television cameras and portable transistorized monitors. This point of view may have been no less optimistic than the original hopes for educational broadcasting entertained by Schramm (1964), in its assumption that new technologies would in fact be made available on a more efficient basis than traditional broadcasting reception equipment. Moreover, as Mattelart's (1979) work suggests, such technology may be all the more likely to derive from western-based multi-national companies, its design and its soft-ware carrying in-built and politically consequential assumptions as to what educational goals should be. In obliging teachers in the Third World to adjust their teaching curricula to the demand for such technology this process might simply accentuate the phenomenon of dependency.

THE QUESTION OF EFFECTS

The role of the mass media in the Third World has therefore received very considerable attention in recent years, both from the critical perspective of dependency theory and from that of developmentally-oriented action research. Yet it is still the case that very little is known about actual media effects in relation to dependency. On the one hand, some of the issues raised are too broad: media structures are related to other components of the international structure of dependency, yet insufficient attention is given to the impacts of specific contents. For instance, if 'reactionary' western media contents do have political impacts, it would seem, prima facie, that such impacts are curiously ineffective in diverting popular discontent, rebellion and revolution in many countries subjected to such contents. The impacts do not seem to rise above the structural conditions for social disintegration. It might even be hypothesized that exposure to western media fare tends to weaken respect for traditional authority, and is therefore dangerous to many different kinds of regime. On the other hand, other issues are raised that focus too specifically on narrowly defined categories of developmentally-related programming, which pay insufficient regard, for example, to the interaction of such programme impacts with the impacts of other programme categories. Overall, there is a shortage of imaginative hypothesis construction in both these two broad areas.

What research there has been on 'media effects' in terms of general media impacts on values, attitudes, and behaviours is strangely repetitive of some of the naively positivistic research, now less common perhaps in the west, in which inferences are drawn from, say, counts of violent incidents, the proportion of all feminine characters who appear in 'subservient' roles, etc. From the analysis of western soap opera is extracted the predictable list of negatively-evaluated concepts — greed, sexism, individualism, etc. — a game that can almost always be played two ways to yield an alternative list of virtues in which, for example, the 'violence' of 'Starsky and Hutch' becomes a mere backdrop to the celebration of comradeship and teamwork. Sophisticated semiological research is comparatively rare in Third-World contexts and even the value of Dorfman and Mattelart's (1975) vaunted analysis of Donald Duck must be assessed in relation to the highly purposeful propagandistic activity of Chilean media during the period of research. The orthodox view of audiences in the West is now one that stresses the social context in which communications are received, and which stresses the individual's capacity for active selection and selective retention. This view does not yet seem to have carried over sufficiently to Third-World contexts in relation to general programming (cf. the review of Latin American research by Beltrans, 1978). Individual capacity for psychological compartmentalization and rationalization is underestimated to an extraordinary degree. Much more attention needs to be given to the processes by which individuals and groups interpret, translate and transform their experiences of foreign culture to relate to more familiar experiences. Perhaps the most useful working conclusion that can be drawn from this brief survey of inter-cultural media communications and the dependency process is that there is a great need for an emphasis on micro-analysis of media impacts at small group and individual levels to engage with and to illuminate the present emphasis on macro-analysis of media and multi-national structures.

REFERENCES

Barghouti, S.M. (1974) 'The role of communication in Jordan's rural development', *Journalism Quarterly*, Autumn.
Beltrans, L.R. (1978) 'TV etchings in the minds of Latin Americans: conservatism, materialism and conformism, *Gazette*, XXIV (1).
Boyd-Barrett, O. (1980) *The International News Agencies*, London, Constable.
Carnoy, M. (1974) *Education as Cultural Imperialism*, New York, McKay.
Carnoy, M. (1975) 'The economic costs and returns to educational television', *Economic Development and Cultural Change*, 23 (2).
Centre for Educational Development Overseas (1972/3) *Survey of Educational Broadcasting in Commonwealth Countries*, London.

Cole, R. (1975) 'The Mexican press system: aspects of growth, control and ownership', *Gazette*, (2).

Dorfman, A. and Mattelart, A. (1975) *How to Read Donald Duck: Imperialist Ideology in the Disney Comic*, New York, International General.

Fett, John H. (1975) 'Situational factors and peasants' search for market information', *Journalism Quarterly*, Autumn.

Hachten, W.A. (1975) 'Ghana's press under the NRC', *Journalism Quarterly*, Autumn.

Hamelink, C.J. (1979) 'Informatics: Third World call for new order, *Journal of Communication*, Summer, 29 (3).

Jamison, D.T. and McAnany, E.G. (1978) *Radio for Education and Development*, Beverly Hills, Cal., Sage.

Jones, G. (1979) *The Toiling Word*, International Press Institute and Friedrich-Naumann-Stiftung.

Katz, E. and Wedell, G. (1975) *The Role of Broadcasting in Development*, Final Report on broadcasting and national development as presented to the Ford Foundation.

Katz, E. and Wedell, G. (1978) *Broadcasting in the Third World: Promise and Performance*, London, Macmillan.

Kearl, B.E. (1977) 'Communication for agricultural development', in Schramm, W. and Lerner, D. (eds) *Communication and Change, The Last Ten Years and the Next*, University Press of Hawaii.

Lent, J.A. (1978) 'Press freedom in Asia: the quiet but completed revolution', *Gazette*, XXIV (1).

Lerner, D. (1958) *The Passing of Traditional Society*, New York, Free Press.

McClelland, D.C. (1961) *The Achieving Society*, New York, Van Nostrand.

Martin R., Chaffee S. and Izcaray, F. (1979) 'Media and consumerism in Venezuela', *Journalism Quarterly*, Summer.

Marvin, C. (1980) 'Delivering the news of the future', *Journal of Communication*, 30 (1).

Matta, F.R. (1979) 'The Latin American concept of news', *Journal of Communication*, Spring, 29 (2).

Mattelart, A. (1979) *Multinational Corporations and the Control of Culture*, Brighton, Sussex, Harvester Press.

Nordenstreng, K. and Schiller, H.I. (eds) (1979) *National Sovereignty and International Communication*, Norwood, (N.J.), Ablex Publishing Corp.

Parsons, T. (1967) *The Social System*, Englewood Cliffs (N.J.), Prentice Hall.

Plowman, E.W. (1979) 'Satellite broadcasting, national sovereignty and free flow of information', in Nordenstreng and Schiller (eds) *National Sovereignty and International Communication*, Norwood (N.J.), Ablex Publishing Corp.

Rao, Y.V.L. (1966) *Communication and Development: A Study of Two Indian Villages*, Minneapolis, University of Minnesota Press.

Rogers, E.M. (1976) 'Communication and development: the passing of the dominant paradigm', *Communication Research*, 3 (2).

Roling, W.G., Ascroft, J. and Wa Chege, F. (1976) 'The diffusion of innovations and the issue of equity in rural development', *Communication Research*, 3 (2).

Salinas, R. and Paldan, L. (1979) 'Culture in the process of development: theoretical perspectives', in Nordenstreng and Schiller (eds) *National Sovereignty and International Communication*, Norwood (N.J.), Ablex Publishing Corp.

Sanders, R. (1978) *Broadcasting in Guyana*, London, Routledge & Kegan Paul.

Santos, T. dos (1976) 'Relaciones de dependencia y desarollo político en América Latina: algunas reflexiones', paper presented at the seminar on Dependency Studies in Latin American Development, Helsinki, Finland, 8-10 September 1977.

Schiller, H.I. (1979) 'Transnational media and national development', in Nordenstreng and Schiller (eds) *National Sovereignty and International Communication*, Norwood (N.J.), Ablex Publishing Corp.

Schneider, I.A. and Fett, J.H. (1978) 'Diffusion of mass media messages among Brazilian farmers', *Journalism Quarterly*, Autumn.

Schramm, W. (1964) *Mass Media and National Development*, Stanford University Press.

Shingi, P.M. and Moody, B. (1976) 'The communication effects gap', *Communication Research*, 3 (2).

Smith, T. (1979) 'The underdevelopment of dependency literature: the case of dependency theory', *World Politics*, XXXI (2).

Trevor-Roper, H. (1967) *Religion, the Reformation, and Social Change*, London, Macmillan.

Weber, M. (1965) *The Protestant Ethic and the Spirit of Capitalism*, London, Allen & Unwin.

Wells, A. (1972) *Picture-Tube Imperialism?* New York, Orbis Books.

III

THE POWER OF THE MEDIA

Introduction

As the preceding section showed, the view taken of the relationship between media and society influences the way in which the power of the media is perceived. Two of the essays in this section — those by James Curran and Tony Bennett — see the media primarily in terms of a struggle for power between competing social forces in which the media are both shaped by, and in turn influence, the course of this struggle. The remaining two essays in this section, by Peter Braham and Jay Blumler/Michael Gurevitch, analyse the influence of the media in a more eclectic way in terms of their effectiveness in shaping human behaviour and consciousness, viewed from a pluralist perspective.

The opening essay by James Curran considers schematically the impact of the mass media over more than a millenium of history. He maintains that the development of new techniques or institutions of communication has given rise to new power centres, ranging from the medieval papacy to modern press magnates. The emergence of these new power centres, he argues, has often generated new tensions within the dominant power bloc. Thus, the priesthood provoked dissension in the middle ages by seeking to transform the power structure; the rise of the book undermined, in turn, the authority of the priesthood in early modern Europe; and more recently professional communicators have become, in some ways, rivals to professional politicians. More generally, he examines the different social contexts in which mass media have amplified or contained class conflicts. In early nineteenth-century Britain, he maintains, conflicts between a substantial section of the press and the dominant class both reflected and reinforced growing fissures within the social structure. More recently, he argues, the media have come to occupy a central role in maintaining support for the social system as a consequence of the close integration of control of the media into the hierarchy of power in contemporary Britain.

Jay Blumler and Michael Gurevitch's examination of the political effects of the mass media draws upon a different research tradition — survey-based research into media effects in western liberal democracies. Their essay challenges the 'limited' model of media influence advanced in the pioneering, highly influential studies into media political effects. The development of television, they argue, has resulted in political communications regularly reaching a segment of the mass audience that is particularly susceptible to political influence. A general decline in the strength and stability of political allegiances has also enabled the media to exercise a more effective influence. And new ways of conceptualizing media influence in terms of their impact on political cognitions rather than in terms of persuasion and behaviour change, they argue, have revealed significant media effects that once tended to be neglected. Their essay concludes with a discussion of convergences between recent pluralist and Marxist approaches to the study of media audiences.

Peter Braham's examination of how the media handle race illustrates two important aspects of the influence of the mass media referred to by Blumler and Gurevitch, namely the power of the media to influence the political agenda and to shape perceptions of reality. The massive media publicity given to Enoch Powell's notorious speech on immigration during the late 1960s helped to define race as a central issue on the political agenda — a place which it has held ever since. The concentration of the media on the manifestations of racial tension has also arguably influenced public perceptions of immigration by tacitly defining the presence of coloured immigrants as constituting a social problem or threat to the white majority. But Braham is at pains to emphasize the limitations of media influence. Enoch Powell, he argues, did not create (though he may have amplified) racial tension: his speech produced an 'earthquake' largely because it expressed anxieties and discontents about race and immigration which were already widespread, but which had received 'insufficient attention in the mass media'. Braham also quarrels with the view that by focusing on the manifestations, rather than the causes of racism, the media are playing a central role in fanning racial hostility. What these causes of racial conflict are, Braham argues, is far from self-evident. But what is clear from historical evidence, according to Braham, is that ethnocentrism and hostility to foreigners are deep-rooted and widely diffused phenomena for which the media cannot be held responsible.

The last essay by Tony Bennett differs from the two preceding it in that it links media systems of representation to their political and social contexts, viewed from a Marxist perspective. He considers the ways in which the mass media — both communist and capitalist controlled — suppressed information about the revolutionary and socialist character of the Republican side during the Spanish Civil War for different propagandist reasons. This profoundly influenced, he argues, the response of the European working class to the Civil War, thereby 'shaping the contours of the political map of prewar Europe'. He also examines the ways in which 'outsiders' such as youth gangs have been stereotyped and stigmatized in the mass media, arguing that their representations have served to strengthen commitment to dominant social norms. His analysis concludes with an examination of the different ways in which the media sustain the dominant political consensus, drawing upon examples of media coverage of industrial relations and the political process.

Bennett also explicitly contests a number of arguments advanced in the two preceding essays. Peter Braham's characterization of the media as 'a searchlight illuminating some areas, while leaving others in shadow' implies a differentiation between objective reality and the media as selective definers of that reality. Bennett argues, however, that 'the "real" that is signified within the media is never some raw, semantically uncoded, "out-there" real. Signification always takes place on a terrain which is always already occupied and in relation to consciousnesses which are always already filled'. Indeed, it is precisely because the media's influence is greatest, according to Bennett, when people are least conscious of its influence — when the ideological categories projected by the media appear neutral and objective — that the measurement and assessment of media influence through survey techniques is so problematic. While these techniques do not generally rely on asking respondents to assess the influence of the media upon them, but rather seek to infer processes of influence by examining the statistical relationships between variables derived from respondents' replies, the value of these techniques remains an outstanding issue of disagreement amongst researchers.

Yet despite these and other disagreements, all four essays in this section are unanimous in opposing the view that the media 'mirror' society, based on the media professionals' claim that they 'report the news as it is'. News does not exist as external reality that can be objectively portrayed on the basis of ascertainable fact: for facts have to be selected and then situated, whether explicitly or implicitly, within a framework of understanding before they 'speak for themselves'. This process of selection and interpretation is culturally encoded and social determined. Yet such constructions largely define our knowledge of the external world of which we have no first-hand experience. This power of definition, all these essays argue, is the basis of 'the power of the media'. All four essays are also at one in repudiating — though in different ways, and with different emphases — the once prevalent academic view that the media have only a marginal influence. They are thus symptomatic of the process of rethinking and reappraisal which has shaped this book, and which is now reshaping more generally the field of mass communications research.

8

Communications, power and social order

JAMES CURRAN[1]

Mass communications are generally discussed as if they were exclusively modern phenomena. Indeed, this assumption is embodied in most social scientific definitions of the mass media. According to McQuail (1969, p. 2), for instance, 'mass communications comprise the institutions and techniques by which specialized groups employ technological devices (press, radio, films, etc.) to disseminate symbolic content to large, heterogeneous, and widely dispersed audiences'. Only modern technology, it is widely assumed, has made possible the transmission of communications to mass audiences; for, as Maisel (1973, p. 160) amongst others would have us believe, 'in the pre-industrial period, the communication system was restricted to direct face-to-face communication between individuals'.

In fact, a variety of signifying forms apart from face-to-face interaction — buildings, pictures, statues, coins, banners, stained glass, songs, medallions, rituals of all kinds — were deployed in pre-industrial societies to express sometimes highly complex ideas. At times, these signifying forms reached vast audiences. For instance, the proportion of the adult population in Europe regularly attending mass during the central middle ages was almost certainly higher than the proportion of adults in contemporary Europe regularly reading a newspaper[2]. Since the rituals of religious worship were laid down in set liturgies, the papal curia exercised a much more centralized control over the symbolic content mediated through public worship in the central middle ages than even the controllers of the highly concentrated and monopolistic press of contemporary Europe.

Centralized control over mass communications is thus scarcely new. An historical comparison with older communication forms — including communications reaching small élites as well as mass audiences — serves, moreover, to throw into sharp relief certain aspects of the impact of communication media that the 'effects' research tradition, relying upon survey and experimental laboratory research techniques, has tended to ignore. Our concern will be with the impact of communications on the power structures of society. In particular, attention will be focused upon the effect of new media in bringing into being new power groups whose authority and prestige have derived from their ability to manipulate the communications under their control; the consequences of their rise in generating new tensions and rivalries within the dominant power-bloc; the wider dislocative effects of new media which by-pass or displace established mediating organizations and groups; the emergence of new media which reflect and amplify increasing conflicts within the social structure; and the central role of the media, when there has been a close integration between the hierarchy of power and control over communications, in maintaining consent for the social system.

This examination will concentrate mainly upon three historical periods — the central middle ages, early modern Europe and modern Britain. It will take the form of a schematic analysis in which we will move backwards and forwards in time in order to elucidate particular aspects of the impact of the media[3]. Inevitably a survey covering so broad a canvas will be highly selective and, in places, conjectural. But hopefully it will serve as a mild antidote to the conventional approach to examining media influence, in which media institutions are tacitly portrayed as autonomous and isolated organizational systems transmitting messages to groups of individuals with laboriously-measured and often inconclusive results, that has dominated media research for so long[4].

COMMUNICATIONS AND POWER

The rise of papal government is one of the most striking and extraordinary features of the middle ages. How did the See of Rome, which even in the early fourth century was merely a local bishopric with no special claim to legal or constitutional pre-eminence, become the undisputed sovereign head of the western Christian Church? Still more remarkable, how did a local church with no large private army of its own and initially no great material wealth and which for long periods of time was controlled by minor Italian aristocrats develop into the most powerful feudal court in Europe, receiving oaths of allegiance from princes and kings, exacting taxes and interfering in affairs of state throughout Christendom and even initiating a series of imperialist invasions that changed the face of the Middle East?

The See of Rome had, of course, certain initial advantages which provided the basis of its early influence. It was sited in the capital of the old Roman empire; it was accorded a special status by the emperors in Constantinople who were anxious to unite their Christian subjects in the west; and it was the only church in western Europe which was thought to have been founded by St Peter.

The papacy capitalized on this initial legacy by spearheading the missionary expansion of the church and by skilfully exploiting the divisions within the deeply fissured power-structure of medieval Europe to its own advantage. Successive popes played off rival monarchies against each other, exploited the tensions and conflicts between monarchies and feudatories and even, on rare occasions, backed popular resistance to aristocratic repression. The papacy also utilized to its own advantage the desire of some leading ecclesiastics to increase their independence from lay control as well as the tensions and rivalries within the Church itself, notably between the episcopacy and the monastic order. The rise of papal government, as a number of scholars (for example, Brooke, 1964; Southern, 1970; Richards, 1979) have convincingly shown, was thus partly the result of the dexterity with which the papacy harnessed the interests and influence of competing power-groups to build up its own power.

But neither the papacy's imperial and apostolic legacy nor its policy of divide and rule adequately account for the transformation of a local bishop into a papal emperor. In particular, it does not explain why (as opposed to how) the papacy should have profited so greatly from its interventions in the power politics of medieval Europe, nor does it adequately explain why the papacy managed quite rapidly to expand its power over the Church far beyond the authority accorded to it by the Roman emperors. The rise of the papacy can only be properly understood in terms of its early dominance over institutional processes of ideological production that created and maintained support for its exercise of power. As St Bernard of Clairvaux wrote perceptively to the Pope in 1150: 'Your power is not in possessions, but in the hearts of men' (quoted in Morris, 1972, p. 14).

The expansion of the Christian Church in early modern Europe provided the institutional basis of papal hegemony. It created a new communications network capable of transmitting a common ideology throughout western Europe. Rome could not exploit this network, however, until it had asserted its authority over the western Church[5]. During the fourth century, the papacy upgraded the status accorded to it by the emperors in the east by claiming leadership of the Church on the basis of scriptural authority. Its claim rested upon a passage in St Matthew's Gospel in which Jesus hails St Peter as 'this rock (upon) which I will build my church . . .' As a title-deed, it left much to be desired, not least because it made no reference to the See of Rome. The omission was made good, however, by the production of a spurious letter, the *Epistola Clementis*, whose author was stated to be Clement, the first historic bishop of Rome, informing St James of the last dispositions of St Peter which designated the bishops of Rome as his successors. This was followed by additional forgeries of which the most influential was the *Donation of Constantine*, which purported to document how the Emperor Constantine had formally handed over large, but mostly unspecified, provinces in the western hemisphere to Pope Silvester; and a collection of canon law called *Pseudo-Isidore*, which included fraudulent canons of the early Christian Councils and equally spurious decrees of early bishops of Rome, representing the pope as the primate of the early Christian Church. Distinguished early popes added to this myth-making by proclaiming as fact obviously false stories about the development of the early Christian Church[6]. The papacy and its allies thus set about reinterpreting history — a practice common to all great ideologies, although in this case conducted with unusual thoroughness by the actual fabrication of historical sources.

The ideological strength of the papacy was based, however, not so much on a single biblical text (important though this was), or on a selective view of history, but on what Kantorowicz (1957) calls 'the monopolization of the Bible' — the selective interpretation of the Bible in a way that constituted a compelling way of viewing the world. Papal and ecclesiastical propaganda provided a teleological view of existence in which all actions of Christians were directed towards the attainment of salvation. According to this perspective, the pope as the supreme ruler of the Church had the duty to direct all men towards the goal of salvation by means of the law. And since every aspect of human life was encompassed within the corporate and indivisible body of the Christian Church, the pope as head of the Church had a universal sovereignty. There was, according to papal ideology, no inherent right to power or property, because these derived from the grace of God and could be revoked or suspended by God's appointed agents. In short, the papacy constructed an ideological system based on two central premises: (a) that all power derived from God; and (b) that the Church was indivisible. These premises provided the foundation for an elaborate superstructure of thought that expanded the bishop of Rome's claim to headship of the Church into a divine-right, absolutist authority over mankind (Ullmann, 1970).

The hierocratic themes of the papacy were mediated within the Church through the established hierarchical channels of communication. The papal curia had the largest collection of records and archives and the most sophisticated team of scholars and polemicists in the western hemisphere during the early and central middle ages. It reiterated with relentless insistence the central tenets of papal propaganda in correspondence, official pronouncements and legal judgements.

To some extent the mediation of papal themes within the institution of the Church also occurred independently of curial supervision. Ullmann (1969) shows, for instance, that the Frankish episcopacy during the Carolingian period stressed the sovereignty of the papacy, and the assumptions that underlay it, in an attempt to establish their autonomy from royal and feudal control. There was thus a natural affinity of interest between the papacy, in remote Italy, and the ecclesiastical hierarchy in other parts of Christendom that resulted in a partly unco-ordinated assertion of the sovereignty of the papacy and the primacy of the clergy in an impersonal ecclesiastical order. This facilitated, in turn, the extension of papal control over the Christian Church in the west. Through increased influence over senior ecclesiastical appointments, insistence upon regular visits to Rome by bishops, and the extension of direct papal control over the monastic order, the papacy was able to exercise increasingly centralized power over the Catholic Church and to harness its resources to the advancement of its power and authority within western Europe.

The Catholic Church translated the sophisticated, hierocratic ideology of the papacy into graphic and readily comprehensible forms in an age when the overwhelming majority of the population — including the nobility —

were illiterate. Such has been the preoccupation of medievalists with literary
sources, however, that surprisingly little attention has been given to the role
of non-verbal communication, and in particular to religious magic, in
shaping the outlooks and perspectives of the mass population in the middle
ages[7]. Yet the whole paraphernalia of ecclesiastical sorcery and ritual was
of crucial importance in mediating an ecclesiastical construction of reality
that underpinned papal hegemony.

The medieval Church acted as a repository of magical power which it
dispensed to the faithful to help them cope with a wide range of daily
activities and secular problems. In this way, it symbolically affirmed the
indivisibility of the Church, while at the same time asserting the magical
potency of God and the special role of the Church as the mediator of divine
power. Thus the rites of passage (baptism, confirmation, marriage, puri-
fication after childbirth, last unction and burial) administered by the
Church invested with religious significance each stage of the life cycle,
thereby affirming that every aspect of human existence fell within the
compass of the Church. Their impact was reinforced by the cluster of
superstitions that developed around each rite. Baptism, for instance, did not
merely signify the entry of the new-born child into membership of the
Church: many believed that it was essential if the child was not to die and
be condemned to an eternal limbo or, as some churchmen insisted, to the
tortures of hell and damnation. Similarly, the Church both sanctioned and
fostered the medieval cult of the saints: the superstitious belief in miracle-
working spirits whose aid could be enlisted through pilgrimages to their
shrines, through acts of propitiation before their images or by simple
invocation. While clergy were mere general practitioners in sacred magic,
the saints were prestigious specialists whose help could be invoked in
situations requiring special skills. St Agatha, for instance, was popularly
thought to be best for sore breasts, St Margaret for reducing the pangs of
labour, and so on. The Church also administered a battery of rituals,
normally entailing the presence of a priest, holy water and the use of the
appropriate incantations, as stipulated in medieval liturgical books, for
blessing homes, purifying wells, preventing kilns from breaking, making
tools safe and efficient, making cattle or women fertile, ensuring a good
harvest or a safe journey. Indeed, there were few secular activities for which
the Church did not issue a form of liturgical insurance policy and few
secular problems for which the Church did not offer a magical specific.

Religious charms, talismans and amulets were worn as prophylactic
agents against evil and bad luck. Such devices were the essential props of
medieval superstition, symbolically expressing the potency of religious
magic mediated by the Church. The Church also daily displayed an
impressive feat of magic in its celebration of mass: inanimate objects were
transformed into flesh and blood, or so it was proclaimed, in the sacrament
of the eucharist. In order to emphasize the mediational role of the clergy, this
demonstration of magical prowess was given special significance through
being employed for a variety of secular as well as spiritual purposes, from

curing the sick and guarding travellers against danger to shortening people's stay in purgatory. In addition to this powerful arsenal of sacred magic, the Church expressed through religious architecture and art basic tenets of papal ideology (Panovsky, 1951; Evans, 1948). The construction of churches towering above their pastoral flock symbolized the looming presence of God over all aspects of life. Sculpture, paintings and glass windows that depicted the divinity of Christ and the macabre tortures of hell served a similar purpose: they were a reminder of God's omnipotence in both the earthly world and the afterlife. As Pope Gregory I commented, the illiterate 'could at least read by looking at the walls what they cannot read in books' (quoted in Innis, 1950, p. 124).

The bizarre superstitions that encumbered popular medieval devotion were not all imposed from above. In part they derived from participation by a superstitious laity. But they had their origin in the sacred magic proclaimed and administered by the medieval Church and were tolerated by the often sophisticated incumbents of the papacy as the expression of simple piety binding God and his children closer together (Thomas, 1973). They served the wider purpose of maintaining the ecclesiological conception of the universe that legitimized papal imperialism.

Indeed, the conscious ideological 'work' that sometimes went into the elaboration of religious ritual is clearly revealed, for instance, by successive modifications made in the liturgical orders of the coronation of the Holy Roman Emperors in the west, a ritual of central importance since it was intended to remove the papacy still further from the authority of the emperors in the east by establishing a western emperor. Scrupulous care was taken to ensure that the ritual investment of the western emperor clearly designated his subordinate status to the pope. Following the coronation of the first western emperor, Charlemagne, the papacy introduced a new rite, the anointing of the emperor with holy oil, in order to symbolize the central theme of papal propaganda that imperial power 'descended' from God through the mediation of the papacy. At the next coronation (A.D. 823) yet another new feature was introduced — the giving of a sword to the emperor by the pope — to stress that the role of the emperor was to defend and protect the pope and carry out, through physical force if necessary, his will as a *filius-defensor*. And finally, to avoid any possible ambiguity and misunderstanding (such as the notion that the emperor was consecrated an autonomous priest-ruler), coronation ceremonies by the eleventh century utilized a liturgically inferior grade of oil, which was used to anoint the emperor, not on the head as before, but on his right arm and between his shoulder-blades. These and other innovations, involving the introduction of new symbols, gestures and prayer-texts, were graphic ways of expressing to an illiterate nobility through one ritual the complex theoretical ideas of papal hierocracy (Ullmann, 1970).

In addition to non-verbal techniques of communication, the ecclesiastical authorities actively proselytized their congregation through conventional methods. Priests reached in aggregate a mass audience through sermons delivered in vernacular languages; the legatine system reached all corners of Europe, and papal legates addressed vast crowds during their tours. The law administered through the ecclesiastical courts both embodied and mediated papal hierocratic themes. And from the thirteenth century onwards, the growing number of travelling friars, who often combined their evangelical role with reporting 'the news' to curious listeners, became an effective propaganda arm of the papacy.

The ecclesiastical hierarchy also decisively shaped élite culture in ways that supported the exercise of papal authority. Monasteries dominated book production until the development of university scriptoria from the thirteenth century onwards. As a result, texts supporting or expounding papal ideology were generally copied at the expense of texts that explicitly or implicitly challenged an ecclesiastical view of the universe. The clerical and monastic order also dominated the transmission of knowledge through formal education during the early and central middle ages. Until the eleventh century, education was confined largely to the clergy and its content was decisively shaped by the ecclesiastical hierarchy from at least the ninth century (Laistner, 1957; Leff, 1958). It was only in the twelfth century that there was a substantial increase in lay education and lay centres of learning, and even many of these centres came under direct or indirect ecclesiastical supervision (Cobban, 1969).

The nature of this cultural domination is illustrated by the steps taken to contain the threat posed by Aristotle. His teaching challenged the dominant perspective of a single political-religious society, an indivisible Church that underpinned papal hegemony. Perhaps for this reason, the principal works of Aristotle were allowed to 'disappear' during the early middle ages. When they were rediscovered, their study was banned at Paris University until such time as they had been 'purified'. And when William of Moerbeke finally translated Aristotle from Greek into Latin in the thirteenth century, he was obliged to use words like *politicus* (political) and *politia* (government) with which most of his colleagues were unfamiliar. Even to make a distinction between religious and political matters, between Church and State, a distinction that directly challenged a key premise of papal ideology, required the learning of new terms. The principal medium of communication between the cultured élite, the universal language of Christendom, was thus itself shaped and defined by the precepts of papal ideology (Ullmann, 1975).

It was thus not simply the power of religious faith that sustained papal authority. The success of the ecclesiastical hierarchy in shaping the dominant culture led, for a long time, to the general (but not total) exclusion of ideas and concepts that might undermine papal ascendancy. Scholars were induced to perceive and, therefore, to 'experience' reality in a way that sustained papal rule regardless of whether they were or were not pious members of the Church.

The papacy's cultural domination, even during the meridian of its power in the central middle ages, was admittedly far from complete. There is ample evidence of a lay culture expressing 'secular' values in song, dance, story-telling and poetry, existing independently of, but overlapping with, a more church-centred religious culture (Southern, 1959). The secular organization of medieval society also often functioned on very different principles from those of the eccesiastical order projected in papal propaganda (Bloch, 1961). And the papacy's direct control over the principal agency of mass communication, the Church, was even at the height of its power far from absolute in practice.

But although the papacy's hegemony was never total, its dual domination over the institutions of mental production and mass communication was nevertheless sufficient to enable it to gain increased authority and power at the expense of adversaries with apparently infinitely greater resources at their disposal. This process of aggrandisement can be briefly illustrated by perhaps the best-known confrontation of the middle ages. In 1075, Pope Gregory VII brought to a head the papal assault on lay control over ecclesiastical appointments by banning lay investiture (i.e. the ritual symbolizing lay conferment of ecclesiastical offices). This was followed by public pronouncements, sermons and pamphlets in a sustained propaganda war. The German monarch, Henry IV, found to his cost that this ideological assault was highly effective, because it drew upon a consensus of opinion that had been built up over the centuries through constant reiteration of ecclesiastical propaganda. When he was excommunicated, temporarily deposed, and the oaths of allegiance made to him by his vassals suspended by the pope, his position became increasingly perilous. His itinerant court did not possess the historical records that would have been needed to challenge effectively the papacy's claim to sovereignty over the Church, and he had no access to an alternative, literate tradition of thought that would have legitimized his authority as ruler independent of the Church. He was king by the grace of God, and this grace had been withdrawn by God's supreme agent. His vassals began to defect with, as Brooke (1964) put it, 'the gates of hell clanging about their ears', though in some cases defections were clearly caused by more opportunistic motives. At the Diet of Tribur, the German princes formally declared that Henry IV would forfeit his throne unless he secured absolution from the pope. The most powerful ruler in the west, who had merely sought to maintain the practice of lay investiture sanctioned by custom for centuries, was forced to go to Italy as a penitent to seek the pope's absolution. While the papal cause subsequently suffered a number of reverses, the German monarchy finally abandoned lay investiture of the clergy after the Concordat of Worms in 1122 (Davies, 1957; Brooke, 1964; Ullmann, 1970 and 1977).

In short, the rise of papal government in the early and central middle ages was based ultimately on the papacy's successful manipulation of élite and mass media to transmit not merely its claims to church leadership but an ideological perspective of the world that legitimized its domination of Christendom. It was only when the papacy's domination of the élite centres of knowledge and mass communications was successfully challenged in the later middle ages that the papacy's ideological ascendancy was broken[8]. With the loss of its ideological control, the papacy's power collapsed. The issuing of excommunications which had brought the most powerful European monarch literally to his knees in 1077 was not sufficient even to insure the payment of papal taxes by the fifteenth century.

*   *   *

Just as the extension of the Christian Church throughout Europe in the early middle ages laid the foundation of papal power, so the development of new media of communication has created new power groups. Perhaps the most notorious of these in British media history have been the press barons. Their rise is of interest, however, as much for the contrast as for the comparison it affords to the rise of the papacy.

In the eighteenth century, press proprietors were, for the most part, unimportant and far from respectable tradesmen. The practice of showing advance copy of scurrilous stories to their victims in order to extract a fee for suppressing their publication, lowered the reputation of those associated with the press generally. In 1777, for instance, it was said of William Dodd, a preacher charged with forgery, almost as corroboration of the charge, that he had 'descended so low as to become the editor of a newspaper' (quoted in Smith, 1978, p. 165). Apart from exceptional proprietors like James Perry, the wealthy owner of the largest-circulation Whig daily in the late eighteenth century, owners of newspapers were not admitted into polite society (Christie, 1970). Even writing articles for the press was judged by aristocratic politicians to be, in Lord Brougham's phrase, 'dirty work' (quoted in Asquith, 1976, p. 277). The low prestige of press proprietors was also a reflection of their lack of independent political influence. Few papers sold more than 1000 copies before 1800, and many papers were heavily dependent upon political patronage in the form of subsidies, sinecures, politically tied advertising and information handouts.

During the nineteenth century the prestige and influence of press proprietors increased as a consequence of the growing circulations they commanded and an increased measure of political autonomy. Leading proprietors and editors were assiduously cultivated by government ministers (Anon, 1935 and 1939; Hindle, 1937) and a growing number of them entered parliament. Their increased political weight was reflected in the substantial legal immunities awarded to the press during the period 1868-88 (Lee, 1976). At the same time, the role of the press was widely reinterpreted as that of an independent fourth estate in order, as Boyce (1978) has argued, to establish for newspapers a 'claim for a recognized and respectable place in the British political system'.

But it was only when newspapers acquired mass circulations that the position of proprietors underwent a fundamental change. *Lloyd's Weekly* was the first Sunday paper to gain a million circulation in 1896, while the *Daily Mail* was the first daily to cross this threshold at the turn of the century. By 1920, the national Sunday press had an aggregate circulation of 13.5 million, with a mass working-class as well as middle-class following.

National dailies subsequently gained a mass readership amongst the working class, growing from 5.4 million to 10.6 million between 1920 and 1939 (Kaldor and Silverman, 1948). The growth of the press as a mass medium was accompanied by increased concentration of ownership, giving leading press magnates ultimate control over vast aggregate circulations. Three men — Rothermere, Beaverbrook and Kemsley — controlled in 1937, for instance, 45 per cent of national daily circulation and 51 per cent of provincial morning circulation, with an aggregate readership (including their evening papers) of over 15 million people[9].

This domination over the principal agency of political communication transformed the social standing of press proprietors. Men whose occupations would have caused them to have been shunned by aristocratic politicians in an earlier age as mere tradesmen were showered with titles and honours. As Northcliffe's sister Geraldine wrote facetiously in 1918, 'in view of the paper shortage, I think the family ought to issue printed forms like Field Service postcards, viz: Many congratulations on you being made Archbishop of Canterbury/Pope/Duke/Viscount/Knight, etc.' (quoted in Ferris, 1971, p. 215). Her facetiousness had a point to it: five of her brothers were given between them two viscountcies, one barony and two baronetcies. Indeed, Viscount Rothermere was singled out for an even greater honour. After campaigning vigorously in his papers for the return of lost territories to Hungary, he was seriously asked by leading Hungarian monarchists whether he would fill the vacant throne of St Stephen as King of Hungary. He contented himself with an address of gratitude signed by one and a quarter million Hungarians (a sixth of the population).

The tsars of the new media also exercised real power. Northcliffe's campaign against the shortage of shells on the Western Front in 1915 reinforced mounting opposition to Asquith, and contributed to the formation of the coalition government under Lloyd George in 1916. Their newspaper fiefdoms helped them to gain high political office, as in the case of Rothermere (in charge of the Air Ministry 1917-18), Northcliffe (Director of Propaganda in Enemy Territories, 1918-19) and Beaverbrook (Minister of State and Production 1941-2, amongst other posts). They also exercised a more intangible but nonetheless important influence in sustaining the dominant political consensus between the wars, and in mobilizing conservative forces in opposition to radical change (Curran and Seaton, 1981).

But the direct influence exercised through their papers was none the less severely circumscribed. When pitted against entrenched political power, the major campaigns initiated by the press barons were relative failures. Rothermere's campaign against 'squandermania' after World War I met with only limited success, and his attempt to force the coalition government's hand by backing anti-waste candidates in parliamentary by-elections failed, despite three notable successes. The Empire Free Trade campaign promoted by both Beaverbrook and Rothermere also failed through lack of sufficient Tory party support, and their subsequent attempt to force through a change of policy by launching the United Empire Party was largely, though not entirely, unsuccessful (Taylor, 1972). These and other failures underlined the fact that the mass audiences reached daily by the press barons had an independent mind of their own. A more realistic appraisal of the power exercised by press magnates reduced their influence on internal politics within the Conservative party. When Rothermere's demand to be informed of at least eight or ten Cabinet ministers in Baldwin's next ministry as a condition of his continued support was repudiated by Baldwin in a famous speech as 'a preposterous and insolent demand' in 1931, the limitations of press power were publicly proclaimed. The point was rammed home a few weeks later when the official Conservative candidate loyal to Baldwin defeated an independent conservative backed by both Rothermere and Beaverbrook in the celebrated St. George's Westminster by-election. The press magnates' ability to address a mass following, based on a cash nexus, proved no match for a party machine, manned only by a relatively small number of activists but able to invoke deeply-held and stable political loyalties.

The contrast between the extensive secular power exercised by the papacy in the central middle ages and the more limited influence of the press barons reflects a number of more important differences. The papacy sought to exercise a universal sovereignty, whereas the ambitions of the press magnates were more modest. The papacy developed a powerful ideological programme that legitimized its claim to divine-right monarchy: the press barons articulated a more defensive 'fourth estate' ideology that sought merely to legitimize their place within the constitution (for example, Northcliffe, 1922; Beaverbrook, 1925). The papacy successfully dominated for a time all the principal institutions of ideological production and imposed a construction of reality that legitimized its supremacy. In contrast, the press barons merely amplified systems of representation furnished by others (politicians, civil servants, judges, the armed forces and so on) that legitimized a power structure of which they were only a constituent element. Furthermore, they were unable to impose even a uniform inflexion of these dominant systems of representation. Their control over the press itself was incomplete; they did not always share the same political objectives; and they had little influence over other agencies of mass communication — books, films, radio, and later television. And by comparison with the papacy, they were faced with a much more unified power-bloc, offering few opportunities for them to play off rival factions in order to build up their own power.

THE DESTABILIZATION OF POWER STRUGGLES

The rise of a new élite, linked to the development of new communications, has tended to destabilize the power structure by generating or exacerbating tensions and rivalries within it. This will be illustrated by examining the conflicts exacerbated by the papacy in the middle ages and by the effect of the modern mass media on the development of the British political system.

The extension of the Catholic Church throughout Europe created, in one sense, a new element of instability in medieval society. As we have seen, the papacy and the ecclesiastical hierarchy sought to regulate social knowledge through its control over medieval communications in order to appropriate some of the power and authority exercised by the traditional leaders of feudal society. This process of aggrandisement was made more disruptive by the fact that the papacy possessed the moral authority to undermine its opponents, without possessing the military means to conquer them. Consequently, the papacy was forced to rely upon others to take up arms on its behalf, and this sometimes led to a positive incitement of fissiparous elements opposed to the nation-building, centralizing strategies of medieval monarchies. Thus, the papacy played a leading part in deliberately provoking feudatories to oppose the German monarchy during the long drawn-out conflict over control of ecclesiastical appointments, thereby contributing to the growing instability of Germany and North Italy in the eleventh and twelfth centuries.

The development of new communications under ecclesiastical control had a destabilizing impact in another, more indirect way. The ecclesiastical hierarchy exploited its control over medieval media to build up monarchical power, which provoked a feudal reaction throughout medieval Europe. Although the initiative often came from medieval rulers, they found in the clergy willing and skilled agents in the ideological reconstruction of their authority, partly because the traditional feudal conception of kingship, and the indigenous northern European traditions from which it derived, constituted a powerful negation of the ideology and new social order which the ecclesiastical authorities sought to impose. According to papal ideology, you will recall, all power *descended* from God and was institutionalized in the form of law-giving by divinely appointed monarchies under the jurisdiction of the papal emperor with absolute authority over the children of God. But according to indigenous feudal tradition, all power *ascended* from below: the monarch was not an absolute ruler, but the first amongst equals bound by the reciprocal obligations of the feudal contract and constrained by natural law enshrined in custom. The early medieval institution of the monarchy was thus a functioning denial of the impersonal ecclesiastical order which the papacy proclaimed, the embodiment of an older, oral ideological tradition that directly challenged the premises of papal ideology.

The ecclesiastical hierarchy sought to refashion the institution of the monarchy through learned tracts, sermons, official pronouncements, liturgical symbolism and ritual. Thus, numerous innovations were made in royal coronation ceremonies, for instance, during the period A.D. 400-1300, in an attempt to suppress the traditional feudal conception of kingship and establish in its place a divine-right monarchy whose power derived through the mediation of the church (Kantorowicz, 1957; Ullmann, 1969, 1975 and 1978). The person of the monarch was deliberately invested with sacred

magic properties, with the result that throughout much of Europe the superstition developed that kings could cure scrofula merely by touching its
victims. Even armed resistance to the king, unless he was deposed by the
Church, was defined by clergy as an act of sacrilege against the Lord's
anointed. In addition to reinterpreting the legitimacy of the monarchy, the
clergy also played a central role in developing court administrations as
effective agencies of authority.

This concerted attempt to transform the position of medieval monarchs
in accordance with the interests and ideology of the ecclesiastical order
posed a major threat to established interests within the hierarchy of power.
It advanced royal authority at the expense of aristocratic power. It implied,
moreover, a fundamental change in the relationship of the monarch to his
feudatories, from that of feudal chieftain with limited powers to that of
divine-right monarch with absolute powers accountable only to God and
his appointed agents. Inevitably this attempt to alter the distribution of
power led to fierce armed resistance, of which the successful baronial revolt
against King John of England in the early thirteenth century was but one
example (Ullmann, 1978)[10].

*   *   *

The rise of professional communicators in modern Britain has been, by
comparison, less dislocative, largely because professional communicators
have more readily accepted a subaltern role than their priestly predecessors.
Media professionals interpret the political system in a relatively passive way
without seeking fundamentally to alter the power-structure of society. An
increasing disjunction has occurred, however, between the British media
and the British political system, with potentially disruptive consequences.

Ironically, the development of the press in Victorian Britain played an
important part in the creation of the modern party system. During the
second half of the nineteenth century, the press forged close ties with the
parliamentary parties and tended to be highly partisan in its political
coverage. The expansion of this press helped to convert what had been, in
effect, aristocratic factions in Parliament into political movements with a
mass following (Vincent, 1972; Lee, 1976).

During the course of the twentieth century, the character of the British
press began to change. An increasing number of newspapers became more
independent of the major political parties[11]. This resulted in papers
providing a more bi-partisan coverage of politics, particularly during the
postwar period (Seymour-Ure, 1977). The popular press also became progressively depoliticized, with some national papers more than halving their
coverage of public affairs as a proportion of editorial space during the last
fifty years (Curran, Douglas and Whannel, 1980). These changes altered the
relationship of newspapers to their readers. By 1979, over a third of
national daily-paper readers bought papers with political allegiances
different from their own. Even newspaper readers buying papers with the
same political affiliation as their own were exposed in these papers to more
'straight' reports of what their political opponents had said and done. And

increasingly the newspaper reading public, as a whole, consumed entertainment rather than public affairs content in the press. While the tradition of a politically affiliated, partisan press reaching a partisan audience has certainly not disappeared, all these changes have weakened the ability of the major political parties to maintain their supporters' loyalty through the press.

The rise of broadcasting has further weakened the position of the political parties. The emergence of television as the principal medium of political communication has resulted in a shift away from consumption of a medium with a tradition of partisanship to a medium which is required to be politically balanced and impartial. This trend has been particularly pronounced during the last two decades. There has been a very rapid growth of public affairs coverage in TV, with a three-fold increase on BBC TV between 1962 and 1974. And while public affairs items in the press only obtained a below-average readership (both before and after the introduction of TV), TV news programmes have secured above-average audiences. More people have thus been exposed to more bi-partisan communications.

The progressive detachment of the mass media from the party system has been confounded by the mutual rivalry between professional politicians and professional communicators. Both groups have competing claims to legitimacy: they both claim to represent the public and serve the public interest. As Gurevitch and Blumler (1977) point out, they are, to some extent, rivals who have different definitions of their roles which produce mutual tension and conflict. This tension is reflected in media portrayals of party politics which are, at times, not so much bi-partisan as anti-partisan. This anti-partisan perspective is typified by this excerpt from a *Sunday Times* editorial:

Mr. Callaghan condemns the income tax cuts forced on the government by the Tories and other opposition parties as looking after the rich and striking a blow at the family budget.... The Prime Minister is a politician and is therefore, no doubt, entitled under the rules of the game to play politics. But a newspaper is equally entitled to remind readers that politics is what he is playing. We must not be tempted by rhetoric to take Ministers' words at face value, and forget what they have said in the past. What the Conservatives have done for the higher tax-payers is precisely what the Government itself would do if it had the political nerve — or if its party would let it. (*Sunday Times*, 14 May 1978)

This editorial makes unusually explicit some of the assumptions that underpin the rhetoric of media anti-partisanship. Prime Ministers 'play politics' whereas The *Sunday Times* is disinterested. Politicians dissemble and lie while The *Sunday Times* fearlessly speaks its mind. Politicians are encumbered by vested interests and party ties, whereas The *Sunday Times* is concerned only with the public interest — even when discussing tax cuts for affluent *Sunday Times* journalists and readers.

Anti-partisanship is present not only in explicit form in political commentary. It is also implicit in the interpretative frameworks within which a good deal of current affairs coverage is set in both the press and broadcasting media. In particular, there is a tendency for politics to be defined in pragmatic, technocratic terms as a process of management and problem-solving; for political conflict to be de-contextualized from the political and economic struggles that underlie it; even, in some cases, for genuine conflicts over principle or of class interest to be represented as mere clashes of personality. Such representations of politics inevitably detract from political loyalties based on class affiliations and political principle.

This anti-partisan bias of the media is the consequence of a number of converging influences[12]. Perhaps the most important of these is a rational-istic, anti-partisan political tradition that has long been particularly pervasive amongst the professional middle class. As Reith, the founder of the BBC (and former engineer) wrote, for instance, in his diary: 'I reflect sometimes on "politics". The whole horrid technique should be abolished. Government of a country is a matter of policy and proper administration, in other words efficiency' (Reith, 11 October 1932). The view that rational, non-party criteria interpreted by disinterested professionals should determine government has a natural attraction: it legitimizes the claim of the professional middle class to stand above sectional interest, to define the public interest, to speak on behalf of us all. A technocratic perspective of politics has thus come to be expressed through the media partly because it is an expression of a more generalized ideology widely diffused within the intermediate strata, of which professional communicators are a part, which legitimizes the prestige, power and status accorded to the professions.

The detachment of the media from the political parties has had only a partially destabilizing effect on the political system. The mass media continue to provide positive support for the principles of representative democracy; they confer legitimacy on the political parties by giving pro-minence to the parliamentary and party political process; and the publicity they give to elections is of crucial importance in assisting the political parties to mobilize their supporters to the polls. But the commercialization of the press, the rise of TV as a bi-partisan political medium of communica-tion, and the anti-partisan bias that characterizes some media political coverage, have all contributed to the marked decline of party loyalties and the increase in electoral volatility during the last two decades[13]. In eroding popular support for the political parties, the media are eroding the basis of Britain's stable political system during the period of mass democracy[14].

THE DISPLACEMENT OF MEDIATING AGENCIES

The introduction of new techniques of mass communication has tended to undermine the prestige and influence of established mediating organizations and groups. By providing new channels of communication, by-passing established mediating agencies, new media have also posed a serious threat to the stable, hierarchical control of social knowledge. The best illustration of this process of displacement, and attendant social dislocation, is provided by the rise of the book in late medieval and early modern Europe.

From the thirteenth century onwards, paper rapidly displaced parchment as the principal raw material of books, thereby making the preparation of manuscripts cheaper, simpler and faster. This important innovation was accompanied by a massive increase in the number of people (mostly women) engaged in the copying of books, with the development of commercial and university scriptoria, and by the establishment of a fully organized international book trade, in the later middle ages. The introduction of printing with moveable metal type for commercial purposes in 1450 was thus the culmination, rather than the beginning, of a major expansion of a book-based culture. Print resulted, however, in an enormous gain in productivity, with output *per capita* engaged in book production rising by well over a hundred-fold, to judge from estimates provided by Eisenstein (1968). Print also led to a sharp reduction in costs, so that the printed works of Luther, for instance, could be purchased in England for 4d or 6d a copy in 1520 — the equivalent of about a day's wage for a craftsman. This increase in output and fall in costs, combined with rising rates of literacy, resulted in a spectacular increase in book consumption. About twenty million books were produced in Europe between 1450 and 1500, rising sharply thereafter (Febvre and Martin, 1976).

This expansion of book production resulted in the mass dissemination of religious texts, and in particular Bibles in vernacular languages. There were, for example, nineteen editions of the Bible in High German before Luther, and Luther's own translation of the Bible was published in whole or in part in no less than 430 editions between 1522 and 1546. This diffusion of the Bible undermined the monopolistic position of the clergy as agents of religious communication, and threatened their authority as mediators of religious knowledge by providing direct access to an alternative, more authoritative source of religious teaching — that of Christ as reported in the scriptures. As John Hobbes wrote disapprovingly in the seventeenth century: 'every man, nay, every boy and wench that could read English thought they spoke with God Almighty, and understood what He said' (quoted in Hill, 1974, p. 154).

It was mainly in order to maintain priestly, hierarchical control over religious knowledge that determined attempts were made to restrict public access to the Bible. The Catholic Church proscribed Bibles printed in languages that people could understand. The English Church under Henry VIII tried a more discriminating approach. Bible-reading was banned in 1543 among the lower orders, namely 'women, apprentices and husbandmen' (Bennett, 1952).

In a less immediately apparent but more important way, the rise of the book undermined the authority of the clergy by diminishing their intermediary role. The prestige and influence of the Catholic clergy (and of the Catholic Church as an institution) derived from their special status as the mediators of divine power. This found concrete and dramatic expression in a variety of rituals symbolizing the role of the clergy in transmitting — and even coercing — supernatural power through their intercession. The development of a book-based culture encouraged a new orientation in which the word of God mediated through print was placed at the centre of religion. This new approach tended to reject the elaborate ritualism and expressive iconography of pre-literate forms of religious communication in which the priest was the principal actor. It frequently repudiated also the efficacy of the rites administered by the priest, thereby diminishing his status as a dispenser of grace. Indeed, in its more extreme form, it fostered an individualistic, private approach to religion that gave precedence to the study of the Bible and private prayer at the expense of the corporate organization of religion, based on collective rituals administered by a professional priesthood. Print thus helped to displace the mediating and intercessionary role of the clergy, and even of the Church itself, by providing a new channel of communication linking Christians to their God.

The development of a lay scribal and print culture also undermined the ideological ascendancy of the Church. The growth of commercial scriptoria and subsequently commercial printing enterprises made it more difficult for the ecclesiastical authorities, who had previously directly controlled the means of book production, to exercise effective censorship. The failure of the Church to maintain its domination over centres of learning in the later middle ages also weakened its grip on the content of élite culture. Through the medium of the written and printed word (as well as in a sense through changing styles of representation in Renaissance art), an anthropomorphic view of the world that stressed man's innate capacity to regulate his environment was expressed that directly confronted the more traditional theocentric view of a divinely ordained and ordered universe that underpinned papal imperialism. Developments in political thought — most notably the modern distinction between Church and State and a belief in the legitimacy of state power as being derived from people rather than from God — was also mediated through books to a larger élite audience, undermining the premises that sustained papal ascendancy (Wilks, 1963; Ullmann, 1977).

The rise of the book, pamphlet and flysheet also to some extent undermined the authority of the Church leadership by expanding the boundaries of time and space: publications increased knowledge of early Church history in which Rome had played an inconspicuous part, and spread information about the greed and corruption of the Renaissance papacy which, though probably no worse than that of the papacy in the tenth and early eleventh centuries, became more widely known. In a more general sense, the rise of the manuscript and subsequently of the printed book also fostered the development of an alternative culture. Although the bulk of scribal and early print output was in Latin and religious in content, the production and dissemination of vernacular texts helped to foster a parallel secular culture based on national languages and dialects, drawing upon indigenous cultural traditions. The ecclesiastical hierarchy in late medieval Europe sought to contain the threat of this 'new learning' through proscriptions and censorship, direct patronage and the creation of what

Southern (1970) calls 'a separate university system' through the Franciscan and Dominican orders. It was unable, however, to neutralize the dislocating influence of new techniques of communication that by-passed the established information order of the Catholic Church.

Indeed, the rise of the book not only subverted the authority of the Church, but also acted as a directly centrifugal force within it. It polarized the Catholic congregation between literate and pre-literate definitions of religious experience and positively fostered heresy. The close connection between Bible-reading and heretical belief has often been observed by historians (for example, Dickens, 1964 and Thomson, 1965). Just why this should have been the case is less than clear without reference to modern media research. This shows that people tend to read, understand and recall elements within a communication selectively, in ways that accord with their prior disposition (see, for example, Cooper and Jahoda, 1947; Hovland, Janis and Kelley, 1953; Klapper, 1966). The widely different responses to the Bible, expressed in different forms of heresy, can be partly explained by the divergent traditions of late medieval and early modern Europe. To see the Bible as 'producing' heresy is somewhat misleading: rather, exposure to the Bible caused prior differences within Christendom, reflecting the different social backgrounds, national traditions and religious orientations of the new Bible public, to be expressed in the form of divergent religious interpretations. Thus, the dissemination of the Bible did not so much create differences within the Catholic Church as cause them to be expressed in the form of differences over doctrine.

Other contingent factors probably reinforced the schismatic impact of vernacular Bibles. Centuries of exegetical analysis and interpretation had produced Catholic doctrines lacking a clear scriptural basis. The Bible is an inherently equivocal text which lends itself to very different interpretations based upon an apparently literal understanding of different parts of it. The failure of the ecclesiastical authorities to prepare the ground adequately for the reception of the Bible also limited their ability to defuse its divisive impact. While the research of historians like Heath (1969) and Elton (1975) clearly calls into question traditional conceptions of a 'corrupt' pre-Reformation Church, there can be no doubt that inadequate, if improved, clerical training and the continuing ritualistic formalism of the late medieval Church prevented effective ecclesiastical supervision of lay responses to the Bible.

The causes of the rise of Protestantism are exceedingly complex, and are only partly to do with religion. But, at one level at least, Protestantism can be viewed as a synthesis of the different disruptive tendencies set in motion by a new technique of mass communication. Protestantism was a movement that was inspired, in part, by access to an alternative source of religious doctrine, the Bible, mediated through print, that competed with hierarchically mediated orthodoxy; it took the form of a fundamentalist reconstruction of Christian dogma based on a literal interpretation of the scriptures; it was a book-centred definition of religious experience that rejected many of the pre-literate, ritualistic forms of religious communication and the central intermediary role of the Catholic priesthood; it was a revolt against papal sovereignty, which the printed word had helped to foster by contributing to the decline of the papacy's prestige and ideological ascendancy; and, in some ways, Protestantism was also the expression of a growing secularism and nationalism that the growth of a lay scribal and print culture had helped to promote.

That Protestantism was, in some respects the product of print is underlined by the way in which Protestant churches sought quite deliberately to supplant traditional, pre-literate modes of religious communication with a new system of communication based on the printed word. Church murals were whitewashed over, church sculptures were destroyed, stained glass was smashed and replaced with pane glass, relics were destroyed, the images of saints were even given to children as toys. Sacramental rites were also suppressed, church ritual was simplified, and the sacred magical role of the priest was de-mystified with the abandonment of celibacy. Bibliolatry took its place with the mass production of the Bible, the training of pastors as biblical experts and a sustained literacy drive aimed at enabling congregations to understand God's teachings through the printed word.

In contrast, the Counter-Reformation in the late sixteenth century resulted in a determined counter-offensive in Catholic countries aimed at containing the disruptive impact of print. The introduction of the *Index*, the proscription not only of vernacular Bibles but also of many religious best-selling commentaries, and the relative neglect of primary education in Catholic countries, all served to reinforce the central role of ritual and iconography in the Catholic Church and to reassert hierarchical control over religious knowledge by the ecclesiastical authorities. The Catholic revival served also to entrench the authority of the priest since, at its deepest psychological level, Tridentine Catholicism was an image-based rather than a word-based experience in which the role of the priest as the administrator of sacred rites was more important than the printed word of God.

The Anglican Church established by the Elizabethan Settlement was, by contrast, a compromise between Catholicism and Protestantism. Its doctrinal evasions were designed to reconcile the sharp divisions over doctrine which a long drawn-out war conducted in print had helped to exacerbate (Davies, 1976); and its liturgy represented an accommodation between the traditional iconography of Catholicism and the bibliolatry of Protestantism (Thomas, 1973). It neither sought to entrench print at the centre of religion nor to exclude it, but merely to contain its social dislocation[15].

MEDIA AND CLASS CONFLICT

There is substantial agreement amongst sociologists writing from different ideological perspectives that the mass media legitimize the social systems of which they are a part (Lazarsfeld and Merton, 1948; Janowitz, 1952; Breed,

1964; Miliband, 1973; Tuchman, 1978; etc.). This consensus is based upon the study of the mass media during a period when control of the mass media has been closely integrated into the power structure of most developed industrial societies.

Control of the media has not always been so successfully integrated into the power structure, as will be illustrated by the rise of the commercial press and subsequent development of a radical working-class press in Britain during the eighteenth and nineteenth centuries. Both developments illustrate the disruptive consequences that follow upon mass media evolving in opposition to the dominant social order[16].

During the early eighteenth century, the middle class in Britain was largely excluded from the institutionalized political process by the limited franchise which gave to the great landed families effective control over small and unrepresentative constituencies. The middle class was also, to some extent, excluded from the central bureaucracy and spoils of office by the patronage system of the dominant landed class who controlled the state. It was denied even the opportunity to participate in a meaningful way in national politics (and therefore to advance its interests) by the consensual political values of the landed élite that discouraged political participation. Central to this consensus was the concept of 'virtual representation' by which politicians drawn from the landed élite were said to represent the public by virtue of their independence and tradition of public service, even though they were not directly elected by the people. Great stress was laid also on the independent, deliberative role of the parliamentarian and the complexity of statecraft in a way that discouraged popular participation in the political process. As Burke put it, the parliamentarian is like 'a physician (who) does not take his remedy from the ravings of the patient' (quoted in Brewer, 1976, p. 237).

Regulation of the press was one means by which aristocratic political ascendancy was maintained. Newspapers were subject to strict legal controls — the law of seditious libel, which was used to prevent criticism of the political system, general warrants issued at the discretion of the authorities against people suspected of committing a seditious libel, and a legal ban on the reporting of parliament. In addition, taxes on newspapers, advertisements and paper were introduced in 1712 mainly in order to increase the price of newspapers and thereby restrict their circulation. Successive administrations also sought to manage the political press by offering secret service subsidies, official advertising and exclusive information to newspapers in return for editorial services rendered to the government as well as giving rewards and sinecures to sympathetic journalists. Opposition groups in parliament countered with similar tactics in order to sustain an opposition press. Consequently, the political press (consisting largely of London papers) was completely dominated by the landed élite which controlled both government and parliament.

Rising levels of press taxation were frustrated, however, by economic growth which created a growing middle-class public for newspapers and a rising volume of advertising which aided its development. The number of local provincial newspapers increased from 22 to about 50 titles between 1714 and 1782 (Cranfield, 1962; Read, 1961). The provincial press also increased its coverage of public affairs, assisted by the improvement in local and postal communications and the increase in the number of metropolitan papers from which it shamelessly plagiarised material. This expansion of a more politicized, regional press fostered the development of a middle-class political culture, centred on the clubs, political societies and coffee-houses of provincial England. In promoting a political awareness amongst its readers, the emergent commercial press helped to lay the foundations for the subsequent middle-class assault on the aristocratic order.

The commercial press in the provinces both catered for and was controlled by the commercial middle class. The majority of newspaper proprietors were merchants, tradesmen, printers or booksellers — people drawn precisely from the class that was politically excluded. Journalists came from more varied backgrounds, but would seem to have been drawn primarily from the petit-bourgeoisie (Cranfield, 1962 and 1977; Rogers, 1972). It was only a matter of time before a section of the commercial press adopted a more critical stance towards the landed élite, if only to attract a larger circulation amongst the expanding middle-class audience.

The person who first successfully mobilized the commercial press was, as Brewer (1976) shows, John Wilkes, who transformed a fairly commonplace occurrence — his imprisonment by general warrant for writing an article attacking the government — into a major political issue. His subsequent exclusion from the Commons, despite repeated re-elections, became a national scandal; and his calculated act of defiance as a magistrate in freeing printers who had published reports of parliament, brought the mobs out into the streets of London in a mass action of support that clearly created amongst the landed aristocracy in parliament something bordering on panic (Rudé, 1962). As Burke commented sardonically (his frantic private notes at the time belie his detachment), MPs responded to the mobs outside parliament like mice consulting on what to do with the cat that tormented them.

The controversies surrounding John Wilkes were the first notable occasions in which the newspaper press defined the central issues on the political agenda in active defiance of the consensus amongst the landed oligarchy in parliament. It was also the first important occasion in which the newspaper press conferred status upon and brought into public prominence a champion of bourgeois interests, enabling him to appeal over the heads of the landed élite in parliament to the disenfranchised constituency that lay outside. The coverage given to Wilkes's campaigns in the commercial press also demonstrated the power of the emergent press (reinforced by printed propaganda) to mobilize discontent on a national scale that was unprecedented in eighteenth-century England: Wilkes received not only the backing of the London mobs, but also the support, manifested in demonstrations, marches and petitions, of people all over the country from Berwick-on-Tweed to Falmouth. Largely as a result of popular pressure, general warrants were declared illegal in 1765 and the ban on the reporting of parliament was effectively abandoned in 1771. The press became increasingly free to subject parliamentary proceedings and government to public scrutiny, and to initiate debate outside the parameter of parliamentary consensus. The politics of oligarchy were at an end: Wilkes inaugurated a new era of political participation sustained by an increasingly independent commercial press.

The 1760s were a watershed in another sense. The commercial press began for the first time to challenge the legitimacy of the political system. Its critique was cautious and indirect at first, taking the form of extensive coverage of American criticism of British imperialism. But the slogan of 'no taxation without representation' used to mobilize resistance in America to the stamp duty was soon linked to the British context. Government was corrupt, incompetent and oppressive, it was argued in the more radical commercial papers, because it was unrepresentative. This led in turn to demands for extension of the franchise, and the formation of an extra-parliamentary pressure group for electoral reform which gained extensive publicity in some commercial papers.

The commercial press expanded steadily during the late Georgian and early Victorian period. Between 1781 and 1851 the number of newspapers increased from about 76 to 563; their aggregate annual sales rose from 14 million in 1780 to 85 million in 1851 (Asquith, 1978). This expansion accelerated with the lifting of press taxation between 1853 and 1861.

Commercial newspapers also became increasingly independent. The ability of governments to control the press through the law was limited by two important reforms. In 1792, the seditious libel law was weakened by Fox's Libel Act which made juries the judges of libel suits. Libel law was further modified by Lord Campbell's Libel Act of 1843, which made the statement of truth in the public interest a legitimate defence against the charge of criminal libel. No less important, there was a spectacular increase in advertising expenditure on the press (reflected, for instance, in a five-fold increase in the advertising revenue of the principal London dailies between 1780 and 1820) which profoundly influenced the character of the commercial press. Increased advertising largely financed the development of independent news-gathering resources that rendered newspapers less dependent upon official information; it also made it possible for more newspapers to employ full-time rather than freelance journalists, thereby reducing the number of casually employed and frequently venal reporters; and, above all, it encouraged a more independent attitude amongst proprietors by making it more lucrative to maximize advertising through increasing circulation than to appeal to government and opposition for political subsidies. The growth of advertising thus provided a material base that encouraged greater independence from aristocratic influence and patronage, whether mediated by governments or by opposition factions in parliament (Aspinall, 1949; Christie, 1970; Asquith, 1975, 1976 and 1978; Cranfield, 1977[17]).

A section of this expanding commercial press fostered a positive class identity amongst its readers by characterizing 'the middle classes' as the economic and moral backbone of England. 'Never in any country beneath the sun', declared the *Leeds Mercury* in 1821, 'was an order of men more estimable and valuable, more praised and praiseworthy than the middle class of society in England' (quoted in Read, 1961, p. 119). The *Mercury*'s assessment was modest by comparison with those that appeared in other middle-class publications of the same period. James Mill in the *Westminster Review*, for instance, hailed the middle class in 1826 'as the glory of England; as that which alone has given our eminence among nations; as that portion of our people to whom every thing that is good among us may with certainty be traced' (quoted in Perkin, 1969, p. 230). By celebrating the virtues of the middle class, and in some cases by attacking the traditional leaders of society as parasitic, decadent and unproductive, commercial newspapers helped to coalesce disparate groups within the middle class by reinforcing a growing consciousness of class.

The commercial reform press contributed, moreover, in a very direct way to advancing middle-class interests and influence. The full enfranchisement of the middle class during the 1830s, the repeal of the Corn Law and the decontrol of trade during the 1840s and 1850s, and the initial reforms of the civil service, universities and armed forces during the 1850s and 1860s, transformed the position of the middle class in Britain. These gains were the culmination of pressure-group campaigns in which the reform press played a central part by generating publicity for reform, raising (in some cases) finance for reform organizations, and gaining converts by representing reform as the universally valid and shared interest of all.

The assault of the reform press on the *ancien régime* in Britain had disruptive consequences in the short term. Some of the campaigns that the reform press backed — from 'Wilkes and Liberty' in the 1750s to electoral reform in the 1830s — came close to inciting popular armed resistance to aristocratic rule. But viewed from a long-term perspective, the rise of the commercial press represented an integrative rather than dislocative influence. It acted as an early-warning system in an increasingly unstable society, alerting aristocratic politicians to the need for accommodation and change in order to preserve the social order.

The commercial press also helped to maintain the initially fragile alliance between the aristocracy and bourgeoisie that developed from the 1830s by providing an internal channel of communication within the new class coalition. Although the aristocracy dominated parliamentary politics until late into the nineteenth century, parliament nevertheless enacted many of the demands of the industrial and professional middle class. The commercial press provided an important institutional means by which middle-class opinion was organized and pressure effectively mounted to ensure that these demands were met, thereby averting a renewed confrontation. The commercial press also furnished a moral framework that legitimized the British capitalist system during a dislocative phase of its development.

Indeed, with the building of mass circulations during the second half of the nineteenth century, commercial newspapers and magazines came to play an increasingly significant role in engineering consent for the social system within the working class.

*   *   *

The development during the early nineteenth century of a militant press, financed from within the working class, posed a more serious threat to the social order. Governments largely abandoned attempts to regulate the radical press through seditious libel law by the mid 1830s because they found that libel prosecutions were often counter-productive. They relied instead upon the so-called security system (requiring publishers to place financial bonds with the authorities) in an attempt to exclude 'pauper' ownership of the press, and press taxes designed to price papers beyond the pockets of working-class consumers. The objectives of these fiscal controls were frustrated, however, by determined resistance. During the early 1830s, radical publishers successfully evaded both the security system and press taxes. This was followed in the next two decades by the organized pooling of financial resources by working people in order to launch and also to purchase newspapers which the authorities sought to exclude from them. People clubbed together on an *ad hoc* basis to buy newspapers, exerted pressure on taverns to purchase radical papers, and bought left papers through branches of political and industrial organizations. As a result of this collective action, leading radical newspapers gained circulations far larger than those of their respectable rivals throughout most of the period 1815-55.

The expansion of this radical press played an important part in the cultural reorganization and political mobilization of the working class during the first half of the nineteenth century. Radical newspapers linked together different elements of the working-class movement, fragmented by sectional affiliations and local loyalties. They extended the field of social vision by showing the identity of interest of working people as a class in their selection of news and analysis of events. By stressing that the wealth of the community was created by the working class, they also provided a new way of understanding the world that fostered class militancy. And by constant insistence that working people possessed the potential power through 'combination' to change society, the radical press contributed to a growth in class morale that was an essential precondition of effective political action.

The radical press also directly aided the institutional development of the working-class movement. Radical papers publicized the meetings and activities of working-class political and industrial organizations; they conferred status upon the activists of the working-class movement; and they gave a national direction to working-class agitation, helping to transform community action into national campaigns.

The Left press also helped to radicalize the working-class movement by providing access to an increasingly radical analysis of society. Initially its critique was limited since it was derived largely from middle-class attacks on the aristocratic constitution and focused mainly upon corruption in high places and regressive taxes. Conflict was defined in these early papers largely in terms of an opposition between the aristocracy and the people (including working capitalists). During the 1830s, however, the more militant papers shifted their attack from 'old corruption' to the economic process that enabled the capitalist class to appropriate in profits the wealth created by labour. Their principal targets became not merely the aristocracy but the capitalist class as a whole, and the institutions that sustained and enforced the domination of the capitalist class. This more advanced perspective sign-posted the way forward towards a radical programme of reconstruction in which, in the words of the *Poor Man's Guardian* (19 October 1833), workers will 'be at the top instead of at the bottom of society — or rather that there should be no bottom or top at all'.

Admittedly, this proto-Marxist analysis was often conflated with the old liberal analysis in an uncertain synthesis. There was, moreover, a basic continuity in the perspectives offered by the less militant wing of the radical press. But the rise of mass readership newspapers that challenged the legitimacy of central institutions of authority, linked to an analysis that came close to repudiating the capitalist system, was none the less a destabilizing influence. Britain's first General Strike (1842) and the political mobilization of the working class, on a mass scale, in the Chartist Movement were symptoms of an increasingly unstable society in which the radical press had become a powerfully disruptive force[18].

COMMUNICATIONS AND SOCIAL CONTROL

As I have argued elsewhere, market forces succeeded where legal repression had failed in containing the rise of a radical press against the background of growing prosperity and the reassertion of ruling-class cultural domination. The operation of the free market, with its accompanying rise in publishing costs, led to a progressive transfer of ownership and control of the press to capitalist entrepreneurs. It also led to a new economic dependence on advertising that encouraged the absorption or elimination of the early radical press and inhibited its re-emergence (Curran, 1978a and 1979a).

Significant changes have occurred since the industrialization of the press in Victorian Britain. Ownership of the press has become more concentrated and has largely passed into the hands of powerful multinational corporations with interests mostly outside publishing; the personal domination of press magnates has been replaced by less coercive controls; political prejudice amongst advertisers has declined, and this has materially assisted the growth of a social democratic press in a depoliticized form. But these changes have merely ameliorated rather than fundamentally changed the control system institutionalized by the so-called free market (Murdock and Golding, 1974; Hirsch and Gordon, 1975; Curran, 1978b, 1979b and 1980; Curran, Douglas and Whannel, 1980; Curran and Seaton, 1981).

By contrast, British broadcasting has developed under the mantle of the state. Broadcasters have gained, nevertheless, a genuine autonomy from political parties and individual administrations as a result of an extended historical process of negotiation and resistance. Such is the compactness of the British ruling class and its continuing cultural hegemony that this increased autonomy has been achieved, however, without the broadcasting system becoming a dissident or seriously disruptive force.

The modern mass media in Britain now perform many of the integrative functions of the Church in the middle ages. Like the medieval Church, the media link together different groups and provide a shared experience that promotes social solidarity. The media also emphasize collective values that bind people closer together, in a way that is comparable to the influence of the medieval Church: the communality of the Christian faith celebrated by Christian rites is now replaced by the communalities of consumerism and nationalism celebrated in media 'rites' such as international sporting contests (that affirm national identities) and consumer features (that celebrate a collective identity as consumers). Indeed, the two institutions have engaged in some ways in very similar ideological 'work' despite the difference of time that separate them. The monarchy is projected by the modern British media as a symbol of collective identity just as it was by the medieval Church. The modern media have also given, at different times, massive and disproportionate attention to a series of 'outsiders' — youth gangs, muggers, squatters, drug addicts, student radicals, trade-union militants — who have tended to be presented as powerful and irrational threats to 'decent' society (Young, 1971; Cohen, 1973; Hall, 1974; Morley, 1976; Hall *et al.* 1978; Whannel, 1979). The stigmatization of these 'outsiders' has had effects comparable to the hunting down and parading of witches allegedly possessed of the devil by the medieval and early modern Church. Moral panics have been created that have strengthened adherence to dominant social norms and encouraged a sense of beleaguered unity, transcending class differences, in the face of a dangerous, external threat.

The mass media have now assumed the role of the Church, in a more secular age, of interpreting and making sense of the world to the mass public. Like their priestly predecessors, professional communicators amplify systems of representation that legitimize the social system. The priesthood told their congregations that the power structure was divinely sanctioned; their successors inform their audiences that the power structure is democratically sanctioned through the ballot box. Dissidents were frequently de-legitimized by churchmen as 'infidels' intent upon resisting God's will; dissidents in contemporary Britain are frequently stigmatized as 'extremists' who reject democracy (Murdock, 1973). The medieval Church taught that the only legitimate way of securing redress for injustice was to appeal to the oppressor's conscience and, failing that, to a higher secular authority; the modern mass media similarly sanction only constitutional and lawful procedures as legitimate methods of protest (Hall, 1974). The medieval Church masked the sources of inequality by ascribing social injustice to the sin of the individual; the modern mass media tend, in more complex and sophisticated ways, to misdirect their audiences by the ways in which they define and explain structural inequalities (Hall, 1979). By stressing the randomness of God's unseen hand, the medieval Church encouraged passive acceptance of a subordinate status in society: the randomness of fate is a recurrent theme in much modern media entertainment (Curran, Douglas and Whannel, 1980). The Church none the less offered the chiliastic consolation of eternal salvation to 'the meek (who) shall inherit the earth'; the media similarly give prominence to show-business personalities and football stars who, as 'a powerless élite', afford easily identifiable symbols for vicarious fulfilment (Alberoni, 1972).

There is, of course, some differentiation in the output of the modern media just as there was in the teaching of the medieval Church. Conflicts have developed between the media and other power centres in contemporary society just as there were conflicts between the papacy, episcopacy and the monarchies of the middle ages. But these conflicts are rarely fundamental and are generally contained within the moral framework that legitimizes the social and political structure. The new priesthood of the modern media has supplanted the old as the principal ideological agents building consent for the social system.

NOTES

1 I would like to express my thanks to Professor Walter Ullmann for his very detailed and helpful comments on the section of this essay dealing with the medieval papacy.
2 By the central middle ages, the Catholic Church was established in a monopoly position throughout most of Europe, extending from Estonia to northern Spain on an east-west axis, and from Iceland to Sicily on a north-south axis. Regular church attendance was maintained not only through the pull of religious belief, but also sometimes by penalties imposed for non-attendance. For evidence about the level of newspaper readership in different European countries, see JICNARS (1979), Hoyer, Hadenius and Weibull (1975) and Smith (1977).
3 General questions about the cultural impact of new media have been largely ignored. For a brief review, see Curran (1977). For an admirable examination of the cultural impact of print see, in particular, Eisenstein (1968, 1969 and 1979), whose analysis is very much more interesting than the better known commentary of McLuhan (1962).
4 This is not intended to imply agreement with the still fashionable denigration of survey-based research methodology. On the contrary, the application of survey methods is now essential for a more adequate development of Marxist perspectives within mass communications research.
5 For a particularly illuminating interpretation of the rise of the papacy, upon which this essay draws heavily, see Ullmann (1969, 1972, 1975, 1977 and 1978).
6 For instance, Pope Innocent I claimed in the early fifth century that St Peter or his pupils were the founders of all the bishoprics in Italy, Spain, Gaul, Africa and Sicily. There is, of course, not a shred of truth in this.
7 Much of the following information is derived from Thomas (1973) whose

research, although mainly concerned with the early modern period, also sheds light on popular religious devotion in the middle ages.

8 A simple summary of these developments is provided in Curran (1977).

9 Calculated from the Royal Commission on the Press (1949) appendices 3 and 4, and readership per copy estimates derived from the Institute of Incorporated Practitioners in Advertising (1939).

10 The ecclesiastic reconstruction of kingship in the middle ages had disruptive long-term as well as short-term consequences. The feudal reaction in England kept alive the concepts of power delegated from below and feudal kingship limited by contract: it paved the way for government by an oligarchy of landed capitalists and, through a relatively peaceful process of transition, to popular participation in a liberal democracy. In contrast, the establishment of theocratic kingship in France, based on the hierocratic principles of divinely-instituted monarchy, blocked the route to peaceful evolution and led to absolutism followed by revolution. Whereas the feudal conception of kingship could evolve naturally through institutionalized channels of negotiation into representative democracy, the papal model of divine-right monarchy permitted only two forms of response — total subjection or total repudiation. The different pattern of development of modern France and modern Britain can thus be explained partly in terms of the failure of the papal conception of divine-right monarchy to take firm root in England, unlike France, during the middle ages.

11 This process of political disaffiliation resulted in half the national daily press in the October 1974 General Election being opposed to the election of a goverment constituted by a single party (Seymour-Ure, 1977).

12 The decline of media partisanship reflects the increasing commercial pressures on newspapers to reconcile the divergent political loyalties of newspaper readers; the progressive displacement of political patronage by advertising patronage of the press; the growth of local newspaper monopoly; the development of a professional ideology that has tended to repudiate the adversary tradition of journalism; the institutionalization of non-partisanship in publicly-regulated broadcasting; the weakening of ties between politicians and journalists, and growing mutual rivalry; and a deep-seated anti-partisan tradition in British political thought that pre-dates the modern party system.

13 A number of political and social changes have also contributed to the decline of partisan allegiance in Britain. For a useful discussion of these, see Butler and Stokes (1976).

14 The changes that have taken place in the British mass media closely resemble those that have taken place in the media in other western industrial societies where there has also been a tendency for partisan allegiance to decline.

15 There are modern parallels in which new media have undermined established institutions by by-passing their internal communication systems. The development of broadcasting and the press independent of ecclesiastical control has probably contributed to the secularization of society and the long-term decline of the Christian churches. The transmission of heterodox views on issues such as contraception, abortion and divorce has probably also contributed to divisions within the Catholic community over these issues. Similarly, the mass membership of the British trade-union movement is also being exposed to hostile coverage of trade unions (Hartmann, 1976 and 1980; Morley, 1976; Glasgow University Media Group, 1976 and 1980; McQuail, 1977; Beharrell and Philo, 1976) mediated by press and broadcasting media that by-pass the much less well-

developed internal communication system of the union movement. This poses a serious threat, in the long run, to the unity and corporate loyalty of trade-union mass memberships. New media have also displaced mediating institutions and groups, although without the dislocative consequences that followed the partial displacement of the priests as mediators of religious knowledge in early modern Europe. Thus the rise of television has undermined the role of parliament as a political forum. It has also undermined the role of grassroots political organizations as mediators of political communications (Rose, 1967). Arguably, this process of displacement has been one factor in the growing demand for increased internal party democracy within the Labour Party: party activists have responded to the decline of their traditional role and status within the party by demanding more power and influence.

16 The role of the printed word in contributing to England's only social revolution, and to 'the revolution within the revolution' constituted by the Levellers' revolt, has yet to be fully explored. But as Siebert (1952) shows, the censorship system began to collapse in the years leading up to the Revolution. The Revolution itself produced an unprecedented spate of polemical literature. Stone (1972) estimates that 22,000 speeches, pamphlets, sermons and newspaper titles were published between 1640 and 1660. For a scholarly, but not very illuminating, study of the early newspaper press during this period, see Frank (1961).

17 These accounts provide a conventional Whig interpretation of the emancipation of the press from the state. Their narrow perspective causes them largely to ignore the growing independence of part of the commercial press from aristocratic control. The limited time-span they cover also causes them to ignore evidence of increased inter-penetration between the press and the political parties in the later Victorian period that belies their claim that the press evolved into an independent fourth estate in the nineteenth century. Government subsidies continued in the form of government advertising allocated to friendly papers well into the nineteenth century (Hindle, 1937); government management of news remained an enduring form of influence (Anon, 1935 and 1939); newspaper proprietors and editors long continued to be intimately connected with one political party or other, whether in or out of office (Lee, 1977; Boyce, 1978); indeed, a number of leading newspapers received political subsidies well into the twentieth century (Seymour-Ure, 1976; Inwood, 1971; Taylor, 1972). The detachment of the press from the political parties, and consequently from government, was a much more gradual and extended process than the accounts cited in the text suggest.

18 For accounts of the rise of the radical press, see, in particular, Glasgow (1954), Thompson (1963), Read (1961), Wiener (1969), Hollis (1970), Harrison (1974), Prothero (1974), Tholfsen (1976), Epstein (1976), Berridge (1978), Curran (1979a) and Curran and Seaton (1981).

BIBLIOGRAPHY

Alberoni, F. (1972) 'The powerless elite: theory and sociological research on the phenomenon of the stars', in McQuail, D. (ed.) *Sociology of Mass Communication*, Harmondsworth, Penguin.

Anon (1935) *The Thunderer in the Making*, History of *The Times*, vol. 1, London, *The Times*.

Anon (1939) *The Tradition Established*, History of *The Times*, vol. 2, London, *The Times*.

Aspinall, A. (1949) *Politics and the Press, 1780-1850*, Home and Van Thal. Reprinted (1973) by Harvester Press, Brighton.

Asquith, I. (1975) 'Advertising and the press in the late eighteenth and early nineteenth centuries: James Perry and the Morning Chronicle, 1790-1821', *Historical Journal*, 17.

Asquith, I. (1976) 'The Whig Party and the press in the early nineteenth century', *Bulletin of the Institute of Historical Research*, XLIX.

Asquith, I. (1978) 'The structure, ownership and control of the press 1780-1855', in Boyce, G., Curran, J. and Wingate, P. (eds) *Newspaper History*, London, Constable.

Beaverbrook, Viscount (1925) *Politicians and the Press*, London.

Beharell, P. and Philo, G. (1977) *Trade Unions and the Media*, London, Macmillan.

Bennett, H.S. (1952) *English Books and Readers, 1475-1557*, London, Cambridge University Press.

Berridge, V. (1978) 'Popular Sunday Papers and mid-Victorian society', in Boyce, G., Curran, J. and Wingate, P., (eds) *Newspaper History*, London, Constable.

Bloch, M. (1961) *Feudal Society*, London, Routledge & Kegan Paul.

Boyce, G. (1978) 'The fourth estate: the reappraisal of a concept', in Boyce, G., Curran, J. and Wingate, P. (eds) *Newspaper History*, London, Constable.

Breed, W. (1964) 'Mass communication and sociocultural integration', in Dexter, L. and White, D. (eds) *People, Society and Mass Communications*, New York, Free Press.

Brewer, J. (1976) *Party Ideology and Popular Politics at the Accession of George III*, London, Cambridge University Press.

Brooke, C. (1964) *Europe in the Central Middle Ages 962-1154*, London, Longman.

Butler, D. and Stokes, D. (1976) *Political Change in Britain*, rev. edn, Harmondsworth, Pelican.

Christie, I. (1970) *Myth and Reality in Late Eighteenth-Century British Politics*, London, Macmillan.

Cobban, A.B. (1969) 'Episcopal control in the medieval universities of northern Europe', in Cuming, G.J. and Baker, D. (eds) *Studies in Church history*, London, Cambridge University Press.

Cohen, S. (1973) *Folk Devils and Moral Panics*, St Albans, Paladin.

Cooper, E. and Jahoda, M. (1947) 'The evasion of propaganda', *Journal of Psychology*, 23.

Cranfield, G.A. (1962) *The Development of the Provincial Newspaper, 1700-60*, London, Oxford University Press.

Cranfield, G.A. (1977) *Press and Society*, Oxford, Clarendon Press.

Curran, J. (1977) 'Mass communication as a social force in history', in *The Media: Contexts of Study* (DE 353-2), Milton Keynes, Open University Press.

Curran, J. (1978a) 'The press as an agency of social control: an historical perspective', in Boyce, G., Curran, J. and Wingate, P. (eds) *Newspaper History*, London, Constable.

Curran, J. (1978b) 'Advertising and the press', in Curran, J. (ed.) *The British Press: A Manifesto*, London, Macmillan.

Curran, J. (1979a) 'Capitalism and control of the press, 1800-1975', in Curran, J., Gurevitch, M. and Woollacott, J. (eds) *Mass Communication and Society*, rev. edn, London, Edward Arnold.

Curran, J. (1979b) 'Press freedom as private property: the crisis of press legitimacy', *Media, Culture and Society*, 1.

Curran, J. (1980) 'Advertising as a patronage system', *Sociological Review Monograph*, 29.

Curran, J., Douglas, A. and Whannel, G. (1980) 'The political economy of the human interest story', in Smith, A. (ed.) *Newspapers and Democracy*, Cambridge, Mass., Massachusetts Institute of Technology Press.

Curran, J. and Seaton, J. (1981) *Power Without Responsibility: Broadcasting and the Press in Britain*, London, Fontana.

Davies, C.S.L. (1976) *Peace, Print and Protestantism, 1450-1558*, London, Hart-Davis, MacGibbon.

Davies, R.H.C. (1957) *A History of Medieval Europe*, London, Longman.

Dickens, A.G. (1964) *The English Reformation*, London, Batsford.

Eisenstein, E. (1968) 'Some conjectures about the impact of printing on western society and thought: a preliminary report', *Journal of modern history*, XL.

Eisenstein, E. (1969) 'The advent of printing and the problem of the Renaissance', *Past and Present*, 45.

Eisenstein, E. (1979) *The Printing Press as an Agent of Change*, 2 vols, Cambridge, Cambridge University Press.

Elton, G.R. (1975) *The Reformation 1520-59*, New Cambridge Modern History, vol. 2, Cambridge, Cambridge University Press (first published 1958).

Epstein, J.A. (1976) 'Feargus O'Connor and the *Northern Star*', *International Review of Social History*, 22.

Evans, J. (1948) *Art in medieval France, 978-1498*, London, Oxford University Press.

Febvre, L. and Martin, H. (1976) *The Coming of the Book*, London, New Left Books.

Ferris, P. (1971) *The House of Northcliffe*, London, Weidenfeld & Nicolson.

Frank, J. (1961) *The Beginnings of the English Newspaper*, Cambridge, Mass., Harvard University Press.

Glasgow, E. (1954) 'The establishment of the *Northern Star* newspaper', *History*, 39.

Glasgow University Media Group (1976) *Bad News*, London, Routledge & Kegan Paul.

Glasgow University Media Group (1980) *More Bad News*, London, Routledge & Kegan Paul.

Gurevitch, M. and Blumler, J. (1977) 'Linkages between the mass media and politics: a model for the analysis of political communications systems', in Curran, J., Gurevitch, M. and Woollacott, J. (eds) *Mass Communication and Society*, London, Edward Arnold.

Hall, S. (1974) 'Deviancy, politics and the media', in McIntosh, M. and Rock, P. (eds) *Deviancy and Social Control*, London, Tavistock.

Hall, S. (1979) 'Culture, the media and the "ideological effect"', in Curran, J., Gurevitch, M. and Woollacott, J. (eds) *Mass Communication and Society*, rev. edn. London, Edward Arnold.

Hall, S., Clarke, J., Critchner, C., Jefferson, T. and Roberts, B. (1978) *Policing the Crisis*, London, Macmillan.

Hanson, L. (1936) *Government and the Press, 1695-1763*, Cambridge, Cambridge University Press.

Harrison, S. (1974) *Poor Men's Guardians: Record of the Struggles for a Democratic Newspaper Press 1763-1970*, London, Lawrence & Wishart.

Hartmann, P. (1975-6) 'Industrial relations in the news media', *Industrial Relations Journal*, 6.

Hartmann, P. (1979) 'News and public perceptions of industrial relations', *Media, Culture and Society*, 1.

Heath, P. (1969) *English Parish Clergy on the Eve of the Reformation*, London, Routledge & Kegan Paul.

Hill, C. (1974) *The Century of Revolution, 1603-1714*, London, Sphere Books (originally published 1961).

Hindle, W. (1937) *The Morning Post, 1772-1937*, London, Routledge and Sons.

Hirsch, F. and Gordon, D. (1975) *Newspaper Money: Fleet Street and the Search for the Affluent Reader*, London, Hutchinson.

Hollis, P. (1970) *The Pauper Press: A Study in Working-Class Radicalism of the 1830s*, London, Oxford University Press.

Hovland, C., Janis, I. and Kelley, H. (1953) *Communication and Persuasion*, New Haven, Conn., Yale University Press.

Hoyer, S., Hadenius, S. and Weibull, L. (1975) *The politics and Economics of the Press: A Developmental Perspective*, Beverley Hills, Cal., Sage.

Innis, H. (1950) *Empire and Communications*, University of Toronto Press (latest edition 1970).

Institute of Incorporated Practitioners in Advertising (1939) *Survey of Press Readership*, London.

Inwood, S. (1971) 'The Press in the First World War, 1914-16', unpublished Ph.D. Thesis, University of Oxford.

Janowitz, M. (1952) *The Community Press in an Urban Setting*, Chicago, Ill., University of Chicago Press.

JICNARS (Joint Industry Committee for National Readership Surveys) (1979) *National Readership Survey*, Institute of Practitioners in Advertising, London.

Kaldor, N. and Silverman, R. (1948) *A Statistical Analysis of Advertising Expenditure and of the Revenue of the Press*, Cambridge, Cambridge University Press.

Kantorowicz, E.H. (1957) *The King's Two Bodies: A Study in Medieval Political Theology*, Princeton, NJ, Princeton University Press.

Klapper, J. (1966) *The Effects of Mass Communication*, New York, Free Press (1966 edn).

Laistner, M.L.W. (1957) *Thought and Letters in Western Europe, 500-900*, London, Methuen.

Lazarsfeld, P. and Merton, R. (1948) in Bryson, L. (ed.) *The Communication of Ideas*, New York, Harper. Reprinted (1964) New York, Cooper Square Publishers.

Lazarsfeld, P. and Merton, R. (1960) 'Mass communication, popular taste and organized social action', in Schramm, W. (ed.) *Mass Communications*, Urbana, Ill., University of Illinois Press.

Lee, A. (1976) *The Origin of the Popular Press*, London, Croom Helm.

Leff, G. (1958) *Medieval Thought*, Harmondsworth, Penguin.

McLuhan, M. (1962) *The Gutenburg Galaxy*, London, Routledge & Kegan Paul.

McQuail, D. (1969) *Towards a Sociology of Mass Communication*, London, Collier-Macmillan.

McQuail, D. (1977) 'Industrial relations content in national daily newspapers 1975', in *Analysis of Newspaper Content*, Royal Commission on the Press Research Series 4, London, HMSO.

Maisel, R. (1973) 'The decline of mass media', *Public Opinion Quarterly*, 37.

Miliband, R. (1973) *The State in a Capitalist Society*, London, Quartet.

Morley, D. (1976) 'Industrial conflict and the mass media', *Sociological Review* 24 (2).

Morris, C. (1972) *Medieval Media: Mass Communications in the Making of Europe*, University of Southampton.

Murdock, G. (1973) 'Political deviance: the press presentation of a militant mass demonstration', in Cohen, S. and Young, J. (eds) *The Manufacture of News*, London, Constable.

Murdock, G. and Golding, P. (1974) 'For a political economy of the mass media', in Miliband, R. and Saville, J. (eds) *The Socialist Register 1973*, London, Merlin Press.

Northcliffe, Viscount (1922) *Newspapers and Their Millionaires*, Associated Newspapers.

Panovsky, E. (1951) *Gothic Architecture and Scholasticism*, Cambridge, Mass., Harvard University Press.

Perkin, H. (1969) *The Origins of Modern English Society, 1780-1880*, London, Routledge & Kegan Paul.

Prothero, I. (1974) 'William Benbow and the concept of the "General Strike"', *Past and Present*, 63.

Read, D. (1961) *Press and People, 1790-1850*, London, Edward Arnold.

Reith Diaries (1975) ed. Stuart, C., London, Collins.

Richards, J. (1979) *The Popes and the Papacy in the Early Middle Ages*, London, Edward Arnold.

Rogers, P. (1972) *Grub Street: studies in a subculture*, London, Methuen.

Rose, R. (1967) *Influencing Voters*, London, Faber & Faber.

Royal Commission on the Press 1947-9 Report (1949), London, HMSO.

Rudé, G. (1962) *Wilkes and Liberty*, Oxford, Clarendon.

Seymour-Ure, C. (1976) 'The press and the party system between the wars', in Peele, G. and Cook, C. (eds) *The Politics of Reappraisal, 1918-1939*, London, Macmillan.

Seymour-Ure, C. (1977) 'National daily papers and the party system', in *Studies on the Press*, Royal Commission on the Press Working Paper, (3), London, HMSO.

Siebert, F.S. (1952) *Freedom of the Press in England, 1476-1776*, Urbana, Ill., University of Illinois Press (latest edn 1966).

Smith, A. (1977) *Subsidies and the Press in Europe*, London, PEP (Political and Economic Planning).

Smith, A. (1978) 'The long road to objectivity and back again: the kinds of truth we get in journalism', in Boyce, G., Curran, J. and Woollacott, J. (eds) *Newspaper History*, London, Constable.

Southern, R.W. (1959) *The Making of the Middle Ages*, London, Grey Arrow.

Southern, R.W. (1970) *Western Society and the Church in the Middle Ages*, London, Penguin.

Stone, L. (1972) *The Causes of the English Revolution, 1529-1642*, London, Routledge & Kegan Paul.

Taylor, A.J.P. (1972) *Beaverbrook*, London, Hamish Hamilton.

Tholfsen, T.R. (1976) *Working-Class Radicalism in Mid-Victorian England*, London, Croom Helm.

Thomas, K. (1973) *Religion and the Decline of Magic*, Harmondsworth, Penguin.

Thompson, E.P. (1963) *The Making of the English Working Class*, London, Gollancz.

Thomson, J. (1965) *The Later Lollards, 1414-1520*, London, Oxford University Press.

Tuchman, G. (1978) *Making News*, New York, Free Press.

Ullman, W.W. (1970) *The Growth of Papal Government in the Middle Ages*, London, Methuen, 4th edn.

Ullman, W.W. (1978) *Principles of Government and Politics in the Middle Ages*, London, Methuen, 4th edn.

Ullman, W.W. (1969) *The Carolingian Renaissance and the Idea of Kingship*, London, Methuen.

Ullman, W.W. (1975) *Medieval Political Thought*, Harmondsworth, Penguin.

Ullman, W.W. (1977) *A Short History of the Papacy in the Middle Ages*, London, Methuen, 2nd edn.

Vincent, J. (1972) *The Formation of the British Liberal Party 1857-68*, Harmondsworth, Pelican.

Weiner, J.H. (1969) *The War of the Unstamped: The Movement to Repeal the British Newspaper Tax, 1830-36*, Ithaca, Cornell University Press.

Whannel, G. (1979) 'Football, crowd behaviour and the press', *Media, Culture and Society*, 1 (4).

Wickwar, W. (1928) *The Struggle for the Freedom of the Press 1819-32*, London, Allen & Unwin.

Wilks, M.J. (1963) *The Problem of Sovereignty in the later Middle Ages*, London, Cambridge University Press.

Young, J. (1971) *The Drugtakers*, London, Paladin.

9

The political effects of mass communication

JAY G. BLUMLER AND MICHAEL GUREVITCH

Public concern about mass communication is chiefly focused on the potential effects of mass media content on audience members. Parents are anxious to protect their impressionable children from the assumed consequences of exposure to extensive portrayals of 'sex and violence' on television; self-appointed guardians of public morality set themselves up as watchdogs, aiming to shield society from the pernicious influence of less savoury media materials; spokesmen of numerous institutions, interest groups and social causes — ranging from the police to trade unions, industry, women's liberation, the elderly, racial minorities, etc. — often rail against broadcast and press distortion or neglect of their affairs; politicians seem to think that ten minutes 'on the box' are worth dozens of hours on the hustings; advertising agencies make a handsome livelihood out of their clients' faith in the persuasive efficacy of the media. Underlying all these reactions is a common assumption: that the mass media do indeed have considerable influence over their audiences; that in this sense they are powerful. It could appear self-evident, therefore, that a priority task of communication research should be to study the effects on people's outlook on the world of the large amounts of time they spend watching television, listening to the radio, going to the movies and reading newspapers and magazines.

Among academics, however, the claims to respect of media effects enquiry are nowhere near so straightforward. Although some communication scholars, particularly those based in the United States, are heavily committed to this line of research, others tend to scorn it as misguided or unenlightening. As a result, media effects research is probably the most problematic sub-area of the field, as well as the one which has changed course most often over the years, partly in response to the ebb and flow of debate over its merits. This chapter, which deals with the *political* effects of mass communication, is accordingly shaped by the four-fold aim of introducing readers to:

1. Some sources of conflicting evaluations of media effects research as such;
2. the main phases in the historical evolution of different ways of investigating and interpreting media effects in politics;
3. some key examples of recent empirical work on such effects; and

4. discussion of the prospects for a convergence of approach even among opposed schools of thought towards the study of audience responses to political communications.

CONTRARY ASSESSMENTS OF MEDIA EFFECTS RESEARCH

Why is the quest for evidence of media effects on audiences so contentious? Particular lines of effects research are sometimes castigated for resting on naive theory or using unreliable methods. Yet if that was all that was wrong, the solution would lie in more mature theorizing and the adoption of improved methodologies — the familiar slow road to gradual progress in all social science endeavour. A root-and-branch scepticism towards effects research, then, must have deeper origins. We believe these can be found in a mixture of technical, ideological and cultural considerations.

Technically, whereas the design of effects research is inevitably intricate and demanding, the evidence that emerges from it often seems 'dusty' — i.e. complex in pattern, difficult to interpret, possibly inconclusive and rarely supportive of a picture of media impact as overriding, uniform or direct. In reaction to this state of affairs, some investigators recoil as if despairing that such a difficult game can ever be worth the candle, while others welcome the very challenge of facing and gradually mastering the inherent complexities of audience response. It is true that different views of the role of theory in social science may also play a part in these contrasting reactions. Most committed effects researchers have not conceived of theory as a valid world-view to be confirmed and filled in by empirical support. They have tended instead to deploy it like a mobile searchlight, hopefully illuminating an ever-increasing range of interrelated phenomena for inclusion in wider understandings. Something like the latter position probably underlies the comment of McLeod and Reeves (1980) that:

There are abundant number of . . . processes and concepts that have been suggested as modifying or interpreting media exposure to effects relationship. . . . For the most part, the most interesting communication theory results from the unravelling of these conditions and interactive relationships, not from the simple assertions that the media set public agendas or that children learn from television. (McLeod and Reeves, 1980, p. 28)

The magnitude of the technical problems of effects research design may be appreciated by considering some of the steps an investigator of political communication impact might have to take. He would probably need to embark on at least the following activities:
1. Specify the sources of media content that he expects to exert an influence on audiences, which might be divisible into different media (TV, press, radio, inter-personal discussion, etc.), or in the case of TV, say, different programme-types (party broadcasts, news bulletins, current affairs and discussion programmes, etc.), or perhaps the appearances of different types

of speakers (Conservative, Labour, Liberal, professional journalists, experts, etc.).

2. Measure the exposure of audience members to the chosen contents, no mean task in circumstances where political messages may be surrounded by much non-political matter (e.g. entertainment programmes on TV) and exposure may be due more to habit than choice, entailing low levels of attention in turn.

3. Postulate likely dimensions and direction of audience effect to be tested, which could include the following foci, each presenting unique measurement problems: policy information; issue priorities; images of politicians' qualities as leaders; attitudes to the various parties' strengths and weaknesses; voting preferences.

4. Specify whatever conditional factors might facilitate, block or amplify the process of effect — such as, say, those of sex, age, educational background, strength of party loyalty, motivation to follow a campaign, acceptance of a medium's political trustworthiness, etc.

Yet after taking all this trouble, the research worker is unlikely to contemplate a sizeable difference of outlook between groups more and less exposed to the relevant media stimulus. It should not be concluded from the modesty of such findings that, say, political campaigning in the mass media is normally ineffectual or that messages and images transmitted through the media are powerless to alter audience perspectives. As we shall see later in this chapter, researchers who in recent years have entered the political field to harvest evidence of effects have not returned entirely empty-handed. But their results have not in the main been simple or clear-cut, and overall may be summarized as showing (1) that the media constitute but one factor in society among a host of other influential variables; (2) that the exertion of their influence may depend upon the presence of other facilitating factors; and (3) that the extent and direction of media influence may vary across different groups and individuals. As Comstock (1976) has put it, commenting especially on the impact of television:

There is no general statement that summarizes the specific literature on television and human behaviour, but if forced to make one, perhaps it should be that television's effects are many, typically minimal in magnitude, but sometimes major in social importance. (Comstock, 1976)

Ideological differences also divide certain proponents and critics of media effects research. Liberal-pluralists are initially more likely than Marxists to pursue research into the political effects of mass communication for a variety of reasons. They are more prepared to regard an election, for example, as a meaningful contest between advocates of genuine alternatives, the rival campaigning efforts of which merit study. They will tend to define political communication as a process in which informational and persuasive messages are transmitted from the political institutions of society through the mass media to the citizenry to whom they are ultimately accountable. They can thus postulate a certain measure of autonomy for the different institutional domains of society, allowing questions to be raised, then, about the influence of materials processed in the media domain on the political and other sectors. They can happily look for the impact of media materials on individual audience members, sampled in surveys or recruited for participation in experiments. They can regard the phenomenon of media power as turning very much on the influence of communication on the outlook of such individuals. Above all, they can treat the issue of media effects — their direction, strength and precise incidence — as essentially constituting an empirical question, one, that is, that is not bound to be settled in a certain way in advance.

To many Marxists, however, the conduct of effects research may seem a dubious or unnecessary enterprise. In their eyes, election campaign rivalry is merely a sort of sound and fury whipped up by Tweedledum and Tweedledee. They are unhappy about the 'methodological individualism' of effects research, believing that history is shaped by confrontations and shifting power relations between opposed social classes. They are little interested in many of the fine-grained informational and attitudinal media effects reported in the literature that seem to them to ignore the predominantly ideological role of mass communication in society. Thus, for Marxists the political communication process is conceived largely in terms of the dissemination and reproduction of hegemonic definitions of social relations, serving to maintain the interests and position of dominant classes — a conceptualization which does not easily lend itself to translation into the form of effects design that was sketched out in a previous page. It also follows that for Marxists the ultimate source of media power is to be located, not at the content/audience interface, but in how media organizations are owned and controlled. Finally, although most Marxists do assume that the mass media exert a significant influence on the political thinking of audience members, for them the issue of its direction is a less open question, requiring empirical probing and determination, than it is for pluralists. They are more likely to take it for granted that mass media materials are typically designed to support the prevailing *status quo*.

Historico-cultural differences between the United States, on the one hand, and many Western European countries, on the other, may also help to explain the much greater involvement in effects research of media academics in North America (see Blumler, 1980). In many European societies, fundamentally opposed ideological options have not only been canvassed in the writings of intellectuals, but have also been organizationally translated into partisan cleavages, involving radical challenges to prevailing distributions of wealth and power, as in the case of Socialist and Communist movements. Yet, since the end of World War II, the reality of socio-political advance towards greater equality in many of these countries has appeared slight and negligible, leaving almost unaltered the seemingly unyielding system of social stratification. Some Europeans have wondered why this should have been so and whether mass communication has played some part in dampening radical impulses among even the working-class 'victims' of inequality. The United States, however, is a society in which the clash of fundamentally opposed ideological and political options has always seemed muted and as if overridden by the appeal of the American dream of equality of opportunity for all. Yet in the latter part of the post-war period, one societal sub-sector after another has been disturbed by unpredictable surges of social change. Even media scholars are accustomed to describe the 1960s and 1970s as a period of 'America in political and social transition' (Becker and Lower, 1979), mentioning such changes in this connection as the decline of the cities, the nation's involvement in and extrication from the Vietnam war, the emergence of unconventional life-styles and sexual mores, and an ever-deepending erosion of confidence in government.

Quite different formulations of the social and political role of mass communication seem to be connected to this contrast. In Europe, academics of a Marxist and radical bent typically regard the mass media as agencies of social control, shutting off pathways of radical social change and helping to promote the *status quo*. In the United States, however, such formulations permeate the literature less pervasively, and the mass media are more often seen either as partial cause agents of social change; or as tools that would-be social actors can use to gain publicity and impetus for their pet projects of change; or as authoritative information sources, on which people have become more dependent as the complexities of social differentiation and the pressures of a rapidly changing world threaten to become too much for them (DeFleur and Ball-Rokeach, 1975). On the whole, a social change perspective is more suited to the conduct of mass media effects research than is a social control perspective.

HISTORICAL DEVELOPMENT OF STUDIES OF POLITICAL
COMMUNICATION EFFECTS

Research into political communication effects has undergone at least two major shifts of direction since its inception. In an initial phase, which lasted from approximately the turn of the twentieth century to the outbreak of the Second World War, the mass media were attributed with considerable power to shape opinion and belief. In the second period, from approximately the 1940s to the early 1960s, they were believed to be largely impotent to intitiate opinion and attitude change, although they could relay certain forms of information and reinforce existing beliefs. And in the current third stage, the question of mass media effects has been reopened; certain previously neglected areas of possible effect are being explored; and a number of freshly conceived roles for communication factors in the political process are being elaborated.

Before telling this story in greater detail, however, it may be useful to identify here certain shifts of paradigmatic or methodological character that seem more central to the state of the art as it is increasingly being conceived at the present time:

1. A shift from focusing on *attitudes and opinions* in the study of media effects to a focus on *cognitions*. Some examples of studies which

represent this new emphasis will be presented on pp. 250-60. This change of focus raises, however, an important question, namely whether changes in cognitions are, indeed, prerequisites for changes in attitudes. While there is no doubt that the two are related, the causal links between them, so far little explored, may be rather complex.

2. A shift from defining effects in terms of *particular changes* to defining them in terms of a *structuring or re-structuring of cognitions and perceptions*. This is related to the previous shift, and is probably most clearly demonstrated in research into the so-called 'agenda-setting function' of the mass media, as well as the role of the media in audience 'constructions of social reality'.

3. A proliferation of models of the mass communication process, which have yielded alternative definitions of the nature of effects. The *linear model*, which specified the components of the communication process as comprising a source, a channel, a message and a receiver, and focused on changes in receivers' mental states induced by stimuli relayed through prior phases of the process, has been complemented by other approaches, including: *'uses and gratifications' studies*, in which the emphasis is placed on members of the audience actively processing media materials in accordance with their own needs (Blumler and Katz, 1974); *convergence and co-orientation models*, which emphasize the exchange of information among individuals in interaction so as to move towards a more common or shared meaning (McLeod and Chaffee, 1973); and a *'chain reaction' model* of communication effect, in which the impact of the mass media is found not only in the addition of effects upon individuals but also in how other people throughout the social structure react to the influenced individuals' example (Kepplinger and Roth, 1979).

4. In considering the sources of communication effect, some shift away from an earlier preoccupation with *partisan advocates*, as originators of messages that might or might not influence voters, to an interest in the less purposive but potentially more formative contributions to public opinion that stem from the political news and reports fashioned by *professional communicators*. In the earlier view, the professionals were conceived of chiefly as 'gate-keepers', admitting or shutting out those messages of advocates that might eventually affect the audience. In recent work, however, they figure more often as 'shapers of public consciousness' in ways that may even dictate what advocates must do to stand a chance of winning electoral acceptance.

5. A broadening of focus away from the near-exclusive concentration of earlier research on *election campaigns*, as sites of measurable political influence, to the study of political effects of media coverage in a variety of more everyday *non-election* circumstances as well.

This last point merits further elaboration. Since highly influential impressions of the scope of the mass media to affect voters' political views have often stemmed from research into election campaigns (in the United States and elsewhere), it is worth noting some of the properties that explain their attraction as a repeated object of study. To begin with, an election is a special, infrequent, yet quite decisive event, during which members of the electorate are subjected to greater outpourings of overtly political communication than at almost any other time. This enables researchers to prepare their fieldwork well in advance. It also produces an outcome (i.e. votes cast for different political parties) which is known, exact, measurable and can be readily related to measures of other variables. Findings of successive campaigns can also be related to each other, thus yielding measurements of trends over time. Moreover, since an election campaign is an occasion for the launching of intensive attempts at persuasion, researchers can not only observe how voters sample and react to the various political offerings, but also put their theories about such processes to a stringent empirical test.

Two limitations of this focus have also attracted criticism. One is that it directs attention to short-term effects (over the campaign period) at the expense of the more gradual cumulation over a longer span of time of media influences on people's political beliefs. Another is that it deals only with manifestly political messages and ignores the more diffuse but possibly more pervasive ideological implications of other forms of media content — such as soap operas, family comedies, adventure serials, advertisements, etc. Some social scientists, however, have attempted to counteract these shortcomings. For example, long-term panel designs, involving interviews with the same voters across several elections, are becoming more common. And at least one major American research programme is devoted to the task of what its initiators call 'cultivation analysis', i.e. an attempt to determine how far certain descriptions of social reality, shown by content analysis to be projected frequently in popular television programmes of all kinds, are accepted as valid by heavy viewers of the medium. Meanwhile, the field continues to develop partly (though not so exclusively as in previous times) through studies of campaign effects. This is understandable, for when citizens are placed in a situation of electoral choice, a whole host of political orientations — information levels, attitudes to parties and leaders, impressions of the issues of the day, policy preferences, perceptions of the wider political system — are brought to the surface and exposed to possible influence.

WHEN THE MASS MEDIA SEEMED OVER-RIDINGLY POWERFUL

The assumption, widely accepted before the 1940s, of massive propaganda impact for the persuasive contents of the mass media, and a concern to test this through effects research designs, had many sources. There was the seeming ease with which World War I war-mongers and Fascist regimes in Europe of the 1930s had manipulated people's attitudes and bases of allegiance and behaviour. That impression was compatible with theories of mass society, current at the time the study of media effects began to take shape, which postulated that the dissolution of traditional forms of social organization under the impact of industrialization and urbanization had resulted in a social order in which individuals were atomized, cut off from traditional networks of social relationships, isolated from sources of social support, and consequently vulnerable to direct manipulation by remote and powerful élites in control of the mass media. Thus, the explosive growth of the media at the beginning of this century, and the global socio-political upheavals in which they were perceived to have played a part, lent urgency to the need to explain systematically and scientifically the role of this new social force and the mechanisms of its power and influence. However, an interest in the effects of assumed-to-be powerful media developed from more 'benign' and pragmatic concerns as well. It was hoped, for example, that the potential of the media could be used for civic education, cultural enlightenment and the diffusion of socially beneficial innovations, while advertisers and politicians hoped to learn more about the design of media messages for marketing purposes and political mobilization. The emergence of effects research in response to both policy problems and practical applications was further facilitated by the academic development of social-psychological concepts, techniques of measurement and statistical methods of survey sampling and data analysis. Once the notion of 'effects' was equated with authoritarian, benevolent or competitive actors initiating changes in audience members' attitudes and opinions, it was almost inevitable that social psychology should become its main disciplinary home.

SOME EXAMPLES OF EARLY ELECTION STUDIES DESIGNED TO TEST THE PRESUMPTION OF MEDIA POWER IN POLITICS

Perhaps the most famous election study conducted in the 1940s was the one carried out by Lazarsfeld, Berelson and Gaudet on the 1940 US Presidential elections, and published under the title, *The People's Choice* (1944). This investigation found that only limited change had occurred during the campaign. About half the electors knew six months before the elections how they would vote, and maintained their party preferences throughout the campaign. Another quarter made up their minds after the parties' nominating conventions in the summer. Only about a quarter of the voters made their decisions during the supposed period of the campaign. Yet political messages seemed little involved even in their decisions. On the whole, late deciders and switching voters paid less attention to the campaign than did more stable ones. Findings concerning the tendency of voters to expose themselves selectively to political messages, i.e. to attend more to political spokesmen and messages with which they agreed than to those of the opposite side, also emerged from this study.

Later in Britain, Trenaman and McQuail (1961) conducted a most carefully designed study of the General Election campaign of 1959. According to their findings, attitudes (as distinct from votes) did undergo a definite swing (in fact favouring the Conservatives), yet no significant association could be found between that movement of opinion and how the voters had followed the election campaign through any of the communication channels they used. In the authors' words: 'within the frame of reference set up in our experiment, political change was neither related to the degree of exposure nor to any particular programmes or argument put forward by the parties' (p. 191).

The image of an election campaign as an occasion for parties and leaders effectively to persuade and influence voters seemed, then, to have been exploded by these and similar studies. Little wonder that two social scientists were moved to remark when discussing this vein of research: 'After each national election students of political behaviour comment on how little effect the mass media appear to have had on the outcome' (Lang and Lang, 1966, p. 455).

REINFORCEMENT AS THE MAIN EFFECT

The leading investigators of campaign communication did not stop short, however, at presenting their finding of little or no communication effect on the voters. They also sought to explain why this was so. Out of these efforts emerged the reinforcement doctrine of political communication impact. This doctrine had several dimensions.

First, the typical outcome of the communication experience was succinctly expressed by Joseph Klapper (1960) in his overview of the then available literature on media effects: 'Persuasive mass communication functions far more frequently as an agent of reinforcement than as an agent of change' (p. 15). In other words, Klapper maintained, when people are exposed to mass media coverage of political affairs they are more likely to be confirmed in their existing views than to be fitted out with new or modified ones.

Second, Lazarsfeld and his colleagues, in their study of the 1940 Presidential election, described the spirit in which voters supposedly attended to political materials thus:

Arguments enter the final stage of decision more as indicators than as influences. They point out, like signboards along the road, the way to turn in order to reach a destination which is already predetermined.... The political predispositions and group allegiances set the goal; all that is read and heard becomes helpful and effective in so far as it guides the voter towards his already chosen destination. The clinching argument thus does not have the function of persuading the voter to act. He furnishes the motive power himself. The argument has the function of identifying for him the way of thinking and acting which he is already half-aware of wanting. (Lazersfeld *et al.*, 1944, p. 83, 2nd edn)

Consequently, certain mechanisms of audience response to political messages were invoked to explain the reinforcement process. Given such labels as selective exposure, selective perception and selective recall, their linking thread was the idea that many people used their prior beliefs, both as compasses for charting their course through the turbulent sea of political messages, and as shields, enabling them to rehearse counter-arguments against opposing views.

Third, it was recognized, of course, that there was a group of 'floating voters' whose prior political anchorages were not firm enough to conform to this reinforcement model. Nevertheless, the findings of early research seemed to suggest that political persuasion was virtually irrelevant to many members of this group who, because they tended to be less interested in political affairs, were also less likely to be reached by political messages.

Finally, a key linchpin of this edifice of interpretation concerned the role of party loyalty in mass electoral psychology. It was assumed that most voters tuned in to political communication through some underlying party allegiance. Typically, this would (a) be acquired early in life; (b) persist through one's life-time; (c) be echoed among many members of the individual's social circles, such as his family, friends, workmates and so on; and (d) guide the majority of the electorate through the maze of issues and events which appear on the political stage.

A 'NEW LOOK' IN POLITICAL COMMUNICATION RESEARCH

The reinforcement doctrine of political communication reigned supreme and virtually unchallenged in academe for a number of years. Even sceptics (e.g. Lang and Lang, 1966), who considered that the dominant perspective overlooked important media roles in shaping public opinion between elections, tended to accept the validity of its interpretation of short-term campaign processes. For example, they tended to agree that 'the minds of most voters' were likely to be 'closed even before the campaign opens'. And since electioneering politicians would be striving mainly to 'activate partisan loyalties', the campaign period was 'inherently . . . less a period of political change than a period of political entrenchment' (pp. 456-7).

It is striking to find, therefore, that from the late 1960s onwards an increasing number of investigators began to proclaim that the book on political communication effects should not be closed after all. The literature began to resound with ever more frequent references to a 'new look in political communication research' (Blumler and McLeod, 1974), to 'new strategies for reconsidering media effects' (Clarke and Kline, 1974) and even to 'a return to the concept of powerful mass media' (Noelle-Neumann, 1974). This new mood reflected three ground-swells of change, each undermining an essential prop of the reinforcement doctrine. These changes inhered in trends in the political environment, in the media environment and in the academic community itself.

Changes in the political environment

The reinforcement doctrine of political communication was part and parcel of an overall view that placed far more emphasis on the underlying stability of the world of politics than on its flux. As Lazarsfeld (1948) put it (p. xx,

2nd edn): 'The subjects in our study tended to vote as they always had, in fact as their families always had.'

Nowadays, however, party loyalty, once the linchpin of electoral psychology, seems to have lost much of its power to fix voters in their usual places. Political scientists in one democratic country after another have documented evidence in recent years of accelerating rates of electoral volatility. In the US, for example, there has been a steady downward trend in Presidential elections since 1952 (only slightly reversed in 1976) in the capacity of self-disclosed 'party identification' to predict how people will actually vote. There has also been a concomitant rise in the number of those identifying themselves as 'Independents'. Similar trends have been reported from Germany, Denmark, Sweden, Norway, Belgium and Holland. For Britain, Butler and Stokes (1974) have assembled an impressive array of evidence indicating 'far greater volatility of party support' in the 1960s than in earlier post-war years. Continuing their work into the 1970s, Crewe (1973 and 1976) has documented further falls, both in shares of the eligible electorate obtained by the Conservatives and Labour at successive elections, and steep declines (ranging from 46 per cent in 1964 to 23 per cent in 1974) in the percentages of voters professing to be 'very strongly' identified with some political party.

Moreover, a number of signs suggest that the combination of weak partisanship and higher volatility rates is no passing phenomenon. For one thing, the power of social class to predict the ultimate destination of voters' ballots is on the wane. That means that people are less likely to encounter a consistent and consistently reinforcing pattern of party loyalties in the work and social circles in which they move. For another, family socialization processes may no longer be capable of transmitting life-long partisan affiliations from parents to children as effectively as had been supposed in the past. It is striking to note in this connection not only that the number of Independent identifications among new entrants to the US electorate went up steadily from 1952 to 1972, but also the lack of evidence that as the newly eligible mature politically they are abandoning their Independent stances for some form of partisan affiliation. So far at least, as they age, the new electors are remaining as Independent-minded as they were when they first acquired voting rights.

It is also important to note that the enlarged group of floating voters can no longer be regarded as consisting only of people who have opted out of the political communication market. Rather are they quite often at least as well informed and politically interested as the typical party loyalist. Some recent studies have even shown a greater use of media information by those making up their minds how to vote during an election campaign than by those with stable preferences throughout a campaign period (Chaffee and Choe, 1980).

There are also indications that more people may be judging political affairs in ways that cut across party lines. They may think in terms of the issues which matter to them, or may look to attractive leadership personalities, or simply respond to political parties with grudging scepticism and mistrust. These increase the uncertainties with which the parties are confronted during election periods, and the parties often respond by redoubling their electioneering efforts and by putting themselves in the hands of public relations and advertising professionals. In these conditions, the probability that political communication will exert an influence appears to increase.

Changes in media environment

At the same time that voters were becoming more footloose, developments in the media were re-shaping the sources of people's political information and impressions. The most important of these was the increasing prominence of television as a medium of political communication.

In terms of the audience, the intervention of television into politics has been dramatic. There is increasing evidence not only that television has by now established itself as the prime source of information about political and current affairs for the majority of the population, but also that reliance on it to follow political arguments and events is particularly heavy and wide-spread at election times. But more important than its overall dominance is how television has helped to restructure the audience for political communication in ways that are at odds with the reinforcement thesis. First, television reaches with a regular supply of political materials a sector of the electorate that was previously less exposed to these materials. In Katz's (McQuail, 1972, p. 359) words 'Large numbers of people are watching election broadcasts not because they are interested in politics but because they like viewing television.' Katz supposed that the forging of a special relationship between television and the less politically-minded electors was largely beneficial: 'Television has "activated" them; they have political opinions and talk to others about them. It can be demonstrated that they have learned something — even when their viewing was due more to lack of alternatives than choice.' But more important, the less interested and less well-informed also constitute a new site for persuasion, since their defences against persuasion are liable to be relatively frail.

A second consequence of the coming of television has been a reduction in selectivity in voters' exposure to party propaganda. A medium which is constitutionally obliged to deal impartially with all recognized standpoints, and which offers favourable time-slots for the screening of the parties' broadcasts, affords little scope for viewers selectively to tune in only to their side of the argument. Moreover, innovations in the formats of election broadcasting, such as face-to-face debates between party leaders, as between the Presidential candidates in the US, further reduce the possibilities of selective exposure.

But perhaps the most potent consequence of television's intervention into politics stems from its seemingly most innocuous feature — its need to maintain an above-the-battle stance in its relationship to party-political conflict. Since broadcasting may not support individual parties, it is obliged to adhere to such non-partisan — perhaps even anti-partisan — standards as fairness, impartiality, neutrality and objectivity, at the expense of such alternative values as commitment, consistent loyalty and readiness to take sides. Thus television may tend to put staunch partisans on the defensive and help to legitimate attitudes of wariness and scepticism towards the politicial parties. Perhaps that explains why some writers have postulated a causal connection between the ascendancy of television and increasing electoral volatility. Butler and Stokes (1974), writing about Britain, for example, conclude: 'It should occasion no surprise that the years just after television had completed its conquest of the national audience were the years in which the electoral tide began to run more freely.' (p. 419, 2nd edn)

Changes in conceptualizing media effects

The third major impulse feeding the renewed interest in the impact of the mass media has been a shift in the conceptual underpinnings of political effects inquiry. In the earlier post-war years, political communication research was almost coterminous with *persuasion* research. More recently, however, greater interest has been shown in the *cognitive* effects of political communication. Instead of focusing on attitude change through exposure to persuasive messages, researchers, pointing out that much political output of the mass media comes in the form of information, have aimed to analyse the political impact of mass communication in terms of its information-transmittal function.

This observation accords with a certain feature of audience psychology. Where overt persuasion is recognized, audience members may be on their guard. But media contents may be received in a less sceptical spirit if people perceive them as information, i.e. as if they have no specific axe to grind. Indeed, when people are asked why they follow political events in the mass media, they tend to give 'surveillance' reasons more often than any other, as illustrated in the following table, which comes from Blumler and McQuail's (1968) study of the 1964 British General Election.

Table 1: *TV owners' reasons (per cent) for watching party election broadcasts:*

1. To see what some party will do if it gets into power	55
2. To keep up with the main issues of the day	52
3. To judge what political leaders are like	51
4. To remind me of my party's strong points	36
5. To judge who is likely to win the election	31
6. To help make up my mind how to vote	26
7. To enjoy the excitement of the election race	24
8. To use as ammunition in arguments with others	10

In addition, a number of recent studies of mass communication content have produced evidence of 'patterning and consistency in the media version of the world' (McQuail, 1977, p. 81). The argument here is that the mass media, on the whole, present a consonant view of certain portions of social reality (e.g. in reporting of race relations, industrial relations, deviance, etc.), thus rendering one view dominant, and encouraging audience members to accept it as if 'obvious' or 'natural'.

The crucial conceptual distinction that has arisen from these reflections is between *attitudes* and *cognitions*. As Becker, McCombs and McLeod (1975) have defined these terms: 'Attitudes are summary evaluations of objects by individuals'; 'cognitions are stored information about these objects held by individuals'. They recognize that evaluations may be based on cognitions and that their interrelations may be complex, but they suppose that cognitions can be measured independently of attitudes and can be assessed 'against some external objective criterion of communicated information'. Hence, the shift in research focus towards a greater stress on how the mass media project definitions of the situations that political actors must cope with, than on attitudes toward those actors themselves.

Probably the most representative example of this approach can be found in attempts to study the so-called 'agenda-setting function' of the mass media. These aim to explore what it means to have a media system that determines which issues, among a whole series of possibilities, are presented to the public for attention. The central concern of agenda-setting research is to test the hypothesis of a 'strong positive relationship between the emphases of mass media coverage and the salience of these topics in the minds of individuals in the audience' (Becker, McLeod and McCombs, 1975, p. 38). What is more, the relationships involved are assumed to be *causal*. As Shaw and McCombs (1977) have put it in a book entirely devoted to this type of research: 'increased salience of a topic or issue in the mass media influences ... the salience of that topic or issue among the public' (p. 12). As such formulations imply, the bulk of agenda-setting studies have focused on 'issues' — their prominence and frequency of display in media portrayals in comparison with their place in audience members' orders of priority. Certain other concerns have also occasionally featured in such research, however, including studies of (a) popular awareness of proposed solutions to the problems arising in key issue domains; (b) how issues get into media agendas (say, from voters' prior concerns, or through politicians' speeches and pronouncements, or via professional journalists' own outlook on society); and (c) the impact of agenda setting on voting behaviour. This last focus reintroduces the complexity of the relationship between attitudes and cognitions. If, for example, immigrants are portrayed in the media as sources of social conflict and problems for society, white audience attitudes toward them may eventually become less favourable (Hartmann and Husband, 1974). Or take the case of American television coverage of the Vietnam war: if in the late 1960s Americans perceived US armed forces as losing ground in the war, even erstwhile hawks might have eventually lost their appetite for continuing involvement (Braestrup, 1977). Thus, media portrayals of social reality may ultimately induce attitude changes towards the various issues portrayed.

SOME EXAMPLES OF RECENT WORK ON POLITICAL
COMMUNICATION EFFECTS

The perspectives described above have so far been presented in terms of
possibilities of media impact. But what evidence have researchers managed
to produce of media effects on the political outlook of audience members?
Some examples of recent studies and findings are outlined below.

Agenda setting during the American Presidential election of 1972

According to agenda-setting theory, an audience member exposed to a
given medium's agenda will adjust his or her perceptions of the importance
of political issues in a direction corresponding to the amount of attention
paid to those issues in that medium. A problem that may interfere with
attempts to test this hypothesis arises when there are few or no differences
between different media in the issues emphasized by them. In such a case
there will be no 'variance' to measure.

During the American Presidential election of 1972, however, McLeod,
Becker and Byrnes (1974) managed to conduct an agenda-setting study in a
city (Madison, Wisconsin) which was served by two rather different newspapers — one quite conservative in outlook, the other more liberal. A
content analysis of the papers confirmed that their election agendas were
indeed different: the more conservative paper devoted more space to
America's world leadership and to the theme of combating crime, while the
liberal paper paid more attention to the Vietnam war and the theme of
'honesty in government'.

The investigators' task was to devise a procedure which would test
whether the issue priorities of readers of the two papers diverged along lines
similar to those of the papers they read. Thus, they had to relate exposure to
the different newspapers to a measure of agreement with the issue agenda
set by the papers. They interviewed two samples, one of first-time young
voters and another of older voters. For the members of both samples, in
addition to finding out what papers people read and their rank ordering of
the importance of six campaign issues, they ascertained the degree of
partisanship, interest in the campaign and degree of reliance on the press as
an election-information source.

The findings were mixed. Generally, the data supported the agenda-
setting hypothesis in the case of the older sample, while the results for the
younger sample were in the right direction, though falling short of statistical
significance. That is, readers of the conservative paper put more stress on
problems of crime and America's role in the world than did readers of the
liberal paper, who gave more weight to Vietnam and corruption in
government. Less interested voters seemed more open to agenda-setting
influence than were the more politically involved ones. Those who were
more dependent on the press as an information source were also more
influenced by their paper's agenda. The authors concluded that there might
be:

two different types of agenda-setting, one a kind of scanning orientation process common to the less involved voters of all ages, and the second a kind of purposive justification confined to the older respondents whereby poorly informed partisans with strong political commitments scan their newspapers as means of filling in information required by that commitment. (McLeod, Becker and Byrnes, 1974, p. 161)

Television and attitudes to the Liberal Party in the British General Election of 1964

Blumler and McQuail (1968) interviewed a sample of Yorkshire voters before and after the British election campaign of 1964. Their findings were among the first to call into question the presumed supremacy of the reinforcement doctrine. Two special features of their study proved crucial. They traced movements in voters' attitudes toward the Liberal Party, as well as to the Conservative and Labour Parties, and they devised a measure of the strength of voters' motivation to follow the election on television. Their assumption was that exposure to campaign messages would have different effects on those who viewed out of political interest, from those who watched political programmes simply because they see a lot of television generally and have little else to do at the time.

As in the British 1959 election study that preceded it (Trenaman and McQuail, 1961), the results showed little sign of an impact of campaign exposure on voters' attitudes to the Conservative and Labour Parties. The relationship between television use and changing attitudes toward the Liberal Party, however, was strikingly different. Overall, attitudes toward the Liberals had improved during the campaign — on average by about half a point on a +5 to —4 scale. When, moreover, the sample was divided according to the amount of exposure to political broadcasts on television, it was found that the rate of shift in favour of the Liberals progressively increased as levels of exposure to Liberal Party broadcasts increased.

Next, strength of motivation to follow the campaign was injected into the analysis. Its effect is shown in Figure 1 (p. 252), which deals separately with those who were rated strong in motivation to follow the campaign, and those whose motivations were medium or weak. The figure suggests that the introduction of a motivational variable has transformed a modest relationship between television exposure and pro-Liberal shift into a strong relationship, and one that was concentrated among the less interested voters. The zig-zag pattern for the more interested voters indicates that there was no consistent pattern between the development of pro-Liberal views and the number of Liberal programmes viewed. But among the less interested (see bottom bars of the figure) there was a strong and progressive relationship between exposure to Liberal programmes and a pro-Liberal shift. The implication is that viewers who were in the audience less out of political interest and more because of attachment to their television sets were most open to influence in their attitudes toward a party about which at the outset they probably had little knowledge and few well-formed opinions.

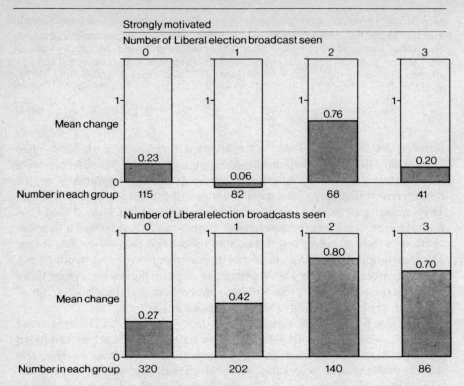

Number of Liberal election broadcasts seen

Figure1a In the sample as a whole, high exposure to Liberal election broadcasts went with attitude change in favour of the Liberal Party

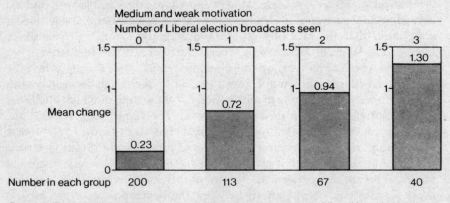

Figure1b The association between pro-Liberal shift and exposure to Liberal broadcasts was confined to those respondents whose motivation for following the campaign was medium or weak

American newspaper endorsements of Presidential candidates

Preoccupation with the role of television in political communication, especially during election campaigns, may cause the role of another important communication channel, the press, to be overlooked. John

Robinson (1974) has argued that the potential influence of the press should not be slighted, especially since newspapers are free to take a political stand, in contrast to television, which is obliged to present all sides of the contest and to assume a 'neutral' stance. In his words (p. 588): 'The newspaper endorsement is a direct message, which appears to reduce the confusing arguments of the campaign to a single conclusion.' But can this have an effect? The title of his article, *The Press as King-maker*, provocatively indicates Robinson's answer. This reports his re-analysis of national survey data for five Presidential elections (1956-72) in which the percentages of respondents voting for the Democratic candidate were calculated according to the candidates endorsed by the newspapers those respondents read. However, since the choice of newspaper may depend, in part, on the reader's political preference — a factor which, if not controlled, may obscure the potential influence of the newspaper — the respondents were divided into three subgroups according to their prior party identifications: Republicans, Democrats and Independents. For Republicans, for example, Robinson aimed to see whether, among those individuals taking a paper endorsing a Democratic candidate, there would be more Democratic votes than among those taking a Republican-supporting newspaper.

Table 2 summarizes the results. It presents the percentages of individuals voting for the Democratic candidate among readers of Democratic-supporting, neutral and Republican-supporting newspapers in the three sub-groups determined by prior party preference.

Table 2: *Percentages of electors voting for the Democratic Presidential candidate by newspaper endorsement and by party identification, 1956-72*

Year	Democrats Dem	Neither	Rep	Difference Dem-Rep	Independents Dem	Neither	Rep	Difference Dem-Rep	Republicans Dem	Neither	Rep	Difference Dem-Rep
1956 a(N=969)	84	74	73	+11	27	22	28	− 1	0	4	5	− 5
1960 b(N=451)	79	79	80	− 1	61	f	48	+13	8	0	8	0
1964 c(N=972)	91	89	87	+ 4	70	71	35	+35	28	32	13	+15
1968 d(N=939g)	62	65	69	− 7	40	35	12	+28	12	4	8	+ 4
1972 e(N=778)	71	61	46	+25	50	34	26	+24	0	6	5	− 5

Source: Robinson (1974)
a Stevenson vs. Eisenhower
b Kennedy vs. Nixon
c Johnson vs. Goldwater
d Humphrey vs. Nixon
e McGovern vs. Nixon
f Less than 10 respondents
g Perceived newspaper endorsement, White voters only

A key column for each group of respondents is the one labelled 'difference, Democratic-Republican'. This records for each election year the excess of Democratic voters coming from readers of Democratic papers over readers of Republican papers. For example, in 1956, 84 per cent of the Democrats reading a paper endorsing the Democratic candidate, Adlai Stevenson, voted for him; 73 per cent of the Democrats reading a paper endorsing the Republican candidate, Dwight Eisenhower, voted Democratic. Thus, the difference in the rates of support for Stevenson between Democrats reading Democratic and Republican newspapers was 11 per cent.

It can be seen that out of fifteen comparisons, the differential of support for the Democratic candidate among readers of Democratic papers exceeded that for readers of Republican papers in nine cases (that is, wherever a plus sign appears in the difference column). Over all cases the average differential was 9 per cent. Among Independents, the differential was typically much higher — averaging 20 per cent across five elections, suggesting that they were especially likely to vote in line with their newspaper endorsements.

Perhaps two conclusions may be drawn from this evidence: first, that people are more open to influence when exposed to a fairly consistent point of view on a given matter; and second, that on this occasion it was the originally less committed voters who were most responsive to such a source of influence.

Media influence on trust in government

Although much political communication research focuses on election campaigns, some social scientists have argued that the periods between elections are just as crucial for understanding the role of the media in the political life of society. This is reflected in the increasing research attention given in recent years to the influence of styles of political reporting on people's faith in their political institutions. Kurt and Gladys Lang (1966) were the first to postulate such an influence. In their words,

The mass media, by the way in which they structure and present political reality, may contribute to a widespread and chronic distrust of political life. Such distrust is not primarily a mark of sophistication, indicating that critical 'discount' is at work. It is of a projective character and constitutes a defensive reaction against the periodic political crises known to affect a person's destiny as well as against what are defined as deliberate efforts to mobilise political sentiment.... How, we may ask, do the media encourage such distrust? ... The answers must be sought in the way in which the mass media tend to emphasize crisis and stress it in lieu of the normal processes of decision making. Such distrust also has its roots in the complexity of events and of problems in which the mass audience is involved. For instance, since viewers bring little specialized knowledge to politics, even full TV coverage of major political events does not allay this distrust. In fact it may abet it. (Lang and Lang, 1966, pp. 466-7)

Attempts to explore these matters empirically started when opinion polls in several countries began to reveal steep downward trends in the readiness of voters to trust their political leaders' management of affairs. A further boost to this line of enquiry stemmed from the Watergate affair.

One example of such research is a study by Michael J. Robinson (1976), an American political scientist who shared the suspicion that certain features of television news-reporting could have been responsible for the sharp decline of popular trust in government in the United States in recent years. He summarized his expectations as follows:

My recent work in television has forced me to build a yet untested theory concerning the growth of political illegitimacy. I have begun to envision a two-stage process in which television journalism, with its constant emphasis on social and political conflict, its high credibility, its powerful audio-visual capabilities and its epidemicity, has caused the more vulnerable viewers first to doubt their own understanding of their political system.... But once these individuals have passed this initial stage they enter a second phase in which personal denigration continues and in which a new hostility toward politics and government also emerges. Having passed through both stages of political cynicism, these uniquely susceptible individuals pass their cynicism along to those who were at the start less attuned to television messages and consequently less directly vulnerable to television malaise. (Robinson, 1976, p. 99)

To test this diagnosis Robinson re-analysed data from a nationwide survey of American voters interviewed during the 1968 Presidential election campaign. The respondents were divided into three groups; those relying on media *other* than television for following political affairs; those relying *primarily* on television and those relying *only* on television for following politics. The extent of agreement with several statements expressing trust or

Table 3: *Respondents' views as to whether or not Congressmen lose touch with constituents after election*

	GROUP A Those not relying on television	GROUP B Those relying on television	GROUP C Those relying only on television
Percent believing Congressman does lose touch with constituents	47% (402)	57% (675)	68% (122)
Controlling for educational level of respondent			
Less than 8 grades	71% (21)	75% (65)	76% (25)
Grades 8-11	58% (97)	66% (216)	69% (48)
Grade 12	46% (127)	54% (217)	62% (39)
Some college	51% (76)	44% (108)	71% (7)
College	29% (56)	46% (56)	100% (1)
Some postgraduate study	32% (25)	30% (23)	50% (2)

Source: Robinson (1976)

mistrust in American political institutions was compared for members of each group. Table 3 presents an example of this work, based on responses to the statement: 'Generally speaking, those we elect to Congress in Washington lose touch with the people pretty quickly'.

The top part of the Table does in fact show more mistrust among those relying on television to follow political affairs than among those who do not rely on television. The same pattern holds in the rest of the Table, where the data have been controlled for the educational level of the respondents. Such control is necessary, because the association of mistrust of politicians with dependence on television could have been due simply to the fact that the less educated respondents were both more prone to mistrust and heavy users of television. But the bottom part of the Table suggests that mistrust and dependence on television went together even when educational level was held constant.

On the face of it, this pattern seems clear and its interpretation straightforward. Nevertheless, its methodological foundations were attacked by Miller, Erbring and Goldenberg (1976) on two grounds. First, they asked, where is the crucial evidence demonstrating the negative and anti-institutional quality of television news, which is supposedly productive of viewer mistrust? Without some analysis of the news content of television, they maintained, a vital link in the supposed chain of causation is missing. Second, they argued, subjective statements about *reliance* on a medium provide no measure of an individual's actual *exposure* to the medium or to that part of its contents that supposedly act as a trigger of mistrust. Controlling for educational level was also, according to these critics, insufficient to rule out the influence of other factors, since other studies have shown dependence on television to go with low levels of political information and interest, independently of levels of education, and those are characteristics that could be related to cynicism and mistrust. Then, as if to clinch these arguments, they examined the relationship between frequency of television news viewing and attitudes similar to those examined by Robinson, and reported little evidence of any effect.

These authors also presented some evidence of their own on the same subject, striving to apply their methodological prescriptions in practice. For this purpose, they looked at change over time, examining data taken from members of a national sample who had been interviewed first in 1972 and again in 1974 and who had on both occasions responded to five statements comprising a so-called trust in government scale. Within the sample, they compared the readers of two kinds of newspapers — whose front-page stories presented, as ascertained by content analysis, above-average and below-average amounts of criticism of politicians or political institutions — to see whether members of the former group displayed a bigger increase in mistrust of government. Their data suggested that mistrust had in fact increased over the two-year period throughout the American public — even among readers of relatively uncritical newspapers. They also found that the tide of increasing mistrust reached higher levels among those with lower levels of formal education. However, the growth of mistrust over time was greater among readers of critical papers than among readers of the uncritical ones. The differential widened considerably when the analysis was confined to *frequent* readers of the two sorts of newspapers. It looked as if frequent readers of the more critical papers were especially receptive to their papers' critical outlook.

The authors concluded their analysis on the following note:

The political meaning of the relationship between newspaper criticism and political cynicism is not entirely obvious. Politics is conflict, and where conflict is involved negativism and criticism will surely exist. Newspaper stories that simply report disturbing events in a fairly objective style will presumably produce discontent. What we have found, however, goes beyond the impact of events and reflects the internal politics of newspapers. The relationships disclosed by the analysis are far too systematic to suggest that they simply reflect a happenstance of presentation style. Only systematic editorial influence could produce such a large variation in degree of criticism across papers. This does not imply only that some newspapers set out to be particularly critical — perhaps to fulfil their function as an adversary press. One must also assume that a systematic avoidance of criticism is occurring in other papers.... Whatever the explanation for the different levels of criticism in newspapers it is quite clear from the evidence that type-set politics have a substantial impact on public attitudes. (Miller *et al.*, 1976)

Two further points are worth noting in connection with these examples. First, they illustrate that research on the political effects of the media need not be confined to the study of election campaigns and indeed can embrace questions other than the impact of the media on voting behaviour. Second, they suggest that the direction of media coverage of political affairs may have repercussions on political legitimacy. Media outlets in a given society may vary considerably in the amount of institutional support or criticism they project, and these may accelerate a growth of mistrust rather than invariably promote the legitimacy of political institutions. This last point stands in some conflict with the premise, shared by some Marxist analysts of the media, that support for the legitimacy of regimes is one of the main consequences of the operation of the media in capitalist societies.

Television and 'the social construction of reality'

Everybody carries a set of more or less coherent images in his mind of the kind of society he inhabits: what it stands for; what its key institutions and power groups are like; the rules of social order that prevail; how values and rewards are allocated and to whom. Of course such impressions are partly formed by people's direct experiences of life. They also reflect their past and on-going involvement with society's traditional agencies of socialization and centres of ritual and myth — e.g. the family, schools, churches, sporting events, festive celebrations, patriotic ceremonies, etc. But one group of media researchers, George Gerbner and his colleagues at the Annenberg School of Communication in the University of Pennsylvania, maintain that television has become for many people a prime source of socially constructed reality which they define as 'a coherent picture of what exists, what is important, how things are related and what is right' (Gerbner *et al.*, 1979, p. 179). Their work, the validity of which is hotly debated, is especially interesting for proposing a way to test the hypothesis that important political influences can stem from messages that in themselves are not in a narrow or conventional sense 'political'.

The Gerbner thesis rests on four main assumptions (each of which is likely to be challenged by critics of this controversial point of view). One is that in modern society people are becoming more and more dependent on vicarious sources of experience: 'the fabric of popular culture that relates elements of existence to each other and structures the common consciousness . . . is now largely a manufactured product', purveyed through mass communications (Gerbner, 1972, p. 37). Second, it is alleged that television, a mass medium which penetrates all sectors of society, projects a view of the world through repetitive and pervasive patterns that are in themselves organically interrelated and internally consistent. Third, viewers tend to absorb the meanings embedded in this fabric, because they use the medium 'largely non-selectively and by the clock rather than by the program' (Gerbner, Gross, Signorielli, Morgan and Jackson-Beeck, 1979, p. 180). A fourth assumption points more directly to the way in which these ideas have so far mainly been tested. This is that 'violence plays a key role in TV's portrayal of the social order' — an assumption, incidentally, which illustrates this group's concern with all forms of programme output and not just informational broadcasting.

The Annenberg research strategy depends on the fact that TV portrayals of social reality are in some respects distorted or exaggerated. Content analysis can show, for example, that characters in television drama are more likely to encounter personal violence than will the average man in the street, and that murder is a more common crime in programme plots (relative to other offences) than in real life. The Annenberg researchers have accordingly asked surveyed sample members to say which of two different statements about social violence is correct, one which is in line with official statistics and one which corresponds more closely to 'television reality'. Their hypothesis is that heavy viewers of the medium will more often give the 'television answer' to such questions than will light viewers. In addition, they suppose that heavy viewers should draw certain conclusions from what they have seen about how to react to the world of violence. For example, they hypothesize that heavy viewers will more often admit to being afraid to walk alone in the city streets at night and will show more mistrust in their dealings with other people.

The findings reported by Gerbner *et al.* in a series of articles have usually confirmed their expectations. Table 4 shows how their results, taken in this case from a New Jersey sample of 447 7th- and 8th-grade school-children (aged 13-14) are usually presented. For each of three sets of data (concerning the prevalence of violence, the danger of urban strolls, and the trustworthiness of other people, respectively) the left-hand column shows the percentage of light TV viewers giving the 'TV answer'. The difference between the responses of light viewers and of heavy TV viewers has been labelled by Gerbner and his colleagues a 'cultivation differential', meaning by this the difference supposedly made by television's 'cultivation' of a certain image of social reality. This difference is shown in the right-hand column. The table presents the results, not only for the sample as a whole, but also for a number of separate sub-groups within it, defined by such characteristics as sex, grade in school, father's educational level (signifying the family's socio-economic status) and media use habits. It can be seen that in this sample the heavy viewers, regardless of subgroup, almost always gave the supposed 'television answer' in higher proportion than did the light viewers. Heavy exposure to television, claim the researchers, indeed results in acceptance of the view of social reality projected by that medium.

Table 4: *Heavy viewers of TV overestimate violence in society and find the world a mean place*

	Percentage over-estimating the per-centage of people involved in violence		Percentage afraid to walk alone in a city at night		Percentage saying that people are selfish rather than helpful	
	Light viewers	Cultivation differential	Light viewers	Cultivation differential	Light viewers	Cultivation differential
Overall	62	+11	64	+10	56	+ 8
Sex						
Male	64	+ 4	45	+15	62	+ 2
Female	60	+17	81	+ 3	50	+13
Grade in school						
7th	68	+12	59	+17	56	+ 3
8th	57	+10	68	+ 5	56	+13
Newspaper reading						
Every day	57	+16	61	+ 7	59	+ 4
Sometimes	66	+ 8	66	+12	54	+10
Network news watching						
Almost daily	53	+26	65	+11	57	0
Once in a while	67	+ 4	60	+10	57	+ 5
Hardly ever	61	+13	68	+12	52	+18
Father's education						
No college	65	+12	60	+11	60	+ 5
Some college	58	+ 8	64	+13	54	+ 3

Source: Adapted from: Gerbner *et al.* (1979)

Other scholars are sceptical about these findings. Although their consistency is impressive, the relationship between television viewing and perceptions of social reality that they imply is rather weaker than the Gerbner notion of the medium as a near-sovereign shaper of culture might have led one to expect. Exact definitions of what counts as a heavy or a light viewer are rarely given in the tables. The order of causation is also problematic. Heavy viewers may bring a more simplistic and wary view of the world to their experience of television instead of taking over that point of view from its programmes. So far, very few efforts have been made to chart the acquisition by heavy viewers of such social beliefs over a longer period of time in which the direction of causation could be more closely examined. Most striking is the failure of the Gerbner team to comment on, or to try to make sense of, the many differences between sample subgroups that their detailed results reveal. Why, say, should heavy viewing males be more afraid to walk alone at night than are equivalent women, when the reverse pattern applies to levels of personal mistrust?

Such neglect probably reflects the concern of Gerbner and his colleagues to demonstrate an *overall* effect of television exposure regardless of population differences. But that is why some critics see them as having naively reverted to 'mass society' notions that were discarded long ago by most other students of mass media effects. It is also the target of critics like Hawkins and Pingree (1980) who contend that differences both of individual psychology and in the forms of mass media content that audience members regularly consume must help to determine how people construct social reality and from what main sources. They argue that the influence of television on people's ideas about society should vary according to a number of intervening variables, including their information-processing ability; critical awareness of television; direct experience of other sources providing confirmation or disconfirmation of TV messages; social structural position; and patronage of various forms of programme content. Underlying all this, of course, there lurks a more profound philosophic difference. The Gerbner position tends to regard the mass media as capable of imposing categories through which reality is perceived, by-passing potential neutralizing factors and engulfing the audience in a new symbolic environment. By their critics, however, media influence is regarded as *essentially* differentiated, filtered through and refracted by the diverse backgrounds, cultures, group affiliations and life-styles of individual audience members. (Note: Since this chapter was written, Gerbner and his colleagues have tilted lances with Paul Hirsch in the pages of *Communication Research*. In the course of this debate Gerbner and his colleagues seem to have taken a more differentiated view of the ways in which television influences the viewers' construction of social reality.)

CONCLUSION: TOWARD A CONVERGENCE OF CONCERN OVER AUDIENCE EFFECTS?

The reader of the first part of this chapter will have learned that empirical enquiry into the audience effects of mass communication is not a universally applauded pursuit. Numerous sources of doubt and criticism were identified there, but at the core of the debate was a polarization of outlook between pluralist and Marxist approaches to the analysis of mass communication systems and processes. We argued that different judgements about the scientific pay-off to be expected from effects studies followed logically from differences between pluralist and Marxist views of society and of the role of the mass media in society. One conclusion which might have been drawn from the discussion is that the gap between the two approaches is so wide as to be unbridgeable. Nevertheless, in this concluding section we wish to consider how abiding such a compartmentalization of outlook is likely to prove, and whether any signs can be discerned of the emergence of a measure of agreement between researchers of different persuasions about some of the issues involved in studying the impact of the mass media.

At the outset of this exploratory journey it should be firmly stated that no papering over of the ideological and theoretical incompatibilities of Marxism and pluralism is envisaged. Holders of the former position are bound to postulate a subordination of mass media institutions to the interests of dominant classes, just as scholars in the latter camp will conceive the media as reacting to and impinging on a wider and much more loosely-knit set of socio-political power groupings. It is not merely unrealistic to expect either side to abandon its theoretical core; such a move if it happened would also dilute what is one of the most exciting sources of significant debate in the field at the present time. Rather, the question for review is whether the two schools can converge in studying audience responses to mass communication so as to put their respective theories to an empirical test at that level.

It may be useful to summarize at this point the conceptual obstacles to that form of convergence. Preoccupation with the effects of the mass media follows naturally from the pluralist tradition's view of society as constituting a plurality of potential concentrations of power (albeit not necessarily equal to each other) which are engaged in a contest for ascendancy and dominance. The mass media are then seen as a central means through which this contest is conducted and public support for one or another grouping or point of view is mobilized. Clearly, questions about the effectiveness of the media as sources of influence and persuasion loom large in this perspective, and the attention of media researchers is thus directed to ways of measuring and assessing such influence and to the socio-logical and psychological variables that intervene in and filter the process of persuasion. The Marxist perspective, on the other hand, starts from Marx's familiar assertion that, 'The ideas of the ruling class are the ruling ideas of the epoch', and so can readily relegate the question of media effects (if defined in terms of their capacity to bring about changes in attitudes and opinions) to near-irrelevance. The social functions of the mass media are conceptualized instead in terms of their ideological role in the production and reproduction of consensus, and the central questions raised focus on explaining how that role is performed and consensus is achieved.

Put in this manner, the differences appear basic. Nevertheless, in some recent work and writing on both sides of the theoretical/ideological divide it is possible to discern the seeds of a measure of agreement, so far as conceptualization of the impact of the media on audiences is concerned, and hence also about the need to study audience-level processes. Interestingly, the first main moves towards convergence of this kind have been taken by those who are actively engaged in empirical effects research. We shall try to illustrate these by briefly looking from this point of view at three already-described lines of work being currently pursued by effects researchers: studies of the agenda-setting function of the media; studies of mass media constructions of social reality; and examinations of the role of the media in influencing — and typically eroding — public trust in government. We shall then conclude by giving our reading of the evidence of the development of awareness among certain Marxist students of the media of a need to examine the reception of mass-communicated messages by audience members.

In considering recent work in the effects tradition we wish to highlight two emergent themes: (1) media effects are conceptualized primarily in terms of the shaping of the categories and frameworks through which audience members perceive socio-political reality; (2) the impact of the media in producing and communicating these frameworks is treated as rooted in characteristics of media organizations and of the professional practices which prevail in them, rather than in features of the persuasion process. Taken together, these themes tend to cast the media in an ideological role in form (though not necessarily in direction) not unlike that proposed by Marxist analysts.

The main thrust of agenda-setting research assigns to the mass media an ability to signal to their audiences what are the most important issues of the day, and so to construct an 'agenda for society'. Thus, according to this thesis, while the media may not be able to tell people *what* to think, they may be effective in telling them what to think *about*. Such a conceptualization reflects a shift from preoccupation with attitude and opinion change in the earlier stages of media effects research towards a concentration on the contributions of the media to the formation of frameworks through which people regard political events and debates. Furthermore, the mass media are seen to perform this role, not by analysing and arguing the merits of different issues, but by the manner in which they select, highlight and assign greater prominence to some issues rather than to others. The setting of the political agenda is thus seen as an implicit outcome of production practices in the media rather than as the deliberate attempt to determine what the public should think. It is consequently at least partially 'hidden' from the audience and may even be 'hidden' from professionals involved in news production themselves, who prefer to think of themselves as passing news events on to the audience instead of shaping them up through the application of value judgements and constructed frameworks of perception. Read in this manner, agenda-setting research appears to converge towards the Marxist view that the ideological role of the mass media has structural roots, embedded in routines and practices of media production, which in turn may reflect interpretative frameworks dominant in society at a given time.

The 'construction of social reality' vein of effects studies is based on a similar conceptualization of the impact of the mass media. Through continual repetition of certain popular plots, story themes, character portrayals and situations with which characters are obliged to cope, the media project certain images of what society and reality are like. Audience members are seen as increasingly dependent on the media for forming such impressions, since so much of the life of society is beyond the reach of their first-hand experience. Consequently, the media are seen as playing a pivotal part, not merely in conveying discrete information to people about social and political events, but in shaping the background canvas of meanings and preferred ways of seeing the socio-political arena, within which such events will be placed. Here too some convergence towards Marxist interpretations of media roles is noticeable. Not only do the media perform an ideological function by cultivating certain ways of looking at the world, but this function may also be traced back to their internal modes of organization and working, and from there to their linkages to the surrounding institutional order. For example, the study by Gerbner *et al.* (1979), with which we earlier illustrated this strand of research, attributed the prevalence of violent contents on American television to the goal of maximizing audience appeal, which was rooted in turn in the commercial imperatives of American television financing. As Gerbner and his colleagues have put it:

Violence plays a key role in television's portrayal of the social order. It is the simplest, cheapest, dramatic means to illustrate who wins in the game of life and the rules by which the game is played. . . . It demonstrates who has the power and who must acquiesce in that power. (Gerbner *et al.*, 1979, p. 180)

Thus, links are forged in that interpretation between a dominant genre on American television, the messages embedded in it, and the economic rationale that sustains the medium's commercial viability.

As previously noted, the work of Gerbner *et al.* has not been immune to criticism, but significantly the most searching criticism has focused not on *whether* the media are involved in the 'construction of reality' but over whether the constructions offered by the media are indeed internally consistent and hence monolithic, or whether they should be regarded as essentially differentiated. Of course the latter position is more in line with a pluralist philosophy. Nevertheless, there appears to be a shared readiness, on both sides, at least to entertain the possibility that the media play an important, perhaps in some cases even a decisive , part in shaping audience members' perceptions of social reality.

A third example of empirical research with similar characteristics can be found in Michael Robinson's examination of the role of television in eroding public trust in American government. In this case influences on people's views about the underlying credibility and validity of institutions of political authority in the United States were seen as deriving from persistent features of political coverage on American television and especially from the tendency of the latter to highlight political conflict and the failure of leaders to cope with major political problems. Thus, this line of research (which has attracted many other contributions since Robinson's piece first appeared) is also concerned with media roles in the maintenance or undermining of legitimacy and depicts media effects (in this case, an increasing political malaise) as originating in certain production practices. Both themes are central to Marxist analyses of mass communication, even though the latter never entertain the possbility that the media may tend to *subvert* authority.

What about the other side of the convergence equation? Are all the moves being taken by only one side of the philosophical divide? Or is there some evidence of a convergence from within the Marxist camp itself towards the traditional preoccupations of effects researchers? At this early stage our answer to these questions is necessarily provisional and forms a mixed assessment. Many Marxists are now undoubtedly concerned to pay more empirical attention than in the past to the audience's response to mass communication. But they wish to develop different methodologies for studying it from those that have hitherto dominated American effects research. In pursuing such approaches, moreover, severe problems have arisen, the solutions to which are not yet clear. And their present efforts still straddle a deeply embedded tension between their new-found empirical commitments and their long-standing ideological convictions.

The growing awareness among Marxists of a need to examine audience reactions to mass-communicated messages stems from two distinct sources. First, the centrality of the concept of *codes* in certain Marxist approaches to the study of the media (see, for example, the discussions by Stuart Hall and Janet Woollacott in this book) emphasizes the importance of analysing the *encoding* and *decoding* poles of the mass communication process. Interest in the encoding process has produced a number of recent studies of media organizations, production practices and the meaning and significance of professionalism in the media. Once the terminology of encoding and decoding is adopted, however, the latter is conceptually distinguishable from the former and stands out as meriting examination in its own right. Second, working from within the Marxist tradition, studies of the audience may be regarded as essential in order to illuminate the processes whereby the mass media facilitate the emergence of 'active consent' in society, particularly in those classes whose supposedly objective interests run counter to the proffering of such consent. As Golding and Murdock (1978) have put it:

To say that the mass media are saturated with bourgeois ideology is simply to pose a series of questions for investigation. To begin to answer them, however, it is necessary to go on to show how this hegemony is actually reproduced through the concrete activities of media personnel and the *interpretive procedures of consumers*. This requires detailed and directed analysis of the social contexts of production *and reception* [our italics].

But how are Marxist scholars actually looking at the audience in these terms? Although no single way has yet firmly established itself, recent writings highlight some key elements of a distinctive Marxist approach. First, it is concerned more with audience *interpretations* of media materials than with their *effects* — with, as Murdock (1980) has put it, 'ways consumers negotiate media meanings and ... the limits to these negotiations'. This last phrase indicates a second feature: the presumption that media fare tends to incorporate and project certain 'preferred' or 'dominant' meanings, which correspond to ruling class interests and set boundaries outside which few audience members would really be free to stray. Third, however, there is scope for a diversity of response *within* those limits, the mapping of which should be plotted against the varying social backgrounds of audience members. Fourth, the material for such an examination should be drawn from free-ranging discussions of selected passages of media material, engaged in by socially homogeneous groups of people, whose acceptance, modification or rejection of the dominant meanings can then be noted by the investigator (Morley, 1980).

At this time of writing the unsolved problems of this methodology are still formidable. There is no antidote to the well-known biases of group discussions, which are notorious for concentrating on themes struck by their most vocal participants and which often focus on what people feel most comfortable conversing about — which may not necessarily reveal everything that they really think about a given topic. There is no antidote to the inherent subjectivity of the investigator, who must decide which passages in lengthy and sometimes rambling group discussions are most significant and revealing. And even if a group of audience members does appear to have accepted the supposedly 'preferred' meanings built into a passage of media material, there is no way of empirically demonstrating that such an acceptance supports the institutional *status quo*. The pressure on Marxist social scientists to face these issues is therefore urgent, for the study of mass communication as a social process without an adequately founded investigation of audience response is like a sexology that ignores the orgasm!

NOTE: This chapter incorporates an edited version of part of the Open University Course Unit on 'The Political Effects of Mass Communication' by Jay G. Blumler. The rest of the chapter represents the collaborative work of both authors, based on an earlier version prepared by Michael Gurevitch. The authors' names appear in alphabetical order.

REFERENCES

Becker, L., McCombs, M. and McLeod, J. (1975) 'The development of political cognitions', in Chaffee, S. (ed.) *Political Communication: Issues and Strategies for Research*, Beverly Hills, Calif. Sage Publications.
Becker, S.L. and Lower, E.M. (1979) 'Broadcasting in presidential campaigns, 1960-1976', in Kraus, S. (ed.) *The Great Debates: Carter vs. Ford 1976*,

Bloomington, Indiana, Indiana University Press.

Blumler, J.G. (1980) 'Mass communication research in Europe: some origins and prospects', *Media, Culture and Society*, 2 (4).

Blumler, J.G. and Katz, E. (eds) (1974) *The Uses of Mass Communication*, Beverly Hills, Calif., Sage Publications.

Blumler, J.G. and McLeod, J. (1974) 'Communication and voter turnout in Britain', in Leggatt, T. (ed.) *Sociological Theory and Survey Research: Institutional Change and Social Policy in Great Britain*, Beverly Hills, Calif., Sage Publications.

Blumler, J.G. and McQuail, D. (1968) *Television in Politics: Its Uses and Influence*, London, Faber & Faber.

Braestrup, P. (1977) *Big Story: How the American Press and Television Reported and Interpreted the Crisis of Tet 1968 in Vietnam and Washington*, Boulder, Colorado, Westview Press.

Butler, D. and Stokes, D. (1974) *Political Change in Britain*, Macmillan, London.

Chaffee, S.H. and Choe, S.Y. (1980) 'Time of decision and media use during the Ford-Carter campaign', *Public Opinion Quarterly*, 44 (1).

Clarke, P. and Kline, F.G. (1974) 'Media effects reconsidered: some new strategies for communication research', *Communication Research*, 1.

Comstock, G. (1976) *Television and its Viewers: what Social Science Sees*, Santa Monica, Calif., The Rand Corporation.

Crewe, I. (1974) 'Do Butler and Stokes explain political change in Britain?', *European Journal of Political Research*, 3, 1, pp. 47-94.

Crewe, I. (1976) 'The erosion of partisanship, 1964-1965', unpublished paper, University of Essex.

DeFleur, M. and Ball-Rokeach, S. (1975) *Theories of Mass Communication*, New York and London, Longman.

Gerbner, G. (1972) 'Mass media and human communication theory', in McQuail, D. (ed.) *Sociology of Mass Communication*, Harmondsworth, Penguin.

Gerbner, G., Gross, L., Signorelli, N., Morgan, M. and Jackson-Beeck, M. (1979) 'The demonstration of power: violence profile no. 10', *Journal of Communication*, 29, pp. 177-96.

Golding, P. and Murdock, G. (1978) 'Theories of communication and theories of society', *Communication Research*, 5 (3).

Hartman, P. and Husband, C. (1974) *Racism and the Mass Media*, London Davis Poynter.

Hawkins, R.P. and Pingree, S. (1980) 'Television influence on constructions of social reality', Mass Communication Research Center, unpublished paper, Madison, Wisconsin, University of Wisconsin.

Katz, E. (1971) 'Platforms and windows: reflections on the role of broadcasting in election campaigns', *Journalism Quarterly*, 48.

Kepplinger, H.M. and Roth, H. (1979) 'Creating a crisis: German mass media and oil supply in 1973-4, *Public Opinion Quarterly*, 43 (3).

Klapper, J. (1960) *The Effects of Mass Communication*, New York, The Free Press.

Lang, K. and Lang, G. (1966) 'The mass media and voting', in Berelson, B. and Janowitz, M. (eds) *Reader in Public Opinion and Communication*, New York, Free Press.

Lazarsfeld, P.F., Berelson, B. and Gaudet, H. (1944) *The People's Choice*, New York, Columbia University Press. Second edn 1948, with preface by P.F. Lazarsfeld.

McLeod, J., Becker, L. and Byrnes, J. (1974) 'Another look at the agenda-setting function of the press', *Communication Research*, 1.

McLeod, J. and Chaffee, S.H. (1973) 'Interpersonal approaches to communication research', *American Behavioral Scientist*, 16 (4).

McLeod, J.M. and Reeves, B. (1980) 'On the nature of mass media effects', in Withey, S.B. and Abeles, R.P. (eds) *Television and Social Behaviour: Beyond Violence and Children*, Hillside, N.J., Lawrence Erlbaum Associates.

McQuail, D. (ed.) (1972) *Sociology of Mass Communication*, Harmondsworth, Penguin.

McQuail, D. (1977) 'The influence and effects of mass media' in Curran, J., Gurevitch, M. and Woollacott, J. (eds) *Mass Communication and Society*, Edward Arnold, London.

Miller, A., Erbring, L. and Goldenberg, E. (1976) 'Type-set politics: impact of news-papers on issue salience and public confidence', Paper presented to the Annual meeting of the American Political Science Association, Chicago.

Morley, D. (1980) *The 'Nationwide' Audience*, British Film Institute Television Monograph no. 11, London.

Murdock, G. (1980) 'Misrepresenting media sociology: a reply to Anderson and Sharrock', *Sociology*, 17 (3).

Noelle-Neumann, E. (1974) 'The spiral of silence: a theory of public opinion', *Journal of Communication*, 24.

Robinson, J. (1974) 'The press as king-maker', *Journalism Quarterly*, 51.

Robinson, M.J. (1976) 'American political legitimacy in an era of electronic jour-nalism', in Cater, D. and Adler, R. (eds) *Television as a Social Force: New Approaches to TV Criticism*, New York, Praeger.

Shaw, D.L. and McCombs, M.E. (1977) *The Emergence of American Political Issues: The Agenda-Setting Function of the Press*, St Paul, Minnesota, West Publishing.

Trenaman, J. and McQuail, D. (1961) *Television and the Political Image*, London, Methuen.

10

How the media
report race

PETER BRAHAM

INTRODUCTION

Since 1948 when the first post-war West Indian immigrants arrived on the
Empire Windrush, the number of black people resident in Britain has risen
to more than one million. Though there has in this period been substantial
white immigration, the word 'immigrant' has come to be generally employed as a synonym for 'black', thereby excluding the large number of
immigrants to Britain who are white and including the large number of
black people who were born here. Thus most people would assume that a
headline which read 'IMMIGRANT BIRTHS UP' would be about an increase in
the black population. Many of the connotations of the word 'black' are to
be found in Britain's colonial past. According to Dilip Hiro for example, in
most white people's minds dark pigmentation is associated with 'dirt,
poverty, low social status, low intelligence, animal sexuality, primitiveness,
violence and a general inferiority' (1973, p. 280). If black people arrived in
Britain with the stigma of slavery and subordinate colonial status attached
to them, as immigrants they came to be associated with undesirable
behaviour such as mugging, and with social problems such as urban decay,
poor housing and overcrowding. The ease with which negative symbols can
be culled from their colonial history and their present status are perfectly
encapsulated in the Daily Express headline, 'POLICE FIND 40 INDIANS IN
BLACK HOLE' (cited in Hartmann *et al.*, 1974, p. 275).

The growth in Britain's black population has given rise to much private
and public debate, to a number of Acts of Parliament — some designed to
control further immigration and others to counter discrimination, to a great
deal of research into race relations, as well as to a great deal of conflict and
hostility. It is against this background that the way the media report race
must be considered. Race and immigration are very controversial issues,
arousing strong emotions. It is therefore to be expected that media coverage
will itself be controversial, that what is reported and the way it is reported
will be very sensitive matters. This will be so whether race is approached
with caution on the grounds that it is potentially explosive, whether it is felt
best that all the tensions and hostility which surround race relations are
fully aired, or whether those within the media maintain there is no

argument as to what constitutes news and that their duty is simply to publish it. Critics of media coverage within academic circles and among the various race relations bodies in Britain say that the media should acknowledge special responsibilities in reporting race and ought to handle race-related stories with kid gloves. In their view to adhere to normal news values will exaggerate the extent of racial conflict and this will inevitably make race relations worse. Most journalists would probably consider these criticisms to be misplaced, mainly because this would be to demand 'news as we would like it to be' rather than 'news as it is'.

Of course, this implies that news is somehow immutable, unchanging and obvious: that it 'reports itself', whereas critics of media coverage would say that news is variously manipulated, manufactured, shaped and suppressed. It is to throw light on what constitutes news in our society that the media coverage of race will be examined.

NEWS AS WE WOULD LIKE IT TO BE OR NEWS AS IT IS

The claimed difference between 'news as we would like it to be' and 'news as it is' is best exemplified by the contrast between editorials and news columns. While the news pages seem to be full of conflict and tension, editorials are likely to emphasize harmony and the need for good race relations. For example, referring to the arrival of the Malawi Asians the *Daily Express* editorialized:

There is bound to be some dismay at the news that a further 25,000 Asian immigrants will be heading for Britain in the next few years.... Yet in a very real sense Africa's loss is our gain. For in the main, these people are not layabouts looking for a cushy billet, but hard-working, ambitious and efficient traders. (10 May 1976)

On the same day, the front page headline in the *Express* ran, '£1,000 PROBLEM OF A REFUGEE — REFUSED WELFARE — BUT I'LL SETTLE FOR A COUNCIL HOUSE', and the story underneath ran:

at Gatwick Airport yesterday Mr. Maroli knew the question to ask. 'How do I get in touch with the British Welfare? I have been told that they can help me?' But Mr. Maroli will have to fend for himself — the Officials at Gatwick knew about his £1,000 nest-egg.

Butterworth's analysis of the reporting of an outbreak of smallpox in Bradford in 1962 is a valuable study of the contrast between what is written in the editorial columns and what appears on the news pages. The *Yorkshire Post* reported under the headline 'ANGER IN BRADFORD' that though there had as yet been no physical violence between blacks and whites, 'there was open evidence that the public as a whole was blaming the Pakistani population ... [and] ... conversation was mainly centred on the lines of "send them home"'. However, in an editorial published four days later the *Post* said that the Pakistani population as a whole cannot be blamed for the outbreak and castigated the 'few hooligans' who had been smashing windows and otherwise threatening innocent Pakistanis and 'who must be given to understand that they have not even the tacit support of the decent majority' (Butterworth, 1966, p. 352 and p. 356). Butterworth concludes that the *Post* often spoke with two voices: 'in its news reporting and presentation it appeared to give circulation to the kind of happenings and opinions which were likely to raise tension and were being condemned in its editorials' (ibid., p. 360), whereas the *Post* defended its news coverage by saying that in the news columns it 'gives the news as it is, not as we should like it to be' (ibid., p. 358).

In contrast, editorial comment often seems to veer towards 'news as we would like it to be'. For example, when *Colour and Citizenship* (Rose *et al.*, 1969) was published most editorial attention was devoted to the survey finding (since challenged) that only 10 per cent of the population was racially prejudiced, which was regarded by the leader writers as evidence in support of the British reputation for tolerance. On the other hand, they paid little attention to the extensive documentation of racial disadvantage contained elsewhere in the book. If we agree that a leader writer may wish to argue one case rather than another — for example, to establish the existence of racial harmony rather than racial conflict — and may even emphasize those facts which lend weight to his argument and play down those facts which would run counter to his argument, it seems strange that such selection or weighting is regarded as out of the question on the news pages. 'News values' it would seem are sacrosanct or somehow beyond the editor's control. As the Press Council put it in response to the evidence submitted by the Community Relations Council to the Royal Commission on the Press: 'It is a complete misconception of the function of the Press to imagine that it can or does control what is news' (*Guardian*, 9 May 1977).

To say as did the *Yorkshire Post* that they print the 'news as it is', or as did the Press Council that news is inviolable, is in effect to say that if the contents of news pages are ugly this is because the press acts as a mirror faithfully reflecting the ugliness of society. Even if this analogy is appropriate it should be remembered that a mirror does not only reflect what is ugly. But it would be much more appropriate to visualize the media acting as a searchlight, illuminating some areas while leaving others in shadow. What appears in the pages of a newspaper is obviously a very small proportion of what happens in the world outside. But it does not follow that the few 'stories' that are printed are representative of the many stories that reach the newspaper office, let alone of those that do not even get that far. A newspaper must have some general criteria to determine which stories are reported and which discarded, though such rules may change dramatically. For example, according to Breichner, news coverage of American blacks by all news media 'constituted almost a boycott or censorship of positive, favourable news — not always by intent, but certainly by habitual neglect' (Breichner, 1967, p. 98). In the South there was at one time an unwritten rule that photographs of blacks should never appear in print (Myrdal, 1944, p. 37), a practice which sometimes had absurd consequences, for example, as late as the 1950s, one Southern newspaper, the *Times-Picayune*, scrupulously scanned photos of street scenes and edited out offending blacks with scissors and airbrush (Harkey quoted in Harland, 1971).

In this case the prevailing attitude to blacks was that they did not form part of the audience — or at least not a part worth catering for. The point was that publishers thought that whites who would form the vast majority of the readership had little or no interest in news about blacks. Where there were particular commercial reasons for seeking a black audience, some newspapers produced a special edition (indicated by one or more stars) in the black community, though apparently most whites were unaware of its existence while many blacks thought they were buying the regular edition (Myrdal, 1944, p. 915). Matters changed with the civil rights movement of the early 1960s in the South and with the civil disorders of the late 1960s in the North. But the change in reporting was more one of quantity than quality. The black struggle for civil rights became almost routine front-page news, but the Kerner Commission observed that the media, 'have not communicated to the majority of their audience — which is white — a sense of the degradation, misery and hopelessness of living in the ghetto. They have not communicated to whites a feeling for the difficulties and frustrations of being a Negro in the United States', and the Commission repeated the criticism that news about blacks continued to be written as if they did not form part of the audience (Kerner Report, 1968, pp. 210-11). But the living conditions enjoyed by blacks in Northern cities were of little interest to whites; they did not constitute a 'problem'. The problem appeared to arise for the white audience only when blacks embarked on actions such as boycotts, violence, demonstrations or disorders which could be seen as a threat to the white majority. Indeed, it might be pointed out that the Kerner Commission itself exemplifies this: it was set up not because of the degradation of living in the ghetto but because this degradation had finally led to disorder. Tunstall (1972) quotes the comment of a British journalist on the vast amount of media coverage of the 1965 riot in Watts (Los Angeles): 'That was a story which commanded attention. Blood on the streets. You can't do better than that'. And Tunstall adds (p. 20): 'Riots in which many people are killed (in a place with whose white inhabitants the intended audience can be expected to identify) fulfil all the requirements of a big news story'.

THE MEDIA DEFINITION OF RACE

To gain a rather more systematic idea of which aspects of race in Britain make news, Hartmann *et al.* (1974) examined every thirteenth copy of the *Guardian*, *The Times*, the *Daily Express* and the *Daily Mirror* between 1963 and 1970. They concluded that there was a quantitative similarity in the handling of race by the four newspapers and that a number of themes emerged as the most salient. These were: immigration (in particular control of coloured immigration); relations between black and white (in particular intergroup hostility and discrimination); legislation to control immigration and counter discrimination; and the politician Enoch Powell.

In their content analysis they eschewed as unreliable any attempt to classify press coverage according to whether a particular attitude is conveyed. Thus an article about, say, immigration control will be placed in the same category whether it takes a restrictionist or an anti-restrictionist position. But they go further than this: in their view to measure the extent to which the various newspapers adopt different positions and display various attitudes is not merely likely to be unreliable, it is also seen as much less important than establishing that otherwise divergent newspapers agree on what the issues are. In other words the role of the media is to be sought in the way that they create awareness of issues and establish what is on the agenda for public discussion rather than in what they say about these issues or in the degree to which what is said may change opinions.

For example, of 'immigration', the topic to which the press devoted most attention, Hartmann *et al.* write:

It did not greatly matter that the material classified under this heading was a mixture of news reports about control measures instituted, or politicians urging stricter control or defending the right of Kenyan Asians to enter, of explanations of how the control measures might be evaded, or of reports of coloured people being refused entry, or of editorials or letters taking up opposing sides on the issue — and indeed the material contained all this. What is important is that central to this coverage is the theme of keeping the blacks out. That, according to our papers is what immigration is mainly about. (Hartmann, 1974, p. 128)

It may be objected that the method of content analysis chosen by Hartmann *et al.* on grounds of reliability leads almost by sleight of hand to this conclusion. For it is one thing to say it is very difficult to measure reliably differences in tone and flavour, and another to say such differences are not very important. Even though it might not be very reliable, a division between 'favourable', 'unfavourable' and 'neutral' items would demonstrate the distinct differences between the various newspapers. It is hard to imagine the *Guardian* or *The Times* publishing something like: 'Cities like Wolverhampton, Leicester, Bradford and Reading . . . the whole character has undergone an astonishing transformation. They now bear a closer resemblance to Bombay or Johannesburg than they do to the rest of England' (*Daily Express*, quoted in Harland, 1971, p. 453). There may also be important differences in content. For example, in its coverage of race the *Guardian* contains a good deal of what may be called 'hard information' on such topics as housing, employment and migration of labour. It is worth citing several of the considerable number of such articles which have appeared in the *Guardian* during the 1970s: 'Black bottom of the heap' (21 June 1974) dealt with employment prospects; 'Race against time' (a *Guardian* 'Extra', 8 July 1975) dealt with black disadvantage; and another Guardian 'Extra' dealt with the problems experienced before, during and after immigration by the Malawi Asians (21 May 1976). Indeed, notwithstanding their general conclusion,

Hartmann *et al.* praise the *Guardian* for giving more substantial coverage to housing, education and employment than the other three papers (p. 129).

Bearing in mind these qualifications, it remains the case that the position of black people in the housing or employment markets receives much less attention in the media than racial conflict and tension, though whether this is a reflection of existing hostility or whether this actually encourages hostility is a moot point. Most of the academic critics of the media coverage of race (for example, Hartmann *et al.*, 1974; Husband, 1975; Halloran, 1974; Critcher *et al.*, 1975; and Troyna, 1982) distinguish between media concentration on the 'manifestations' of racial conflict and the media neglect of the distribution of scarce social resources which they regard as the 'underlying basis of racial conflict'.

The extent to which race relations are painted in terms of conflict is illustrated by the kinds of headlines which are often used. It is only to be expected that headlines about race will be designed to dramatize events just as political disagreements are dramatized as 'clashes', 'storms' and 'rows'. Nevertheless headlines such as 'A MILLION CHINESE CAN ARRIVE HERE NEXT WEEK IF THEY WANT TO' (*Daily Express* quoted in Seymour-Ure, 1974, p. 118) are hardly likely to 'keep the temperature down'. Hartmann *et al.* found that 'race' was frequently combined in headlines with 'conflict' or 'violent' words, so that race and colour came to be associated with hostility, violence and dispute as in 'Colour Bar', 'Racial Clash' and 'Race Hate' (Hartmann *et al.*, 1974, p. 158).

This almost automatic association is illustrated by a front-page story which appeared in the *Evening News* in July 1973 under the headline 'SCHOOL MOBS IN LONDON RACE RIOT'. The report described pitched battles between pupils from rival South London Comprehensive Schools in which 'the mob of black youths stormed into Kingsdale School. They attacked mainly white pupils.... Passers-by cowered in doorways as white and black youths clashed'. However, in the next day's paper the headmaster of one of the schools was quoted as saying that there had been no *racial* clash, 'As far as I could see they were all coloured'. Following a complaint to the Press Council, the adjudication was that 'the *Evening News* story was inaccurate in a number of details.... The words "race riot" in the headline were unjustified ... [and] the newspaper should have published a retraction' (Press Council, 1974, pp. 29 and 32).

The picture which is presented by critics of media coverage of race relations is that press concentration on conflict has altered only in the sense that if the coverage of the 1960s can be encapsulated in the phrase 'Keeping the Blacks Out', the reporting of the 1970s might be encapsulated in the phrase 'The Black Problem Within'. But in a more fundamental sense there has been little change: in both decades the press has presented a white audience with the image of a black threat to a white society.

But those factors which are peculiar to coverage of race relations are inextricably linked and overlaid with the operation of normal news values. This can be illustrated by the press coverage of the arrival of a number of

Malawi Asians in 1976. This coverage was inaugurated by a report which appeared in the *Sun* under the banner headline, 'SCANDAL OF £600-A-WEEK IMMIGRANTS' (4 May). It reported that two families comprising thirteen individuals had been accommodated for some five weeks by the West Sussex County Council at a four-star hotel at a weekly cost of £600. The *Sun* continued to give the story extensive coverage for nine days and some of the developments of the story can be deduced from various headlines which appeared on 5 May:

Daily Express:	MORE ASIANS ON THE WAY TO JOIN 4-STAR MIGRANTS
Daily Mail:	WE WANT MORE MONEY SAY £600-A-WEEK MIGRANTS
Daily Telegraph:	MIGRANTS 'HERE JUST FOR THE WELFARE HANDOUTS'
Sun:	ASIANS OFF TO THE WORKHOUSE
The Times:	HOMELESS ASIANS LIKELY TO BE MOVED TO WORKHOUSE BY END OF WEEK COUNCIL SAYS.

(Evans, 1976)

It is not hard to see elements in this story which would have aroused the interest of 'our merciless popular press' even had the individuals concerned not been black immigrants: 'spongers', free-spending welfare officials, wasting of public money, and so on, will usually make a good story. But in this case the racial aspects provided an added dimension sufficient to push the story onto the front pages and keep it there for some nine days. This dimension may consist of fears of an unending flow of black immigrants (perhaps attracted by welfare handouts), the belief that immigrants live off the welfare state, and the strong passions aroused by immigrants' entitlement to council accommodation. In short, what made it a good story was that the threat implied by black immigrants was sufficient to ensure that 'race was news'.

Because race was news in this case does not mean that race is always news, or that stories about race are not subject to the normal criteria of news value. But the operation of news values and the definition of news are extremely elusive. The journalist, perhaps quite prudently, is not much concerned with analysing why a story is 'news'; it is enough he has — or believes he has — a nose for the kind of story which, in the words of a distinguished American newspaper editor, makes the reader say 'Gee Whiz'. It is left to the outsider to try to go beyond this cliché — that 'news is news', to try and arrive at some understanding of the way in which all sorts of newspapers select which news is fit to print, though it should go without saying that such an understanding in no way equips us to say which stories will see the light of day or reach the front page. In the most general terms, however, we can say that news values tend to neglect background material. Events are likely to appear as sudden and unexplained or as having only direct and immediate causes. The underlying state of affairs which social scientists would say helps explain or gives rise to a particular event tends to be absent or to be taken for granted in the news reports. And of these dramatic and immediately-caused events, those which are readily associated with conflict, tension, threat and violence are the most likely to make news. The authors of *Colour and Citizenship* allege that the tremendous publicity that race receives has less to do with 'actual conflict' than with the conflict which editors think is inherent in race (Rose *et al.*, 1969, p. 740). The idea that conflict and violence make news may serve as a rule of thumb whether it is applied in the popular press in the words of a cigar-chewing editor greeting news of a murder committed in horrifying circumstances, 'Don't forget we're in the bad news business'; or whether it is applied to the quality press in the more sober words of the Press Council: 'Bad news has always been a more salutory instructor than good news and its publication is necessary to the efficient functioning of society' (*Guardian*, 9 May 1977).

There may be aspects of the way the media report race which are special to race in so far as a large black presence in a predominantly white society may be automatically depicted as a threat. But even if it can be justly claimed that there is thus what amounts to a special 'racial angle' in news coverage it does not follow that each omission and commission of media reporting of race should be explained in such terms. For example, it is easy to assume that the instinctive association of black people with threat and conflict explains why the press devotes little attention to such background issues as the position of black people in education, housing and employment, without stopping to consider that the press — guided by considerations of news value — may generally devote inadequate attention to such background areas whether or not the people concerned are black.

NEWS FRAMEWORKS

News values not only govern what will be selected as newsworthy, but will also help determine how a particular story is presented to the reader. Whatever ingredients a story has to recommend it, it will be more acceptable, however unexpected or dramatic it appears, if it can, at the same time, be readily slotted into a framework which is reassuringly familiar to both journalist and reader.

The coverage of race relations is very likely to change in tone and scale according to whichever views currently prevail about the state of race relations throughout the media as a whole or within an individual newspaper. For example, a race riot or disturbance could be portrayed as an isolated incident, the result of a conspiracy or as part of a growing wave of racial unrest. The sort of considerations which might influence an editor's decision on how to treat the story might include: is race currently regarded as particularly newsworthy, perhaps because we are in the middle of a 'long hot summer' of racial unrest? How are other newspapers running the story? Are politicians making play of the event or are they trying to play it down? And are there other events which either magnify or overshadow the event in question?

Reporting is not simply a matter of collecting facts, whether about a race riot or about anything else. Facts do not exist on their own but are located within wide-ranging sets of assumptions, and which facts are thought to be relevant to a story depends on which sets of assumptions are held. These sets of assumptions are referred to as 'news frameworks'. It stands to reason that journalists faced by the need to meet their deadlines must have a set of preconceptions of what is related to what, a sort of 'ready reckoner'. If both journalists and readers associate race relations with conflict and see black immigration as a threat, then reporters and editors, presented with a vast number of events from which to choose, pressured by deadlines and constrained by the limited amount of space available, may simply treat news about race relations in a way which fits in with this definition. In other words, what they are doing, as they must, is to present the news which is unfamiliar by virtue of just having happened — in as familiar and easily digestible a fashion as possible.

Of course, there may be circumstances in which a newspaper goes out of its way to highlight an issue. For example, an editor may pursue a campaign about, say, rising crime in order to demonstrate that 'law and order is breaking down' or 'violence is on the increase', even though crimes of violence may be decreasing even as the campaign becomes more shrill (Davis, 1973). But there need be no campaign or conscious decision for the media definition to begin to distort the reporting of race relations (or any other subject). Indeed, the distortion may be most pervasive where the media definition is not employed consciously, where there is no campaign.

This distortion could occur in two ways. First, events which conform to this framework might have a better chance of being reported than those which conflict with it. For example, an announcement in 1970 that the birth-rate among New Commonwealth immigrants was rising received a great deal more coverage than the news that immigration from the New Commonwealth was declining. Whereas seven out of the eight national dailies carried the birth figures (five on the front page), only four of them carried the figures on immigration (only one on the front page) (Hartmann and Husband, 1974, p. 167). Second, an event may be reported not as it happened, but as it is expected to happen (Murdock, 1973, Knopf, 1973). Combining these two possibilities, we can speculate that once a decision is taken to give an event publicity, based on its 'consonance' with the prevailing news framework, it may then be reported in such a way as to conform to this framework.

The extent to which the media definition of race influences or distorts the reporting of events is a matter of controversy. Max Wall, editor of the *South London Press*, says that

Today any newspaper which attempts to cover community relations, even remotely adequately, is aware of constant surveillance, not only from those working in the field, but by social and political groups, trade union organizations, university researchers and often the minority press. (Wall, 1978, pp. 463-4)

Thus, according to Wall, reporters on the *South London Press* — although they inevitably make errors of both fact and judgement — are 'instructed to check, check and check again all stories with any ethnic content — to an extent far beyond that felt necessary in other fields' (Wall, 1978, pp. 463-4). On the other hand, according to Harold Evans, the former editor of the *Sunday Times*,

Racial stories tend to be reported against only the flimsiest background of verifiable fact.... There is persistent carelessness in sources. Odd individuals without any real following at all are elevated into 'spokesmen' for immigrant groups, though a moment's enquiry would show that they are spokesmen for no-one but themselves. (Evans, 1971, p. 45)

If either of these two views is to be accepted then we must conclude that there *is* something special in the way the press reports race: either particular care is exercised (partly because of the expected surveillance by numerous outsiders), or there is unusual ignorance and carelessness.

Perhaps the perfect illustration of Evans' contention was the *New York Times*'s coverage in 1964 of the 'Blood Brothers' — an alleged organization of Black teenagers in New York who were said to be pledged to maim or kill any white person venturing into Harlem. The *Times* cited four isolated and unsolved slayings of whites in hold-up attempts and credited them to the Blood Brothers. According to one commentator, despite denunciations of the story from every responsible social and anti-delinquency agency in Harlem and despite, as another commentator put it, the difficulty — as those who work in Harlem know only too well — of getting 400 Negroes organized to do anything, 'the *Times* continued to pursue it with its competitors panting in its path — and with the Blood Brothers' membership growing from 30 to 400 and then dropping to 90 in successive editions' (Poston, 1967, p. 68; also Klein, 1967, p. 148). Moreover, this was not an isolated example, for as Poston explains, there was hardly a year without a season of black scare stories: 'One paper may pick up a legitimate and dramatic story of racial conflict and then the season is on. A competitor will seek a "new angle" only for the story to be topped by a third and a fourth rival' (Poston, 1967, p. 67).

This process of a dramatic story being launched in one paper with other papers rushing to produce 'new angles' was repeated in reports that a black power group was trying to take over Manchester City Council (Kushnick, 1970). It was also an example of reporting in line with prevailing assumptions rather than by careful probing of sources and evidence. The story broke on 4 September 1970 in the *Guardian* under the headline 'Black Power Bid to Rule Manchester', and in the Manchester edition of the *Daily Telegraph* under the headline, 'Black Power Attempt Poll Sabotage'. The essence of the plot was revealed the following day by the *Daily Sketch* (similar reports were carried in the *Daily Mail*, *Manchester Evening News*, *Scottish Daily Express* and *Western Daily Press*) under a three-inch banner-headline, 'BLACK POWER ELECTION PLOT': it involved a plan to swamp the city council elections by putting up more than 100 candidates for a single seat, and the report relayed claims from the plot's instigators that they had launched similar campaigns in several major cities.

By contrast, a report which appeared in the *Sunday Times* on 6 September claimed that inquiries 'into the so-called Black Power bid to seize political control of seven major cities' seemed to show that the organization which had been reported as being responsible for the Black Power election plot — the Campaign for Relief of Need (CARN) — might be controlled not by blacks but by white right-wingers. The report claimed that two of CARN's organizers had long associations with various right-wing organizations. These associations were further explored in the 'World This Weekend' (BBC Radio 4) on 6 September and in the *Guardian* on 7 and 8 September.

It may be thought that the press would seize on this dramatic reversal of events and so extract further mileage from the story. But in spite of exposures carried by the *Sunday Times* and the 'World This Weekend', the press stuck to the original story and gave no hint of these developments as is shown by some of the headlines which appeared on 9 September:

Sun:	'94 BLACK POWER MEN "IN ONE HOUSE" GET POLL BAN'
Daily Mail:	(Manchester Edition):
	'Lord Mayor Foils Black Election Plot'
Daily Mirror:	'Ban on Black Power Election Plot'
Daily Sketch:	'95 at One Address Foils a Black Power Votes Plan'
Daily Express:	'Black Power Poll Bid Fail'
Daily Telegraph:	'Ban on 94 Black Power Nominees'

Why these newspapers should uniformly ignore the new information provided on 6 September is not altogether clear. Perhaps it was because the original idea of a 'Black Power Election Plot' was so good a story that to reveal that it might actually be a plot to discredit Black Power in particular and therefore black people in general would be too tame an ending. Or perhaps it was, as Kushnick suggests, that the press ignored new evidence because the original story fitted so well with the framework of attitudes held by the British public about Black Power. In any event this 'media blindness' was not confined to the press. As Downing recorded, BBC TV News

Took with the utmost seriousness the claims of a Manchester West Indian to be a colonel in the black power movement, and to have discovered a loophole in electoral law which would enable him to flood Manchester City Corporation with black power advocates.... Later in the year the whole affair was exposed by a '24 Hours' item; the news section, however, maintained a stony silence in the face of their own gullibility. (Downing, 1975, p. 115)

It may seem that the reporting of the 'Black Power Plot' is an extreme case; that the safest conclusion is that once the media had ignored contrary evidence (or at least had not let it alter the framework within which the story was being reported), it simply became too embarrassing to admit that they had — partly by virtue of the sheer intensity of coverage — perpetuated a hoax on themselves. What makes the case of general interest is the nature of the prevailing assumptions themselves and the ease (rather than the tenacity) with which the media were able to adhere to this ready-made framework, in which blackness appears to be automatically coupled with threat and conflict. It must be borne in mind, however, that just as 'bad news' is more newsworthy for journalists than is good news, so 'bad reporting', in the sense outlined by Evans, is more noteworthy for media critics than is careful reporting. The reporting of the Blood Brothers or of the Black Power Plot may thus be typical of slipshod or careless reporting without being typical of all reporting.

What most media critics do hold to be typical of all reporting is that the media have concentrated on the threat perceived by the white majority to be implicit in black immigration and in the black presence; and that they have neglected the extent of discrimination and disadvantage experienced by blacks except in so far as these very conditions seem to contribute towards the supposed threat, for example, by fostering anti-social behaviour. They seek to give the impression that in all important respects the media have presented their audience with an unvarying picture of race and immigration in Britain. Husband, for example, writes that the 'news consensus' suggests that the bulk of the white population

receiving news media definition of events would find a statement that black immigration is a threat and a problem quite reasonable ... the news media have reported race relations in too uncritical a way: they have reflected racist assumptions and reported without adequate analysis racist behaviour and racist policy. (Husband, 1975, pp. 26-7)

It is true that because news values favour stories about racial conflict rather than about racial harmony, media reporting is likely to portray black immigration as a threat. But it is also true that other factors have influenced coverage of race relations.

THE CHANGING CONSENSUS

Foremost amongst these have been considerations of 'media responsibility' which have been invoked by many media controllers in order to keep down the temperature of race relations. The most notable expression of these considerations during the 1960s came from the then Director-General of the BBC, Sir Hugh Carlton Greene, who said:

In talking about the BBC's obligation to be impartial I ought to make it clear that we are not impartial about everything. There are, for instance, two very important exceptions. We are not impartial about crime ... nor are we impartial about race hatred. (Quoted in Harland, 1971, p. 21)

Whereas this permitted plenty of coverage of crime but excluded giving a platform to those who advocated robbing banks, in the case of race relations this precept was interpreted as meaning that merely to exclude those who advocated 'race hatred' was insufficient, and that it was best to have as little coverage of any kind, based on the proposition, allegedly adopted by liberal-minded producers of such programmes as 'Panorama', that to focus on racial problems at all would merely serve to stir them up (Seymour-Ure, 1974, p. 112). Moreover, as long as those who expressed strongly anti-immigrant opinions were confined to the unsavoury political fringes, those who controlled the media felt they could be safely ignored.

If in the Britain of the mid-1960s the media did then proclaim a consensus on the subject of race and immigration, it was not, as the media critics contend, simply that black immigration was a threat, it was also that black immigration was a threat that had already been greatly diminished by the passage of stringent new immigration laws, and which would be diminished still further if the presence of black people was not made the subject of media controversy. The problem that resulted was — contrary to Husband's contention that media coverage reflected racist assumptions — that the media gave little or no airing to opinions which, though they appeared unsavoury to media critics and media controllers alike, were very widely shared among the general public. As Enoch Powell remarked: 'There's very little connection here between the manner in which these subjects are discussed . . . and the realities as they are known by the citizens of this country' (1970 TV interview, quoted in Downing, 1975, p. 134). It seemed in the end that the attempt to play down racial conflict and hostility had been counter-productive. At least this was the view expressed by the BBC to the Select Committee on Race and Immigration. In its evidence the BBC departed from its position of the mid-1960s to state unequivocally that there could be no manipulation of the audience by the suppression of certain stories, nor could there be any departure from its policy of truth in order to achieve racial harmony (Toynbee, 1976).

According to Jeremy Isaacs, a former producer of 'Panorama', it was Enoch Powell who demonstrated that the media consensus had been counter-productive:

Television current affairs deliberately underplayed the strength of racist feelings for years, out of the misguided but honourable feelings that inflammatory utterances could only do damage. But the way feelings erupted after Enoch Powell's speech this year was evidence to me that the feeling [i.e. presumably, against black immigration] had been under-represented on television, and other media. (Quoted in the *Guardian*, 13 November 1968)

The main purpose of the speech on immigration which Enoch Powell delivered in Birmingham in 1968 was to sweep away what he saw as an artificial consensus. It could be argued that he succeeded in this purpose in so far as many opinions which would formerly have been labelled as 'unsavoury', and could therefore have been safely ignored, were now regarded as expressions of legitimate attitudes and fears, and as such could be given circulation in print and on the air. Much later, however, Powell paid tribute to the resilience of the old consensus:

One cannot but grudgingly admire the success with which those in authority, political and official, and the 'best people' of all parties and of none, have succeeded in burying out of sight the greatest problem overhanging the future of Britain. (1975 speech, quoted in Evans, 1976, p. 11)

Powell challenged, in particular, two important elements of the consensus. First, he pointed out that the threat of black immigration had not been ended by the various Immigration Acts because the rights of dependents of existing immigrants remained untouched. Second, he questioned the viability of a *peaceful* multi-racial Britain in face of a black presence which would grow irrespective of any immigration laws which might be passed, as growing numbers of blacks would be born here.

The speech received extremely wide coverage (an opinion poll taken a few days later revealed that 96 per cent of respondants were aware of the nature of the speech) because Powell had chosen to speak out on a subject that everyone else of repute in politics had chosen to avoid. He chose to speak in a way, moreover, which he believed expressed the feelings of the general public and which was designed, in his own words, 'to bring out the sense of oppression, the sense of being victimized which is felt in these areas' (i.e. of coloured immigrant settlement) (quoted in Seymour-Ure, 1974, p. 113). The result was, in Seymour-Ure's words, 'an earthquake': London meat-porters and dockers — hardly traditional supporters of Conservative politicians — marched in his support; thousands of other workers laid down their tools; and Powell received 110,000 letters (containing something like 180,000 signatures) all but 2000 of which expressed approval for what he said. The speech and its immediate consequences dominated the headlines for a full eight days.

Although many of the newspapers condemned what Powell had said in their editorials, and most condemned the way in which he had said it, this was outweighed by the sheer intensity and duration of coverage, an intensity which signified that what could now be taken for granted in public debate over race and immigration had changed. As a report in *The Times* observed:

Over the past six days Mr. Powell has stirred the national emotions more than any other single politician since the war. Not even Aneurin Bevan at his most acerbic so inflamed opinion — and so cut across traditional political loyalties. (quoted in Seymour-Ure, 1974, note 16)

Powell has remarked that as a politician he regrets only what he has refrained from saying rather than anything he has actually said; and that as a politician what he says should aim 'to provide people with words and ideas which will fit their predicament better than the words and ideas which they are using at the moment'. In his Birmingham speech (and in later speeches on the same subject) Powell was concerned to give voice to a public opinion which had been unable to find public expression although he knew it to exist.

Powell would claim that he did not seek to change public opinion but only to give voice to the feeling — albeit an unfocused feeling — which already existed. The change that Powell did seek was in the attitude of those in control of the media — 'the best people' — so that instead of suppressing stories about the discontent and hostility which resulted from black immigration and settlement, the media should illuminate 'the greatest problem overhanging the future of Britain'. It may be objected that this is disingenuous in that whatever the discontent surrounding race and immigration, the moment a politician of Enoch Powell's prominence draws attention to it, it is amplified and so a problem of a different magnitude is created. But whatever validity this objection has should not distract us from drawing the correct lesson from the coverage of the speech, and from the impact of that coverage on future coverage of race and immigration: namely, that the speech could only have created an 'earthquake' in a climate where anxiety and discontent about race and immigration were both widespread and deep, and where this anxiety and discontent had been accorded insufficient attention in the mass media.

The effect of Powell's speech was to convince those media controllers who required convincing that any special responsibility to avoid worsening or inflaming a delicate situation, which had often led them in the past to suspend or downgrade normal news values, was now clearly outweighed by the need to keep public confidence. After the speech, for example, the *Wolverhampton Express and Star* received 5000 letters supporting Powell and only 300 opposing him. A subsequent poll conducted by the newspaper recorded a 'vote' of 35,000 for Powell and only a tiny number against him. As the editor of the paper remarked:

We cannot build up the sort of reader-editor relationship which establishes the local paper as a local ombudsman on matters like unemptied dustbins, uncut grass verges, unadopted roads, unlit streets, excessive council house rents and all that sort of thing, and then snap it off shut on a major social issue like this. To do this would be to betray that faith which readers would have in us and the social function of newspaper production. (Jones, 1971, pp. 16-17)

CONCLUSION

Much has been claimed about the power of the media to determine what are regarded as major social issues and the sorts of questions most people have in their minds about them. According to Spiro Agnew, for example, the small group of men who control the media 'decide what forty-five million Americans will learn of the day's events in the nation and the world . . . these men can create national issues overnight' (quoted in Burns, 1977, p. 59). Particular reference has been made to the power of the media to influence the state of race relations. For example, UNESCO declared that the media can have a crucial role in encouraging or combating racial prejudice; and Harold Evans believes that what the media publishes about ethnic groups can directly affect ethnic tensions. The coverage of Powell's speech, however, indicates that the power of the media might be much smaller than is often supposed and that it was Powell who changed the definition of the situation so that the focus of debate became a concern with the consequences of a large and growing black presence, and that the media controllers saw no alternative but to pass on this message.

Even if as Evans says, 'the way race is reported can uniquely affect the reality of the subject itself' (1971, p. 42), the effectiveness of the media message depends on how well it accords with various feelings, dispositions and circumstances already present in a particular society.

Where prevailing beliefs are hostile to immigrants in general or to black immigrants in particular, stories which present black people in a favourable light may be widely seen as evidence that the media are not giving a true picture, whereas 'selective perception' will exaggerate the amount of material unfavourable to blacks which is *perceived* to be in the media. If the media message is uncongenial it is likely to be distorted or rejected in order to fit in with the recipient's outlook, because people tend to react to the media according to their initial attitudes. The editor of one provincial newspaper, for example, noted that news about black immigrants is read by many whites who live in areas of high immigrant density, many of whom, in his experience, regard any favourable reference to black immigrants as evidence of media bias (Jones, 1971, p. 19). On the other hand, it can be presumed that the majority of his readers would not question items which could give an unfavourable impression or which could be used to reinforce stereotypes: for example, they may see reports of crimes committed by members of immigrant groups as proof that most blacks are criminally inclined.

This is not to concede, as Husband argues, that the contents and impact of the mass media coverage of race should be assessed on the basis that 'We are a society with racist beliefs entrenched in our culture and racial discrimination evident in our laws and in our behaviour' (Husband, 1975, p. 23). If we bear in mind that the reception accorded to black immigrants has been far less violent than that which met Irish immigrants to Britain in the nineteenth century, it could equally well be argued that the hostile predisposition referred to by Jones can be explained in terms of traditional dislike of foreigners and resentment at the influx of immigrants (of whatever colour) into particular local communities.

If the media now presented a picture more in keeping with this resentment and did more, as Powell wished, 'to bring out the sense of oppression, the sense of being victimized', so satisfying their white audience, they have, as we have seen, been roundly criticized from another source. Critics of media coverage argue that there has been undue concentration on the *manifestations of tension* — such as hostility and conflict — at the expense of such topics as housing, education and employment which 'might be thought to represent major social resources, competition for which would seem to be among the underlying roots of tension' (Hartmann *et al.*, 1974, p. 132). This amounts to saying that the media have concentrated on the effects, the tip of the iceberg, rather than on social structure and the distribution of resources, a concentration which would presumably be explained in terms of news values. But the housing and employment markets, and the study of discrimination and disadvantage within them, cannot be arbitrarily designated as 'background' factors with the implication that they are *causative* (i.e. if you take away shortages of housing and jobs, race relations will become universally smooth). It is just as plausible to argue that competition for housing and jobs provide a *pretext* for expressions of ethnocentrism or racialism.

This cautionary note does not, however, dispose of the criticism that media coverage of race has ignored structural factors. The press has, for example, given little consideration to the context within which New Commonwealth immigration occurred. The great bulk of this immigration took place in an era of excess demand for labour and as such was welcomed by both government and employers. Until social and political considerations were judged to outweigh economic interests, black immigration seemed the easiest means of filling the gaps left by indigenous workers who were increasingly demonstrating their refusal to perform a whole range of jobs characterized by low wages, unsocial hours and poor conditions, whereas, except for the occasional mention of poverty and unemployment in the Third World and the attractions of a steady job and comparatively high wages in Britain, little or nothing of this economic aspect has been presented in the media.

Against this it has been argued that it is a misconception to treat 'the problem' of the mass media as primarily a cognitive one: that news is not a surrogate form of social enquiry; and that media critics are wrong in treating media men

as if they have signed up to be professional sociologists and have fallen down on the job ... where the measure of distortion is precisely the extent of discrepancy between their account and that given by the favoured sociological theories of the media scholars'. (Anderson and Sharrock, 1979, pp. 369 and 383)

The irony is that the sociological definition of race relations which has been the product of lengthy 'scientific enquiry' is itself open to grave criticism. In particular, the sociological definition has been unduly influenced by the American experience and the wealth of research which is available about that experience. The consequence has been that race *per se* has generally been unquestioningly accepted as the key to understanding the position of black people in Britain; it is regarded as sufficient to refer to a 'society where racism is entrenched' or in which the connotations of blackness are wholly negative. On the other hand, the parallels which may be drawn between the position of black immigrants in Britain, and that of the more than eleven million migrant workers who work in the North-European industrial triangle to perform the jobs which indigenous workers no longer wish to perform, have received — until the appearance of certain publications in the early 1970s (Castles and Kosack, 1973, Bohning, 1972) — insufficient attention. Thus it can be said that both the media definition and the sociological definition have 'fallen down on the job', though editors may reasonably point out that it is not their task to provide an adequate sociological definition of race.

The standards by which the press should be judged, according to the Royal Commission on the Press, included the need to provide 'a clear and truthful account of events, of their background and their causes; a forum for discussion and informed criticism' (Royal Commission, 1949, Para. 362). Measured against these standards, the performance of the press may leave something to be desired. Perhaps this is because such standards have little to do with newsgathering and rather more to do with scientific enquiry. News, by contrast, has more to do with what is happening now than what has evolved over many years; as Walter Lippmann put it: 'the news does not tell you how the seed is germinating in the ground but it may tell when the first sprout breaks through the surface' (quoted in Daniel, 1968, p. 8).

As far as reporting race relations is concerned, once the contradiction between 'keeping the temperature down' and following 'news values' was resolved in favour of the latter, it became inevitable that the bulk of media coverage (with the exception of the quality press to which media critics pay insufficient attention) would be formulated in a way which would both reflect the changing consensus and hold the attention of the mass audience. Thus the news framework is constructed around the problem of the black presence and within it news values revolve around conflict and tension.

REFERENCES

Anderson & Sharrock (1979) 'Biasing the news: technical issues in "media studies"', *Sociology*, 13 (3).
Bohning, W. (1972) *The Migration of workers in the United Kingdom and the European Community*, London, Oxford University Press, for the Institute of Race Relations.
Breichner, J. (1967) 'Were broadcasters colour blind?' in Fisher, P. and Lowenstein, R. (eds) *Race and The News Media*, New York, Praeger.
Burns, T. (1977) 'The Organization of Public Opinion', in Curran, J. *et al*, (eds) *Mass Communication and Society*, London, Edward Arnold.
Butterworth, E. (1966) 'The 1962 smallpox outbreak and the British press', in *Race*, 7 (4).
Castles, S. & Kosack, G. (1973) *Immigrant Workers and Class Structure in Western Europe*, London, Oxford University Press, for the Institute of Race Relations.
Critcher, G. *et al*. (1975) *Race in the Provincial Press*, Birmingham, Centre for Contemporary Cultural Stories, University of Birmingham.
Daniel, W. (1968) *Racial Discrimination in England*, Harmondsworth, Penguin.
Davis, F.J. (1973) 'Crime news in Colorado newspapers', in Cohen, S. and Young, J. (eds) *The Manufacture of News*, London, Constable.
Downing, J. (1975) 'The balanced (white) view', in Husband, C. *White Media and Black Britain*, London, Arrow.
Evans, H. (1971) 'A positive policy', in *Race and the Press*, London, Runneymede Trust.
Evans, P. (1976) *Publish and Be Damned*, London, Runneymede Trust.
Halloran, (1974) 'Mass media and race: a research approach, in *Race as News*, Paris, Viesco Press.
Harland, P. (1971) 'Reporting race: some problems', in *Race and the Press*, London, Runneymede Trust.

Hartmann, P. *et al.* (1974) 'Race as news', in Halloran, J. *Race as News*, Paris, UNESCO.

Hartmann, P. and Husband, C. (1974) 'The mass media and racial conflict', in Cohen, S. and Young, J. (eds) *The Manufacture of News*, London, Constable.

Hiro, D. (1973) *Black British, White British*, Harmondsworth, Penguin.

Husband, C. (1975) *White Media and Black Britain*, London, Arrow.

Jones, C. (1971) 'Immigrants and the news', in *Race and the Press*, London, Runneymede Trust.

Kerner Report (1968) *Report of the National Advisory Commission on Civil Disorders*, London, Bantam.

Klein, W. (1967) 'The new revolution: a postscript', in Fisher, P. and Lowenstein, R. (eds) *Race and the News*, New York, Praeger.

Knopf, J. (1973) 'Sniping — a new pattern of violence', in Cohen, S. & Young, J. (eds) *The Manufacture of News*, London, Constable.

Kushnick, L. (1970) '"Black power" and the media', in *Race Today*, December.

Murdock, G. (1973) 'Political Deviance: the press presentation of a militant mass demonstration', in Cohen, S. and Young, J. (eds) *The Manufacture of News*, London, Constable.

Myrdal, G. (1964) *An American Dilemma*, New York, Harper & Bros.

Poston, T. (1967) 'The American negro and newspaper myths', in Fisher, P. and Lowenstein, R. (eds), *Race and the News Media*, New York, Praeger.

Rose, E. *et al.* (1969) *Colour and Citizenship*, London, Oxford University Press, for The Institute of Race Relations.

Royal Commission on the Press (1949) Report (Cmnd 7700) London, HMSO.

Seymour-Ure, C. (1974) *The Political Impact of the Mass Media*, London, Constable.

Toynbee, P. (1976) 'Media's name is mud when race is news', *Observer*, 20 June.

Troyna, B. (1982) 'Reporting the National Front: British values observed', in Husband, C. (ed.) *Race in Britain: Continuity and Change*, London, Hutchinson.

Tunstall, J. (1971) *Journalists at work*, London, Constable.

Wall, M. (1978) 'Caution or Credibility', in *New Community*, Journal of the Commission for Racial Equality.

11

Media, 'reality', signification

TONY BENNETT

THE MEDIA AS 'DEFINERS OF SOCIAL REALITY'

In making the national press awards for 1977, James Callaghan referred to
the media as a 'mirror held up to society'. The analogy is, of course, a
hackneyed one. The concept of the mirror with its attendant series of
questions — do the media offer a faithful reflection of reality, or do they
mirror the real in a one-sided, distorting way? — has haunted the study of
the media since its inception. The difficulty with the analogy, however,
consists in the suggestion that a dividing line can be drawn between 'reality'
or society on the one hand and the world of representations on the other. It
implies that the media are secondary and derivative, somehow less real than
the 'real' they reflect, existing above society and passively mirroring it
rather than forming an active and integral part of it. Like a mirror, it is
suggested, they reflect only what is placed in front of them by the structure
of the real itself.

In truth, this difficulty is not limited to media studies. The theory of the
sign developed in the work of Ferdinand de Saussure, the founder of
modern linguistics, posits a duality between the world of signification and
that of 'reality' — a duality kept alive by Saussure's distinction between the
sign and referent — and, correspondingly, implies that the former is in some
way subordinate to and governed by the latter (see MacCabe, 1978, chapter
4). The world of signs can only signify the reality which is given to it; the
media can only reflect what is already there. Subalterned to the reality it
mirrors, the world of signs is granted only a shadowy, twilight existence; it
'hovers' above 'reality' as an ethereal appendage to it, deriving such
substance as it has merely from what is reflected within it.

More recent developments in the theory of language have pulled in a
direction directly contrary to this, stressing not only the independent
materiality of the signifier — the 'fleshiness' of the sign — but also the
activity and effectivity of signification as a process which actively
constructs cognitive worlds rather than simply passively reflecting a pre-
existing reality. Indeed, whereas once the priority of signified over signifier,
of 'reality' over signs, used to be stressed, this relationship seems now often

to have been reversed as the signifier is held to pre-exist and have priority over the signified. Sign orders world.

An apparently similar perception backgrounds the contention that the media should be viewed as 'definers of social reality'. True, the phrase retains a certain duality, a crucial ambiguity of formulation — first there is reality, the 'real real', and then there are the media, its 'definers' — which as we shall see, remains the source of important theoretical difficulties. Given this qualification, the contention is one that allow the media and the terms of signification they propose something other than a secondary, reflective role in social life. For to suggest that the media should be viewed as 'definers of social reality' is to suggest that *what* 'events' are 'reported' by the media and the *way* in which they are signified have a bearing on the ways in which we perceive the world and thus, if action is at all related to thought, on the ways in which we act within it. It is to affirm that the media *are* agencies of mediation, that in reporting events they also propose certain frameworks for the interpretation of those events, moulding or structuring our consciousness in ways that are socially and politically consequential. Viewed in these terms, the media are not *apart from* social reality, passively reflecting and giving back to the world its self-image; they are *a part of* social reality, contributing to its contours and to the logic and direction of its development via the socially articulated way in which they shape our perceptions.

My aim in this essay is to illustrate the sorts of claims that have been made within this tradition of media theory by commenting on three different levels of media practice at which the reality-defining role of the media has been approached and conceptualized. The first concerns the propaganda function of the press. It is a matter of public knowledge that each newspaper treads a certain party line and that, in seeking to recruit public support for the political philosophy it favours, seeks to 'sell' a particular political definition of the events it reports. This is reflected in its editorial columns, use of language and photographs, headline layouts and so on. I will thus be concerned, at this level, with media practices that deliberately report events in a manner which serves to promote particular political views in the pursuit of particular political objectives, be these implicit or explicit.

Next, I shall consider the role played by the way in which the popular press signify the activities and behaviour of various groups of 'outsiders'; that is, groups whose behaviour is viewed as transgressing or threatening the cohesiveness of dominant social norms — drug-users, criminals, soccer hooligans, 'mods' and 'rockers' and so on. My concern here will be with the part that this area of media practice has played in the development of a law and order ideology since the mid-1960s. Finally, consideration will be given to the extent to which the culture of consensus politics can be said to provide the dominant background against which the media project the events they report. Our interest here will centre chiefly on the television news and on the extent to which, although neutral in party-political terms

— and obliged to be so by law — they are, in the words of the last Director General of the BBC, Sir Charles Curran, 'biased in favour of parliamentary democracy' (cited in Hall *et al.*, 1976, p. 57). At this level of analysis, I shall be principally concerned not with conscious bias but with the 'unconscious' bias which results from the implicit, taken-for-granted assumptions of consensus politics embodied in the ideologies and working practices of professional communicators.

However, I shall also be concerned to point to some of the difficulties associated with this tradition of media theory, particularly with regard to the way in which its implicit retention of the mirror analogy impedes an adequate theorization of the politics of signification. Owing to limitations of space, however, it will be necessary to present these criticisms in programmatic form rather than as part of a fully developed critique.

POLITICS AND THE MEDIA

In his essay 'Looking Back on the Spanish Civil War', Orwell wrote:

Early in life I have noticed that no event is ever correctly reported in a newspaper, but in Spain, for the first time, I saw newspaper reports which did not bear any relation to the facts, not even the relationship which is implied in an ordinary lie. I saw great battles reported where there had been no fighting, and complete silence where hundreds of men had been killed. I saw troops who had never seen a shot fired hailed as the heroes of imaginary victories; and I saw newspapers in London retailing these lies and eager intellectuals building emotional superstructures over events that had never happened. I saw, in fact, history being written not in terms of what happened but of what ought to have happened according to various 'party lines'. (Orwell, 1974, p. 233)

In order to understand Orwell's comments on the press coverage of the Civil War, it is necessary to sketch in the background to the struggle in Spain. In broad terms the political situation in Spain from 1930 to the end of the Civil War can be understood in terms of a struggle for power between three contending political forces: the bourgeois republican parties (the Republican Union, the Catalan Left, the Basque Nationalists) subscribing to a bourgeois-democratic programme of reforms; right-wing bourgeois forces of a pro-monarchy and fascist hue led by Franco; and a variety of working-class political forces subscribing to a variety of communist, socialist and anarcho-syndicalist ideologies. During the greater part of the early 1930s, nominal power was held by a succession of administrations headed by bourgeois-republican forces. The basis upon which power was exercised, however, was an excessively fragile one, the bourgeois-republican democracy being susceptible to successive challenges from both the left and the right. The final blow came in the July of 1936 when Franco initiated a fascist uprising by calling on the army to support him in establishing an authoritarian state.

To appreciate the political logic of the Civil War, it is important to note that the resistance to Franco came from the workers who, in Barcelona,

Madrid, Valencia and Malaga armed themselves, put down the garrisons and, through a series of anti-fascist round-ups, established control over those provinces and thus forced on the bourgeois-republican forces the defence of their own republic. Furthermore, in doing so, the workers' forces pushed the logic of events beyond the parliamentary-democratic phase by seizing control of industry, placing it on a war-time footing, and placing the fleet under the control of elected sailors' committees. In the countryside, there was a mass seizure of the land by the peasantry; property titles, mortgages and debt records were burnt and peasants' committees formed to organize the supply of foodstuffs to the town workers. It *could* be argued, then, that what was at issue in the Civil War was not *merely* the defence of traditional bourgeois-democratic rights and liberties, inasmuch as there existed in the republican camp a situation of 'dual power', of proletarian forms and institutions existing side by side with bourgeois ones.

So much for the line-up of political forces in Spain. To understand the direction and significance of the struggle for the definition of the political realities involved in the Civil War, our analysis must shift to the international level. For the events in Spain occupied a position of nodal political significance inasmuch as it clearly held implications for, and offered opportunities to, the three major political principles operative in Europe at the time — bourgeois-democratic, communist and fascist. So far as the latter were concerned, it was clear to Hitler and Mussolini that Franco's victory, especially if procured through the assistance of German and Italian arms, would offer them an important extension in the sphere of their influence and significantly alter the balance of power in Europe. They accordingly offered Franco, quite openly, military, financial and diplomatic assistance on a large scale.

The situation for France and Britain was more delicate. On the one hand, the victory of Franco was clearly not in their interests if it would give Hitler a footing in the Iberian peninsula. On the other hand, the successful pursuit of the Civil War in a revolutionary proletarian direction could hardly be expected to recruit their support either. For it, too, especially if achieved with Russian assistance, would have altered the balance of power in Europe. Equally important, it would have offered the working classes of England and France a revolutionary example which, in the appropriate circumstances, they might have wished to imitate. The western press, so Orwell alleges, accordingly pursued a combination of three strategies with regard to the definitions it imposed on events in Spain.

First, it significantly overplayed the extent of Russian involvement on the side of the republican forces, thereby suggesting that the struggle in Spain was not a struggle waged by the toiling masses for their own interests but one in which the Spanish people were being used to further the global political objectives of the USSR. This interpretation, Orwell argued, significantly limited support for the republican forces among both working-class and bourgeois-humanist forces in Britain. The fact that the more specifically proletarian aspects of republican Spain — the workers' committees running the factories, the mass seizure of the land by the peasantry, the initially democratic structure of the army, etc. — were underplayed or simply not mentioned at all, also served to limit the development of ties of international proletarian solidarity with the Spanish working class. Time and again, in *Homage to Catalonia*, Orwell records his sheer disbelief, on returning from the front to France and England, at the number of not only 'fellow-travellers', like himself, but also working-class militants in those countries who were simply not aware of the proto-revolutionary aspects to the conflict in Spain. This was reinforced by the tendency to report the events in Spain within a 'democracy versus fascism' political construction at the expense of stressing the respects in which the activity of the Spanish workers had also placed revolutionary socialist objectives on the agenda. Again, Orwell is instructive here. For he records that many of the trade-union militants and members of the liberal intelligentsia, himself included, who went to Spain to join the International Brigade believed that they were going to the defence of democracy in an abstract sense, and he notes that it was only by directly participating in the struggle in Spain that he gradually became aware of its specifically proletarian and socialist aspects.

Although with some qualifications, Anthony Aldgate's recent study of the British newsreel companies' coverage of the Spanish Civil War confirms the general thrust of Orwell's criticisms. However, Aldgate suggests that the specific inflection of the events in Spain effected by the newsreels was determined less by any outright hostility to the republican cause than by the need to recruit support for the government's policy of non-intervention, itself dictated by Britain's commitment to the political initiatives being made at the time for disarmament in Europe. In view of these considerations, Aldgate argues, the early newsreel coverage of the Civil War tended to sympathize with neither the republican nor the insurgent forces but sought rather to draw a contrast between the miseries of war-torn Spain and the ordered, peaceful and improving quality of life in Britain in support of fostering an anti-war climate of opinion. This also partly explains why the part played in Spain by *both* the Soviet Union *and* the fascist forces of Hitler and Mussolini tended to be underplayed as part of an attempt to limit the significance of events in Spain, to present the War as a purely local dispute (this being contrary to the policy pursued within the press) and thereby — through controlling definitions in this way — to reduce the chances of the Civil War becoming the touchstone that might spark off a general European conflagration.

Given this qualification, however, the newsreels can by no means be exonerated from the charge that their coverage was biased against the republican forces, although this was effected more by omissions — but highly significant omissions — than by any explicitly biased editorial comment. Whilst the Russian assistance to the republican forces was occasionally dealt with, for example, all the major newsreel companies maintained a virtually total conspiracy of silence concerning the assistance Hitler and Mussolini rendered the insurgent forces — a conspiracy that was maintained by such tricks of the trade as simply not mentioning the fact that the planes which bombed Guernica had been supplied by the Luftwaffe (although *The Times* had printed this information — see Aldgate, 1979, pp. 159-60). Similarly, Aldgate records that the existence of the International Brigade was scarcely ever acknowledged and that, when it was — as in a 1937 Paramount newsreel — it was only to suggest that such Brigades consisted wholly of the unemployed, thereby suggesting that the volunteers who went to Spain did so out of necessity rather than out of principle, and that, once in Spain, they were used for road making rather than for fighting, none of which was true. Perhaps more important, however, was the way in which — quite contrary to historical record — several newsreels insinuated that it was the republican rather than the insurgent forces which were responsible for the disorder in Spain. Commenting on the contrasting ways in which the republican and insurgent forces were typically represented — the former as un-uniformed, apparently ill-disciplined and, not infrequently, engaged in church burnings (some of which were clearly stage-manged) or other acts of desecration; the latter as neat, orderly, professional and disciplined, usually associated with symbols of traditional Spain — Aldgate remarks:

All in all, despite the fact that the Nationalists constituted a rebel, Insurgent army, it takes little effort to conclude that the imagery surrounding it is that of traditional, conservative Spain, fighting to preserve its heritage. While the duly elected Republican Government is presented as maintaining an undisciplined army bent upon destruction and upheaval. (Aldgate, 1979, pp. 116-17)

To return to Orwell, his concern — and his indignation — were more particularly exercised by the role played by the Communist Party press in mediating the Spanish Civil War to the international labour movement, and this, in turn, can only be understood in terms of the opposition between Stalinist and Trotskyist policies at the time. Trotsky's prognosis of the situation in Spain was clear (see Trotsky, 1973). He recommended that the workers' committees in the army and industry should be built on so as to create Soldiers and Workers' Councils capable of posing a serious alternative to the Cortes (or parliament) as a form for the organization of state power. He further urged that the war should be pursued as a revolutionary war, waged both to defend and extend the socialist ground already won in the republican camp, and that such socialist gains — particularly the virtual abolition of land ownership — should be extensively publicized in a propaganda war aimed at both undercutting Franco's support among the peasantry in the territory he occupied and deepening, extending and developing the support offered Spanish workers by the international labour movement. Above all, whilst advocating that communists should co-operate with bourgeois, anarchist and socialist forces in defence of the Republic, Trotsky recommended that the communist forces in Spain should at all times retain their organizational, propagandistic and programmatic independence in order not to be politically compromised by the pursuit of collaborationist policies.

Viewed in terms of its effects, however, Trotsky's prognosis was not particularly influential in mediating the events of the Spanish Civil War to either the Spanish or the international working class. In Spain itself, the Partido Obrero de Unificación Marxista (POUM) came closest to embracing a Trotskyist position, but the links between this organization and the international Trotskyist Left Opposition were severed when André Nin led POUM into a coalition government in 1936. Internationally, of course, Trotsky's analysis of the Spanish situation was circulated only within the pages of the *Bulletin* of the Left Opposition. Put simply, the Trotskyist forces lacked a mass newspaper through which to make their definition and interpretation of the Spanish situation count, to make it a widespread part of working-class consciousness and thus an effective ingredient within that situation itself.

Not so the Communist Party. In accordance with the logic of socialism in one country, the policy of popular frontism was officially adopted by the Comintern in 1935. Briefly, according to the prognosis of the Comintern, revolution was no longer an objective possibility in Europe; the issue of the day was 'democracy versus fascism'. Politically, this meant that communists should seek alliances with socialist and bourgeois-democratic opponents of fascism and that the Soviet Union should seek treaties of alliance with the western democracies, France and Britain in particular, against Hitler. This entailed that distinctively communist objectives were to be temporarily abandoned in favour of an ameliorative political stance which would facilitate the building of such alliances. Given this perspective, it was highly inconvenient that the Spanish workers took to barricades in the way they did. For whilst the Comintern would clearly have forfeited all credibility on the left had it failed to intervene in support of the Spanish workers, it would have proved impossible to forge the alliances required by the political perspective of the Popular Front had that intervention assumed too direct or revolutionary a character.

The logic of events in Spain was accordingly redrawn in accordance with Popular Front conceptions. The issue, it was said, was not socialism versus fascism but democracy versus fascism. The first task was to defend the bourgeois-democratic forms of the Republic against the insurgent forces and to consolidate this ground before going on to develop a struggle for socialism against bourgeois democracy. The strategy of the Communist Party in Spain was thus that communists should enter into formal alliance with the bourgeois-democratic forces in the Republic and, as the price of doing this, abandon the distinctively proletarian forms of organization that had been created in the republican camp in order to make sure of a solid front with the bourgeois-republican forces in defence of democracy. The disbanding of workers' and soldiers' committees; the return of factories and of the land to private ownership; the disarming of workers' militias — all of these measures were initiated and implemented by administrations which included members of the Spanish Communist Party.

The Communist Party press, reflecting the Comintern's position, sought constantly to interpret the Spanish situation in terms of the logic of the Popular Front and, as Orwell noted with incredulity, accordingly excluded virtually all mention of the distinctively proletarian edge which the Spanish workers and peasants had themselves given to their struggle. It sought also to discredit Trotskyist forces in Spain by presenting the leaders of POUM as fascist *agents-provocateurs* bent on encouraging the Spanish proletariat to take an increasingly revolutionary stance in order to justify a direct German invasion of Spain.

Looking back, much of this seems scarcely credible. Yet it needs to be borne in mind that we have been made aware of the proletarian dimensions of the struggle in Spain only posthumously. For, at the time, there was a large degree of complicity between the ways in which the communist and the western capitalist press reported (or did not report) and interpreted events in Spain. Both, for their different reasons, were instruments of darkness. A footnote which underwrites the point is the difficulty Orwell had in obtaining a publisher for his *Homage to Catalonia* for it was, initially, rejected by both capitalist and left-wing publishing houses for political-ideological reasons which should require no further comment.

It would be wrong, of course, to suggest that Orwell's study of the press coverage of the Civil War could be viewed as a model of sociological analysis. It was too impressionistic for that, lacking both methodological rigour or any sense of theoretical distance. It was, moreover, clearly partisan in the respect that Orwell does not conceal his sympathy for the Trotskyist prognosis of the political logic of the War. However, I would count this in its favour. To speak of the political role of the media is not an abstract undertaking. It can be done only through a study of the role played by the media in concrete, historically determined political conjunctures; and to study these, it is necessary to deal not only with the media but also with the political issues at stake in those conjunctures. One does so at a price, of course. For it is not possible to offer an analysis of a given political conjuncture without being drawn — as Orwell was — into the maelstrom of political debate and, thereby, of politics itself. It is, however, misplaced to imagine that one might stand aloof from this arena.

Perhaps the greatest value of Orwell's study, however, consists in the fact that it deals with events that were of a momentous, world-historical significance in relation to which — although their impact may not be quantifiable — the part played by the media was politically consequential in ways that may not seriously be doubted. In 'Looking back on the Spanish War', Orwell argues that, no matter what might have happened on the ideological front, the disposition of military and international forces was such that the Republic would probably have been lost anyway. But he also records that there are different ways in which a defeat may be suffered. As he wrote in *Homage to Catalonia*:

For years past the communists themselves have been teaching the militant workers in all countries that 'democracy' was a polite name for capitalism. To say 'Democracy is a swindle', then 'Fight for Democracy!' is not good tactics. If, with the huge prestige of Soviet Russia behind them, they had appealed to the workers of the world in the name not of 'democratic Spain', but of 'revolutionary Spain', it is hard to believe that they would not have got a response. (Orwell, 1974, p. 68)

There is, of course, no way of telling what might have happened had the Communist Party issued such a revolutionary call or what might have happened — both in Spain and internationally — had an alternative, say Trotskyist policy, been pursued. Maybe total disaster. Maybe an under-mining of the political stability of France and England. But is clear that the way in which the Spanish Civil War was lost created considerable disillu-sionment and, indeed, disarray within the ranks of the European left, just as it is clear that, in terms of their coverage of the Spanish situation, the media — capitalist and communist — did not function as a passive mirror but, through the way in which they defined and interpreted that situation, actively contributed to shaping the contours of the political map of pre-war Europe.

Yet Orwell's study also clearly exemplifies the central difficulty associated with the proposition that the media should be viewed as definers of social reality. For the proposition is one that keeps alive the concept of media as mirror at the same time as it contests it. 'This kind of thing is frightening to me,' Orwell wrote of the press coverage of the Spanish Civil War, 'because it often gives me the feeling that the very concept of objective truth is fading out of the world' (Orwell, 1974, p. 235). The definitional frameworks to which Orwell points are, by implication, all distorting ones; they are measured as being in some way false in relation to that 'real real' of 'objective history' — a real that exists prior to and independently of signi-fication. But this is merely to keep alive the notion that there may be forms of signification that are adequate in relation to the 'real real' they are alleged thus to re-present, forms which are, so to speak, neuter in that they allow the real to reveal itself 'as it really is'. The mirror analogy, therefore, is not so much abandoned as simply re-worked: there are mirrors and mirrors, it is implied. Some may be partial and distorting, but the possibility of a form of representation that does genuinely re-present or mirror the real is retained as the standard against which the distorting effects of such 'false mirrors' may be assessed. In spite of appearances, politics is thus evacuated from the world of signs. Implicitly, signification is allowed an effectivity only in so far as it is, simultaneously, deception. The sphere of ideology, as a sphere of struggle, is defined not by the clash and reverberation of sign versus sign — of competing systems of signification locked in combat — but by the simple opposition of truth versus falsehood.

THE DEVIANT IN THE MEDIA

The attribution of a reality-defining role to the media hinges on two pro-positions. The first is that the news is a manufactured product, not necessarily in the sense that it is contrived or invented but in the sense that it is the product of a culturally encoded and socially determined process of making which displays, in its content and form, the technical and ideological forces which bear on its construction. The second is that the power which the media derive from their reality-defining capability is attributable largely to the service they perform in making us the indirect witnesses to events of which we have no first-hand knowledge or experience.

Both of these propositions are central to the tradition of media theory concerned with the definitions the media impose on the behaviour of various groups of 'outsiders'; that is, of those groups — drug-addicts, criminals, soccer hooligans, homosexuals — whose behaviour is viewed as transgressing dominant social norms, be these enshrined in law or in custom and convention (see Cohen and Young, 1973). Briefly, it is contended that, by casting such groups in the role of 'folk-devils', the media serve to strengthen our degree of commitment to dominant social norms and, thereby, to create a climate of opinion supportive of the operations of society's law-enforcement agencies and of the extension of their powers. Developments within this area of media theory, however, have been greatly indebted to the more general theoretical realignments which have characterized the recent history of the sociology of deviance in this country, particularly as represented by those associated with the National Deviancy Symposium (see Cohen, 1971).

In classical criminology, the concept of criminal behaviour was largely regarded as an unproblematic given. Criminality or any other form of deviance, that is, was viewed as a property inherent within certain types of acts themselves. Given this, the primary analytical task was held to be that of explaining such behaviour within reference to the, so it was felt, abnormal causes (social, psychological or even biological) which must be responsible for it. The contemporary focus within deviance theory, by contrast, is concerned more with the social processes within which the attribution of deviance is made. Deviance, that is, is no longer regarded as an attribute immanent within certain acts but as a label which is attached, via a series of complex social processes, to those types of behaviour which transgress either legally codified rules or normatively enshrined codes of behaviour. It is thus, it is argued, a term whose use reflects the relative power of certain social groups to impose the label — and, of course, the punitive practices of the legal and penal systems — on those whose behaviour is incompatible with the socially dominant concepts of legality and normality which are ideologically buttressed and sustained by those groups. Although this does not deny the cogency of inquiring why it is that the members of some social groups are more likely to engage in such forms of behaviour than are the members of other groups, it does entail a shift of interest away from the behaviour of the so-called deviant towards an examination of the social and cultural processes whereby the attribution of the label of deviance is made to some acts but not to others and of the functions which the nomination of such acts as deviant fulfils in relation to the wider social order.

These developments within sociology have been influenced by and, in turn, contributed to parallel developments in the field of historical scholarship. Particularly relevant here are those studies of witch persecutions — witches being the deviants *par excellence* of earlier, theological universes — undertaken by English and American historians (see, for example, Macfarlane, 1970). These suggest that, in periods of disorientating social, political and economic crisis, the responsibility for such crises will be projected onto vulnerable groups of 'outsiders' who, by virtue of their divergence from dominant social norms, are structurally well placed to serve as scapegoats. Dramatized in the form of show-trials, their behaviour serves, in a way that conforms with the Durkheimian logic of the social function of deviance, to reinforce, by negative example, the threatened power of dominant consensual norms.

Whilst it might be tempting to argue that such irrational forces play no part in modern political processes, recent experiences preclude any such sanguine conclusion. The treatment of Jews in Hitler's Germany; the Moscow show-trials of the 1930s; the persecution of communists in the McCarthy era; Powellism — all of these are contemporary instances which may be cited. Sociologists working at the meeting point of media theory and deviance theory have argued that the presentation of deviance by the media in recent years has exhibited a similar logic in producing, through their symbolization and dramatization of the behaviour of 'mods' and 'rockers', drug users, soccer hooligans, political extremists and so on, a gallery of 'folk-devils', a modern demonology. By the devices of exaggeration and stereotyping, by wrenching such forms of behaviour from any societal context that might help to explain them, it is argued that social tensions have been signified within a semiology of law and order which has served to reinforce the strength of dominant consensual norms. Involved as the unwilling participants in a kind of modern morality play in which they serve as the negative symbols of disorder, thereby pointing to the need for society to mount a permanent patrol along its normative boundary-lines, the behaviour of such 'deviant' groups is so defined that they appear both to crystallize and to be responsible for the acute instability that has characterized British society since the 1960s.

It may be objected that the obvious difficulty with theories of this nature is that they are couched at such a level of abstraction as to render either their confirmation or disconfirmation difficult. Indeed, it may further be argued that there is a real difficulty in imputing any effectivity of whatever kind to the media if, as is often argued, the influence they exert on the social world is necessarily an indirect one determined by the influence they exert on the actions of individual members of the audience via their impact on their consciousness. For it is by no means easy to know how one might sift out, in both quantitative and qualitative terms, the discrete and differential impact that the media might have in influencing our view of social reality and hence our actions within it. To show that the media propose certain definitions of reality is one thing; but it cannot be inferred from this that such definitions are necessarily accepted in the sense that they are effectively taken for real and acted upon. One cannot, in other words, infer 'audience response from the nature of the message they receive' (Hall *et al.*, 1976, p. 52).

This is clearly a general problem; indeed, it is perhaps the most important single outstanding theoretical difficulty in need of exploration in media sociology. Currently, far from being resolved, there are few signs that the problem has even been adequately conceptualized (a notable exception being David Morley's work on the 'Nationwide' audience — see Morley, 1980). So far, inquiries in this area have largely taken the form of audience research based on sampling and questionnaire techniques. Whilst clearly helpful in some areas — the impact of the media on voting behaviour, for example — it is equally clear that there are some questions, vital and important ones, which cannot be tackled in this way. For, in speaking of the impact of the media on the terms in which we see the world, we are speaking of an ideological process which, in so far as it concerns the formation of consciousness, is one which those subjected to it — you, me, all of us — tend to be unconscious of. It escapes our consciousness inasmuch as it constitutes the framework within which our consciousness is produced. This is not to say that the operations of ideology are necessarily invisible; but it is to say that their invisibility is a condition of their effectiveness. They have to be *made* visible. It therefore follows that the proposition that the media are influential in proposing certain ideologically derived definitions of reality is one that cannot be dependent for its validation solely upon the subjective reports of those whose consciousness is said to be produced, without their being aware of it, by this process. It is a proposition that would automatically lose its theoretical power were it to be operationalized in this way.

A further difficulty with such approaches consists in the methodological individualism they exhibit in according priority to the study of the individual and her or his consciousness over the study of groups, group formation and the institutional structure of society. Much of the more general theoretical and methodological value of recent studies concerned with media representations of deviance consists in the fact that they are not liable to this criticism. For they have addressed the question of media effects not solely or even primarily as an issue that concerns the consciousness of individual members of the audience but have sought rather to theorize the media-society connection in terms of the impact which this area of media practice has exerted on the practices of law-enforcement agencies.

Stanley Cohen's *Folk Devils and Moral Panics: The Creation of the Mods and Rockers* — a study of the local political reactions to the media sensationalization of the 'mods' and 'rockers' incidents of 1964 — offers a useful illustration of some of the issues involved here. Cohen argues that, in the seaside resorts concerned, the local business communities, perturbed lest the sensationalism of the press reports reduced the volume of their summer trade, were anxious that the impression should be created, nationally, that, in future, such occurrences would be well under control. As a consequence, there emerged — as evidenced in public meetings, letters to the local newspapers — a number of 'moral entrepreneurs' who further amplified the media's already exaggerated inflation of the 'mods' and 'rockers' problem by calling on the police and the courts to adopt new and more severe strategies in relation to it. Tear-gas, more police, national service, corporal punishment — all of these proposals were mooted and debated in the columns of the local press.

The police, not surprisingly, were not unresponsive to the manifestation of such a supportive climate of opinion at grass-roots level. Apart from cancelling weekend leave so as to increase the police presence on the streets, Cohen records that a variety of new tactics were adopted in an attempt to nip any potential trouble in the bud, by what is known, euphemistically, as preventive police work. These tactics included confining likely trouble-makers to one part of the resort, usually the beach; preventing people whose appearance suggested that they might be 'mods' or 'rockers' from congregating at certain previously designated 'trouble-spots'; the harassment of so-called potential trouble-makers by, for example, the confiscation of studded belts as dangerous weapons or by giving them 'free lifts' to the roads leading out of town or to the railway station (see Cohen, 1972, p. 93 for details). Inasmuch as these tactics involved an infringement of the liberty of the youths concerned prior to the actual commission of any offence, their constitutional and legal propriety was questionable. The behaviour of certain of the local magistrates, however, was perhaps even more disturbing. For, sensitized to the 'mods' and 'rockers' menace by the media and by the crusading activities of the local 'moral entrepreneurs', they seem not only to have passed unduly severe sentences on the offenders brought before them and to have used their power to remand in custody as a form of pre-trial additional punishment but, particularly in the trials which followed the incidents at Margate over the Whitsun weekend of 1964, to have used the court-rooms to further develop and elaborate the dramaturgy of 'mods' and 'rockers'. This was particularly true of one Dr. George Simpson, who gained a certain national fame — or notoriety — through his harangues from the bench on the subject of hooligans and the severity of the sentences he passed.

The attractiveness of Cohen's study consists in the fact that it deals with the effects of media definitions of reality not by regarding the media as isolable variables whose discrete and differential influence must be precisely measured and quantified. Rather, it places those definitions within a wider social process, seeing the media's practices as having consequences for and, in turn, being influenced by the reality defining practices of other social agencies and institutions — the police, the courts, local political and interest groupings and so on. The effect that is attributed to the joint practices of such agencies and institutions is that of the creation of an 'amplification spiral' whereby the scope and significance of an initial 'problem' — that is, of what is defined as a problem by such agencies — is subject to increased magnification as the reality-defining practices of such agencies reciprocally sustain and complement one another. In the case of the 'mods' and 'rockers' incidents of 1964, this 'amplification spiral' worked as follows: first, the national media dramatized the confrontations that took place at such resorts as Eastbourne and Margate; the moral crusaders and the local press then took up the problem; the police responded by introducing new policing measures; these led to an increase in arrests and the magistracy responded by further dramatizing the 'mods' and 'rockers' in their court-room speeches — all of which was reported in the media, thereby adding another loop to the spiral.

In this case, the moral panic sparked into life by this circuit of amplifying significations soon worked itself out — if only because changes in teenage fashions deprived the initial dramaturgy of much of its signifying potency. And, of course, one could argue that the immediate, tangible consequences of the panic were limited in import — a localized abuse of police power, a few wrongful arrests and a handful of unduly harsh sentences. In their *Policing the Crisis* (also discussed in chapter 4 of this collection), however, Stuart Hall and his co-authors argue that such moral panics — when viewed collectively and cumulatively — have played a major role in so orchestrating public opinion, via the production of a generalized law-and-order crisis, as to have recruited support for a significant extension of the arbitrary and coercive powers at the disposal of the state.

This thesis is set within the wider context supplied by an application of Gramsci's concept of hegemony to the contours of post-war British history. Briefly, the authors of *Policing the Crisis* contend that the period since the early 1960s has witnessed the development of a deep and sustained crisis of hegemony in this country, a crisis which has rendered the production of popular consent to ruling-class political and economic objectives increasingly problematic and which, thereby, has occasioned the need for the state to accumulate a reservoir of coercive powers which might be used to exact such compliance forcibly. The end of the post-war boom and the continued declining international competitiveness of the British economy, it is argued, have resulted in a marked sharpening of class conflict as an increasingly militant, unionized working class has resisted attempts to resolve the economic crisis by capitalist means — that is, by allowing unemployment to increase, the attempts to impose income restraints, cuts in the social services and so on. This resistance took its most highly effective and dramatic form in the miners' strike in the winter of 1973-4 which, in challenging the ability of an elected government to govern, bore clear testimony to an attenuation of ruling-class authority.

If, at the political level, the resolution of this crisis has been sought by means of strengthening the powers of the state — particularly in regard to the sphere of industrial relations — Hall and his colleagues argue that support for such policies has been recruited chiefly by the way in which the crisis has been ideologically signified as a crisis of law and order. Whereas, in the earlier part of this period, such moral panics as that exemplified by the 'mods' and 'rockers' scare tended to be discrete and of short duration, it is contended that, particularly during the 1970s, there has operated a 'signification spiral' whereby hitherto discrete and localized problems — rebellious youth cultures, student protest, industrial militancy, flying pickets, mugging — have been pulled into a seamless web of associations. Presented as manifestations of a common problem — the breakdown of respect for the authority of the law — it has thereby been suggested that they are susceptible to a common solution: an increase in the scope of the law and a strengthening of the means of its enforcement.

There is not the space here to survey the details of this study. The most that can be attempted is a brief adumbration of the more important theoretical and methodological advances that are registered within it — or at least in those parts of it which bear most directly on the study of the media — and of the problems that remain. Perhaps the most important advance consists in the contention that the signifying or reality-defining practices of the media should not be viewed in isolation. In examining the axial, coordinating signifying role accorded to the figure of the 'mugger' within the ideology of law and order between 1972 and 1976, *Policing the Crisis* stresses that this was produced not merely by the media but by and within the context of the symbiotic relationships that exist between the media and other reality-defining agencies — particularly, in this case, the courts, senior police officers and leading political spokespersons. The media did not 'invent' the law-and-order crisis *ex nihilo*. Nor were the policies they pursued the effect, in any direct or obvious sense, of the structure of media ownership. Nor was there a ruling-class conspiracy in which political leaders and media magnates colluded in manufacturing a crisis of law and order. Rather, Hall and his colleagues speak of a much more subtle process whereby the definitions of the media and the discourse of the powerful — the framing definitions supplied by prominent public figures — tend to sustain and reinforce one another owing to the close ties of dependency that exist between them, the media depending on prominent public figures as a primary source of newscopy just as the latter depend on the media for placing their diagnoses and prescriptions before a wider audience.

Although, in this way, the pitfalls of conspiracy theory are avoided, some difficulties remain. The overall thesis of the book is that the law-and-order crisis has been constituted via a specific ideological inflection of Britain's economic crisis and that the effect of this ideological inflection has been to deliver popular support for the pursuit of specific political strategies in relation to the economic crisis:

There is, of course, no simple consensus, even here, as to the nature, causes and extent of the crisis. But the overall tendency is for the way the crisis has been ideologically constructed by the dominant ideologies to win consent in the media, and thus to constitute the substantive basis in 'reality' to which public opinion continually refers. In this way, by 'consenting' to the view of the crisis which has won credibility in the echelons of power, popular consciousness is also won to support the measures of control and containment which this version of social reality entails.' (*Policing the Crisis*, pp. 220-21)

The central difficulty with this formulation consists in the secondary role it appears to accord to the sphere of the ideological — secondary in the sense that it is conceived as a response to an economic crisis that is pre-given to it. The effect of this is to reproduce the antinomies — sign/world, signifier/signified — with which we have become familiar in relation to Orwell's work by conceiving these as analogous to the relationship between ideology and the economy. For such formulations as 'the way in which the crisis has been constructed' suggest that it is possible to speak first of a crisis (an economic crisis) and then of the mode of its ideological signification. It is to suggest that a crisis may be held to exist prior to and independently of the way in which it is ideologically signified. It would be a mistake, however, to press this objection too strongly. The problems associated with the residual economism to which they subscribe are ones that the authors of *Policing the Crisis* are fully aware of, and the determinancy that is allocated to the economy is, indeed, in Althusser's famous phrase, that of the last instance which never arrives. If the ideology of law and order is held to constitute a specific discursive inflection of economic crisis, the role allotted to that ideology is a far from passive one; its role in structuring the terms of political debate so as actively to influence the forms adopted for the political regulation of that crisis is, indeed, the very *raison d'être* of the book.

Perhaps the most important aspect of the book from the point of view of our concerns here, however, has to do with the extent to which it undermines the view that the media should be theorized as 'definers of social reality'. For the ideology of law and order is not primarily assessed in terms of its accuracy as measured against some independent index of the 'real' extent and distribution of crime. There is some element of this, it is true, but the preponderant emphasis is placed upon the *articulating* role of this ideology, on the ways in which it pulled together and connected, around the image of the mugger, a series of linked ideologies concerning, *inter alia*, the rebelliousness of post-war youth, the 'lawlessness' of trade unions, race, immigration and Empire. In short, the concern that is focused in *Policing the Crisis* is not that of the relationship of ideology to 'reality' but that of the relationship between ideologies. The effectivity that is attributed to the discourse of law and order is understood not in terms of its codification of a reality presumed to be external to it but in terms of the position it has occupied in relation to associated discourses which, conjointly with it, are held to constitute a dimension of reality itself — fully physical and material — and not a secondary, ontologically debased reflection or transformation of a 'more real' reality.

It is perhaps necessary to add that this break is not made quite so clear or so cleanly as it might be. In part, this is a result of the often somewhat unsatisfactory coupling that the study seeks to effect between a wide range of extraordinarily diverse bodies of theory. *Policing the Crisis* is, indeed, extremely confusing in this respect and, at times, has the appearance of a huge melting-pot into which virtually every available tradition of analysis has been poured with insufficient attention being paid to the problems involved in thus combining them. This constant elision of theoretical difficulties results in the often superficial and misleading grafting of one tradition of analysis on to another in what can only be regarded as an over-hasty quest for synthesis. It is thus noticeable that, although the stress that is placed on the articulating role of the ideology of law and order is ultimately derived from the work of Antonio Gramsci and Ernesto Laclau, the route through which this perspective is reached is supplied by previous studies of the role played by the media, construed as definers of social reality, in the orchestration of moral panics. It is in the disparity between these two perspectives and the languages appropriate to them that the central tensions of the book are located.

THE IDEOLOGY OF TELEVISION NEWS

The fourth and most important filter [Richard Hoggart has argued, speaking of the processes by which the news is constructed] — since it partly contains the others — is the cultural air we breathe, the whole ideological atmosphere of our society, which tells us that some things can be said and that other had best not be said. It is that whole and almost unconscious pressure towards implicitly affirming the *status quo*, towards confirming 'the ordinary man' in his existing attitudes, that atmosphere which comes from the morning radio news-and-chat programmes as much as from the whole pattern of reader-visual background-and-words which is the context of television news. (Glasgow University Media Group, p. X)

The level of analysis which Hoggart introduces here is concerned with the much less visible ideological pressures which, inherited by reflex from the dominant political culture and embodied in the codes and conventions of the working practices of professional journalists, give to the news — the journalistic form in which the 'facts' are said to be represented free from bias or comment — its distinctive ideological skew. This level is, in many senses, the most important aspect of the reality-defining practices of the media if only because its ideological underpinnings are the least visible. We expect the editorial columns of our daily newspapers to relay certain party lines and may thus interpret what they have to say with due caution, whilst most readers display a certain degree of scepticism in relation to media sensationalism. 'The news', by contrast, presents itself and is widely taken to be an impartial record of the key events of the day. It presents itself as 'truth', as raw, unprocessed reality; as the world narrating itself.

Although canons of impartiality are embedded in the news format of the daily press as well as in the news bulletins of the broadcasting media, the ideological role played by the latter is probably of the greater importance — both because of the sheer scale of their impact and because their claims to neutrality are more clearly articulated, and more widely credited, than are those of newspapers. The audience for the major news bulletins of all three channels is significantly larger than the readership of any national newspaper — ITN's 'News at Ten' had an estimated nightly audience of between 12 and 15 millions in 1977 — and, as the Annan Report confirms (para. 17.2), the amount of time devoted to news programmes has increased dramatically in recent years. The BBC's news coverage, for example, more than doubled between 1962 and 1977. Perhaps more important, as the Annan Committee again reported, an increasing percentage of the public has come to rely on television as its primary source of news and, according to surveys conducted by Professor Himmelweit, both the BBC and ITN news bulletins are widely regarded as being more trustworthy and impartial than newspapers. Finally, of course, impartiality is an official requirement placed on the broadcasting companies by the charters which govern them. Television news may therefore be taken as an extreme and limiting case: if it is possible to demonstrate the operation of ideological categories here — the acknowledged pinnacle of impartiality in the media world — similar claims made by journalists working in other media will thereby be called into question.

This is not to suggest that the broadcasting media have ever claimed to be impartial in any truly philosophical sense. As Reith said of the BBC's operations in the midst of the General Strike: 'since the BBC was a national institution, and since the government in this crisis was acting for the people, apart from any emergency powers or clauses in our licence, the BBC was for the government in the crisis too ...' (cited in Hood, 1972, p. 415). Both the BBC and the ITV companies have the right — which was fully endorsed by the Annan Committee — to waive the constraint of impartiality in their coverage of those events and issues which are considered (by whom?) to challenge the constitution, the national interest or public order. Northern Ireland is a case in point where the media have been, so to speak, officially biased — albeit not altogether openly so in the respect that such official bias has, by now, been naturalized through systematic exclusion of any alternative perspective.

However, whilst it is possible to itemize cases of overt bias and explicit censorship, it is arguable that the ideological effectivity of the news is greatest in those areas where the operation of the particular signifying conventions which constitute the news and seem to secure its impartiality — the use of actuality footage or of live interviews, framed by the apparently impersonal and neutral narrative of the presenter, for example — conceal the operation of another, ideologically loaded set of signifying conventions. *Bad News*, the Glasgow University Media Group's study of the television news coverage of industrial disputes in 1975 affords a good illustration of this. For although not partial in the sense of favouring a Conservative versus a Labour Party position in relation to these issues, this study convincingly argues that the way in which such stories were actually handled — the criteria of newsworthiness that were used, the place that they occupied within the structure of the news bulletin as a whole and so on — produced a markedly anti-union inflection.

The authors suggest, for example, that, compared with the Department of Employment statistics relating to industrial stoppages in 1975, the news bulletins by no means offered a balanced or accurate picture of the history of industrial stoppages during that year. They focused disproportionately on the key mass-production industries, particularly the car industry, which occupied a key position in the drive for exports, and on those industries — notably transport and communications — where industrial disputes created a maximum of inconvenience for the general public. The result, it is alleged, was that industrial disputes were signified within a 'unions versus the national interest/general public' semiology of the public world, suggesting that strikers were holding the nation to ransom or hindering the decent, orderly, non-striking citizen from going about his/her daily business. This effect was reinforced by the typical placement of industrial dispute stories within the structure of the news programme. 'The close proximity between economic and industrial items, which is particularly clear on BBC 1, suggests that items about particular industrial situations are likely to be juxtaposed with items (usually shorter) on the general state of the economy, with a resultant strong implication of a causal connection' (*Bad News*, p. 118). Clearly, the implication of such a causal relationship was to favour certain explanations of the economic difficulties of the period — those that attributed the chief blame to the unionized working class — over others — those, for example, that have attributed Britain's long-term economic difficulties to the declining international competitiveness of the economy stemming from the obsolescence of its capital stock and a persistently low rate of investment.

The Glasgow Media Group also argue that the ways in which management and union representatives were interviewed, and the ways in which such interviews were inter-cut and articulated in relation to one another within the structure of the pertinent news items — although formally impartial in the sense that they recognized that there were two sides to such disputes — tended to favour the management interpretation of such disputes. Whereas management representatives tended to be interviewed in their offices, surrounded by all the trappings of authority, reason and responsibility, union representatives were more likely to be interviewed by out-door broadcasting units against the setting of a mass meeting, or pickets at a factory gate — in other words, against a background of activity and disorder which stripped them of any semblance of power, authority or reason and, at times, of the elementary requirement of audibility. (It is worth nothing that current TUC guidelines concerning their use of the media advise union representatives to refuse to be interviewed in such circumstances.) A further effect of structuring interviews in this way, the Glasgow Media Group suggest, was that of constructing an opposition between 'facts' and 'events' homologous to that between management and unions. Whereas management representatives were usually looked to to provide the 'facts' against which to view the dispute, the labour side was looked to for 'events' — for filmable happenings — with the result that, in visual terms, the source of discord was most typically *seen* to be the workers — in pickets, mass meetings, rallies — a discord which was projected against an orderly backcloth of 'facts' as established by management. Finally, the structure and content of interviews with union leaders was said to be almost *a priori* prejudicial to the union interpretation of disputes in the respect that such union spokesmen were usually asked to provide an explanation or justification for their union's action. In being thus provided with an opportunity to exculpate themselves, the inevitable implication was that — in striking — unions were axiomatically engaged in a culpable act.

Bad News and its successor, *More Bad News* (1980) are both useful and important studies, particularly in the degree of close attention they pay to the routine practices of television news. Yet there are limitations to both, particularly so far as the alternatives they envisage are concerned. The concern of *Bad News*, it is stated in the introduction to *More Bad News*, was to show how 'viewers were given a misleading portrayal of industrial disputes in the UK when measured against the independent reality of events' (p. xiii). This is to imply that the standards against which news coverage is being assessed and found wanting are those of a truthful representation of reality 'as it really is', reflecting a politics of the sign based on the notion of truth versus falsehood. Indeed, as Ian Connell has argued, it often seems that the demands of this alternative would be met if the statutory require-ments of balance, impartiality and neutrality were scrupulously met (Connell, 1980). Connell's objection to this is not merely that this is impossible, resurrecting, as it does, the dream of forms of representation that are neutral and through which reality might be revealed as if without mediation. He also argues that to castigate the broadcasting media for their failure to be impartial in some absolute, philosophical sense misses the more essential point that they achieve their ideological effectivity *precisely through* their observation of the *statutory* requirements of balance and impartiality. (The statutory requirement, it should be noted, is merely that the media should exhibit 'due impartiality', taking account of 'not just the whole range of views on an issue, but also of the weights of opinion which holds these views' — a formula which clearly justifies the media according a privileged weight to the views of those political parties which can claim popular support as evidenced by the returns of the ballot-box.)

The basis for this argument is to be found in work earlier undertaken by Ian Connell, together with Stuart Hall and Lidia Curti, on the subject of current affairs television. Hall, Connell and Curti argue that it is television's very commitment to impartiality and the fact that, within a limited sphere — notably, the political terrain constituted by the parties which define the arena of legitimate, parliamentary politics — it genuinely *is* impartial that secures its most significant, and least noticed, ideological effectivity. For the effect of the broadcasting agencies operating in a genuinely impartial way within such limited terms of reference (limited because of what they exclude: the perspectives of all political groups — the communist Left, 'terrorists' — which fall outside the framework of consensus politics) is that they contribute to the reproduction of the unity of the parliamentary political system as a whole:

'Panorama', above all other Current Affairs programmes, routinely takes the part of the guardian of unity in this second sense. It reproduces, on the terrain of ideology, the political identification between Parliamentary system and the Nation. As a consequence, the agenda of problems and 'prescriptions' which such a programme handles is limited to those which have registered with, or are offered up by, the established Parliamentary parties. It is these authoritative prescriptions, alone, which are probed to discover which appears most appropriate to the task of maintaining the system. (Hall, Connell and Curti, 1977, p. 91)

It is in this way, by actually fulfilling their statutory requirements, that the media may be said to collude with the major established parties in limiting the very way in which problems are defined and the horizons within which solutions may be sought, but in a way that seems not to violate the liberal-democratic requirement that equal space be given to contending points of view. It is a 'double-dupe' system, an ideological form which effects a contraction of the sphere of public debate whilst simultaneously engendering the illusion that that sphere is entirely free and open. The response that this requires, as Connell quite rightly argues, is not that the media should be required to become 'genuinely impartial' but rather 'the formation and implementation of quite different editorial criteria' (p. 32). It requires a politics in which sign is opposed to sign, and not truth to falsehood.

CONCLUSION

My primary purpose in this essay has been to summarize and illustrate some of the central areas of debate within the tradition of media theory concerned with the reality-defining role of the media. Yet I have also sought, although in a much lower key, to call into question the way in which the signifying role of the media is conceived and represented within this tradition. For, although confirming the activity and effectivity of the media as a critical area of signification, the notion that the media are somehow ontologically secondary in relation to a more primary, more basic 'real' is kept alive within the very terminology 'definers of social reality'. To raise this objection is not merely a semantic quibble. The validity of positing a duality between the plane of signification and that of 'reality' has long since been called into question in linguistics and literary and film criticism. To suggest that media studies should be brought into line with these is not a question of theoretical fashion, of being up-to-date for the sake of it. It is rather a question of politics, a question of how to conceive the politics of the sign and how to enter the domain of signification as an arena of political struggle. For the formulation 'media as definers of social reality' admits of only one politics: one in which the power of allegedly distorting systems of signification is opposed by the truth, by a system of signification which effaces itself in allowing the real to speak through it without hindrance or modification. The objection to this is not merely that it is impossible. It also misconceives the political task which is not to oppose truth to falsehood, but *to take up a position* in relation to dominant systems of signification — a matter that can only be broached if the focus of analysis shifts away from the investigation of the relationship between sign and 'reality' to that of the relationship between signs, the play of signification upon signification within a structured field of ideological relationships.

REFERENCES

Aldgate, A. (1979) *Cinema and History: British Newsreels and the Spanish Civil War*, London, Scolar Press.

Annan Committee (1977) *Report of the Committee on the Future of Broadcasting*, London, HMSO.

Cohen, S. and Young, J. (eds) (1973) *The Manufacture of News. Deviance, Social Problems and the Mass Media*, London, Constable.

Cohen, S. (1972) *Folk Devils and Moral Panics: the Creation of the Mods and Rockers*, London, MacGibbon and Kee.

Cohen, S. (ed.) (1971) *Images of Deviance*, Harmondsworth, Penguin.

Connell, I. (1980) 'Review of *More Bad News*', *Marxism Today*, August.

Derrida, J. (1978) *Writing and Difference*, London, Routledge & Kegan Paul.

Glasgow University Media Group (1976) *Bad News*, London, Routledge & Kegan Paul.

Glasgow University Media Group (1980) *More Bad News*, London, Routledge & Kegan Paul.

Hall, S., Critcher, C., Jefferson, T., Clarke, J. and Roberts, B. (1978) *Policing the Crisis: Mugging, the State, and Law and Order*, London, Macmillan.

Hall, S., Connell, I. and Curti, L. (1976) 'The "unity" of current affairs television', *Working Papers in Cultural Studies*, (9).

Hood, S. (1972) 'The politics of television', in McQuail, D. (ed.) *Sociology of Mass Communications*, Harmondsworth, Penguin.

MacCabe, C. (1978) *James Joyce and the Revolution of the Word*, London, Macmillan.

Macfarlane, A. (1970) *Witchcraft in Tudor and Stuart England*, London, Routledge & Kegan Paul.

Morley, D. (1980) *The 'Nationwide' Audience*, London, British Film Institute.

Orwell, G. (1974) *Homage to Catalonia*, Harmondsworth, Penguin.

Trotsky, L. (1973) *The Spanish Revolution, 1931-39*, New York, Pathfinder Press.

Index

Adorno, Theodor, 8, 31, 42, 45, 46, 59, 91, 92; *see also* Frankfurt School

advertising, 243, 247; and American broadcasting, 159; and British broadcasting, 145-6; and economic growth, 187; and international broadcasting, 179-80, 181-3; structuralist analysis of, 99-100

Agatha, St, 206

agenda-setting function of the media, 241, 249, 250, 251, 262

Agnew, Spiro, 282

Aldgate, Anthony, 291-2

alienation, 37, 165

Althusser, Louis, 8, 9, 23, 31, 48, 49, 51, 53, 75, 77, 78, 82, 105, 110; and the reproduction processes of capitalism, 52; on ideological state apparatuses, 24, 88; on ideology, 24, 52-3; on the concept of interpellation, 24

American Dream, the, 61, 240

American sociology, 39-41; *see also* behaviourism

American Telephone and Telegraph Company, 134

amplification spiral, 299-300

Anderson, Perry, 35

Anglia Television, 139

Anglia Television Group Ltd, 139

Anglican Church, the, 220

Annan Report, 167; on the impartiality of television news, 303-4; on the *Yesterday's Men* controversy, 168

Annenberg School of Communication, 257, 258

anomie, 37, 62

Arendt, Hannah, 32, 36

Aristotle, 208

Arnold, Matthew, 32, 35

articulation, theory of, 79-84

Ascherson, Neal, 140

Asquith, Herbert, 211

Associated Communications Corporation, 123, 138

Associated Newspapers, 139, 143

ATV, 120, 170

ATV Network Ltd, 138-9

audience: effects of mass communications on, 249, 260-1, 262; media perceptions of, 169

avant-garde films, 24, 107

Bachrach, P., 64-5

Baldwin, Stanley, 212

Bank of England Nominees, 138

Baratz, M., 64-5

Barthes, Roland, 9, 23, 66, 79; and semiology, 94, 95, 97, 98, 99, 100

base/superstructure, 22, 27, 47-8, 108

Baudelaire, Charles, 45

BBC, 100, 152, 167, 171; and relations to the state, 49, 87-88; formation of, 155-7; relationships between BBC and ITV, 157-9; *see also* broadcasting

Beaverbrook, Lord, 211-12

Beaverbrook Group, 119

Becker, Howard, 13, 63

behaviourism, 8, 56-8, 61, 93

Bell, Daniel, 37, 40, 60

Benjamin, Louis, 138

Benjamin, Walter, 45, 98

Bennett, Arnold, 38

Bennett, Tony, 8, 199-201
Bensman, Joseph, 39
Berelson, B., 15, 243
Berger, Peter, 67
Berle, Adolf, 128, 133-6
Bernard of Clairvaux, St, 204
Bernstein, Alex, 139
Bernstein, Basil, 79
Bernstein, Cecil, 139
Bernstein, Lord, 139
Bernstein family trusts, 138
Blumler, Jay, 13, 20, 151, 199-200, 215
Bon, Gustave Le, 32
Bond, James, structuralist analysis of, 95-7
book, rise of the, 216-20
Bourdieu, Pierre, 79
bourgeois culture, 44, 91; ideology of, 264
bourgeoisie, the, 41, 44, 46, 47, 50, 105
Boyd, Gavin, 139
Boyd-Barrett, Oliver, 116
Braham, Peter, 199-201
Bramson, Leon, 32
Brecht, Bertolt, 47
Breichner, J., 270
Brewer, J., 222
broadcasting, 87; and relations to the state, 120-1, 155-7, 160-2; and the British political system, 214-16, 227-8; development of commercial broadcasting in Britain, 157-8
Brooke, C., 209
Brougham, Lord, 210
Brown, William, 139
Brunce, Richard, 140
bureaucracy, theories of, and the media, 162-70
Burgelin, O., 93
Burke, Edmund, 221-2
Burnham, James, 128
Burns, Tom, 152, 159, 161, 167, 171
Buscome, Edward, 101
Butterworth, E., 269-70

Callaghan, James, 215, 287
Camargo, M., 79
Campaign for Relief of Need, 278
Campbell, Lord, 223
Cantril, H., 92

capitalism, 8, 26, 41, 44, 50, 91, 127, 135, 142, 178, 186; advanced, 8, 41; and relationships to the media, 126, 132, 134; monopoly, 44, 91; theories of, 125, 144-5, 147
Carey, James, 2
Carnoy, M., 191
Carter, President J., 103
chain reaction model of communication effect, 241
Chandler, Raymond, 96
Charlemagne, Emperor, 207
Chibnall, S., 14
Chomsky, Noam, 71
Christ, Jesus, 204
Clark, Robert, 138
class, 47-50, 51; and class relationships, 103, 239; capitalist class, 125, 126, 129, 132, 135, 137, 141, 143, 144; consciousness, 141; struggle, 26, 108-9; *see also* bourgeoisie, proletariat, middle class and working class
Coase, R.L., 156
cognition, media effects on, 240-1, 249
Cohen, Stanley, 14, 298-300
Cold War, 40, 96, 108
Collins, Norman, 138
Complaints Commission, 167
commercial press, development of, 220-5
commercial television, rise of, 157-8
commonsense theory, 73, 76-7
communications industry, ideology of, 126
Communist Party, 42
Community Relations Council, 270
Comstock, G., 238
Comte, Auguste, 125
Congress, US, 256
Connell, B., 127
Connell, Ian, 22, 305-6
connotation, 79, 99
consciousness: concept of, 50-1; critical, 142; popular, 147; public, 241
consensus: the media and, 60-2; break-up of, 62-5
consent, the production of, 85-8
Conservative Party, 212, 246, 252
conspiracy theory, 143
Constable, John, 98

Constantine, Emperor, 204
consumer sovereignty, 144-5, 147
consumerism, the media and economic
  development, 186-7
content analysis, 64, 92-3, 250, 258;
  analysis/semiology compared, 94
Coser, Lewis, 165
Counter-Reformation, 220
Coward, Rosalind, 72
creativity, and autonomy, 163, 165
cultivation analysis, 242
cultural dependency, 174, 177
cultural imperialism, 180, 182, 187
cultural pluralism, 184
cultural theorists, 32, 35, 38, 45
culturalism, 8, 109; and approaches to
  the study of the media, 26-8
culturalists, and structuralism, 27
culture, 23, 27, 40, 44, 45, 53, 102, 182,
  259; imports of, 179, 180, 181, 193;
  industry, the, 8, 26, 31, 41-7, 91, 105,
  125-6, 129; see also folk, mass and
  popular culture
Curran, James, 7, 8, 18, 145, 146, 199
Curran, Sir Charles, 87, 289
Curti, Lidia, 306-7

Daily Express, 37, 140, 268-9, 271, 274,
  278
Daily Mail, 210, 274, 277-8
Daily Mirror, 271, 278
Daily Sketch, 277-8
Daily Telegraph, 274, 277-8
Daily Telegraph Ltd, 138
Darna, Charles, 131
democracy, 40-1
Democratic Party (US), 253-4
denotation, 79, 99
dependency theory, 174-5, 177, 178,
  180, 192, 193, 236
determinism, 104, 105, 144, 178, 181
deviancy theory, 7, 9
deviants, media representations of,
  62-5, 67, 295-303
discourse theory, 7, 74-77, 108; and film
  analysis, 93, 106
dissonance theory, 12
Dodd, William, 210
dominance, concept of, 84-5
Dowing, J., 278

Durkheim, Emile, 32, 63, 162-3

Eastern Counties Newspapers, 139
Eckersley, Peter, 155, 156
Eco, Umberto, 9, 70, 96, 97
effects studies, 13, 16, 56, 58-9, 242,
  261; see also media effects
Eisenhower, Dwight, 254
Eisenstein, E., 217
election broadcasting, 247
election campaigns, study of, 243-4,
  246, 248, 252, 254, 257; see also
  general elections and presidential
  elections
Eliot, T.S., 32, 35
élites, 31, 36, 37, 40, 107, 116; and
  control over media, 183, 184, 243;
  élite theory and pluralism, 128-9; in
  the Third World, 176, 178, 184,
  187-9; theories of, 34, 41
Elizabethan Settlement, the, 220
Elle, 97-8, 99
Elliott, Philip, 18, 163
Ellis, John, 72
Elton, G.R., 219
EMI, 133, 138, 143
empiricism, 38, 39; and theory in media
  research, positions compared, 12-16,
  23
Engels, Frederick, 22, 42, 47, 84
Epstein, E., 160
ethnomethodology, 67
ETV, 191
Evans, Harold, 277, 279, 282
Evening News, 273

false consciousness, 26, 50, 105, 110
Fascism, 11, 42, 242
Federal Communications Commission,
  155
feudal society, 37
film noir, 94
Financial Times, 119
Fiske, J., 100-3
folk culture, 36; tales, Russian, 95-6
Fox, Charles James, and Libel Act of
  1792, 223
Franco, General Francisco, 289-90
Frankfurt School, 8, 23, 31, 47, 58-9,
  105; and the culture industry, 44,

91-2; critique of liberal pluralism, 45-6
Freud, Sigmund, 45
Friedrich, Carl, 36
functionalism, 53, 176

Galbraith, John, 128
Gallagher, Margaret, 116
gangster films, study of, 93, 95; *see also film noir*
Garnham, Nicholas, 25, 68
gatekeeper, concept of, 153
Gaudet, H., 243
Gemeinschaft, 58, 182
General Elections, studies of (1959), 243-4, 252; 1964, 248, 252; *see also* election campaigns
Gerbner, George, 257-60, 263
Giddens, Anthony, 125
Gill, Jack, 138
Glasgow Media Group, 69, 303-6
Golding, Peter, 1, 18, 25, 26, 68
Goldsmith, Sir John, 131, 145
Gone With the Wind, 159
Grade, Sir Lew (later Lord), 123, 138
Gramsci, Antonio, 9, 23, 27, 53, 74, 78, 80, 84-5, 108, 110, 300, 303; and common sense, 73; *see also* hegemony
Granada Group Ltd, 120, 138
Granada Television, 138
Greeley, Horace, 131
Green, Sir Hugh Carlton, 279
Greene, Sir Hugh, 160
Gregory I, Pope, 207
Gregory VII, Pope, 209
Grundberg, Carl, 42
Guarantee Nominees, 138
Guardian, 139, 271-2, 273, 277-8
Guevera, Che, 44
Gurevitch, Michael, 7, 8, 13, 20, 151, 199-200, 215
Gurney, May Holdings, 139

Hall, Stuart, 8-9, 14, 23, 67-8, 79, 83, 92; and television news, 306-7; and the analysis of news photographs, 99; and the definition of cultural studies, 26-27; *et al.* and *Policing the Crisis*, 108-10, 300-3
Halloran, James, 1

Hanson, Sir James, 139
Hartley, John, 100-3
Hartmann, P., 15, 272
Heath, P., 219
Hegel, Georg Wilhelm Friedrich, 45, 46, 49
hegemony, 9, 27, 53, 108, 115, 239; post-war crisis of, 300; theory of, 79-83, 85
Hemingway, Ernest, 38
Henry IV, Kaiser, 209
Henry VIII, 217
Himmelweit, Professor, 304
Hiro, Dilip, 268
Hirst, Paul Quentin, 25, 50
Hitler, Adolf, 42, 289-90, 293
Hobbes, John, 217
Hoggart, Richard, 26, 153, 303
Hollywood, 24, 146, 147
Horkheimer, Max, 31, 42, 91; *see also* Frankfurt School
Husband, C., 279-80, 283
Hutchinson Publishing Group Ltd, 120

iconography, 98
ideology: and discourse theory, 74-5; and hegemony, 79-83; and the class struggle within language, 76-9; and the structuralist study of language, 66-72; class basis of, 105; concepts and theories of, 10, 42, 47-8, 50, 92, 97, 100, 103, 108; in film and television, 102-3, 106-8; Marx's views on, 47-8; papal, 205-8, 212-14; professional, 19-20, 21, 152, 162, 179; reductionist analysis of, 102-3, 104, 105; relative autonomy of, 83-4; the end of ideology, 60-2, 64
Illiffe, Lord, 119
Imperial Tobacco Pension Fund, 138
imperialism, 174, 180
Independent Television Corporation, 170
industrial society, theories of, 125, 127, 147
instrumentalism and media theory, critique of, 126-8, 135, 137, 141-3
interactionism, 67

Ironside, 103
Isaacs, Jeremy, 280
ITV, 88

Jacobson, Roman, 68
James, St, 204
Jameson, Frederick, 94-5
Janowitz, Morris, 39
John, King, 214
Johnson, Richard, 23
Jones, C., 283

Kantianism, 70
Kantorowicz, E.H., 205
Katz, Elihu, 12, 13, 247
Kemsley, Lord, 211
Kerner Commission, 271
Keynesianism, 43
Klapper, J., 12, 13, 244
Klute, 106
Kotz, D., 133
Kushnick, L., 278

labelling theory, 296-7
Labour Party, 246, 252
Lacan, Jacques, 9, 23, 24
Laclau, Ernesto, 9, 80, 84, 108, 303
language: referential theories of, 74-7;
   structuralist analysis of, 66-72;
   theories of and the media, 287-8; *see
   also* linguistics
law and order, media representations of,
   300-2
Lazarsfeld, Paul, 12, 13, 15, 39, 58, 152,
   243, 244
Leavis, F.R., 35, 38
Leavis, Q.D., 38
Leeds Mercury, 224
Lent, J.A., 181
Lerner, D., 186
Lévi-Strauss, Claude, 9, 23, 66-7, 70-3,
   94
Liberal Party, 252
liberal-pluralism, 9, 31, 39, 40, 41, 45,
   153, 238; and relationships to Marxism, 2, 7-8, 11, 23; *see also* pluralism
liberalism, 33, 34
linguistics, 7, 9, 22, 23, 51, 66, 93-5,
   107-8
Lipset, Seymour, 60

Lloyd George, David, 211
Lloyds Bank, 45
Lloyd's Weekly, 210
London Weekend Television, 120, 131,
   138
Luckmann, Thomas, 67
Lukács, Georg, 51, 64-5; and ideology,
   49-50
Lukes, Steven, 64-5, 125
Luther, Martin, 217
LWT (Holdings) Ltd, 138

MacCabe, Colin, 8, 287; and the classic
   realist text, 106-8
McCombs, M., 13
McCorn, R., 15
McKensey Report, 168
McLeod, J., 13, 237
McQuail, Dennis, 1, 15, 202
Maisel, R., 202
managerial revolution, 128-9, 130-2,
   134
managerialism, theory of, 132-3, 134,
   136
Manchester Evening News, 139, 277
Maoism, 44
Marcuse, Herbert, 8, 14, 15, 42, 43-4,
   45; *see also* Frankfurt School
Margaret, St, 206
Marx, Karl, 37, 41, 42, 45, 141; and the
   reproduction processes of capitalism,
   52; base superstructure metaphor, 22,
   47-8; experiences as a journalist, 130-
   1; media ownership in capitalist
   societies, 125-7; on ideology, 22,
   47-9, 83-4, 103-5
Marxism, 41, 46, 47, 49, 52, 174; and
   alliance with semiology, 97, 103, 106,
   108-9; and capitalism, 51-2, 104-5,
   128, 132-6, 257; and culture, 23, 110,
   144-5; and ideology, 2, 7-9, 22-4, 28,
   32, 47-50, 53, 98, 103-4, 109 (*see also*
   ideology); and the media, 1-2, 7-8,
   11, 13, 14, 18, 19-22, 31-2, 42, 53, 91,
   106, 108, 116, 142, 153, 238-40, 257,
   260-4; relationship to liberal-pluralism, 1-2, 7-8, 11, 16, 20-1, 23-4, 26
   (*see also* neo-Marxism); reproduction
   processes of, 51-2
mass communications, 12, 13, 22, 30-2,

91
mass culture, 36, 40, 57, 91
mass man, 35-6
mass media: and the medieval Catholic Church, power compared, 226-8; effects of, 151, 193, 236, 237, 239, 240, 242, 244, 245, 260, 262; theories of, 30-4
mass psychology, 32, 33; and elections, 245-6
mass society, 12, 23, 36-7; outlook and early American media research, 36-41; theories of, 8, 12, 31-2, 42, 57-8, 62, 242
materialism, 25, 110
Matisse, Henri, 45
Matta, F.R., 183
Matthews, Victor, 140
Matza, David, 67
Mean, Gardiner, 128, 132-6
media: allocative control of, 122-5, 132, 134, 140; and social change, 240; and the relationship to ownership, 122-3, 127, 144-5, 179, 181, 239 (see also ownership); as definers of social reality, 27, 63-5, 200-1, 257-60, 262-4, 287-308; control, nature of, 152, 155, 159, 161, 171; corporate control of, 123-9; effects on attitudes, 240-1; effects on violence, 14-15, 18, 92, 109, 193, 236; effects on voting behaviour, 15-18 (see also election campaigns); imperialism, 180; institutions, 16, 17-18; interactions with socio-political environment, 20-1; media control over communication channels, 152, 166, 178; messages, 12, 16, 18, 21, 30, 39, 40, 92, 98-9, 151, 238, 262-3; operational control of, 122; political economy of, 18-19; power of, 11-28, 115-16, 236, 238-40, 243, 245; research, the 'critical paradigm', 65-88; sociology, 40, 48; technology, 237-8
Merton, Robert, 62
methodological individualism, 239
M & G (Unit Trust), 138
middle class, 34, 35
Midland Bank Trust, 138
Miliband, Ralph, 41, 141, 143

Mill, James, 224
Mill, John Stuart, 32; and the tyranny of the majority, 33-4
modernization, 186, 188
mods and rockers, media representations of, 298-300
Moerbeke, William of, 208
Montagu, Samuel (Nominees), 138
Monty Python, 167
Morley, David, 15, 298
Morning Advertizer, 126
Morning Post, 126
Morning Star, 143
Mosca, Gaetano, 32
Muir, Frank, 132
Mussolini, Benito, 290
myth, 66, 71, 72, 74, 97, 98, 101, 182, 257

National Coal Board Pensions, 138
Nazism, 36, 40
Neilsen Marketing Research Territory, 159
neo-Kantianism, 70
neo-Marxism, 117, 127, 134, 144, 176, 178
New York Daily Tribune, 131
New York Times, 277
news: frameworks and the reporting of race, 275-9; values and the reporting of race, 269-75
News International Ltd, 138
Newton, F., 164
Nietzsche, Friedrich, 32; and mass society theory, 34
Nin, Andre, 293
Nordenstreng, K., 178, 181
Northcliffe, Lord, 211
Northern Ireland, television coverage of, 161
Norwich Union Life Insurance, 139
Now Magazine, 131

Observer, 119, 135, 138
Ortega y Gasset, José, 34
Orwell, George, 289-95
ownership of the media, 26, 118-47, 152; legal and economic aspects, 122-3, 142-3; of media conglomerates, 118-20, 140-1; of newspapers, 119; of

television, 138-9; of the record industry, 120

Pahl, R., 122
Pakula, Alan, 106
Panofsky, E., 98
Panorama, 298
papacy, and press barons, power compared, 212
Pareto, Vilfredo, 32
Paris-Match, 101
Parsons, Talcott, 60
Partido Obrero de Unificacion Marxista (POUM), 293-4
Peacock, Michael, 131-2
Pearl Assurance, 138
Pearson, S., and Son, 119, 141, 143
Pêcheux, Michel, 76
Penguin Books, 119, 141
Pentagon Papers, 140
Perry, James, 210
Peter, St, 204
phenomenology, 66
Picayune Times, 271
Pilkington Committee, 161
Plato, 45
pluralism, 1-2, 8-9, 14, 19, 21, 40, 239; and conception of élites, 129; and neo-Weberianism, 175, 176; criticisms of, 56-62, 64-5, 85, 103, 107; relationship to Marxism, 20, 21, 23-4, 26, 260-1
political communication, effects of, 245, 247, 248, 254
political economy, 8, 76; approach to the study of the media, 25-6
Popper, Sir Karl, 46
popular culture, 147, 258
positivism, 7-8, 39, 57, 180, 193
Poulantzas, Nicos, 52, 144
Powell, Enoch, 200, 280-3
power, contrasting models of, 64-5, 123-4, 127
presidential elections, study of, 246; 1940, 243, 244-5; 1956-72, 250, 255
press, the: and the British political system, 214-16, 226; control of, 221-2; radical, and working class politics, 221, 225-6
press barons, power of, 210-12
Press Council, 270, 275

Presse, Die, 126
print culture, and the rise of Protestantism, 219-20
proletariat, the, 50
propostion, the entailment of, 74-5
Propp, V., 95, 97
Prudential Assurance, 138
psychoanalysis, 66, 75, 108; Freudian, 72; Lacanian, 72
Public Enemy, 93
Punch, 126

race, media definitions of, 200, 268-85, 279-82
Radiotelevision Italiana, 170
Rank Organization, 137, 139
Reagan, President Ronald, 103
realism, classic realist text, 106-8; in the cinema, 106, 108
Reeves, B., 237
reflection theory, 51, 64, 103, 287-8
Reform Bill (1867), 35
Reich, Wilhelm, 32
Reith, John, 216, 304; and the role of broadcasting, 155-6
Republican Party (US), 253-4
Resler, H., 140
Richfield, Atlantic, 119, 135, 138
Robinson, John, 253
Robinson, Michael J., 255, 256, 263
role/goal conflict, 166-7
Roman Catholic Church and control over medieval communications, 203-10, 212-14
Romulus Films, 139
Rothermere, Viscount, 211-12
Royal Commission on the Press, 141, 144
Russian Formalism, 95

Saint-Simon, Claude Henri, 125, 128
Sapir-Whorf hypothesis, the, 66
satellite communications, 177, 179, 180
Saussure, Ferdinand de, 23, 66, 68, 94, 97, 287
Schiller, H.I., 176-8, 181
Schumpeter, Joseph, 40, 41
science fiction, 97
Scottish Daily Express, 277
Scottish Daily News, 145

Screen, 24, 106-8
Scrutiny Group, 38
Seaton, Jean, 18
Seiden, Martin, 129
semiology/semiotics, 7, 9, 22, 53, 66, 84, 92-3, 94, 95, 97, 98, 100-2, 105, 107, 110, 193
Seymour-Ure, C., 281
Shelley, Percy Bysshe, 45
Shils, Edward, 39, 45, 60
sign, the, 94, 97, 98; multi-accentuality of, 77
signification, 10, 24, 27, 51, 53, 93, 101, 102, 107, 110, 177
signifier/signified, 90, 94-7, 99, 101
signifying practice, 64, 77-8, 106; systems, 47, 48, 49, 51, 92, 94, 97, 98, 100, 108, 109, 110
Silvester, Pope, 204
Simpson, George, 299
Smith, Anthony, 156, 160
social action analysis, 153-4
social conflict, 125, 249, 255
social control, 63, 153, 159
social order, 63, 262
social stratification, 239
social structure, 46, 241
socio-cultural imperialism, 177
sociological tradition, the, 34
South London Press, 275
Southern Television Ltd, 139
Spanish Civil War, 200, 289-95
Spy Who Loved Me, The, 96
Stalinism, 36, 42
Star, 145
Star Wars, 96
Starsky & Hutch, 103
Stevenson, Adlai, 254
Stewart, Sir Ian, 139
structural analysis, 95, 124-5, 127; functionalist, 176, 188; *see also* functionalism
structuralism, 2, 7-9, 22-8, 53, 67, 73, 93, 94, 98, 105, 108, 110; *see also* language, structuralist analysis of
subcultures, 62
subject, theories of, 72, 77, 80, 108
Sun, 274, 278
Sunday Times, The, 215, 277-8
Sweeney, The, 96, 103

systems analysis, 152-3

Telefusion Ltd, 139
television: bardic function of, 101-3; news, 100, 262-5; political use of, 247-8, 252
Thames Television, 133, 138
Thames Valley Broadcasting, 133
That Was the Week that Was, 167
Thompson, E.P., 26
Thomson, D.C., 137, 139
Times, The, 45, 141, 271-2, 274, 281
Tocqueville de, Alexis, 32
Tönnies, Ferdinand, 32
Toscanini, Arturo, 46
totalitarianism, 36, 40, 184
Townsend, Marquis of Kaynham, 139
Tracey, Michael, 153, 158, 161, 167, 169, 171
Trade Unions, and the media, 69, 82-3, 100, 304-6
Trafalgar House, 119; BPM Holdings, 138
Trenaman, J., 15
Trevor-Roper, Hugh, 186
Trident Television Ltd, 139
Trotsky, Leon, 292-3
Tunstall, Jeremy, 151, 167, 271
Tyne Tees Television, 139

Ullmann, W.W., 205
UNESCO, 282
United Empire Party, 212
United Newspapers, 139
Universal Instruments, 119
University of Colombia, 42
uses and gratification studies, 241

Veron, E., 71
Vidich, Arthur J., 39
Vološinov, V.N.: and ideology, 77-80; and theory of language, 50-1
Vroey, M.De, 134

Wall, Max, 276
Watergate, 255
Weber, Max: on bureaucracy, 162; on the protestant ethic, 186
Weberian, neo-, 176, 177
Wedell, G., 181

Wednesday Play, The, 167
Weimar Germany, 42
Wells, A., 187
Wemyss, Earl of, 139
West Unit Nominees, 138
Westergaard, J., 140
Western Daily Press, 277
Westinghouse Electric, 140
Westminister Review, 224
Whale, John, 129
Whannel, Garry, 14
Wheldon, Huw, 158
White, David, 153
Wilkes, John, and the struggle for press freedom, 222-3, 224
Wilkinson, John, 139

Williams, Raymond, 23, 26, 104, 105, 147, 156
Wilson, H.H., 157
Winkler, J., 122
Wolverhampton Express and Star, 282
Woollacott, Janet, 7-9
working class, 35, 42, 102, 105, 146, 147, 239
World War, First, 11

Yesterday's Men, controversy over, 167-8, 171
Yorkshire Post, 269-70
Yorkshire Television, 139

Zeitlin, M., 133